# HINDENBURG

# HINDENBURG

## POWER, MYTH, AND THE RISE OF THE NAZIS

ANNA VON DER GOLTZ

OXFORD
UNIVERSITY PRESS

# OXFORD
UNIVERSITY PRESS

Great Clarendon Street, Oxford OX2 6DP

Oxford University Press is a department of the University of Oxford.
It furthers the University's objective of excellence in research, scholarship,
and education by publishing worldwide in

Oxford New York

Auckland Cape Town Dar es Salaam Hong Kong Karachi
Kuala Lumpur Madrid Melbourne Mexico City Nairobi
New Delhi Shanghai Taipei Toronto

With offices in

Argentina Austria Brazil Chile Czech Republic France Greece
Guatemala Hungary Italy Japan Poland Portugal Singapore
South Korea Switzerland Thailand Turkey Ukraine Vietnam

Oxford is a registered trade mark of Oxford University Press
in the UK and in certain other countries

Published in the United States
by Oxford University Press Inc., New York

First published 2009
First published in paperback 2011

British Library Cataloguing in Publication Data

Data available

Library of Congress Cataloging in Publication Data
von der Goltz, Anna.
Hindenburg: power, myth, and the rise of the Nazis / Anna von der Goltz.
p. cm.
Includes bibliographical references and index.
ISBN 978–0–19–957032–4 (acid-free paper) 1. Hindenburg, Paul von,
1847–1934. 2. Presidents—Germany—Biography. 3. Germany—Politics and
government—1918–1933. I. Title.
DD231.H5V66 2009
943.085092—dc22
[B]                                    2009019323

Typeset by Laserwords Private Limited, Chennai, India
Printed and bound by
CPI Group (UK) Ltd, Croydon, CR0 4YY

ISBN 978–0–19–957032–4 (Hbk)
ISBN 978–0–19–969586–7 (Pbk)

*To Heide*

ANNA VON DER GOLTZ is a Leverhulme Early Career Fellow in Modern History at the University of Cambridge. From 2006 until 2011 she was a Junior Research Fellow at Magdalen College, Oxford. Her work on the Hindenburg myth won the German History Society Essay Prize in 2006 and the prestigious Fraenkel Prize in 2008. She is currently pursuing research on '1968' and has edited a collection of essays on the subject. From January 2012, she will teach German and European History at Georgetown University, Washington, DC.

Praise for *Hindenburg*

'Impressive, innovative, convincing'
Wolfgang Kruse, *HsozKult*

'[a] lucid study . . . Anna von der Goltz does an expert job in deconstructing the Hindenburg legend . . . his destructive effect on German politics has rarely been analysed better'
David Cesarani, *Literary Review*

'This book . . . offers important new insights. It demonstrates like no previous study the dynamism and universal appeal of the Hindenburg myth as arguably the most important unifying factor of the Weimar Republic.'
Gerd Krumeich, *Süddeutsche Zeitung*

'Anna von der Goltz sets the stage brilliantly.'
*The Canada Post*

'This is a profound study that will help any reader, German or not, better to understand this unique era in German history.'
*Contemporary Review*

# *Acknowledgements*

This book is a slightly revised version of my doctoral thesis submitted to the University of Oxford in 2007. While working on it, I accumulated many debts of gratitude that it is a pleasure to record here. I have been exceptionally fortunate in enjoying the backing of not just one, but two supervisors: Nicholas Stargardt and Hartmut Pogge von Strandmann. Nick's constructive criticism, academic support, and extraordinary generosity with his time made being his graduate student a great experience. Hartmut's historical curiosity and enthusiasm provided great encouragement and his knowledge of German archives was indispensable. I can hardly express how grateful I am to both of them for investing so much trust and time in my work.

I would also like to thank my examiners Jane Caplan and Richard J. Evans for a challenging viva, for reading the script so thoroughly, and for making valuable suggestions for improvement.

My research would not have been possible without the generous financial support of a number of institutions. The Faculty of Modern History at the University of Oxford provided funds during the early years and the Arts and Humanities Research Council supported the project throughout. A Domus Scholarship from Merton College saved me from having to re-apply for money as the years went on. I would also like to express my thanks to everyone at Magdalen College for taking a leap of faith and offering me a Prize Fellowship before my thesis was completed.

The staff of the archives and libraries in Berlin, Bonn, Freiburg, Koblenz, London, Marburg, and Oxford I visited offered kind and thoughtful guidance. Many other people also contributed to this study in more ways than they may be aware. John Röhl first introduced me to the First World War as an undergraduate and his support has meant a lot to me. Over the years, I have also benefited immensely from conversations with and advice from Paul Betts, Bernhard Dietz, Robert Gerwarth, Robert Gildea,

Christian Goeschel, Ruth Manning, and Patrick Porter. The participants of research seminars at the University of St Andrews, at the German Historical Institute in London, at Oxford, and in Menaggio, Italy, offered friendly and valuable suggestions. Furthermore, I should like to thank the OHM Editorial Committee for including my script in this series. I have greatly enjoyed working with everyone at OUP.

I am especially indebted to my editor, Seth Cayley, my production editor Kate Hind, and to Kay Clement and Carolyn McAndrew who copy-edited and proofread the script. The mistakes that remain are, of course, my responsibility.

Last but not least, I would like to mention some of those people, who have assisted me in more indirect—but no less important—ways: my close friends, Kim and Sarah in particular, who made life feel a lot less lonely than it could have done; my grandfather, who supported me in many other ways, for which I will always be grateful; and, above all, Nico, who has been incredibly patient and encouraging, and who contributed an extraordinary amount to the happiness in my life while writing this book.

The one to whom I owe the most comes last: my wonderful mother Heide Menge. It is a true joy to dedicate this book to her!

*Anna von der Goltz*
*December 2008*

# Contents

*List of Illustrations*     xi
*List of Abbreviations*     xiii

Introduction     I

1. The 'Victor of Tannenberg'     14

2. Surviving failure     43

3. Anti-democratic politics     65

4. Electing 'the Saviour'     84

5. Buying the icon     104

6. Hollow unity     124

7. The 'inverted fronts' of 1932     144

8. 'The Marshal and the Corporal...'     167

9. Hindenburg after 1945     193

Conclusion     211

*Notes*     219
*Bibliography*     287
*Index*     319

# *Illustrations*

Cover  Volksblock poster by Walter Riemer (1925): 'What hides behind this mask? Thus vote for Marx', *BAK*, poster no. 002–014–018

1.  Postcard of the 'Iron Hindenburg' nailing statue in Berlin, 1916, *DHM*, picture collection ............ 29

2.  Poster by Louis Oppenheim (1917): 'Those who subscribe to the war loan give me my most beautiful birthday present! von Hindenburg' (1917), *BAK*, poster no. 001–005–072 ............ 40

3.  Photograph of a *Reichsblock* election car with 'The Saviour' poster and Imperial flags in 1925, *BAK*, photograph no. 183–1989–0816–500 ............ 92

4.  'Reich President v. Hindenburg in the new Opel car', *Die Woche*, no. 40, 1 Oct. 1927, copy in *BA-MA*, N429, no. 12, 49 ............ 117

5.  An advertisement for brandy featuring Hindenburg and Hitler before the Nazi ban on using their images in May 1933, *BAB*, R601, no. 11, n. p. ............ 121

6.  Hindenburg during the celebration of his eightieth birthday at Berlin's sport stadium (1927), *BAK*, photograph no. 102–04875 ............ 131

7.  Nazi cartoon: 'A dishonest game behind an honest mask', *Die Brennnessel*, 9 March 1932, *BAB*, R1501, no. 126042, 339 ............ 155

8.  Photograph of a Hindenburg election car in Berlin in 1932, *BAK*, photograph no. 146–2004–0137 ............ 160

9.  Nazi poster: 'Never will the Reich be destroyed if you are united and loyal', *BAK*, poster no. 002–042–153 ............ 172

10. Photograph of Hitler speaking at Hindenburg's funeral at the Tannenberg Memorial on 7 August 1934, *BAK*, photograph no. 183–2006–0429–502 ............ 184

11. Photograph of the reburial of the Hindenburgs and the Prussian Kings at night-time in Marburg's Elizabeth Church, August 1946, *StM*, NL Bauer                                    195

12. Photograph of Hitler and Hindenburg shaking hands outside the Garrison Church in Potsdam on 21 March 1933, *BAK*, photograph no. 183-S38324                                    200

# Abbreviations

| | |
|---|---|
| ADGB | Allgemeiner Deutscher Gewerkschaftsbund |
| *AdsD* | *Archiv der sozialen Demokratie der Friedrich-Ebert-Stiftung, Bonn* |
| *BAB* | *Bundesarchiv Berlin* |
| *BA-FA* | *Bundesarchiv-Filmarchiv* |
| *BAK* | *Bundesarchiv Koblenz* |
| *BA-MA* | *Bundesarchiv Militärarchiv Freiburg* |
| *BBC* | *Berliner Börsen-Courier* |
| *BBZ* | *Berliner Börsen-Zeitung* |
| *BIZ* | *Berliner Illustrirte Zeitung* |
| *BL* | *Berliner Lokalanzeiger* |
| *BT* | *Berliner Tageblatt* |
| BVP | Bayerische Volkspartei. |
| CDU | Christlich Demokratische Union |
| *CEH* | *Central European History* |
| DAG | Deutsche Adelsgenossenschaft |
| *DAZ* | *Deutsche Allgemeine Zeitung* |
| DDP | Deutsche Demokratische Partei. |
| DGC | Deputy General Command (Stellvertretendes Generalkommando des Armeekorps) |
| *DHM* | *Deutsches Historisches Museum, Berlin* |
| DNVP | Deutschnationale Volkspartei. |
| *DRPS* | *Deutscher Reichsanzeiger und Preussischer Staatsanzeiger* |
| *DS* | *Deutschen-Spiegel* |
| *DTAZ* | *Deutsche Tageszeitung* |
| DVP | Deutsche Volkspartei. |
| *DZ* | *Deutsche Zeitung* |
| *EHQ* | *European History Quarterly* |
| ev. ed. | evening edition |

| | |
|---|---|
| *FAS* | *Frankfurter Allgemeine Sonntagszeitung* |
| *FAZ* | *Frankfurter Allgemeine Zeitung* |
| FDP | Freie Demokratische Partei |
| fn | footnote |
| *FR* | *Frankfurter Rundschau* |
| *FZ* | *Frankfurter Zeitung* |
| GDR | German Democratic Republic |
| *GG* | *Geschichte und Gesellschaft* |
| GHQ | General Headquarters |
| *GStA PK* | *Geheimes Staatsarchiv Preussischer Kulturbesitz, Berlin Dahlem* |
| *GWU* | *Geschichte in Wissenschaft und Unterricht* |
| *HA* | *Hannoverscher Anzeiger* |
| *HZ* | *Historische Zeitschrift* |
| *IWK* | *Internationale Wissenschaftliche Korrespondenz zur Geschichte der deutschen Arbeiterbewegung* |
| *JCH* | *The Journal of Contemporary History* |
| *JMH* | *The Journal of Modern History* |
| *KAZ* | *Königsberger Allgemeine Zeitung* |
| KPD | Kommunistische Partei Deutschlands. |
| *KV* | *Königsberger Volkszeitung* |
| *KZ* | *Neue Preussische Zeitung (Kreuz-Zeitung)* |
| *LAB* | *Landesarchiv Berlin* |
| *MGM* | *Militärgeschichtliche Mitteilungen* |
| *MNN* | *Münchener Neueste Nachrichten* |
| morn. ed. | morning edition |
| MSPD | Mehrheitssozialdemokratische Partei Deutschlands. |
| NCO | Non-commissioned officer |
| NL | Nachlass (Personal Papers) |
| NSDAP | Nationalsozialistische Deutsche Arbeiterpartei. |
| NVA | Nationale Volksarmee |
| *NYT* | *New York Times* |
| OHL | Oberste Heeresleitung (Supreme Army Command) |
| *OZ* | *Ostpreussische Zeitung* |
| PDS | Partei des Demokratischen Sozialismus |
| *RF* | *Rote Fahne* |
| RfH | Reichszentrale für Heimatdienst |

| | |
|---|---|
| RjF | Reichsbund jüdischer Frontsoldaten |
| SPD | Sozialdemokratische Partei Deutschlands |
| SS | Schutzstaffel |
| *StM* | *Stadtarchiv Marburg* |
| *SZ* | *Süddeutsche Zeitung* |
| *TAZ* | *Tageszeitung* |
| USPD | Unabhängige Sozialdemokratische Partei Deutschlands |
| *VB* | *Völkischer Beobachter* (Berlin edition, unless stated otherwise) |
| *VfZ* | *Vierteljahrshefte für Zeitgeschichte* |
| VVV | Vereinigte Vaterländische Verbände |
| *VZ* | *Vossische Zeitung* |
| *WaM* | *Welt am Montag* |
| WP | Wirtschaftspartei |
| *WTB* | *Wolffs Telegraphisches Büro* |
| *ZfG* | *Zeitschrift für Geschichtswissenschaft* |

# Introduction

On 27 April 1925, the day after Paul von Hindenburg had won the first presidential elections of the Weimar Republic, the liberal weekly *Welt am Montag* offered a striking explanation for the victory of the retired Field Marshal of the First World War. It had not been possible to persuade the 'ignorant' with compelling and irrefutable arguments against Hindenburg's candidacy, the leading article argued,

> because for them he is not at all a sharply delineated person with clear character traits, but a mythical slogan, a fetish. They need only look at him, hear his name, and the last of their reason goes up in smoke, they sink into a state of befuddlement . . .[1]

The left-liberal *Frankfurter Zeitung* took the same line. It conceded self-critically that it had been 'one of the gravest mistakes to spare the Hindenburg legend's life' after Germany's military collapse and revolution in 1918. As a result of this omission, the article concluded admonishingly, the 'Hindenburg legend continues to live on among large parts of German society'.[2] Both newspapers could find no explanation more convincing for republican defeat than the alluring appeal of what they termed the 'Hindenburg legend' or the 'Hindenburg myth', which had supposedly drawn German voters to the polls the previous Sunday.

In 1932, Hindenburg would win a second presidential election battle fought under fundamentally altered political conditions. This time, left-wing journalist Carl von Ossietzky was equally certain that no political programme had brought about this victory. Only 'Hindenburg has triumphed, a piece of legend', the future Nobel laureate maintained.[3] Thus, both in 1925 and 1932—the only two times in German history that the people could elect their head of state directly and secretly—a majority opted for the mythical Hindenburg.[4]

Today remembered first and foremost critically for the role he would play in the collapse of Weimar democracy by appointing Hitler as Reich Chancellor on 30 January 1933, a myth surrounding Hindenburg as invoked by these Weimar journalists seems a somewhat curious phenomenon. Interviewed in 2003, during a controversy surrounding a possible retraction of Hindenburg's honorary citizenship of Berlin, the city's one-time mayor, Walter Momper (SPD), summed up this present-day sentiment with the verdict: 'there is no one who stands up for Hindenburg with enthusiasm'.[5] As the pointed election commentary of 1925 shows, however, matters looked entirely different then. If the papers' analyses are to be believed, Hindenburg was a figure enthralling enough to let voters' capacities for critical thinking evaporate and to paralyse republican defences. In the seventh year after the First World War had ended—having brought in its wake the collapse of the German monarchies, near civil war, hyperinflation, and a reviled peace treaty cementing German war guilt, the loss of substantial territory, and a reduced army—Hindenburg, who had led the German armies between 1916 and 1919, remained *the* undisputed living national hero in Germany.

How, then, did this man acquire the extraordinary, mythical stature that enabled him to capture the presidency in 1925 and to defend it in 1932? How did his myth manage to survive military failure in 1918, and why was the sheer presence of his name on the ballot enough to mesmerize a critical mass of voters? Admiring and trusting Hindenburg were, of course, not the only factors that motivated voters' choices and dominated people's concerns in the complex period of Weimar. Nevertheless, the suddenness, intensity, longevity, striking political and social breadth, and the political deployment of Hindenburg's adulation, in short, the power of his myth between 1914 and 1934, was a political phenomenon of the first order that merits detailed examination. How this little-known General, whose career to normal retirement age had provided no real foretaste of his heroic status after 1914, became a national icon and living myth, catching the imagination of millions of Germans, and what this phenomenon tells us about one of the most crucial periods of the country's history, is the subject of this book.

\* \* \*

Much has been written about Paul von Hindenburg. A bibliography compiled by the National Socialist Cultural Community a few years after the President's death, already listed no fewer than 3,000 works on the deceased.[6] The volume of studies since has grown considerably. The historiography to date, however, consists first and foremost of assessments of Hindenburg's military leadership and political role as head of the third Oberste Heeresleitung (OHL) during the First World War[7], of biographical approaches, which either focus on the period of 1914–1918[8] or concentrate on Hindenburg's politics until 1934.[9] Some of these studies—even from the post-1945 era—have to be considered hagiographic.[10] In addition, the very fact that Hindenburg was a key player in Weimar politics in the second half of the 1920s and, in particular, during the era of the so-called presidential cabinets between 1930 and 1933, means that his part in the political decision-making process has been analysed in the standard works on the history of this period.[11] The overwhelming majority of these works is concerned exclusively with political and military matters. Hindenburg's talents as a military commander, the ambivalent nature of his relationship with Erich Ludendorff, his own political ideas, and his stance towards Kaiser Wilhelm II are themes addressed in the literature. Furthermore, many specialized studies have shed light on various aspects of Hindenburg's record as President.[12]

For a long time, the consensus had been that Hindenburg was a personally weak and untalented military leader and an apolitical and perhaps not particularly intelligent Reich President, who was largely steered by others—a consensus summed up by John Wheeler-Bennett's evocative description of Hindenburg as a 'wooden titan', imposing on the outside but hollow within.[13] Those charged with pulling the strings in the background were first and foremost Erich Ludendorff during wartime and the so-called camarilla during his presidency, allegedly comprising his son Oskar, his State Secretary Otto Meissner, and various figures from the East Prussian agrarian conservative political milieu and German big business.[14] Only recently has this paradigm been thoroughly questioned, with newer studies revising the idea of an all-powerful camarilla and highlighting Hindenburg's independent thought and acute political understanding. Werner Maser, Harald Zaun, and, most recently, Wolfram Pyta have revealed a political figure much better-informed and in command of his decisions than previously thought and—though not its focal point—this study makes a further contribution to revising the idea of an apolitical and weak-willed Hindenburg.[15]

While Hindenburg's politics are an important issue, the thrust of this book is different. Although it is widely acknowledged that the Field Marshal had entered the realm of myth during his lifetime, little research has been done on what that myth meant.[16] How did it come into being, how was it communicated, appropriated, transformed, and how did it function between 1914 and 1934, and beyond his death? Those historians who invoke the phenomenon usually treat it first and foremost as a political issue, a factor in German political history, debated endlessly by party politicians and in the political press.[17] Here, however, the Hindenburg myth will be investigated as a political *and* cultural phenomenon, which did not just occupy those involved in German politics, but penetrated much broader sections of society in its myriad forms. The mythical narrative sheds a great deal on how power was brokered and what hopes, wishes, and fears the German population harboured between 1914 and 1934.

* * *

The study of political myths—central components of cultural memory—is largely based on the notion of socially constructed memory.[18] It owes much to the theoretical works of French interwar sociologist Maurice Halbwachs. In his pioneering work Halbwachs argued that images of the past are not static, but in flux; different socio-political groups constantly contest them.[19] The problem of memory is thus one of social power. Analysing what a society or community remembers—and how—is a way of reading the cultural distribution of power within that society and gives us clues to the needs and wishes of its members.[20] Rather than commemorating 'objectively', each age reconstructs the past within images that suit its present needs. Politicians and opinion-makers intent on furthering a more current agenda often appropriate such constructed images of the past.[21] Far from being a method pursued only by authoritarian regimes or dictatorships, the deployment of the past to meet more current practical ends is a phenomenon that can also be witnessed in pluralist democratic societies.[22]

The application of Halbwachs's model of how the memory of individuals is converted into collective memory has since led to extensive research into the history of commemorative practices in the public sphere.[23] The politics of memory and commemoration in the fragmented political culture of the Weimar Republic with its lack of a historical consensus has been subject to particularly close scholarly attention.[24] It took some time until the theoretical sophistication of this area of research began to have an impact on the study of political myths. As late as the mid-1990s one historian bemoaned that in spite of the cultural turn historical scholarship had mostly ignored the study of myths.[25] This has changed in recent years; scholars have discovered the history of myth as a fruitful subject.[26]

After 1945 the notion of myth was largely discredited in Germany. The National Socialists' powerful appropriation of older political myths during their rise to power and the aesthetics of their rule meant that myths were seen first and foremost as possessing dangerous emotional connotations, causing people to depart from rational behaviour. Myths appeared as hazardous weapons from the arsenal of political propagandists, especially in authoritarian societies and dictatorships, which ran counter to the values of an enlightened democratic society.[27] In the period under investigation, however, the term did not yet entail these negative connotations, but was largely considered a positive social force.[28] Even the German philosopher Ernst Cassirer, dubbed the 'father of the modern study of myths'[29] who described myth as a potentially destructive force in his highly influential *The Myth of the State* published after the Second World War, had subscribed to a more positive understanding of the concept in the 1920s.[30] This 1920s consensus on myth as a constructive force may explain why Hindenburg's contemporaries frequently interpreted his mythical exaltation in a positive light without fear that such candour would discredit the cult.[31] Contemporary society considered myth a binding force, a social glue, which appealed to people on an emotional level serving to integrate different groups within society. Myth seemed to be an almost natural force, which belonged to all forms of human life 'like roots to a plant'.[32] Especially during the 1920s, as some contemporary observers noted, people were 'starving' or 'longing' for myth in Germany, thus expressing the belief that myth was somewhat organic.[33]

Hence, in this study the term 'myth' will not be used in its colloquial form as a deliberate falsification or an outright lie. It differs from the term 'legends' in this respect. Legends are commonly defined as stories based on half-truths and distortions of reality.[34] By contrast, the aim here is not to contrast the 'real' Hindenburg with the mythical one. Naturally, some of the factual distortions that lie at the heart of the narrative surrounding him will be discussed, but the aim of this study is neither to uncover the real 'Victor of Tannenberg' nor to prove that Hindenburg was not worthy of his adulation.[35] Instead, the Hindenburg myth itself will take centre stage and will be analysed as a complex communicative process, in which the motives of both myth-purveyors and consumers have to be examined.

The term 'myth' is defined as an 'order of images with a metaphysical claim'.[36] Myths are symbolically charged narratives that purport to give a true account of a set of past, present, or predicted political events and are accepted by a social group.[37] They are told to explain or justify present conditions and as social constructions of reality, they appeal to the emotional dimension of human thought.[38] By reducing complex events to simple processes (e.g. by creating a dichotomy of 'good versus evil', 'hero and coward', or 'us versus them') myth-purveyors seek to simplify reality for the purpose of increasing affective mass unity.[39] This is a viable avenue, because reducing the multiplicity of standpoints creates a feeling of community and belonging—myths integrate.[40] They also generate meaning by acting as a filter of reality, a lens through which events and human actions are perceived.

Furthermore, they have a normative function: the protagonists of mythical narratives—the mythical heroes—often embody a set of values and serve as role models appealing to societies or social groups to emulate their virtuous stance.[41] Equally, mythical figures have much to reveal about the society in which they are worshipped: as the symbolic expression of its hidden conflicts, fears, hopes, longings, and needs they give us vital clues to the 'collective unconscious of a society'.[42]

As manifestations of collective memory, myths are dynamic. They consist of different layers—what Levi-Strauss termed 'les véritables unités constitutives du mythe'—and are therefore by nature polyvalent in their form.[43] Their function is not always clear-cut. It can, in fact, vary considerably depending on the respective social and political context in which they surface. Myths can thus create legitimacy for an existing political order, but they can also destabilize conditions—depending on how and by whom they are deployed and which particular mythical layer is emphasized at which point.[44] Myths are embedded into the binding forces of social groups or societies. In times of crisis they are often especially potent and prolific, as Ernst Cassirer was one of the first to recognize.[45] The period under investigation, which was defined by the experience of the First World War, Germany's military collapse and revolution in 1918/19, and the politically, economically, and socially unstable years of the Weimar Republic was the perfect 'incubator for political myths', the 'natural soil' in which they 'found ample nourishment'.[46]

'Mythophilia' and by definition the worshipping of individual heroes had generally been on the rise in Europe since the mid-nineteenth century, particularly in Germany, not least due to the promise innate in myths of filling the void left by the decline of religious thinking in the era of secularization.[47] Thomas Nipperdey identified the 'inclination to historical myths, monumentality and pathos' as one of the negative aspects of the Wilhelmine period.[48] As early as the 1860s, the historian Jacob Burckhardt had observed 'intense longing for great men' in Germany and Thomas Carlyle's lectures *On Heroes, Hero-Worship and the Heroic in History*, in which he hailed hero-worship as one of the most efficient means of stabilizing a social and political order, went through numerous German editions.[49] Leo von Klenze's *Walhalla* monument near Regensburg, a pantheon of German heroes, had opened in 1842, and turned into a magnet for tourists. After 1871 a large number of memorials to individual heroes—especially Otto von Bismarck and Kaiser Wilhelm I—were erected throughout Germany and German schoolchildren were instilled with a sense of their historic glory in the *Kaiserreich*'s history lessons that focused overwhelmingly on the role of 'great men'.[50] Heroic thinking in 19C

Myths and mythical hero figures are rarely new inventions. It is easier for them to gain potency if they correspond to the structure of a society's imagination and build upon semantic and semiotic traditions.[51] The dominant hero figure of the latter half of the nineteenth century was, of course, the 'Iron Chancellor', and Hindenburg was often hailed as a 'new Bismarck' based on the two men's visual and political associations.[52] Hindenburg's image was also composed of different elements of other historical narratives. His myth was closely entwined with the notion of German 'innocence' for the outbreak of war in 1914, the saviour theme, the 'stab-in-the-back' legend, and the 'spirit of 1914'. He was firmly embedded in this mythical network of Weimar Germany and served as the supreme individual living link between these collective moments and tales.[53]

Furthermore, Hindenburg's adulation owed much to even older German patterns of thought. In some important respects, he met the criteria of a classic hero figure—ideals worshipped in the nineteenth century in figures as diverse as Arminius or Hermann, who had defeated the Roman troops in the Teutoburg Forest in AD 9, in Siegfried, the hero of the *Nibelungen* saga popularized as the German national epic since the beginning of the nineteenth century, and in the legend of the medieval Hohenstauffen Emperor Friedrich I Barbarossa, who would allegedly awake one day from his long sleep inside Mount Kyffhäuser to restore the German *Reich* to its former greatness.[54] All three had gained prominence as a reaction to the Napoleonic occupation and the wars of liberation at the beginning of the nineteenth century.[55]

The archetypal hero of the classic heroic saga was almost exclusively male and an aristocrat who embodied the values of medieval society resurrected by German romanticism: honour, loyalty, obedience, and piety.[56] Indeed, the one great German heroine, Queen Luise of Prussia, supposedly embodied them all in a heightened degree.[57] As the personification of German wartime virtues, Hindenburg fitted this description perfectly. In sacrificing his comfortable life in retirement in Hanover, he personified another key element of heroism: leaving one's home to experience 'adventures' in a 'strange and faraway land' (in his case German military headquarters in the east).[58] Though he could hardly be said to be either youthful or athletic (usually a further precondition for heroic status), this did not stop illustrators from portraying Hindenburg as a youthful and athletic giant into old age.[59]

\* \* \*

Some scholars have turned to Max Weber's concept of 'charismatic authority' to explain the adulation of heroic political leaders.[60] In his seminal work on what constitutes legitimate rule the sociologist described trust in a 'charismatic leader' as one of the binding social forces that can lend legitimacy to a social order. Charismatic rule is based on the exceptional belief in the heroic power and model function of a leader who is thought to possess extraordinary qualities.[61]

The concept has first and foremost been applied to Hitler and Bismarck. Since Weber's notion of plebiscitary democratic leadership found expression in the Weimar constitution at least in part—the President was elected by popular vote and could dissolve the Reichstag—an analysis of Hindenburg as 'charismatic leader' might seem like an obvious choice.[62] On closer inspection, however, in Hindenburg's case the blanket concept of 'charismatic authority' poses almost as many questions as it provides answers. Whilst its emphasis on the charismatic leader functioning as a projection screen for the needs and wishes of a society is certainly useful, it does not tell us much about the daily face of charisma—the communication of a leader's popularity, the role of the media, of everyday objects, symbolic displays and rituals.[63] Most importantly, Weber insists that the charismatic leader has to prove his worth time and again to sustain his authority. He cites the case of a Chinese monarch under whose rule a series of natural catastrophes occurs and whose troops are defeated in the field. As a consequence, his followers lose their trust in his exceptional qualities and his authority falters; he can no longer sustain his charismatic rule.[64] As we will see, Weber's insistence on the leader having to prove his worth continuously to guarantee the loyalty of his following, cannot be applied to Hindenburg's mythical standing in a clear-cut manner.[65] Hindenburg did not deliver victory in 1918. Nor did he 'save' Germany from perceived international humiliation, civil war, or hyperinflation in the postwar years. Nor could he avert the increasing political polarization, economic crisis, and record unemployment of the late 1920s and early 1930s, and he did not, as the majority of his voters of 1932 had hoped, save Germany from Nazi rule. Thus, Hindenburg did at least as much to disappoint the expectations his devotees had invested in him as he did to turn desperate hopes into confident expectations in the first place. And yet, he kept the status of a mythical hero throughout the period of 1914 to 1934. Those who subscribed to his myth largely clung to their beliefs for twenty years and more, although the political system in which they lived and all its other symbols (including the national flag) were overthrown not once, but twice during this time. The belief in Hindenburg's mythical qualities was less ephemeral and more enduring than a close reading of Weber would suggest.[66]

How far was such mythical adulation an exclusively German phenomenon? Should the personality cult surrounding Hindenburg be considered a further stride on Germany's 'special path', ultimately ending in dictatorship and war?[67] Parallels to the hero worship of Hindenburg certainly suggest themselves in other countries and periods even though they cannot be discussed in detail here.[68] In wartime Britain, not just a civilian leader like David Lloyd George was revered, but Herbert Kitchener, idolized until his sudden death in 1916, determined the British iconography of wartime.[69] In the Second World War, Winston Churchill seemingly embodied key British virtues such as resilience and fighting spirit and has remained a popular icon to this day.[70] In France, Philippe Pétain emerged as *the* hero of the First World War, his fame, like Hindenburg's, resting on a defensive battle—Verdun—and he would also be portrayed as the 'saviour' of the French as the leader of the Vichy government. The trust of large parts of the French population in Maréchal Pétain also proved remarkably enduring even after the pitfalls of the policy of collaboration his name sanctioned became evident. The Pétain myth, in fact, shaped and defined French politics from the First World War to the post-1945 period, in similar ways the Hindenburg myth left its mark on German history between 1914 and 1934.[71] A hundred years earlier, Napoleon Bonaparte had also entered the realm of myth during his own lifetime. At the core of his myth lay not just his glory as a victorious military leader, but also notions of non-partisanship and a conciliatory political role—not all too different from Hindenburg's reputation as towering above the fray of party politics. Napoleon's myth, too, was a broad and complex phenomenon that lasted beyond his death and represented much more than romantic nostalgia for the Imperial past. And like Hindenburg, Napoleon was the subject of a 'cult of objects'.[72] In Italy, the country that invites comparison with Germany most frequently due to its relatively late unification and strong regional characteristics, Guiseppe Garibaldi, the hero of the *Risorgimento*, a potent and plastic symbol of Italian nationalism, was exalted to mythical heights during his lifetime. As in Hindenburg's case, the Garibaldi myth was the result of an 'intricate process of negotiation between actor and audience' whose authorship was not always clear-cut, as Lucy Riall has shown recently.[73] Socialist regimes, be it Communist China or Soviet Russia, have equally witnessed heroic leadership cults around Mao Zedong, Lenin, and Stalin.[74]

Notwithstanding these parallels, which show that worshipping mythical figures was not limited exclusively to Germany, however, the Hindenburg myth merits investigation because its consequences were extremely serious: it was followed by National Socialism. While this outcome was far from coincidental, it was, as this study will assert, not inevitable from the outset. Public displays of unity between Hindenburg and the 'young leader' Adolf Hitler, such as the infamous 'Day of Potsdam' of March 1933 were, of course, milestones in both the history of Hindenburg's mythical adulation and in showcasing the 'people's community', a key element of Nazi propaganda. Focusing exclusively on Hindenburg's image in the early years of the Nazi regime, however, entails the danger of buying into Nazi propaganda by reducing the hero worship of Hindenburg to a linear process, which was always going to result in Hitler coming to power—when, in fact, it is precisely the complexity of Hindenburg's idolization that makes the phenomenon worth investigating. For it was not just based on right-wing notions of authoritarian leadership but also more collective national values, such as salvaging something positive from war and defeat, preventing chaos, and about self-affirmation and German virtues in the face of crisis. The polyvalent and multi-layered nature of the narrative also meant that different groups could deploy the myth, at different times, and for different purposes. It did not serve the same clear-cut rationale for twenty years; its function changed repeatedly depending on the conditions of its deployment. This plasticity made the Hindenburg myth a much more powerful political weapon than a clear-cut symbol strictly consigned to the echelons of Weimar's political right could ever have been. As this study will show, it was precisely because he managed to cut across party political lines like almost no other figure in this period of political polarization that Hindenburg's myth—and, by extension, his actions—could wield such influence over the course of German history.

Weimar's political landscape was fragmented into numerous different social-political milieux, with at least nine different political or professional affiliations having been identified by scholars as the loci of group identities—the liberals, Social Democrats, left-wing intellectuals, Communists, political Catholics, the industrial elites, agrarian conservatives, right-wing nationalists, and the Nazis.[75] When analysing the political and cultural codes to which they subscribed, they can be reduced to three blocks—the republicans, who were essentially in favour of Weimar democracy, the nationalist right, which opposed it and favoured authoritarian rule, and the Socialist block, which extolled class warfare.[76] As we will see, only the latter, comprised of the left-wing of Social Democracy and the Communist Party (KPD) founded after the revolution in 1918, was immune to Hindenburg's appeal from 1914 to 1934. All other seven subgroups—albeit at different times and in qualitatively different ways—subscribed to significant elements of the mythical narrative, and there we must include the moderate Social Democratic majority, which had supported the war and the Republic. He thus did not quite achieve, but bordered on a catch-all appeal.

In terms of myth-making, Hindenburg's exaltation was somewhat special. Without a permanent propagandistic myth-maker, or, to use Claude Lévi-Strauss's term, 'bricoleur', in the fashion of Joseph Goebbels to Hitler (at least prior to 1933), his mythical adulation was promoted by a variety of players.[77] Acknowledging Hindenburg's own role in promoting and safeguarding his fame is especially crucial, because his much-trumpeted personal modesty, lack of ambition and political interest, as well as his non-existent vanity were such central elements of the mythical narrative.

According to his admirers, Hindenburg regarded the cult that had accreted around his name with growing irritation and did nothing to further this adulation. The liberal publicist Theodor Wolff, for instance, proclaimed that Hindenburg gained popularity precisely because he did not look for it. 'It is unthinkable that anyone else on whom the eyes of the world rest, is freer of pose, less concerned with making a positive impression…than him', he wrote in 1932.[78] Such convictions have turned out to be remarkably long-lived.[79] Although replacing the notion of a Hindenburg, who was entirely free of vanity and did nothing to further his cult, with that of a highly image-conscious politician obsessed with his public standing may be tempting, such a turnaround would be oversimplified. The truth probably lies somewhere in between these two extremes: there is plenty of evidence to revise contemporary ideas about Hindenburg's indifference towards his public standing, but there were also limits to his attempts to control the way he was portrayed, especially, as we will see, in ostentatiously apolitical media.[80] Hindenburg's vanity or image-consciousness cannot explain every twist and turn of his career.[81]

Since the main focus of this study will be on Hindenburg's mythical adulation during his lifetime, rather than on the posthumous deployment of his myth, it differs from other works on myth and memory in some important respects. Myths surrounding political ideas, such as that of the 'national community', or heroes of a previous era, such as the myths of Bismarck or Hermann the Cherusker in the Weimar years, are confined to the realm of discourse and commemoration. Thus, their capacity as projection screens for contemporary ideas and the influence exerted on them by present agendas is much more clear-cut. As a living myth, Hindenburg could still influence the way he was perceived, and he could and did make decisions that contradicted his erstwhile reputation. In that sense, the future Nobel laureate Carl von Ossietzky only grasped part of the phenomenon when he described Hindenburg as 'a heroic frame onto which anyone can clamp whatever colourful web of illusions he desires'.[82] In fact, there was a tension inherent in the Hindenburg myth between the projected needs and wishes of his followers and his political actions. Because he made decisions that often contradicted the expectations of his diverse adherents, Hindenburg was no empty vessel waiting to be filled with whichever dreams and wishes people harboured at a particular moment in time. They could not simply mould him into the mythical figure they desired, but had to work with what they got from him. His actions were constantly incorporated into the mythical narrative, making it an ever-evolving phenomenon. This inner tension and need for ongoing adaptation, and the fact that despite so many ruptures between 1914 and 1934 the myth managed to survive make its history particularly worth examining.

# I

# The 'Victor of Tannenberg'

In the beginning was Tannenberg. Paul Ludwig Hans Anton von Beneckendorff und von Hindenburg—to give his full name—the son of a Prussian aristocrat and a non-aristocratic mother born in Posen on 2 October 1847, was virtually unknown to the German public before the famous battle of August 1914.

Hindenburg's normal military career ended in 1911, when he retired. At the age of eighteen, in 1866, he joined the recently established Third Regiment of Foot Guards and was thereby admitted to the esteemed Prussian officer corps, membership of which went hand in hand with greatly increased social prestige. During the Austro-Prussian war of 1866, young Hindenburg fought in the famous battle of Königgrätz; four years later, during the Franco-Prussian war, he took part in the crucial battles of Saint-Privat and Sedan. When Wilhelm I of Prussia was crowned German Emperor at Versailles on 18 January 1871, the 23-year-old Hindenburg had the honour to be present as his regiment's representative. After successfully concluding his training at the Prussian Military Academy, he was admitted to the prestigious Prussian General Staff and would later spend several years teaching tactics at the Academy. He continued to rise up the ranks steadily, eventually becoming an Infantry General—the third highest rank in the Prussian army—in 1905.

Hindenburg had always been known to delegate many tasks to his subordinates—a key feature of the later and more well-known stages of his military and political career—and renowned for his calmness and equanimity, major strengths that would also become central to his public image. A devout Protestant and Prussian aristocrat, he was deeply attached to his monarch and the traditional Prussian values of loyalty, honour, piety, and obedience. As a member of the Prussian military establishment Hindenburg was naturally anti-liberal and conservative in his political outlook. He was however, no conservative *Altpreuße* suspecting German unification of macerating Prussia's character; rather, his attachment to the ideal of a unified German nation meant that he had welcomed unification in 1871.[1] A family man, married happily to his wife Gertrud with whom he had a son and two daughters, with a soft spot for hunting, long walks, and military marches, his was not a particularly dazzling character. Personable and usually well-liked by those who met him face-to-face, but not a great orator or brilliant intellectual, Hindenburg never excelled in creativity or strategic thinking throughout his solidly successful career, exhibiting little of the military genius that would later be attributed to him. Nevertheless, his name was mentioned as merely one of seven in discussions about who would succeed Alfred von Schlieffen as Chief of the General Staff in 1906. Even though Hindenburg was by no means a favourite and duly lost out to Helmuth von Moltke the younger, the fact that he was even considered to become the Kaiser's chief military adviser shows that his career prior to 1911 was, in fact, a remarkably thriving one.[2] And yet, the German public scarcely took notice of Hindenburg's departure in 1911; well-known in military circles only, his career seemed to have passed its natural zenith at the age of 64. He had certainly distinguished himself, but that was all. After the outbreak of war, however, he would have greatness thrust upon him.

In August 1914, he was called back to active service to command the Eighth Army in East Prussia when it had run into difficulties under its previous commander, Maximilian von Prittwitz und Gaffron. Hindenburg was not chosen for his strategic brilliance, but as a good delegator and calm and composed presence. His foremost task was to provide a backbone to the ambitious and more junior Major-General Erich Ludendorff, who had just proven his talents at the Battle of Liège. Wilhelm Groener, who would eventually succeed the impulsive Ludendorff in 1918, claimed with hindsight that 'the *only* reason for . . . [Hindenburg's] appointment was that due to his phlegm he would not interfere with Ludendorff's decisions'.[3] While Hindenburg's re-activation still went unnoticed, the events of late August 1914 proved to be the turning point.

In Germany, as, in fact, in most belligerent countries, the successful psychological mobilization of the population rested largely on the idea of fighting a defensive war. Accordingly, the German government had gone to great lengths to ensure that the German people believed that they were being attacked.[4] As some of the very few battles fought on German soil during the entire war, the events on Germany's Eastern Front in the first few weeks of August 1914 proved to be pivotal.[5]

The Russian Army had marched into East Prussia in early August 1914, occupying large parts of the province. The invasion played a crucial role in emphasizing the idea of Germany defending herself—an idea otherwise increasingly hard to maintain in the light of Germany's invasion of neutral Belgium. Newspaper reports about Russian atrocities against the civilian population only strengthened the German people's sense of collective victimhood, the seeds of which had been carefully sown by stoking up Russophobia and the fear of encirclement in the prewar years. This strategy had been crowned by remarkable success, even among Social Democrats.[6] Describing the Russian soldiers on the Eastern Front, Social Democratic war correspondent Wilhelm Düwell invoked the image of 'semi-barbarians, who scorch, murder, loot, who shoot at Samaritans, who vandalize medical stations, and spare neither women nor the injured'. Those were the true pillars of tsarism, he concluded, 'the scourge of Europe'.[7] Such depictions could build on much older stereotypes of a people characterized by Slavonic barbarism and aggression—stereotypes even many Social Democrats subscribed to.[8] In fact, their support for the war on 4 August 1914 was the logical consequence of their repugnance of tsarist autocracy, a cornerstone of Marxist ideology and a Social Democratic 'article of faith', as well as the result of their equally long-established commitment to national defence.[9]

Liberal publicists were no less eager to point out that Russia occupied a special place amongst Germany's enemies. In the words of Theodor Wolff, the chief editor of the *Berliner Tageblatt*, 'a difference exists between the French, who defend their country, and the great Russian mass, which follows the Tsar's orders without any national driving force'.[10] For him the 'overthrow' and 'weakening of the [Russian] colossus . . . was the moral idea of this great fight'.[11]

Once the Russian occupation had ended, the atrocity stories in the German press largely turned out to be exaggerated.[12] Nevertheless, the notion of a brutal Russian bear violating Germany's innocence had established itself as a powerful image in the collective mind of the German people. Not only would such notions be carefully kept alive by propagandists, but they also provided a welcome counter against stories of atrocities committed by German troops in Belgium, a recurrent theme of Allied propaganda.[13]

This sense of victimhood is vital for understanding the public's responses to the outbreak of war. The belief that German society had welcomed war with unanimous enthusiasm, captured by the so-called 'spirit of 1914', and united in a renewed sense of community, has long since been revised. In its stead a more complex picture has emerged of an 'August experience' characterized by a combination of duty-bound patriotism and fervent nationalism with an undercurrent of real anxiety, apprehension, and fear.[14] In that sense, many Germans—even if supportive of the war—perceived August 1914 as a moment of crisis and uncertainty. Myths are particularly prolific during such moments since they offer desperate individuals the opportunity to repress their fears.[15] The public enthusiasm that accompanied the news of the victory at Tannenberg in late August and early September 1914—as well as Hindenburg's subsequent adulation—have to be viewed against the background of people's heightened senses, their uncertainty and anxiety about what this war would bring. Focusing on Tannenberg and Hindenburg was one way of bottling up more sombre thoughts.[16]

Furthermore, having followed the extensive news coverage of the Russian occupation, many Germans probably felt genuinely liberated from the yoke of 'barbarism'.[17] But Tannenberg was also hailed as an outstanding victory for other reasons. The fighting, having lasted several days, had resulted in the total defeat of the Second Russian Army under its commander Alexander Samsonov on 29 August 1914. Capitalizing on the failure of all co-ordination between Samsonov's army and Paul von Rennenkampf's First Russian Army in East Prussia, the Germans had moved rapidly from the eastern part of the province to assemble opposite the southern Russian army, surrounding it on three sides. The battle resulted in 50,000 Russian dead and wounded, and 92,000 soldiers taken prisoner against German casualties of 10–15,000—despite the Germans' inferiority in numbers.[18] Subsequently, the Germans turned eastwards, where, in a series of confrontations in early September, known as the Battles of the Masurian Lakes, they temporarily pushed the First Russian Army out of Germany and took an additional 125,000 Russian prisoners—although this time the German armies suffered nearly as many casualties as the Russian.[19] The total defeat of the Second Russian Army at Tannenberg and the sheer number of prisoners taken made this victory stand out remarkably against the battles waged on the Western Front. In this modern conflict on an unprecedented scale, which would increasingly become characterized by military stalemate and trench warfare, Tannenberg was an old-fashioned and decisive victory, reminiscent of German successes in the wars of unification. The battle would even be referred to as a modern Cannae—one of the most famous battles of encirclement of all time—on more than one occasion.[20]

Tannenberg's simultaneity with the Battle of the Marne on the Western Front further enhanced its propagandistic use. Initially, the German public had been promised a swift victory in the west, with Paris being taken within six weeks. After some early successes, however, the western campaign became stuck, resulting in the large-scale withdrawal of the German armies at the river Marne in September 1914. This major setback, as well as Helmuth von Moltke's subsequent breakdown and resignation as Chief of the General Staff, were not debated openly in Germany's censored press.[21] Instead the German victories on the Eastern Front were emphasized in the daily army reports to gloss over the defeat at the Marne. The news of Tannenberg was, of course, greeted enthusiastically in the German press and public in late August, but that enthusiasm only reached its height after the defeat at the Marne had become evident to German officials in mid-September.[22] By emphasizing information on the eastern campaigns when positive news from the Western Front was lacking, the German military carefully orchestrated continued belief in their prowess and prospects of a swift victory. Tannenberg thus proved to be a powerful tool in the battle for the hearts and minds of the German population—a promise of further victories to come.

The clever naming of the battle can equally help to explain why it grew to mythical proportions, rivalling Verdun as the most famous battle of the First World War in German memory. The first semi-official dispatches of the German wire service, Wolffs Telegraphisches Büro (WTB), did not cite the catchy name 'Tannenberg', but spoke of three-day-long clashes in 'Gilgenburg and Ortelsburg'.[23] Equally, an instruction by General von Kessel of 29 August stated that flags should be raised on all public buildings to commemorate 'the victory at Gilgenburg'.[24] The name 'Tannenberg' was not mentioned until 31 August, but the events would soon thereafter be known exclusively by this name. 'Tannenberg' triggered association with one of the greatest humiliations in German public memory, the defeat of the knights of the German Order by Polish and Lithuanian armies in July 1410. After Poland's partition in the eighteenth century, 1410 became a symbol for the Polish struggle for independence. The celebratory commemorations staged in Cracow on the occasion of the 500th anniversary of the battle in 1910 had brought back to life the memory of the German defeat and had caused heated public reactions in Germany. A victory with the same name, albeit against Russia, offered a welcome opportunity to overcome this painful recollection in 1914.[25]

Different individuals claimed credit for the idea of re-naming the battle, including Max Hoffmann, one of the lesser-known architects of German victory in East Prussia, Erich Ludendorff, and finally, Hindenburg himself. As he wrote to his wife on 30 August 1914:

> I have asked H.M. [His Majesty] to name the three-day-long fights the Battle of Tannenberg. At Tannenberg, situated between Gilgenburg and Hohenstein, the Poles and Lithuanians defeated the German Order in 1410. Now, 504 years later, we have taken revenge . . .[26]

This christening demonstrated Hindenburg's acute sense of the politics of memory;[27] it ensured that the German public instantly perceived it as a victory of historic proportions—and in making himself Tannenberg's godfather Hindenburg equally guaranteed that his own name would forever be associated with this supposedly seminal event. The fact that news of the triumph was still coming in on 2 September, the anniversary of the Battle of Sedan, which had spelt victory for the German armies in the Franco-Prussian war of 1870–71 and had been commemorated every year since, created even more of an historical aura. The conservative *Deutsche Tageszeitung* promptly hailed Tannenberg as 'The Sedan of the Russian Army'.[28]

Contrary to Verdun or Langemarck, which would come to symbolize the creation of a hardened and new type of German soldier and the loss of youthful innocence respectively, Tannenberg's hero was one man alone: Hindenburg.[29] Although his contribution to the military planning and execution of the battle is often described as being of very little substance—Max Hoffman once commented sarcastically that Hindenburg's input had been no greater than that of his own daughter Ilse[30]—he was almost solely credited with the victory. Kaiser Wilhelm II's congratulatory telegram, calling Tannenberg a victory 'unique in history', which would guarantee Hindenburg 'never-ending glory', was printed on the front page of the major papers.[31] As early as 29 August a biographical sketch of Hindenburg was circulated to all the major newspapers by the wire service Wolffs Telegraphisches Büro.[32] Thus, the Germans immediately learnt that he had fought in the legendary battles of Königgrätz and Sedan and had been present at Versailles in 1871, and was thus in many ways the embodiment of Wilhelmine Germany's glorious past. The liberal *Berliner Tageblatt* was quick to offer insights into Hindenburg's personality when informing its readers that 'the 67-year-old [*sic*] gentleman had overcome his physical frailties with iron energy' and had grabbed his 'tried and tested sword and brandished it with the same calm and cold-bloodedness against the Russians' that he had displayed against the French 44 years earlier.[33] The notion of the 'cool' and 'calm' Hindenburg that was to become a pillar of his myth was thus born as early as August 1914. Even more inventive reports portrayed him as having spent the years of his retirement single-handedly devising a gigantic trap for a Russian invasion, exploring paths and plumbing the quicksands in East Prussia, in which the enemy was to be engulfed in a perfect battle, finally fulfilling his plans in August 1914.[34] He was soon celebrated as the 'Russians' Slayer', the 'Conqueror of the Russian Bear', and 'Liberator of East Prussia'.[35] Others who had conducted the Battle of Tannenberg, most notably Ludendorff, initially did not feature at all in the coverage of events. In the words of Theodor Wolff, within two weeks of the battle Hindenburg, on the other hand, had become Germany's 'new hero'.[36]

The 'Victor of Tannenberg' was another of his many sobriquets and probably the most enduring one.[37] Equally, the name 'Hindenburg'—not the much longer and less catchy 'von Beneckendorff und von Hindenburg'—soon became a label in its own right. More than a decade later the poet Wilhelm von Scholz reminisced about the fear the German population had felt before the news of victory in East Prussia had reached the home front, and described the moment the public had first heard this name. 'Hindenburg' had sounded 'dark, dull, heavy and German' and its 'promising sound' would be invoked frequently throughout his career.[38] Soon after, the first images began to circulate. According to Scholz, they matched the name: Hindenburg was no 'elegant, dashing' man, but a 'heavy, mighty . . . General with a square head'. He thus embodied a specific type of masculinity; he was no youthful or athletic warrior, but symbolized virile gravitas through his rectangular features and broad frame. The early character sketches highlighting his equanimity, as well as his evocative name and physical appearance thus all contributed equally to his evolving image as a tranquil and determined guardian of Germany who would contain the 'Russian tidal waves' and stand firm as a rock no matter what.[39]

People's perceptions of him would remain closely linked with the events of August 1914 for the next 20 years. The quickly developing Hindenburg cult and the legendary narrative constructed around Tannenberg worked reciprocally—Hindenburg's fame would keep the memory of Tannenberg alive until well into the 1920s and 1930s, whilst the battle's propagandistic deployment, not least in the struggle against the notion of German war guilt, continued to nurture the Hindenburg cult.

At the same time, the emerging Hindenburg myth comprised more than the military genius allegedly exhibited at Tannenberg. A dichotomy existed between Hindenburg's cold-bloodedness and readiness to wage violent battles on the one hand—after all 50,000 Russians had been slaughtered in East Prussia—and his calm, decency, generosity, personal modesty and willingness to make sacrifices on the other.[40] In that sense, the character traits ascribed to him mirrored not only idealized descriptions of medieval chronicles glorifying kings, but also Christian narratives of religious martyrdom and hero epics of the nineteenth century. In these tales heroic deeds were always bound up with courage and self-sacrifice. The greatest of all virtuous acts was to put one's life on the line for the greater good, because this affirmed the worthiness of the ideal for which the sacrifice had been made. In the nineteenth century—and even more so in the twentieth—heroic 'sacrifice' no longer necessarily meant blood-sacrifice, but had taken on an ethical dimension: selfless effort for the community rather than death on the battlefield.[41] The fact that Hindenburg had traded his comfortable retirement in Hanover for active service was thus a crucial element of the mythical narrative: he had displayed the very willingness to make substantial sacrifices for the fatherland asked of all enlisted men (the fact that he did not actually have to put his life on the line on the battlefield was irrelevant). Far from having been conscripted, Hindenburg had volunteered, as he had allegedly not been able to bear the thought of letting down Kaiser and country. As he himself would note in his memoirs not without pathos—suggesting his own or his ghost writer's awareness of the traditional structure of hero epics—he had remained in Hanover 'in longing expectation' until the Kaiser's call to duty came on 22 August 1914.[42] In this sense, Hindenburg served as a shining example of self-sacrificial devotion, the ideal-type of the German soldier, ready to fulfil the highest duty of all: protecting the fatherland against its enemies' onslaught. The strong sense of duty which, as Hindenburg insisted, had driven him to serve, would also become a recurrent theme, in so doing resting on a concept which had long been established as a fundamentally Prussian-German ideal.[43]

Hindenburg's calmness, tranquillity, and strong nerves were, equally, perhaps even more central to his public veneration. Remaining calm and composed in the face of intense pressure was a bourgeois virtue extolled in newspaper opinion columns across Germany in 1914 and would gain in importance in the years to come. The rhetoric of stoical self-possession and sang-froid was tied closely to the notion of defensive warfare and Hindenburg seemingly symbolized these typically masculine virtues like no other—a further advantage over Ludendorff who had allegedly 'lost his nerves' at Tannenberg and whose 'fickle, womanish changes of mind' would be noted by contemporaries as well as later immortalized in Alexander Solzhenitsyn's *August 1914*.[44] The German population's supposed superior mental strength, which would ultimately lead to German victory despite the numerical inferiority, would become one of the most long-lasting paradigms of German war propaganda. Hindenburg, whose 'calm' and 'cold-bloodedness' the *Berliner Tageblatt* had celebrated as early as 29 August, was a key role model in this regard, soon exemplified by the rhetoric of the Field Marshal as a 'rock in the ocean'—the ultimate stoical object defying the enemy's onslaught.[45]

A number of older, well-established legendary tales fed into the Hindenburg narrative, ultimately making his myth more potent and more readily accessible. The newly minted Field Marshal was soon likened to 'Barbarossa', the medieval Hohenstaufen Emperor Friedrich I, who, legend had it, slept in the Kyffhäuser Mountain until he would one day return to resurrect the German Empire. Hindenburg's quiet life in Hanover in the pre-war years, his victorious return to active military duty in 1914, and the widespread enthusiasm which marked the public reaction to Tannenberg, explain why Hindenburg's appearance on the public stage was hailed as a Barbarossa-style return.[46] The 'Hermann' myth, one of the most enduring national tales of the previous century also intensified Hindenburg's sudden adulation. Just as Hermann had fought the Romans triumphantly, Hindenburg was now allegedly uniting the Germans against the Slavonic onslaught.[47] And finally the Bismarck cult, which had gripped Germany in the decades preceding the First World War, in its turn, no doubt boosted Hindenburg's glorification—not least as a result of the two men's striking physical resemblance.

The German population began to worship Hindenburg as its new war hero practically across the board—he appealed equally to Protestants and Catholics, to people in the countryside and urban centres. Because of his anti-Russian—and thus anti-Tsarist—credentials, moderate Social Democrats sang his praise alongside conservative Prussian junkers, just as members of the educated liberal bourgeoisie bought into the mythical narrative.[48] Hindenburg himself sometimes made fun of the universality of his appeal. When a delegation of senior Social Democrats travelled to the military headquarters in Kreuznach to congratulate him on his seventieth birthday, he joked 'that he was quite popular with the comrades and would soon have to acquire a red beret'.[49] Only more radical left-liberals, such as the members of the *Schaubühne* circle, and some Socialists, including the anti-war Karl Liebknecht and the pro-war Eduard David, took a more critical and judicious stance towards Hindenburg's adulation.[50] A myth which rested on militarism went against the core of their political beliefs and smacked of the 'petty bourgeoisie'.[51]

In spite of these few dissenting voices, soon after the outbreak of war Hindenburg became Germany's major symbol of victory against the enemy and of unity at home—a function traditionally performed by the Emperor in wartime, or perhaps on occasion by the Chief of the General Staff, but certainly not by the commander of a single German army. Wilhelm II seemed unable to perform the unifying leadership role expected of a Supreme Warlord. The formidable rise of the modern mass media after the turn of the century—especially the expansion of the illustrated press—had turned Wilhelm II into the first 'media monarch'.[52] The last German Kaiser, however, seemed unable to match his symbolic promises. His popularity had begun to decline as early as 1905/6 after a series of domestic scandals and had deteriorated even more rapidly after the so-called '*Daily Telegraph* Affair' of 1908. Wilhelm responded by increasingly retreating from public life and entering a kind of 'internal emigration'.[53] According to Thomas A. Kohut, his subjects had started to turn their backs on Wilhelm when he proved incapable of fulfilling their glorified images of themselves and their country.[54]

Chief of Staff Moltke's resignation in September 1914 and its initial cover-up only extended the public void that Hindenburg began to fill surprisingly quickly. Walter Nicolai, head of the intelligence department of the OHL, Section IIIb, later remarked that 'Hindenburg's glorification had not been looked for or been created by propaganda.' Instead, the people had apparently 'subconsciously gone down the path we needed them to go down, the path of unity and determination'.[55] This statement can certainly not be upheld in its entirety, but in terms of the genesis of the myth in

1914 it bears a kernel of truth. There is no evidence to suggest that its construction was carefully orchestrated by official German propaganda at the outbreak of war. In fact, the necessary infrastructure was not even in place in the first months of the war to engineer a large-scale publicity campaign of that sort.[56] Once the public passion for their war hero had caught fire, however, the German government happily stoked the flames. Eager to promote the Field Marshal as a boost to morale, the military and political establishment soon found that the Hindenburg myth helped to gloss over problems faced at home and at the front. In a letter Matthias Erzberger, the exceptionally well-informed leader of the Centre Party's parliamentary group, sent to Chancellor Bethmann Hollweg on 23 June 1915, he revealed:

> I have learned from a most trustworthy source that there is a movement at work . . . to start a campaign to move Field Marshal von Hindenburg ostentatiously more into the foreground. I would welcome if Your Excellency promoted such a move yourself . . .[57]

Erzberger's source seems to have been trustworthy indeed: only six days later Wilhelm's aide-de-camp Hans Georg von Plessen noted in his diary that he had urged the Kaiser to visit Hindenburg in Posen or in Lodz—a visit he considered extremely important to convince 'the world' that there was no truth in all the 'talk that the latter was being treated badly'.[58] Although reluctant to listen to Plessen initially, the Kaiser met Hindenburg in Posen a few days later. The Empress, accompanying her husband on the trip, took photographs of Wilhelm and Hindenburg together to be published as postcards to raise money for the Red Cross. 'One has reasons to hope that the *gossip* about a disparity between H. M. and Hindenburg has been thwarted effectively in this way', Plessen confessed to his diary on 2 July 1915.[59]

It is thus obvious that the political and military elites capitalized on Hindenburg's popular appeal once they had recognized its propagandistic potential. The seeds had been sown at the outset when phrasing the official army reports and when disseminating the Kaiser's telegram and Hindenburg's biographical sketch via WTB. Journalists had done their share by singling out Hindenburg and hailing Tannenberg as a historic victory.

At the same time, however, parts of the German population participated very actively in raising Hindenburg's public veneration to extraordinary heights. Many Germans wanted to believe in a traditional war hero, symbolizing past glory, providing fatherly stability, embodying the newly-found sense of political unity, and upholding the belief in eventual military victory. Such sentiments were not mere escapism. In Hindenburg his followers cherished not only the 'good old times', but simultaneously the very values needed in order to survive the First World War: determination, fighting skill, strong nerves, calmness in the face of pressure, trust in God, patriotism, patience, willingness for sacrifice, and a sense of duty to the fatherland. The catchphrase 'Hindenburg will sort it out' captured the idea that despite all the hardship suffered at home and at the front, everything would be alright if one only put one's trust in Hindenburg's heroic qualities.[60] The act of trusting in his ability to 'sort it out' brought about a passive acceptance of reality, whilst also representing a more active coping strategy; it would create the vague sense of optimism needed to endure a prolonged conflict originally promised to last only a few months.

## Shaping the myth from below

Ordinary people helped to shape the mythical narrative in numerous poems, brochures, and songs written and published on private initiative. Newspapers printed hundreds of Hindenburg poems, which had been sent in by their readers, and enough Hindenburg songs and Hindenburg anecdotes existed to publish entire collections.[61] These anthologies were not compiled and disseminated by a government department, but appeared because there was enough demand to sustain a market. Similarly, the mass of Hindenburg memorabilia that started flooding the whole country after Tannenberg, was as much an expression of the already existing Hindenburg cult as it helped to spread his fame even further.

Robert Breuer of the *Schaubühne* spoke of a strategic calculation behind the mass production of Hindenburg kitsch: 'the penetration of people's in-stincts with hope and trust in the symbol of victory'.[62] Whilst such products undoubtedly had this effect there was little strategic top-down control. The German government had issued no propagandistic guidelines for the production of children's toys, and yet miniature statues of Hindenburg were sold by the thousands.[63] Hindenburg's image could be found on all sorts of commercial articles—be they purely decorative and thus probably most appealing to female bourgeois shoppers, or objects of everyday use, including household goods such as cups, glasses, plates, teapots, cutlery, card games, boxes of matches, and other tobacco products consumed disproportionately by lower class Germans. Mouth organs with Hindenburg design were among the most popular models sent to soldiers at the front and by 1915, 150 different cigar makers sold the brand 'Hindenburg Cigar'.[64] The producers of such goods obviously realized that Hindenburg sells.

But even if solely commercial interests drove the producers, their goods could have far-reaching effects. The flood of everyday Hindenburg kitsch bought by his devotees caused the myth to penetrate people's private lives and made the Field Marshal a physical reality in the sanctuary of the home. People put up pictures or drawings of the Field Marshal in their living rooms, replacing or complementing religious images or depictions of the Kaiser. The way one Peter Eck described his young son's daily routine—albeit tongue-in-cheek—testified to the mythical Hindenburg's domestic ubiquity:

> One has to imagine, when the little boy wakes up in the morning, the first thing he sees is a framed etching of the Field Marshal, who looks at him admonishingly. Then the frightened boy frantically demands his morning milk. Naturally, the porcelain mug is decorated with the full-body image of Hindenburg. Next to the bed, a real-size Hindenburg is keeping guard. From the cover of a picture book the Liberator of East Prussia smiles at him . . . Even on the plate the boy uses for his porridge, Hindenburg's characteristic head can be found . . . When my son wants to play with tin soldiers, he has at least an entire battalion of Hindenburgs in all imaginable sizes at his disposal. (. . .) Not surprising that the boy is a proper Hindenburg-maniac ['Hindenburgomane'].[65]

Considering their insatiable demand for new playthings, it is perhaps not surprising that the authorities began to consider toys useful in 'instilling in children a national, upright, and patriotic spirit'.[66] Young people often carried their convictions into the parental home and were therefore directly targeted by German propagandists, who were aware of such channels of opinion.[67] Hindenburg's presence in private family homes intensified the relationship people felt they had with the Field Marshal, and firmly embedded him in people's daily lives. Peter Eck's son allegedly referred to him as 'Uncle Hindenburg', which suggests that he regarded him as an imagined member of his family. Likewise, the phrase 'Our

Hindenburg', which crept up in numerous anecdotes and publications, reflects that he was considered national property, whose ownership lay with the people.[68]

The iconography of Hindenburg images was nearly always similar and some of the artists portraying him on posters and postcards during the war would be equally involved in drawing up Hindenburg posters and designing Hindenburg celebrations in the Weimar years, thereby creating a comforting and powerful visual continuity.[69] Hindenburg's massive square head, his bushy moustache, his broad shoulders, and decorated uniform featured in almost all depictions. In the present day, Hindenburg's appearance fails to strike up the kind of admiration his contemporaries reserved for his looks. His heavy frame which seems a little overweight to today's observer was considered the embodiment of masculine gravitas, and Hindenburg was perceived as a true giant of a man.[70] In reality, at 1.83 metres (6 feet), Hindenburg was tall but far from gigantic even by contemporary standards.[71] The more popular he became, however, the taller he appeared in depictions, mirroring people's perceptions of the Field Marshal as a true colossus. And even in the early years of the First World War, cartoons and other drawings typically featured Hindenburg as a giant in shining armour, crushing the Russian armies with his fist or killing the Russian bear with an enormous sword.[72]

## Saying it with nails

The 13-metre-high 'Iron Hindenburg' nailing statue, erected in front of the column of victory in Berlin on 4 September 1915, was perhaps the most famous visual manifestation of the Hindenburg myth. The statue was the flagship of all the nailing statues that 'mushroomed' on the territory of the Central Powers during the First World War.[73] This peculiar ritual was based on a medieval Austrian tradition, involving travelling blacksmiths driving nails into trees in the cities they visited.[74] From March 1915 onwards, the ritual was modified to raise money for war widows and orphans, and nailing statues were erected on hundreds of town squares. Local papers urged people to donate anything from one to 100 Reichsmark in order to hammer a nail into a wooden statue. In most cases such sculptures depicted patriotic symbols, such as the Iron Cross, victory columns, or a coat of arms, biblical figures such as Saint Michael, or historical ones, such as

Barbarossa or Roland.[75] The advantage of this form of fundraising was that, unlike those who had subscribed to the war loans, no one would have to be reimbursed once the war ended. They also provided a public outlet, if one were needed, for the home front to testify to its own readiness for sacrifice. In that sense the nailing ritual performed a variety of functions. In addition to raising funds, the statues were a useful means of continuously mobilizing the home front psychologically, and symbolizing the bond between the population at home and those who fought. The physical act of driving a nail into a wooden structure was meant to pass on the home front's strength and belief in military victory to the soldiers on the battlefield.[76]

Wilhelm II personally authorized the erection of the 'Iron Hindenburg' on the Königsplatz between the victory column and the Siegesallee in Berlin in early August 1915.[77] The statue was the biggest of its kind in Germany. Designed by the sculptor Georg Marschall and carved out of Russian alder wood by over eighty sculptors in merely six weeks, it was thirteen metres in height and twenty-six tons in weight. The German public had been closely informed about the construction of what would become one of Berlin's most famous and recognizable landmarks.[78] In fact, the omnipresence of stories about the statue caused Hans Sachs, an art critic, to remark satirically that, 'the man who had drilled Hindenburg's right nostril had his picture printed in the illustrated press and subsequently became a European celebrity'.[79]

The sculpture, with its strong legs apart, earnest facial expression and the giant arms resting on a sword expressed what Hindenburg had come to entail: its design re-enforced the image of the Field Marshal as the protector of German soil, and the sword on which his arms rested triggered associations with the Teutonic knights who had fought in the first Battle of Tannenberg in 1410.[80] High-brow artistic considerations had clearly come second to the prospect of quick financial gain, and the sight of the colossus provoked outrage in the art world. The sculptor Hugo Lederer, whose Bismarck memorial in Hamburg had served as a model for the Hindenburg statue, called the memorial a 'slap in the face of aesthetic feeling' and generally regarded the nailing ritual as a 'barbaric act of the worst kind'.[81] Louis Tuaillon, a fellow sculptor and senator of the Royal Academy of Arts in Berlin, went even further when he complained to Berlin's mayor, Adolf Wermuth, that the statue was 'distasteful', 'trivial', a 'crime against the soul of the people', and an 'international humiliation'. He concluded by observing that Berliners should thank God for the lack of foreigners in

**Fig. 1.** Postcard of the 'Iron Hindenburg' nailing statue in Berlin (1916).

their city during wartime, because the label 'barbarian', regularly attached to the Germans by Entente propaganda, would have been hard to cast off in the light of this artistic catastrophe.[82] Along similar lines, critic Robert Breuer labelled the statue 'ridiculous' and exclaimed that it was 'a stupidity, not worthy of touching the sole of the feet of the genius it depicts: it's blasphemy.'[83]

The mayor of Berlin, on the other hand, remained entirely unmoved by such allegations. Despite the fact that the city of Berlin had been completely uninvolved in the statue's design, he was happy to take full responsibility for its erection, because for him, aesthetic concerns and, he claimed, the financial gain of the enterprise, were much less weighty than, 'the spirit that carries the event and should be kept alive by it: the spirit of boundless readiness for sacrifice for the Fatherland.'[84]

Neither did those who participated in the nailing ritual seem to share the reservations of the art world; instead, the spirit Wermuth had described sometimes genuinely captured them. Far from being repelled by the idea of symbolically crucifying a living person, a father, who had spent a day 'nailing' the 'Iron Hindenburg' with his children, likened their experience to a 'patriotic pilgrimage' in an article he sent to an army newspaper.[85] He described being greeted by Germany's wooden war hero from a distance when walking up the Siegesallee, fighting his way through the 'wall of people' around the memorial, queuing for a whole hour, and feeling more and more uplifted with every metre that brought him closer to his 'great hero'. Once he had passed the entrance gate, he felt that he stood on 'sacred soil', which put him in a 'spiritual mood', all the time being watched by the Iron Hindenburg, who seemed sombre, but 'proud of his numerous admirers'.[86] People were only allowed to drive nails into Hindenburg's coat, the uniform, and the sword so as to spare his hands and face and avoid directly wounding his flesh. After the father had climbed the scaffolding, his heart was 'throbbing in his chest' when he hammered his nail into Hindenburg's wooden leg, and his oldest son even said a quick prayer before hitting the hammer as hard 'as if he wanted to beat his enemies to a pulp'. When his youngest son accidentally hit his thumb instead of the nail, his brother was envious, because his younger sibling had been so 'lucky to be injured in the service of the fatherland'.[87] As we can see, people who participated in the nailing ritual sometimes felt that they were not only donating money for a good cause, but also contributing physically to the war effort. To a small boy, an injured thumb became a war injury endured proudly, and the certificate people were given after they had made their nailing donation was likened to a medal obtained for bravery in combat. The 'Iron Hindenburg' was a participatory memorial, encouraging people to travel to the centre of Berlin to perform a patriotic duty. Whereas ordinarily memorials come alive through rituals staged in front of them or around them, the 'Iron Hindenburg' already incorporated audience participation—in that sense the memorial itself was the ritual, its violation of high-brow aesthetics no obstacle to its popular appeal.

The events around the Königsplatz also shared many of the characteristics of a fair. On sunny days military bands played patriotic songs, vendors sold all kinds of Hindenburg souvenirs, entire school classes travelled to the memorial, and the scaffolding was bedecked with ribbons in the Imperial colours of black, white, and red. The nailing ceremony was regularly embedded in extensive public festivities and the Berlin press willingly participated in encouraging the population to attend and make their donations by emphasizing the theme of civilian indebtedness to Hindenburg's self-sacrifice.[88] During the unveiling ceremony on 4 September 1915, Chancellor Bethmann Hollweg highlighted, in the presence of Crown Princess Auguste Wilhelm and Hindenburg's family, that the German population owed the Field Marshal 'never-ending gratitude'.[89] By 5 p.m. on that first day alone, 20,000 people had driven nails into the wooden frame, suggesting that the nailing of the 'Iron Hindenburg' was extremely popular at the outset, attracting crowds of people to one of Berlin's most central squares.[90] There is, however, some evidence to suggest that the ritual became less popular as time went on, due to the 'waning of faith' on the home front.[91] The statue, which would remain in front of the Reichstag during the first Weimar years, was never fully covered in nails, and when it was finally taken down in 1921, the body was sold as firewood, only the head ending up in a Berlin museum.[92]

At the outbreak of war in August 1914, the law of siege had been introduced, banning political demonstrations in the whole of Germany. The law had been enforced strictly in most cases, apart from those in which public gatherings had been spontaneous and patriotic and had posed no danger to the *Burgfrieden*, such as during the early days of August 1914. The celebrations staged in front of the 'Iron Hindenburg' were therefore exceptional occasions, when larger crowds could gather legally and listen to public speeches. Nailing the 'Iron Hindenburg' was strongly linked to celebrating Hindenburg, so the temporarily erected statue also served as a memorial to Germany's most popular war hero, turning the Königsplatz into a site of Hindenburg commemoration. At second glance, such public festivities could sometimes carry a more hidden meaning. Hindenburg's sixty-eighth birthday provided a good example of how subversive messages could be conveyed under the cover of seemingly innocent—and officially promoted—Hindenburg worship. For 2 October 1915, the semi-official 'National Foundation for the Surviving Dependents of Fallen Soldiers', an umbrella organization overseeing the nailing ritual throughout Germany, had planned a patriotic 'Hindenburg Hurrah' to attract more people to the statue.[93] Celebrations lasted the entire day, and after dusk five massive spotlights lit the statue to enable participants to climb the scaffolding until well into the night. The keynote speaker of the day was Count Ernst von Reventlow, a well-known journalist who would later be active in the *völkisch* movement and the Nazi party. In his speech, Reventlow did not limit himself to patriotic birthday wishes, but far exceeded conventional praise of Hindenburg when he called for the unrestrained hatred of England, a nation he considered Germany's ultimate enemy. Indirectly calling for unrestricted submarine warfare, which the German government was not yet in favour of at this stage, he argued that 'one should not have ostensible moral reservations when waging war against England'.[94] Invoking the mythical narrative of Hindenburg's determination and strategic brilliance, he called for Germany to be led by the 'Hindenburgian spirit' whilst waging war against England with all means at her disposal. 'From Hindenburg... [the Germans] must learn how to will, how to be victorious, how to move forward, and how to exploit victories.' 'Just as the Field Marshal always knows what he wants and what he can achieve, so should the statesman.'[95]

According to his Chief of the Civil Cabinet, Rudolf von Valentini, Wilhelm II was furious when he found out about Reventlow's remarks and launched an investigation into the matter, involving the head of the 'Welfare Foundation', Emil Selberg, Prussian Interior Minister Friedrich Wilhelm von Loebell, as well as the Berlin Chief of Police Traugott von Jagow.[96] The Kaiser covered Jagow's report, which justified his inaction on the grounds that Reventlow's speech had been a 'spontaneous display of emotion' and therefore to be welcomed, with angry marginal comments. Wilhelm considered 'Reventlow's speech... malicious rabble-rousing' against his government and neither Selberg nor Jagow could convince him that it had been a display of innocent patriotism.[97] His marginal notes suggest that he was also displeased with the passages citing Hindenburg as a glorious role model.

Although this episode did not cause any major public outcry, Kaiser Wilhelm's angry reaction and continued interest in the investigation illustrate that he was highly sensitive towards criticism of him or his government disguised as praise of Hindenburg.[98] He duly ensured that similar events would be banned in the future.

As we can see, Wilhelm had recognized the danger Hindenburg's larger-than-life reputation entailed for his own public standing as early as 1915. Whereas the Hindenburg myth had been advantageous as a propagandistic tool during the previous autumn, it was now becoming clear that the government did not automatically possess a monopoly over its exploitation. State Secretary of the Navy Alfred von Tirpitz, for example, tried hard to gain Hindenburg's support for his own proposal for unrestricted submarine warfare, because he had recognized that his opponents were working to win the Field Marshal for their cause. He regarded the 'saviour's' endorsement as vital to push through his objectives.[99] All sorts of political messages could quite simply be tagged on to the popular hero Hindenburg. Invoking the Hindenburg myth was a powerful weapon that was already escaping the control of the government and the military. For this purpose, the 'Iron Hindenburg' in Berlin provided a public, yet still fairly inconspicuous stage for voicing dissent under the cover of seemingly innocent and patriotic Hindenburg worship. The example set by Reventlow in 1915 would evolve into a pattern that could be observed even more frequently once Hindenburg had retired for the second time in 1919—the difference being that after the war, public appearances of the real Hindenburg would provide the cover for staging political demonstrations.

## The third supreme command

By 1916, Hindenburg's nimbus had long since started to overshadow Wilhelm II's; and had certainly eclipsed Chief of Staff Erich von Falkenhayn's public standing.[100] The *Times* correspondent in Germany noted this changing hierarchy of affections as early as 1915 when standing before a large shop window in Hamburg, which contained

> figures of the most prominent contemporary Germans in various sizes, which were graduated so as to indicate their relative positions in popular esteem.

In the centre stood Hindenburg alone, commanding, dominating, wrapped
in his military cloak. In front of him stood the Kaiser, about a quarter of
the size of the popular general... In ordinary times the shopkeeper would
probably have incurred prosecution for lése majesté had he placed the Kaiser
in a position so subordinate.[101]

Moreover, worshipping Hindenburg and Wilhelm II were two rather
distinct phenomena. The latter was venerated not just as Wilhelm the
person, but also—and probably more so—as the Kaiser and King of
Prussia. Martin Kohlrausch has explained this focus of public loyalties with
reference to the constitutional role of the monarchy and the inherent
'bipolarity' of Wilhelm II's adulation.[102] Hindenburg's mythical status,
on the other hand, was not the result of a 'bipolar' role. There was
something very Hindenburg-specific about his glorification; his rank of
General and then Field Marshal, or his role as Commander of the Eastern
Front alone, do not offer a sufficient explanation. Even invoking his
subsequent promotion as Chief of the General Staff remains unsatisfactory
since Moltke or Falkenhayn never enjoyed a remotely comparable degree of
popularity.

As illustrated not least by the Reventlow episode, the Kaiser observed
Hindenburg's popularity with extreme jealousy.[103] His concerns were motivated by more than sheer vanity, however. Wilhelm was worried that
Hindenburg's mythical adulation and popular support had introduced a
plebiscitary element into German politics that would consequently undermine the monarchical idea. Wilhelm II's fears were not entirely unfounded.
Hindenburg was generally considered to be more folksy and popular, while
in March 1916 the Berlin Chief of Police, Jagow, reported: 'the popularity of His Majesty the Kaiser and King has suffered substantially'.[104] Yet
Wilhelm had, in fact, sown the seeds of this development himself. Throughout his rule, he had not just relied on his Imperial aura, but had sought
far-reaching contacts with the public at large—he had travelled extensively
and given numerous public speeches. His own efforts to personalize politics,
to shift the focus from the royal institution to the individual and become
the 'people's Kaiser', had introduced a quasi-democratic element into the
legitimation of the monarchy. Personalizing the monarchy, however, entailed the danger of someone else eventually taking on this public role.[105]
Once war had broken out, that someone turned out to be Hindenburg.

By 1916 operations on the Western Front had become stuck in the
trenches, German casualties were mounting, and the food shortages

resulting from the British naval blockade and German administrative incompetence were beginning to take their toll on morale at home.[106] In comparison, Hindenburg's and Ludendorff's campaigns on the Eastern Front had been relatively successful, ever increasing Hindenburg's following and exerting pressure on the Kaiser and government to extend his responsibilities. Failure to suitably 'rope Hindenburg's laurels in' was beginning to undermine morale and thus the reputation of the civilian and military leadership.[107] Twelve months earlier, Wilhelm II's aide-de-camp had already urged his monarch to recognize the 'great national popularity Hindenburg enjoyed'. Plessen had predicted that Wilhelm would cause 'serious damage to himself when he did not treat Hindenburg accordingly'.[108]

Wilhelm, the 'media monarch', was of course keen to guard his own image. He strongly resisted the idea of appointing Hindenburg as his Chief of the General Staff, precisely because he considered the Field Marshal's popularity a threat to his own standing.[109] The Kaiser and Falkenhayn had even initially vetoed all moves to promote Hindenburg to the rank of Supreme Commander of the whole eastern front.[110] As Adolf Wild von Hohenborn, former Prussian War Minister and close confidant of both Falkenhayn and the Kaiser, observed, Wilhelm was eventually won over in July 1916 and agreed to place all troops in the east under Hindenburg's command, because of 'national psychology' ['Völkerpsychologie'].[111]

Nevertheless, the military situation on the Western Front continued to be a source of grave concern. Falkenhayn's strategy of attrition to 'bleed the French army white' resulted in dreadful losses for both the French and Germans, and the Battle of Verdun marked a new and grisly phase in the history of warfare.[112] At the same time, the British offensive at the Somme began, putting Germany in a very serious military situation. When, contrary to official expectations and predictions, Romania entered the war on the Entente side on 28 August 1916, Wilhelm finally realized that Falkenhayn had to be replaced. Hindenburg was the only viable option; 'the hero's' appointment had been 'in the air' for some time. In Wild von Hohenborn's words, 'if Hindenburg couldn't sort things out, no one could'.[113] Bethmann was equally certain that

the name Hindenburg...is the terror of our enemies and electrifies our army and our people, who have boundless faith in him. (...) even should we lose a battle, God forbid, our people would accept such a setback under Hindenburg's leadership, as they would a peace over his name.[114]

Fittingly, Hindenburg and Ludendorff—the 'Siamese Twins' or 'Hindenburg, Ludendorff & Co.' as they were frequently referred to[115]—were appointed to the Supreme Command, henceforth known as the Third Supreme Command, on the second anniversary of Tannenberg, 29 August 1916.[116] Hindenburg became Chief of the General Staff and Ludendorff his First Quartermaster-General. The appointment was first and foremost a propaganda coup. Placing the mythical Hindenburg at the head of the OHL was a move designed to bolster people's trust in the military leadership, to renew the belief in victory both among soldiers and people at home, and generally to inject a fresh incentive into Germany's war effort.[117]

All available evidence suggests that Hindenburg's appointment was indeed hugely popular. First, the censored press showed its unanimous support:[118] the *Berliner Tageblatt* lauded Wilhelm's decision and asked 'Did the Emperor know the secret wish of the people?'[119] The *Deutsche Tageszeitung* emphasized Hindenburg's role as an integrative figure who was not 'just the subject of the love and admiration of the whole German people, but has become the unifying force for all Germans'.[120] Equally, the *Frankfurter Zeitung* praised 'Hindenburg-Ludendorff' as 'the entity around which all Germans . . . have gathered with overflowing hearts, ready to fight anew, and full of the belief that victory will be ours'.[121]

Similarly, the secret monthly reports on the mood of the population collected by the Interior Ministry largely support the picture painted in the press. According to the 5th Deputy General Command in Posen, the concern caused by Romania's entry into the war had 'been replaced by a calmer assessment of the situation, brought about by Hindenburg's appointment'.[122] The 11th Deputy General Command reported a 'renewed feeling of hope' from Kassel[123] and the Württemberg Büro für Sozialpolitik noted that 'the workers have received the naming of von Hindenburg as Chief of the General Staff with great enthusiasm . . . Even the most radical Socialist newspapers have always expressed complete confidence in his magnificent leadership . . .'.[124]

Official Germany was equally far from immune to Hindenburg's appeal. Even someone like Moritz Freiherr von Lyncker, Chief of the Kaiser's Military Cabinet, who had not favoured the Field Marshal's promotion from the outset, spoke of the great sense of calm people had started to feel at Supreme Headquarters since 29 August.[125] In decidedly more enthusiastic terms, Wild von Hohenborn remembered his first encounter with Hindenburg as 'unforgettable'.[126] Even in January 1917, after his dismissal had been brought about by none other than his cherished Field Marshal, he wrote to a friend that 'it would be a crime to undermine or diminish the belief in our hero with a single line. He is the chosen one of the people and that needs to remain so.'[127] Along similar lines, Karl von Einem, Commander of the Third Army, considered it 'God's gift that we have this man who is a pole in our torn nation.'[128] Even the jealous and volatile Wilhelm II warmed, if only temporarily, to the new head of his armies and 'felt like heaven with Hindenburg'.[129] A letter Wilhelm's aide-de-camp General Hans von Plessen sent to a confidante the day of Hindenburg's appointment perhaps sums up the mood of exaltation the event generated most appropriately:

> It took a load off my mind! My soul breathes freely again! I envisage favourable prospects for the war and its end and the salvation of the fatherland and of our dynasty! I have trust again! Fat Hindenburg is a splendid fellow ['Der dicke Hindenburg ist ein Pracht-Kerl']! You cannot possibly imagine how happy I am ...![130]

As we can see, those involved in the myth-making process often genuinely subscribed to the ideas they were promoting. Naturally, once Hindenburg had been appointed, efforts to use his name and image for propaganda purposes were stepped up. A new battle cruiser was christened in Hindenburg's name, the massive arms and munitions programme introduced in the autumn of 1917 was labelled the 'Hindenburg Programme', and in the public debate on war aims, a victorious peace with annexations favoured by conservative and Pan German politicians became known as the 'Hindenburg Peace' (as opposed to the 'Scheidemann peace' of renunciation without annexations promoted by the political left).[131]

Hindenburg's fame was further disseminated in films shown at home and at the front, and in Posen a 'Hindenburg Museum' was established to collect all kinds of Hindenburg artefacts with the aim of stimulating people's patriotic feeling.[132] Especially Chancellor Bethmann Hollweg invoked Hindenburg's name when trying to legitimize policies regulating matters not usually within the state's control, such as the distribution of foodstuffs.[133] His endorsement was valuable political currency and could often provide greater legitimacy than legal orders. Especially when voluntary participation was required, the mythical appeal of the popular war hero was successfully used to galvanize people.[134] The 14th Deputy Army Command in Baden explained in a report of June 1917: 'After all, the people believe in Hindenburg... The government strengthens the necessary trust in its policies if the public knows that they have Hindenburg's endorsement.'[135]

Hindenburg's appointment caused a short-term upsurge in morale in the summer of 1916. It could not, however, stop the erosion of the monarchical idea.[136] Instead, Hindenburg's role as Chief of the General Staff has been poignantly described as that of a 'surrogate monarch'.[137] In fact, he eclipsed Wilhelm II in the eyes of the public even more strongly after his promotion. Almost all available reports on Wilhelm's public standing after 1916 highlight people's loss of support and admiration for their monarch. In an article published on the occasion of Wilhelm's birthday in January 1917, Konrad Lehmann even dared to describe the withering away of the monarchical idea since the outbreak of war with explicit reference to Hindenburg's greater glorification.[138] Around the same time, the 2nd Deputy Army Command in Mecklenburg noted that people in the district were increasingly concerned about the future of the throne.[139] In non-Socialist workers' associations, which had traditionally celebrated the Kaiser's birthday, no such festivities were organized in 1917 for lack of interest.[140] And in all this, according to Professor Matschoss from the War Press Office, one of the most commonly voiced criticisms of the Kaiser was that he 'did not get on with Hindenburg, that his entourage kept trying to turn the public mood against Hindenburg, and on the other hand people are saying "It'd be better to get rid of the Kaiser and to keep Hindenburg than the other way round".'[141] Whilst such implicit calls for the Kaiser's abdication certainly reflected the new quality of people's grievances, blaming Wilhelm for mistreating Germany's national hero was nothing new. After all, Plessen had recognized this mood as early as June 1915; Hindenburg's and the Kaiser's increasingly divergent images were thus defining features of Germany's public mood for most of the war.[142]

In the spring of 1917, members of the Supreme Command's press office, Section IIIB, and the War Press Office became so concerned about Wilhelm's diminishing popularity that they started searching for ways in which the Kaiser could be 'brought closer to the people'.[143] This had to be done by 'systematically bringing about suitable occasions which can be used tactfully and appropriately'.[144] Highlighting the Kaiser's veneration for the 'people's hero' was an obvious way of enhancing Wilhelm's standing. In July 1917 Wilhelm's advisers persuaded him to invite the Field Marshal and his wife to accompany the Kaiser and the Empress to their traditional Sunday worship at the Berlin Cathedral. A cinematographer was asked to film the party strolling through the Lustgarten after the service. 'Those present could see with their own eyes how H. M. honoured the Field Marshal', Plessen noted in his diary.[145] By 1917 the emphasis was no longer on Hindenburg showing reverence to his monarch. In contrast, Wilhelm had to seize every public opportunity to stress his unity with the Chief of the General Staff. Even the film on Wilhelm's birthday in January 1917 focused on Hindenburg congratulating the Kaiser at the General Headquarters in Bad Kreuznach.

Hindenburg's seventieth birthday 10 months later provided a further occasion for an open display of the Kaiser's veneration for his Field Marshal as well as invidious comparison with the public restraint of the Kaiser's celebrations.[146] Great public festivities accompanied the event on 2 October 1917 and all communal institutions were ordered to join in.[147] Celebrations were staged in many different towns and schools, and at the 'Iron Hindenburg' in Berlin airplanes dropped thousands of war loan campaign flyers onto gathering crowds. 6,000 additional nails were driven into the statue on that day alone.[148] The celebrations took on regal proportions; indeed, their scale and press coverage far outshone the festivities on Wilhelm's wartime birthdays.[149] To highlight his admiration, Wilhelm II officially conferred the title 'national hero' onto Hindenburg, cementing the latter's role as an integrative figure.[150] The papers reported that the Kaiser had travelled to Hindenburg's headquarters personally, had been among the first to congratulate him on the day, and had given Hindenburg a marble bust of himself as a gift. Pictures showing Hindenburg and the Kaiser together at lunch were distributed throughout the country. Furthermore, the Supreme Command's Picture and Film Section made two documentary films to mark the occasion—*Our Hindenburg* and *Hindenburg—70th Birthday at General Headquarters*. Both were highly structured documentaries and often used the same footage. *Our Hindenburg* featured the Field Marshal in every single shot—be it planning strategy with Ludendorff or walking through jubilant crowds of people. The latter had a human-interest format and included staged scenes of the birthday

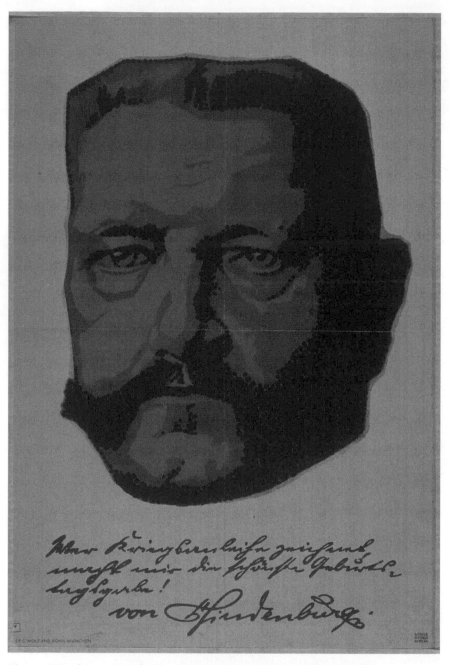

**Fig. 2.** War loan poster by Louis Oppenheim: 'Those who subscribe to the war loan give me my most beautiful birthday present! von Hindenburg' (1917).

celebrations and of the Kaiser's departure and arrival at the German General Headquarters.[151]

Not only desperate monarchists deployed Hindenburg's birthday in the hope of bolstering the image of the Kaiser; it also provided the theme for the biggest German advertising campaign to date: the campaign for the seventh war loan.[152] The official guidelines issued by the institution in charge, the Reichsbank, advised speakers to emphasize the fact that Hindenburg's brilliant military leadership made Germany invincible.[153] Bruno Paul, one of the founding fathers of the Werkbund, an association of modern designers, and Louis Oppenheim, the chief graphic designer and advertising agent employed by the Reichsbank, designed two posters for the campaign.[154]

Oppenheim's sketch portrayed the Field Marshal's face as if carved in stone on a memorial relief—clearly alluding to his popular veneration and his alleged rock-like qualities. Likening the Field Marshal's body to matter that withstands the ravages of time recast his age as an advantage rather than a drawback. The poster also featured a message in Hindenburg's handwriting at its bottom: 'Those who subscribe to the war loan give me my most beautiful birthday present.' As if personally answering his well-wishers, Hindenburg guaranteed that those subscribing to the war loan were pledging their loyalty in the way he approved. Their subscription to the war loan was phrased in quasi-familial terms—they had to give generously, because Hindenburg had asked for a present worthy of his own sacrifices and deserved no less on his birthday. At a campaign rally staged at Circus Busch in late September, Baron von Wangenheim voiced the expectation that 'the German people will splash out on their best son.' At the same event, the Catholic politician Erzberger alluded to the commercial value of Hindenburg's image rather flagrantly: the soldiers had turned Hindenburg into their 'Field Marshal' ('Generalfeldmarschall') and it was now the home front's task to turn him into their 'Cash Marshal' ('Geldmarschall').[155] Given the difficult economic situation in the late summer of 1917, such appeals to people's generosity were still proving remarkably successful.[156]

\* \* \*

Within three years of the outbreak of war, Hindenburg had gone from being a little known retired Infantry General to Germany's national hero, a supreme symbolic figure, eclipsing even his monarch, Wilhelm II. The

Field Marshal had quickly become ubiquitous in German public life. People read about him in the papers, saw his picture in the illustrated press, watched him at the cinema, sent postcards and purchased products adorned with his iconic portrait, hung his framed picture on their walls, celebrated his birthday and sang his praise in schools, drove nails into the wooden frame of his larger-than-life statue in Berlin, or harboured hopes of a victorious 'Hindenburg Peace'. Hindenburg's popularity and omnipresence had turned his image into a source of political legitimacy, a commercial and political currency of immense value, readily deployable to further a variety of agendas. While his fame was promoted from the top down to aid military and civilian morale and to bolster the monarchical idea, the Hindenburg myth also took on a life of its own. As the next few years would come to show, his myth would not only outlive the reign of the Hohenzollern dynasty, but even managed to survive German military defeat—a defeat which the trust in his leadership had promised to avert in the first place.

# 2

# Surviving failure

Whilst Hindenburg's appointment as Chief of the General Staff in August 1916 had been extremely popular with the German population at large, its long-term impact on morale is somewhat more complicated to measure. Hindenburg's personal standing no doubt continued to be strong after mid-1916, but the limits of his nimbus's influence on soldiers' morale, and the home front's willingness to hold out were slowly becoming apparent. Whilst the secret reports on the mood of the population all emphasized the renewed hope people had felt after the appointment, they warned simultaneously that 'generally one should not overlook that a certain war-weariness dominates the mood'.[1] Equally, the Deutscher Nationalausschuss, an influential organization founded in 1916 to lobby for an 'honourable peace', agreed in a letter to Ludendorff in September 1916 that Hindenburg's appointment had been greeted with general enthusiasm, but cautioned 'we cannot conceal from ourselves that the mood not just at home but also at the front needs *lasting* strengthening and support'. As the organization warned, 'patriotism is endangered when hunger begins'.[2] The Berlin Chief of Police equally qualified his assessment when pointing out that 'the food shortages largely damage' the renewed sense of security.[3] Most of the secret reports from across the country identified the shortages in basic supplies, ranging from butter, fat, and potatoes to winter coal, as the main source of official concern in terms of morale.

Evidently, the trust in Hindenburg had managed to buoy up morale in the short term. Yet trusting his leadership could not alleviate the soldiers' and population's day-to-day worries, which had grown steadily the longer the fighting had gone on. The supply of foodstuffs and other basic goods had become the most pressing concern for many on the home front—and due to the manifold lines of communication also became a growing concern for those fighting in the trenches.[4] In the words of the 4th Deputy General

Command in Saxony the food shortages constituted the 'Achilles' heel of the people's mood.'[5]

Nevertheless, the majority of informants continued to emphasize Hindenburg's strong personal standing from 1916 until the war's last year.[6] At the same time, however, their language often juxtaposed his towering reputation with the worsening of the mood in general. In March 1917, the 18th Deputy General Command, reporting from Frankfurt, alluded to the flagging power of the Hindenburg myth, not in terms of people's devotion, but in terms of the difference that devotion ultimately made:

> Every economic measure is seen as a source of concern especially by people in urban areas, just as much as every military measure associated with the name of Hindenburg, which thereby lends it an aura of infallibility, is seen as a source of strong trust.[7]

Similarly, Heinrich Scheüch, head of the War Office, described the bottom-line of all incoming secret reports in September 1917 as '[t]rust in the army and the OHL on the one hand, grave concern about the economic endurance and mistrust of the civilian authorities on the other'.[8] For the population at home—especially those from lower- and working-class backgrounds—the events on the battlefield often seemed far removed from their daily worries, and news of military victories did not always take centre stage. In September 1917, after the French and British offensives in Champagne and in Flanders had come to a halt, the 17th Deputy General Command in Danzig reported to Berlin that in the light of the economic difficulties,

> even the great events in the west and east have not created any real enthusiasm. This was illustrated by the fact that Field Marshal Hindenburg's plea . . . to raise all flags to celebrate the great victories, was not met with the same reception the great military commander's every word usually is. The weariness was too great and the poorer parts of the population are not stirred by anything but the lack of food.[9]

In the following months military or political news could still not compete with economic news for people's attention.[10] The 14th Deputy General Command in Baden pointed out that people's willing participation in the celebrations staged on Hindenburg's seventieth birthday had shown that trust in the OHL, and particularly in Hindenburg, was still infinite.[11] And while Berlin's Chief of Police agreed that the enthusiastic birthday festivities had 'strengthened and fed' the trust in the military leadership, he considered that 'on the other hand, they have not managed to destroy or even diminish the deeply-rooted and widespread discontent among large sections of the population.'[12]

Such language suggests that the relationship between the belief in victory, the war-weariness of the population, and people's subscription to the Hindenburg myth was a complex one, entailing a high degree of ambivalence and ambiguity. As opposed to war-weariness simply replacing the more optimistic outlook of the first years of the war, a longing for peace could exist alongside the hope of eventual German victory and coincide with trust in Hindenburg's leadership. Disillusionment with the army leadership and mistrust of the ability of the German troops to win the war were not the main issues at stake. Hunger and cold were much more immediate concerns and the underlying reasons why morale was plummeting.

During the so-called 'turnip winter' of 1916/17, the prices of basic foods increased 800% or more across the country compared to the years prior to 1914. Millions of Germans without special provisions had to survive on an estimated 700–900 calories per day, 50–30% of allotted normal rations, and on a diet almost entirely lacking in protein and fat. Consequently, the mortality rate among civilians began to rise significantly.[13] The food situation was worsening at a time when the OHL had issued its ambitious 'Hindenburg Programme' designed to increase German arms and munitions production substantially to bolster the country's flagging war effort and bring about an outright victory. Black marketeering in the countryside and non-compliance with rationing orders issued by the civilian authorities were responsible not just for the emerging social cleavages between town and country, but also for the growing difficulties in supplying the workers in the arms and munitions industries.[14] Following the example set by propagandists in previous years, Hindenburg's appeal was used to galvanize support to boost food supplies for those labouring in the crucial industries. Two Hindenburg letters of September and November 1916 urged people in the countryside to make voluntary contributions to improve urban rations.[15] The Field Marshal's pleas proved more successful than official rationing orders. In December 1916 the War Food Office reported that Hindenburg's letters had been crowned with 'extraordinary success'. The 5th Deputy General Command in charge of Posen and parts of Silesia concurred that after some initial difficulties 'the great reputation of the name

Hindenburg has . . . now led most groups in the countryside to comply with his demands . . .'.[16]

The efforts to collect foodstuffs from the countryside were soon termed the 'Hindenburg Donation', a name suggesting to donors they were paying their dues to him personally. Leaflets with the Field Marshal's image were distributed urging people to abstain from black marketeering and to show greater general awareness of the urban population's plight.[17] The relative successes of the 'Hindenburg Donation' and the campaign for the seventh war loan using his image and birthday provide some of the last clear evidence that deploying the Field Marshal's mythical appeal could notably alter the population's behaviour in wartime. Yet, at a time when the Germans were entering the fourth year of a war originally promised to be of short duration, with military casualties mounting and civilians starving at home, the effectiveness of Hindenburg-related propaganda was bound to reach its limits eventually.

## Rumour and anti-Hindenburg agitation

After a period of political apathy described in the secret mood reports, many Germans started to take an active interest in military and political news again in the winter of 1917/18.[18] The victory on the Eastern Front, culminating in the armistice with Russia and peace negotiations at Brest-Litovsk, renewed the hope that German victory in the west was now within reach. As a consequence, the mood both at home and at the front had improved since December in spite of continuing problems with food supplies.[19] The spring offensive of 1918, aimed at breaking through French and British lines in the west before the anticipated arrival of fresh American troops in the autumn, was accompanied by a last upsurge of morale in Germany that found expression in the eager subscription to the eighth war loan.[20] Such sentiment was, however, relatively short-lived and founded less on new enthusiasm for war than on expectations of an imminent end to the fighting.[21] As a result, the disappointment was ever greater when the offensive came to a first halt. As the 21st Deputy General Command stationed in Saarbrücken noted in April, the overall mood was one of 'nervous tension'. People reacted much more strongly to news of military successes, but also responded much more emotionally to 'every little setback' that occurred.[22] Apathy quickly followed the brief moment of exaltation. By June 1918, 'numbness and indifference' were the overarching feelings at the home front.[23] At the same time, however, according to one informant, many Germans still sought comfort in the idea that the lull signified that this time the OHL 'was planning something quite great, because they needed so much time for preparation'.[24] Even now, the Hindenburg myth remained a lens through which people viewed reality and the thought that Hindenburg might yet be able to 'sort things out' was often more appealing than facing up to the uncomfortable fact that Germany would not win the war.

In the early years of the war, the Hindenburg myth had corresponded to German soldiers' interpretations of war as a heroic enterprise, of fighting out of a sense of duty, and defending their home.[25] Towards its end, however, official attempts to galvanize soldiers' fighting spirit by invoking the Hindenburg myth were increasingly out of touch with reality on the battlefield. In a letter one particular soldier sent to his family he described how a messenger had angrily shown him an order he had had to carry through intense barrage. Only when he was caught in the barrage had he stopped to look at what the order comprised—it instructed all regiments to cut from newspapers a letter from Hindenburg thanking the population for the participation in the festivities on his birthday and to put it up in the soldiers' quarters and their shelters in the trenches. 'Because of this order two people have had to run through a heavy barrage', the letter concluded defiantly.[26] In the light of such senseless risking of lives just to disseminate Hindenburg's gratitude, it is perhaps no surprise that for a Bavarian soldier in January 1918, the whole war had become a 'Hindenburg-Elendschwindel'.[27] By this stage, leaflets had started to appear referring to Hindenburg as a 'butcher' and by July, Independent Social Democrats were campaigning against him and Ludendorff as 'protractors of the war'. In September, concerned military informants reported that some soldiers were labelling the Field Marshal a 'mass murderer', whom they would 'not let get away' with what he had done.[28]

Until the late summer of 1918 the reports of the Deputy General Commands, on the other hand, testified to the population's trust in Hindenburg's leadership almost unanimously.[29] In the summer of 1918, however, even their language began to change subtly. In early September, the 10th Deputy General Command in East Prussia noted that enduring trust could only be observed in the 'level-headed sections of the population'—a semantic qualification not hitherto found.[30] The Oberkommando in den

Marken responsible for Berlin and Brandenburg was even more concerned: 'It is most regrettable that the trust in the OHL, which had thus far been unshakable, has started to waver disturbingly.'[31] Likewise, the Württemberg War Ministry reported that 'the trust previously placed in the military leadership has been undermined'.[32] Other informants observed that most people still believed in Hindenburg's and Ludendorff's military superiority, but irrespective of this no longer thought that Germany could win the war due to the shortage of manpower and materiel.[33]

In late July the War Press Office had already issued an order to the effect that faith in Hindenburg and Ludendorff had to be strengthened to sustain soldiers' willingness to fight. The fact that it deemed such a move necessary suggests that this faith had indeed started to dwindle noticeably.[34]

Whilst such alarmed voices imply that attitudes had begun to change, the assessments were by no means undivided. The East Prussian 20th Deputy General Command reported as late as October that trust in the OHL had remained 'untouched'—a fact apparently also mirrored in private letters surveyed by the local censorship committee. The Bavarian 6th Deputy General Command confirmed that the trust in the OHL was 'unlimited' and the 17th Deputy General Command even reported from the east that it had increased during the course of the previous month.[35] According to the 9th Deputy General Command in north western Germany an appeal Hindenburg had issued to his former regiment in late August urging its members not to give up their belief in victory had seemed like a 'salvation from all anxieties'.[36] Even the editors of the liberal *Vossische Zeitung* and the Social Democratic *Vorwärts* were convinced as late as September 1918 that Hindenburg's public appeals had a much greater effect on the population than administrative decrees.[37]

Generally speaking, soldiers voiced criticism of the army leadership much less frequently than grievances about their immediate superiors—or, for that matter, the Kaiser. Those censoring soldiers' letters reported overwhelmingly that the OHL had been beyond reproach since 1916 and was not even blamed for the social cleavages between officers and men that had been undermining morale among German troops.[38] Moreover, the reports on the mood of the population, which testify to the somewhat dwindling trust in Germany's military leadership, report the withering away of support for the OHL overall, but do not usually mention Hindenburg's name in isolation—in stark contrast to previous years when Hindenburg's veneration had almost always been singled out as the backbone of trust in the OHL.[39] It is therefore difficult to establish whether those surveyed had really changed their opinion of Hindenburg personally or had actually lost faith in Ludendorff or the OHL as an institution.

Instead of turning against Hindenburg more thoroughly and directly, the German people increasingly found a release valve for their apprehension and fear in rumour and hearsay. The virulence of all kinds of rumours within Germany and at the front in the spring and summer of 1918 gave vivid expression to the population's mounting insecurity and nervousness.[40] Such tales often reflected the values of those spreading and believing in them simultaneously and were both a manifestation and a source of insecurity. Virtually all aspects of the war had given rise to incredible reports since 1914—food supplies, illusory peace negotiations, imagined battles, and inflated numbers of enemy prisoners captured were all subjects of the rumour epidemic.[41] From late 1917 onwards, however, people's anxieties began to express themselves for the most part in stories about Hindenburg. Whilst the majority of such rumours probably originated within Germany itself or was fed back from the trenches, the Allied press, too, was fanning the flames. Whereas anti-monarchical propaganda had previously been the main concern of the military intelligence department, the War Press Office noted in November 1917 that 'attacks against the OHL, particularly against Field Marshal Hindenburg, are obviously on the increase'.[42] From January 1918 'Propaganda against the OHL and its members' was a separate section of its enemy press surveys and by April this comprised no less than 24 pages—the largest single segment of the reports.[43]

In late 1917, the British press started publishing stories about 'Hindenburg's nervous breakdown'.[44] The following July, the *Daily Mail* spread the rumour that he was seriously ill. Only two weeks later, the *Daily Express* informed its readers that the Field Marshal had suffered a stroke during an argument with Wilhelm II and had died shortly afterwards. The same story had surfaced in the Dutch *Nouvelles Haag*. Some French and Swiss papers had allegedly uncovered a more interesting cause of death: a Russian NCO had killed Hindenburg when the latter visited the Eastern Front after the peace of Brest-Litovsk.[45]

Although the average German had no direct contact with the foreign press (it had been formally banned in 1917) such news trickled into Germany through various sources, not least the domestic press.[46] Visitors to Germany noted that countless stories about Hindenburg's death were circulating in the summer of 1918. In southern Germany, tales of a duel between the Bavarian Crown Prince and Hindenburg during which Rupprecht had shot dead the Field Marshal were spreading particularly rapidly.[47] Another variant of Hindenburg's alleged demise had him severely injured by shrapnel from a bomb dropped by a British aeroplane.[48] These stories were so prevalent in Germany that Hindenburg himself issued an appeal on 2 September 1918 urging people to stop spreading them because they were undermining the German war effort.[49] A month earlier, he had already felt the need to assure his old friend and former corps chief Franz von Seel that he was fine 'in spite of all rumours to the contrary'.[50]

Rumours often mirrored recurrent themes of the war and served as a prism of the Hindenburg myth. Since Hindenburg was 70 years of age, stories about his frail health were easily believable. Tales about arguments with the Kaiser showed that the population was aware of Wilhelm's jealousy and the differences between him and his Field Marshal. Rupprecht of Bavaria's victory in the imaginary duel may have mirrored the growing perception that Prussia and the southern German states were at odds politically.[51] Hindenburg's Russian assassin probably symbolized those soldiers and NCOs with leftist political views who had begun to regard him as the embodiment of the prolonged conflict. Invoking British air bombardment as a cause of death played on the fear of air warfare that had begun to grip soldiers on the Western Front and was severely undermining morale in 1918.[52] And finally, Hindenburg's alleged nervous breakdown signified that in spite of his famed sang-froid, the military situation was now deemed so serious that even he was thought to be losing his nerves.

Strikingly, such rumours for the most part did not reflect badly on Hindenburg's personality.[53] Some of these stories had Hindenburg lose out to the Bavarian Crown Prince or to the Russian NCO who had allegedly shot the Field Marshal. And even if falling somewhat short of blaming the Kaiser directly for Hindenburg's death, the rumour about their argument sees the latter off as the innocent victim of a stroke. Rumour-mongers did not usually portray Hindenburg as personally incompetent and almost never as a perpetrator. He was increasingly perceived as powerless, but also overwhelmingly as a victim himself—thus mirroring the self-perception of many Germans. Given that he had embodied not just the belief in German victory but also the core values needed to survive the war since 1914, the prevalence of rumours about his incapacity or death signified the slow demise of these convictions. In short, his rumoured downfall represented the German people's unwillingness and inability to continue 'holding out'. After all, how was Hindenburg going to 'sort it out' if he was severely ill, injured, or no longer alive?

The themes of Hindenburg rumours reveal that for many of his admirers it was more comfortable to imagine that he had died than to make him a target for blame. Maintaining one's blind trust may have been irreconcilable with experiencing the hopelessness of Germany's military situation in the summer of 1918, but the response was not a straightforward debunking of the Hindenburg myth. On the contrary, the Field Marshal's image remained a refractor through which events were viewed. As the rumours illustrate, it proved easier to square the long-held belief in Hindenburg's near-superhuman qualities with his death than his failure of judgement.

That many of these rumours surfaced repeatedly in the newspapers of the Entente or of neutral countries also illustrates that opinion-makers outside Germany had started to pick up on their potential power. Non-German journalists and propagandists had clearly identified the Hindenburg myth as a source of political legitimacy. Their articles were intended to enlighten the German public about its political leaders' hypocrisy by laying bare the mechanisms of Hindenburg's veneration. They also refrained from attacking the Field Marshal more openly—suggesting that the papers' editors bought into the mythical narrative or judged the German population unfit for a more critical approach. According to the French *Matin* for instance, 'the Kaiser had decided to push [Hindenburg] . . . into the background to prevent the old dog from becoming the subject of a cult, which he [the Kaiser] wants to preserve for himself.'[54] In July 1918, the Dutch *Nouvelles Haag* suspected a cover-up when reporting that 'the Germans keep his death secret not to demoralize the people, who believe in Hindenburg as their "saviour".'[55]

The Swiss *Freie Zeitung* was one of the few publications—and the most vocal one—to scrutinize the Hindenburg myth more closely.[56] Founded in May 1917 by a group of German political émigrés living in Bern, the paper provided the most important forum for German war critics and radical republicans outside Germany. Hugo Ball, Ernst Bloch, Kurt Eisner, Carl von Ossietzky and Walter Benjamin were among its regular authors and it had a large readership in Germany—not least as a result of the authors' intimate knowledge of German politics and the fact that they wrote in

German.[57] In September 1917, the *Freie Zeitung* pinpointed Hindenburg's veneration as an obstacle on Germany's path to democracy:

> The best means to accelerate the German revolutionary process is to take away the most steadfast pillar of German authority. This pillar is called . . . Hindenburg. Those who help to defeat Hindenburg work towards revolutionary success. Those who knowingly or unknowingly, directly or indirectly, help to strengthen Hindenburg, are fighting against the German revolution, against German democracy.[58]

However insightful this passage may have been, it remained the exception. Only a very small number of observers recognized the Hindenburg myth's full potency and even fewer were prepared to face the consequences by attacking it as a potential threat to democratic development in Germany. With German defeat starting to look likely, the search for scapegoats would soon begin instead.

## Finding scapegoats

Although Hindenburg and Ludendorff had entered the public stage more or less simultaneously in 1914 and had worked closely ever since, their images had diverged from the outset. Ludendorff never exuded the same kind of emotional appeal as Hindenburg.[59] As the chief editor of the prestigious liberal daily *Vossische Zeitung* phrased it on the occasion of Ludendorff's 53rd birthday: Ludendorff was 'admired', but Hindenburg was 'loved'. The Field Marshal had generously shared his fame with his subordinate, the editor Georg Bernhard opined, but the gratitude people had originally felt for Hindenburg had long since transformed itself into the genuine love of 'a great human being'.[60] Ludendorff had enjoyed popular admiration and achieved the status of one of Germany's greatest war heroes, but was respected first and foremost for his strategic talent and military leadership. He had never been loved 'as a human being'.

By October 1918 Ludendorff had fallen out of favour both with the German public and the new political leadership under Prince Max von Baden. His erratic nature, his political ambitions, his growing difficulties with the Kaiser, and his contradictory statements concerning Germany's military situation had all contributed to his fall from grace. After the Austro-Hungarian peace note of 14 September and the collapse of Bulgaria's war effort in late September, the OHL had had to recognize that only an immediate armistice would prevent further disaster. It thus announced Germany's military bankruptcy at a conference in the Belgian resort town of Spa on 28–29 September and urged the Imperial government to sue for peace immediately.[61] When Ludendorff changed his mind concerning Germany's fighting capabilities again publicly merely a few weeks after his announcement at Spa, now arguing that the German army could after all win—without the military situation having changed substantially—his position was no longer tenable.[62] As the leader of the Social Democrats and future Reich President Friedrich Ebert observed, the whole people now pointed to 'Ludendorff... as the guilty one'.[63]

On the basis of the OHL's admission of military failure, and to gain more favourable peace terms from the Allies, negotiations were conducted about constitutional reform and the formation of a new government backed by a parliamentary majority. Max von Baden's reform government, established on 3 October, represented a decisive step on the path from constitutional to parliamentary monarchy.[64] Baden sent the government's first peace note to the American President Woodrow Wilson the day he was appointed. The new Reich Chancellor was keen on Ludendorff's dismissal, not least because he sought to curb the political power the OHL had accumulated since 1916, but saw himself faced with one significant problem: Hindenburg's future.

On 17 October 1918, Baden's October government deliberated the OHL's dismissal for the first time. The Chancellor enquired whether the German people would be able to endure both Hindenburg's and Ludendorff's resignation. State Secretary Conrad Haußmann of the liberal Fortschrittliche Volkspartei argued that the government ran the risk of being accused of having deprived Germany of her two greatest strategists at a particularly difficult time. This 'would have catastrophic consequences, in particular because of Hindenburg', he warned—suggesting that he was convinced of the myth's continued potency.[65]

Wondering whether it would be possible for the Kaiser to 'persuade Field Marshal Hindenburg to make the ultimate sacrifice of staying on without Ludendorff', State Secretary Siegfried von Roedern was the first to raise the possibility of dismissing the Quartermaster-General only.[66] Though pessimistic concerning his chances of success, Baden discussed the matter with the Kaiser and others. During the conversation, State Secretary Wilhelm Solf supported the plan and made the case that 'Hindenburg's departure would obviously be very regrettable because of his high esteem which even large parts of Social Democracy share. Not so in Ludendorff's case.'[67] In a telegram Baden sent to Wilhelm II on 25 October, he once more urged the Kaiser to dismiss Ludendorff and to do 'everything possible to persuade Hindenburg to stay'.[68] Gustav Stresemann, deputy leader of the National Liberal Party and future Foreign Minister during the Weimar years, echoed Baden's sentiment even more ardently in a letter to Robert Friedberg, a fellow National Liberal politician:

> I hope you agree if I urge you to do everything to prevent Hindenburg from leaving . . . [I]n my opinion . . . the German people still has, can have, and has to have great trust in Hindenburg, because there is no doubt that he has protected the homeland against superior forces for 50 months and has . . . won the greatest world-historical victories. We must under no circumstances be . . . tainted with the odium of having overthrown Hindenburg. In my opinion, the Kaiser's abdication would be easier to endure than Hindenburg's departure. I cannot even begin to imagine how history would judge us if we were somehow persuaded to get involved.[69]

According to Friedrich von Berg, Wilhelm's Civil Cabinet Chief, the Kaiser had initially agreed with the plan to dismiss Ludendorff, but changed his mind again because he feared running the risk of Hindenburg resigning simultaneously. After a heated argument on 26 October, however, Wilhelm accepted Ludendorff's resignation—but he declined to accept Hindenburg's own offer to go.[70]

Major-General Hans von Haeften, the OHL's government envoy and one of Germany's chief wartime propagandists, was one of the first to hear the news and rushed to see Baden, who was in the company of Vice Chancellor Friedrich von Payer, Solf, Roedern, and others. When he delivered the news of Ludendorff's dismissal

> [a]ll those present jumped up apprehensively and besieged me with the words: 'and Hindenburg?' 'He stays', I answered briefly. A lively 'Thank God' was the response . . .[71]

As we can see, the members of Baden's reform government and other German politicians from various political parties were keen on Ludendorff's dismissal in October 1918, but tried to avoid Hindenburg's exit at all costs in spite of the OHL's admission of military bankruptcy—first and foremost because they feared the public's wrath and were concerned about their historical legacy if they were to be associated with the dismissal of Germany's national hero. When reminiscing about the events one year later, Conrad

Haußmann, now a member of the newly-founded DDP, therefore took great pride in the fact that Ludendorff's dismissal and Hindenburg's staying in office had been 'engineered by Max von Baden's government'.[72]

The public reaction to Ludendorff's dismissal seemed to vindicate these calculations; the decision was largely greeted with support. A detailed survey of the press coverage compiled for Ludendorff's successor in the 'fourth OHL', General Wilhelm Groener, found that the whole press cited his 'political actions' as 'the reason for his overthrow'.[73] Most opinion columns on the dismissal also offered their take on Hindenburg's remaining in office. The papers interpreted the departure of his right-hand man as a painful loss for the Field Marshal practically across the board. Staying in office represented a 'sacrifice' for Hindenburg, a 'sacrifice' he had supposedly endured based on his long-standing and sternly Prussian idea of duty to the fatherland.[74] Georg Bernhard went as far as labelling the decision an act of 'superhuman sacrifice'. Hindenburg had allegedly remained at his post because he was aware of what 'his name meant for Germany at this difficult time'.[75] The editor of the prestigious *Vossische Zeitung* lauded the Field Marshal for providing mythical credibility at a moment of crisis. Disloyalty towards his long-term aide or a refusal to take full responsibility for Germany's military situation by resigning as well was not the interpretative framework. Instead, selflessness, sacrifice and steadfast loyalty towards the German people were the key themes invoked by journalists assessing Hindenburg's retention.[76] The Field Marshal himself fed this rhetoric in letters to his family and old acquaintances, in which he declared that 'his heart was bleeding', but that he regarded staying as his 'duty'.[77] Commentators viewed his decision to stay on strictly within the parameters of the mythical narrative that had surrounded him since 1914. Mirroring the fact that Hindenburg's reputation had long since risen above Germany's military fortunes several conservative papers, including the *Kreuz-Zeitung* and *Der Tag*, predicted that the German people would forever honour his name even if he did not return victorious.[78] Even the *Vorwärts*—albeit especially forceful in its vilification of Ludendorff—quickly exempted the Field Marshal himself. Although the SPD's mouthpiece recognized that his myth had been deployed as a political weapon in the past, it was convinced that others had pulled the strings:

> Ludendorff was a type of political General, Hindenburg is not, [and] does not want to be one in the future. If his name has often been abused for matters

not entirely within the military sphere that is mainly because of his former adviser who was not just a soldier, but also a hot-blooded, pan-German, conservative politician.[79]

Ludendorff had been discredited especially among workers and ordinary soldiers precisely because of his active drive and political ambitions.[80] Hindenburg had been worshipped as a strong leader at a difficult time, but ruthless determination had never been considered his trademark. On the contrary, his outward passivity and tranquillity had always been components of the mythical narrative in their own right—in the euphemistic guise of 'strong nerves' and 'calmness'—and had endeared him to members and supporters of the more moderate and leftist parties who had always feared Ludendorff's authoritarian zeal. The Quartermaster-General may have appeared to be masterminding the OHL's military and political moves, but, in the end, that also made it easier to blame him for its failures. Whereas the radical segments of the German right, such as the Pan-Germans, continued to favour their associate Ludendorff and were suspicious of Hindenburg due to his alleged lack of political understanding, this was precisely what liberal and Social Democratic commentators considered an asset.[81] This basic framework of interpretation would remain intact after the revolution, when Ludendorff's public image deteriorated still further, which underlined once more the extent to which his and Hindenburg's images—as well as their political fortunes—diverged.[82]

Whilst the left zeroed in on Ludendorff as the culprit, the General, in his turn, had prepared the ground for the vilification of the democrats as early as September 1918. Since he judged the military situation as hopeless, it seemed wise to grant greater powers to the parties and thus place on them the responsibility for terminating the war effort. Ludendorff had thus planted the seeds for the infamous 'stab-in-the-back' legend, according to which Socialist and Jewish agitators on the home front had betrayed the German army, leading to German military collapse before the fighting had even stopped. After his return from exile in Sweden in early 1919, he embarked on a campaign to spread this narrative and gave a series of interviews portraying Socialist activists as the real culprits.[83] Within one year after the revolution in November 1918—courtesy of Hindenburg's backing—the 'stab-in-the-back' would assert itself as a powerful political narrative and anti-republican political tool deployed by German Nationalists and, later, Nazi propagandists in their quest to undermine the legitimacy of the Weimar Republic.[84]

Hindenburg's enduring heroic status meant that scapegoats had to be found on both sides of the political spectrum. A more balanced assessment of the causes of Germany's military collapse was severely hampered by the survival of the Hindenburg myth. The 'stab-in-the-back' legend and worshipping the Field Marshal were two sides of the same coin. One did not follow from the other in a strictly causal sense, but they were born out of similar desires and served a similar purpose—namely to avoid asking difficult questions about German defeat and to uphold the notion that the country had fought a just war.

## Revolution and a fateful 'pact'

Just as keeping Hindenburg in office had been the new government's and Wilhelm II's central aim when orchestrating Ludendorff's dismissal, it was also a consideration of Baden and others in discussions about the future of the Hohenzollern dynasty—discussions that acquired ever greater urgency when the peace notes exchanged with the Wilson government made it clear that the Allies would not conclude a peace settlement with a German *Reich* ruled by the current Kaiser. Bowing to Allied pressure, the war cabinet openly debated the possibility of Wilhelm II's abdication during a meeting on 31 October 1918. The Prussian Interior Minister Bill Drews opined that the troops would not fight against peace in the name of the Kaiser. His assessment was prescient: even if no large-scale mutinies broke out within the army, naval mutinies would soon break out in Kiel after the sailors had been ordered to 'sacrifice' themselves in a final—and impossible—battle. But Drews was convinced that the damage inflicted on the army by the abdication 'could be avoided if Hindenburg was made commander-in-chief.' An opinion poll among officers in Spa on 9 November 1918 partially confirmed this assessment.[85] Not all officers, however, were equally steadfast in their insistence on Hindenburg's retention.[86] Moreover, in early November, war-weariness had reached such depths that images neither of the Kaiser nor of Hindenburg could be shown in soldiers' cinemas, because audiences regularly booed them.[87] At the top of government, the fear of being 'tainted with the odium of having overthrown Hindenburg' nevertheless persisted in spite of such signs of grass-roots discontent.

On 9 November, the revolution reached Berlin after it had already broken out in numerous other places in the *Reich*. Around lunchtime, Reich Chancellor Baden, acting on his own authority, announced Wilhelm II's abdication as German Emperor and King of Prussia. Shortly afterwards, Scheidemann declared the creation of a German Republic at Berlin's Reichstag, pre-empting Karl Liebknecht's declaration of a Socialist Republic based on the Soviet model two hours later. Early the next morning, the Kaiser got on a train to Holland, where he would remain in exile until his death in Doorn in 1941. Whilst the Kaiser 'fled'—following Hindenburg's recommendation—the Field Marshal remained at his post.[88] The debate about his role in engineering Wilhelm II's departure would occupy German monarchists for some time and would taint the relationship between Hindenburg and his former monarch considerably in the years to come. The Field Marshal, however, would always publicly reject the accusation that he had advised the Kaiser to go into exile.[89]

In November 1918, Hindenburg succeeded Wilhelm II as commander-in-chief. As early as 10 November he sent a message to all army groups explaining how to behave in the new situation brought about by Wilhelm's abdication. The growth of the soldiers' councils in the army could not be prevented, but he urged officers to bring them under their control.[90] Two days later, the new Council of the People's Delegates—the interim government under Friedrich Ebert's leadership—issued an order, approved even by the Independent Social Democrats, informing the revolutionary soldiers' councils that their first duty was to prevent chaos and work towards successful demobilization: 'after the unspeakable suffering and incredible privations every one of our soldiers should return home in the shortest possible time'. 'If individual units stream back arbitrarily, they will seriously jeopardize themselves, their comrades, and the homeland. The consequence will be chaos, with famine and want.'[91] The revolutionary government understood that if the army officers lost their power of command, the ensuing breakdown of organization and discipline would make the orderly withdrawal of the three-million-strong army across the German frontier impossible within the fifteen days allowed by the armistice that had been signed by representatives of the new democratic government at Compiègne on 11 November. Any German soldier left behind would potentially become the Allies' prisoner of war.[92]

The revolutionary workers' and soldiers' councils established across German towns in November 1918 were often dominated by Majority Social

Democrats and, for the most part, complied with the new government's demands for co-operation with the old army. When the OHL's GHQ moved from Spa to Wilhelmshöhe on 14 November, however, representatives of the local council even exceeded the call for pragmatic collaboration. They raised the Imperial flag and the soldiers wore ribbons in the Imperial colours of black, white, and red. Albert Grzesinski, a Majority Social Democrat and leader of the local council, who would go on to become Berlin Police Chief and Prussian Interior Minister, further issued a statement appealing to the population to greet the Field Marshal with all due respect:

> Hindenburg belongs to the German people and the German army. He led his armies to glorious victories and did not leave his people in a difficult hour. Never has Hindenburg in the greatness of the fulfilment of his duty been closer to us than today. He stands under our protection.[93]

Such displays of reverence for the Imperial Field Marshal by groups that had sought to overturn the very social and political order he had represented clearly illustrate the patriotic fervour of the soldiers' councils and the broad and enduring appeal of the Hindenburg myth during the revolution. They also hint at the fact that, far from being damaged by German military defeat, Hindenburg's mythical standing was further enhanced among those working towards German democracy in 1918/19 because he had not 'left his people' at a moment of crisis.

The co-operation between the old army and the provisional government, laid out in the so-called 'Ebert-Groener Pact' of 10 November 1918, according to which the government promised to curb the powers of the soldiers' councils and to fight Bolshevism in return for the army's support with demobilization, is one of the most important—and most controversial—aspects of the German revolution of 1918/19.[94] The Field Marshal's immediate backing of the alliance silenced not least the right-wing critics of cooperation with the Social Democrats.[95] His mythical standing provided the symbolic backbone of this fateful collaboration and was thus a crucial component of the German revolution from above.

In a concrete sense, war did not end for the German home front with the signing of the armistice on 11 November—the naval blockade was not lifted until July 1919 and political violence in the streets of German cities aggravated feelings of insecurity and the sense of crisis.[96] Millions of soldiers still stood on French and Belgian soil and others would continue to fight Lithuanian and Polish troops on Germany's eastern borders. The very mood of crisis people in warring nations live through often expresses the search for continuity and stability.[97] Crucially, the fear of political and economic chaos and the wish for order were the central driving forces behind the decisions of the leading Majority Social Democrats during and after the revolution. Ebert, Scheidemann, and Gustav Noske all considered the prevention of 'chaos' and the re-establishment of 'tranquillity' their top priorities in 1918/19—and all put their faith in the old Imperial elites, especially the army, rather than in the revolutionary councils to realize these aims.[98] Hindenburg's wartime image as a 'rock in the ocean', containing the 'Russian tidal wave' and famed for his stoical calmness and 'tranquillity', corresponded directly to their desire to contain the chaotic 'floods' of the revolution.[99] Salvaging the Hindenburg myth from war and revolution was attuned to this widespread wish for order that was a result of the disruption experienced in previous years[100]—an experience the members of the revolutionary councils had shared with more conservative forces.

According to the historian Hans Delbrück, editor of the *Preussische Jahrbücher*, Hindenburg's leadership of the army at this dangerous and highly difficult time was a 'historical necessity'.[101] One of Groener's closest advisers would later also reminisce about the gratitude the German public owed Hindenburg for staying, 'because it could not have worked without his nimbus'.[102] Evidently, Friedrich Ebert agreed.[103] Whenever members of his interim government and leading Independent Social Democrats criticized Hindenburg in the months after the revolution, Ebert justified his co-operation with the old elites with reference to the Field Marshal's importance in expediting demobilization and preventing chaos. There was no legitimate reason to question his position, because 'demobilization required the avoidance of any unnecessary disturbance of army unity'.[104]

Philipp Scheidemann formed a new government the following March after the elections to the National Assembly, and Ebert became Germany's first Reich President. During a cabinet discussion about the eventual dissolution of the OHL in March 1919, Ebert's assessments of the autumn were echoed by many of those present. The general consensus was that this had to occur in 'friendly agreement' with Hindenburg, who had made a 'great sacrifice' by staying on.[105] The DDP's Eugen Schiffer warned that any government propaganda under the headline 'down with Hindenburg' was going to have severe consequences. The new Prussian War Minister Walther Reinhardt, who had headed the army's Demobilization

Department in late 1918, thought that Hindenburg's presence still made a significant impression on Germany's enemies. He appeared as a 'Roland' to them, he argued. He also agreed with Schiffer that the Field Marshal's departure had a downside, because his commitment to the democratic process kept many people from working against the new government, especially the less wealthy younger members of the officer corps.[106] The memories of Hermann Hoth, an officer in his mid-thirties at the time, corroborated Reinhardt's assessment:

> Anyone who remembers the military defeat in 1918, the desperate pessimism of those first few weeks when Germany seemed to drown in the stream of Spartacus uprisings, will recall that the eyes of those who were looking for security were not directed towards Berlin . . . but to the General Headquarters in Wilhelmshöhe where Hindenburg . . . kept back the waves of turmoil firm as a rock in the ocean. I was probably not the only one who gained the courage and motivation to work for the reconstruction of Germany from the example set by the Field Marshal.[107]

The revolutionary government's room for manoeuvre in 1918/19 is perhaps the most heatedly debated issue in the historiography of the Weimar Republic. It is not the purpose of this study to revisit the polemical condemnations of the Majority Social Democrats for their deliberate 'betrayal' of the revolution.[108] Consensus now exists, however, that the latitude of the democratic leadership was considerably greater than making a forced choice between two options—a council system based on the Soviet model and a parliamentary democracy co-operating closely with the old elites. While the revolution undoubtedly introduced real and lasting change in Germany, the democratic leaders missed the opportunity for a more thorough re-assessment of the *Kaiserreich*'s political symbols.[109] The Hindenburg myth was one such symbol. Instead of revising his image in 1918/19 along with Ludendorff's and the Kaiser's, the provisional government relied on his veneration to cushion the blow of military defeat. SPD politicians even went as far as using the 'Iron Hindenburg' statue in Berlin as a platform for speeches against the Treaty of Versailles.[110]

In the debates in Baden's reform government and Ebert's revolutionary government about Hindenburg's possible departure, the belief in the potency of his mythical glorification transpired as the underlying reason for advocating his retention in office. Hindenburg's name and reputation were sources of legitimacy neither Baden nor Ebert and their respective circles thought they could afford to lose if they wanted to avoid chaos and curb political violence. Even if they considered the trust in Hindenburg in their own ranks volatile in autumn 1918, as did the MSPD leaders, they still subscribed to the notion that the Hindenburg myth was a compelling force able to sway public opinion at large.[111]

From the summer of 1918 onwards, there had been growing signs that segments of public opinion were turning against Hindenburg. Those working towards democratic reform, most notably the Majority Social Democrats, however, chose not to stoke the flames. They did not attempt to accelerate the revolutionary process by taking 'away the most steadfast pillar of German authority', a course the astute *Freie Zeitung* had urged as early as 1917. They did not do so for fear of the consequences—resulting from their continued belief in the potency of the Hindenburg myth—and because of their own inability to turn against a myth, which symbolized 'order' and 'tranquillity'—the central issues occupying the new government in 1918/19.

To be sure, taking away this 'pillar' would have been no easy task. Given that Hindenburg did not just embody the Prussian militarist tradition, but also the broader virtues of wartime Germany, his myth acting as a lens through which people viewed events, debunking it would have meant questioning the purpose of Germany's fight. By largely salvaging the Hindenburg myth after the defeat, the German population could substantiate the faith in its own virtues. Wanting to believe in the justness of Germany's cause and in the idea that millions of soldiers had given their lives—and the home front faced years of deprivation—for a legitimate reason were perhaps logical concerns. Whilst three-quarters of the electorate may have been ready to bid farewell to the semi-absolutist *Kaiserreich* by voting for the pro-republican parties of the 'Weimar coalition' (SPD, Centre Party, and DDP) in the elections for the National Assembly in January 1919, only months after the armistice, they were overall not yet able to reconsider the meaning of the war.[112]

On 3 July 1919, five days after the controversial peace treaty had been signed—not by him, but by representatives of the democratic government at Versailles—Hindenburg finally retired from the OHL which would be dissolved the next day, to return to Hanover, where the local population gave him a rapturous welcome.[113] The night before his departure a farewell celebration at the German GHQ marked his second retirement. On this occasion, Wilhelm Groener, who had 'consciously spread the old Hindenburg's glory for political reasons' in previous months,[114] expressed his take on the function of the Hindenburg myth in no uncertain terms:

> The personality of the Field Marshal represents the passage from an old period to a new one. He is the bearer of the great and silent forces of the past for the future of our people. Simple dignity and the ultimate fulfilment of duty are the main character traits which have not only affected us ... but also affected the whole people. Looking towards the future, we should honour our Field Marshal with a thundering hurrah and swear that we will follow his example until the end of our days.[115]

Hindenburg thus entered retirement not as a military leader marred by defeat, but as a dutiful commander-in-chief and national hero, 'loyal' to his people at a crucial time, whose myth salvaged the key values of a bygone era for the new German state. Had he refrained from meddling in political affairs after July 1919, the democrats' lack of critical engagement with his wartime myth might not have become a problem. One could even speculate that he might, in fact, still be remembered as a force of stability, continuity, and tranquillity that expedited demobilization and helped to ease the transition from monarchy to Republic in 1918/19. But Hindenburg would not leave the public stage for long and republicans would soon pay a heavy price for using him as a mythical prop in the war's aftermath. Their reliance on Hindenburg's reputation in 1918/19 led to their self-elimination as credible critics of right-wing agendas promoted by means of deploying the Hindenburg myth in the years to come. This largely self-inflicted paralysis was to have severe consequences which it took republicans considerable time to recognize. After the Field Marshal's election victory in 1925, the *Frankfurter Zeitung* published a leader on the events in 1918/19 so insightful it is worth quoting at length:

> We did not see it before, but we see clearly today that it was one of the gravest mistakes to let the Hindenburg legend stay alive ... In all the years that have passed since the collapse, we have critically examined many Generals of the First World War, most notably Ludendorff, Hindenburg's aide, but Hindenburg was left aside. (...) This reluctance had honourable and humane motives ... He did not flee, as the Emperor did, and he did not decline to work with the soldiers' councils. He just remained at his post, and under his leadership the difficult task of an orderly retreat of the army was fulfilled. That was undoubtedly an achievement ... However, there was another component, which contributed to Hindenburg's extraordinary standing in

the people's minds: German romanticism . . . Even though we lost the war, there were also great accomplishments. Especially a vanquished people need those accomplishments symbolized in difficult times. Hindenburg was such a symbol, and even those who should have known better, salvaged his name. This consideration was honourable, but mistaken. We should have told ourselves that a people so taken with romanticism as the Germans have no greater need than the truth, always and everywhere. This omission was a mistake, which has now taken its toll.[116]

\* \* \*

The Hindenburg myth did not coincidentally survive the military collapse.[117] Towards the end of the war, people's mounting insecurity and sense of crisis had manifested themselves in countless rumours about Hindenburg, partly fanned by Allied propaganda. Moreover, the success of pro-Hindenburg propaganda had begun to encounter its limits. Of course, German soldiers and the home front could not have held out indefinitely simply because they trusted the Chief of the General Staff. Given that the Field Marshal had eclipsed Wilhelm II and outshone Ludendorff in the public's perception, it is nevertheless striking that he was, for the most part, not blamed for Germany's defeat. The democratic left vilified reactionary German politics represented by Ludendorff instead, whilst the right found its scapegoat through the 'stab-in-the-back' theory.

Hindenburg's 'corona' did not completely 'fade when defeat became inevitable'.[118] In fact, his myth survived in 1918/19, because it still corresponded to the social expectations of large sections of German society: to salvage something positive from war, to continue believing in the justness of Germany's cause, and to re-create a sense of order, tranquillity, and continuity after the disruption of wartime. But as the *Frankfurter Zeitung* would finally recognize six-and-a-half years after the revolution, the democrats' reluctance to criticize the Hindenburg myth, and their reliance on it during the transition, turned into a heavy burden for the young Republic.

# 3

# Anti-democratic politics

Hindenburg never faded completely from public imagination after his retirement, or indeed throughout the Republic's 'crisis years' of 1919 to 1923,[1] not least guaranteed by the continued presence of Hindenburg memorabilia in German homes, which had been amassed during wartime. On the occasion of the Field Marshal's 72nd birthday in October 1919, Wilhelm von Gayl, an East Prussian Nationalist politician and protagonist in promoting Hindenburg's fame in the early years of the Republic, hailed him as a 'bible, a gospel of inner freedom'. Although Germany was going through a dark period, he had not lost faith in its resurrection, Gayl explained, because everywhere he travelled, all palaces, classrooms, and pubs were adorned with Hindenburg's picture.

> His image, looked upon by children's eyes, should not be missing from any German home. 'Hindenburg' should be the word our boys learn along with father and mother... As long as our society worships its heroes, as long as children say 'Hindenburg', there will be hope.[2]

Echoing Groener's thoughts on Hindenburg's retirement in the summer, Gayl's article sketched out what function Hindenburg-worship served for anti-republicans on the right. Keeping his memory alive was a way of re-affirming the belief in key nationalist values they felt had been lost in the revolution.[3] For these right-wingers, who regarded hero-worship by definition as positive, Hindenburg was an ideal educational figure whose commemoration would accelerate the resurrection of the 'good' forces within German society. His myth would inspire future generations of Germans to strive towards toppling the despised 'system' of Weimar—personified by figures like Matthias Erzberger, who had signed the armistice in 1918.

Hindenburg, a living myth, played a key role in connecting the various narrative strands of Weimar's anti-republican 'mythical network'.[4] He was the embodiment of different elements of other potent political tales of the interwar period: the Bismarck myth, a widespread anti-republican tale about strong leadership, the notion of German innocence in 1914, a powerful tool in the anti-democratic fight against the 'shameful peace' of Versailles and the 'war guilt lie', and the myth of the 'spirit of 1914', a narrative of social and political unity that acquired an increasingly anti-parliamentarian character after the war.[5] Hindenburg, a strong leader of Bismarckian qualities, had 'saved' Germany from the invading Russians in 1914, thereby confirming Germany's innocence in 1914 and proving the injustice of the Versailles Treaty and its infamous §231 on German war guilt. The rapturous public response to Tannenberg and Hindenburg's broad social and political appeal in wartime seemingly testified to the reality of the 'spirit of 1914'—a spirit republicans had allegedly betrayed by calling off the Burgfrieden and sapping the home front's endurance through pacifist agitation. They had thereby destroyed German unity and founded the Weimar Republic on treason and defeat.

Above all, however, the Hindenburg myth was entwined closely with the 'stab-in-the-back' legend, about to become a 'mainstay of conservative-nationalist ideology' in 1919, but nevertheless successful far beyond the circle of uncompromising anti-republicans, because large parts of the population were equally reluctant to admit German defeat.[6] The idea of a 'stab-in-the-back' of the army by the German home front would become increasingly radicalized and merge with the notion of an 'unvanquished army' undefeated in the field, but robbed of the fruits of victory by treacherous Socialists at home.[7] Whilst it acted as a catalyst to republican destabilization in the long run, the narrative was naturally advantageous for Hindenburg's image as it shed a positive light on the OHL's record and exempted him not just of most, but virtually all responsibility for German defeat. The twin myths of 'Hindenburg' and the 'stab-in-the-back' worked reciprocally and were mutually re-enforcing. The liberal journalist Theodor Wolff summed up their interconnectedness pointedly in November 1919: 'The unfortunate scapegoat theory could not emerge if the infallibility theory had not risen on the other side.'[8]

Hindenburg's public appearances and official statements guaranteed extensive press coverage. Because his veneration was not a homogeneously right-wing affair, but also penetrated republican circles, especially among the bourgeoisie, those worshipping him could spread anti-republican ideas inconspicuously and without the smack of party politics. The events in

Berlin in November 1919 were the first example of just how effective anti-republican agitation disguised as innocent Hindenburg celebrations could be.

## Popularizing the 'stab-in-the-back'

Hindenburg testified at a hearing of the Parliamentary Investigation Committee on the Causes of the Collapse at the Reichstag in Berlin on 18 November 1919. If one had to pinpoint the public breakthrough of the 'stab-in-the-back' idea, this would be the pivotal moment.

The investigation committee had been set up in August 1919. Its main tasks were the investigation of the 'war guilt' question and establishing responsibility for the causes of Germany's military collapse. Expert opinion from military, naval, and civilian specialists was heard and extensive documentary material collected to be published in a final report.[9] The anti-democratic right had denounced the work of the committee as a nest-besmirching enterprise from the outset. To avoid further right-wing outrage the committee had decided not to summon Hindenburg as a witness. Ludendorff, however, had been called upon to testify on the OHL's involvement in the decision to declare unrestricted submarine warfare in 1917 and to reject the Entente peace offers of 1916 and 1917. But when he, clearly aware of the potency of Hindenburg's image, refused to appear unless the Field Marshal was summoned alongside him, the committee was forced to backtrack and eventually asked Hindenburg to attend.[10]

The committee was anxious to show its admiration for the Field Marshal. On 18 November, the table in the Reichstag witness box was decorated with a large bunch of chrysanthemums, tied with ribbons in the Imperial colours. Moreover, it had been agreed that Hindenburg would not be cross-examined by a member of the largest parliamentary group, the Social Democrats, but by the DDP's Georg Gothein, a man of old Prussian civil service traditions. Nevertheless, Hindenburg dodged all direct questions and produced a typed document, which he had drafted together with his host in Berlin, Karl Helfferich, a DNVP politician and key player in the nationalist struggle against republican politicians such as Walther Rathenau and Matthias Erzberger.[11] Hindenburg read the whole memorandum without paying the slightest attention to Gothein's repeated attempts at interrupting him. He laid out Germany's innocence in 1914 and blamed divergent party interests, which had allegedly led to the 'disintegration of the German people's will to conquer', for the military collapse. His closing remarks, however, proved to be the most fateful:

> As an English General has very truly said, 'The German Army was stabbed in the back.' It is plain enough upon whom the blame lies. If any further proof were necessary to show it, it is to be found in the utter amazement of our enemies at their victory.[12]

Citing the words a Swiss newspaper had attributed to British General Sir Frederick Maurice, Hindenburg thus lent his mythical authority to the 'stab-in-the-back' allegation. His endorsement popularized the narrative immediately; conservative commentators proclaimed a 'victory of the truth' within 24 hours.[13] Hindenburg had not invented the narrative, but broadened its dissemination considerably. His statement was printed in all the major daily papers the day after his testimony and debated endlessly in the opinion columns. He was therefore midwife to an idea German society had been pregnant with since the revolution—an idea that burdened the young republic with accusations of treachery, thereby intensifying political polarization and shifting the political climate decisively to the right.

Hindenburg's endorsement put the democratic camp in a near-impossible position. Republican commentators faced the complicated task of defying a narrative granted the Field Marshal's official approval, whilst avoiding personal and direct criticism of a man whose mythical adulation had lent legitimacy to their cause until a few months previously. Even if Theodor Wolff had recognized the danger of the 'infallibility theory' about Hindenburg, which strengthened the allegations of democratic treason, he insisted in the same article: 'Tannenberg remains Tannenberg. [Hindenburg] . . . is one of those historical figures to whom the people's feelings [*Volksgefühl*] will always flow.'[14]

Condemning the 'stab-in-the-back' as a fabrication, whilst steering clear of criticizing its now most famous proponent, led others to revert to further vilifying the Field Marshal's former second-in-command. Exempting Hindenburg from the responsibility for his own public proclamation, the *Frankfurter Zeitung* was convinced that 'You could hear Ludendorff's voice through Hindenburg's words'.[15] *Vorwärts* dared to declare its disappointment with Hindenburg, whom the SPD 'respected', but then quickly changed the subject:

> Let us not speak of the old gentleman...whose misfortune commands respect! [H]e remains a likeable old Commander. An old man in a foreign world...Let us speak of Ludendorff only.[16]

Only the left-wing *Welthühne* spotted the irrationality inherent in 'people's rage stopping short of the old Field Marshal and turning, without logic, purely emotionally, against his aide.' By still worshipping Hindenburg, people were 'worshipping themselves', the poet Kurt Tucholsky remarked with characteristic acuity. 'One has to lose a war to be celebrated like this', he concluded with resignation.[17]

## 'The enemy is on the right'

Hindenburg's visit to Berlin did not just forestall many of the intricacies of Weimar's politics of memory, but also produced a new style of right-wing anti-republican agitation. Whereas the Republic had hitherto been threatened predominantly by radical left-wing violence—above all, during the Spartacist uprising of January 1919—Hindenburg's visit to Berlin in November 1919 was accompanied by the first display of organized and subversive agitation by the anti-democratic right in the streets.

Reminiscent of October 1915, when Hindenburg's birthday had enabled Reventlow to defy the state of siege with his speech at the 'Iron Hindenburg', the Field Marshal's presence provided a welcome cover for right-wing agitators in November 1919. A state of siege banning all political demonstrations was again in place at the time, but spontaneous public displays of enthusiasm for the Field Marshal could not be banned for fear of appearing ungrateful to Germany's war hero. These public pledges of support for Hindenburg, however, were from the outset highly politicized, with agitation against the investigation committee, the democratic government, and the Weimar 'system'. Increasingly, they also had anti-Semitic overtones—blaming 'the Jews' for the collapse of the German war effort—which Ludendorff stoked up in his Reichstag statement of 18 November 1919.[18]

When Hindenburg arrived at Zoologischer Garten station in the morning of 12 November, nearly a week before his testimony, a Reichswehr guard of honour greeted him and a military band played marching songs. The Free Corps leader Colonel Wilhelm Reinhard had organized the reception in defiance of orders to host a low-key affair.[19] The time of Hindenburg's arrival had not been publicized, but when his train pulled into the station at 8 a.m., thousands of people, carrying flowers and cheering loudly, greeted the Field Marshal, who had difficulties reaching his car.[20] The presence of such a large crowd early in the morning suggests that his right-wing hosts had either leaked his time of arrival strategically or staged the whole affair outright. Far from constituting quiet, patriotic worship, Hindenburg's appearance clearly had political connotations. Displaying the Imperial colours, members of the audience denounced the investigation committee and its 'Jewish inventors' loudly.[21] Socialist counter-demonstrators, meanwhile, interrupted the celebrations by singing the 'International' and one female counter-demonstrator, shouting noisily, condemned Hindenburg as a 'mass slaughterer'. A fight between the rival groups ensued, forcing the soldiers in attendance to intervene.[22] Similar scenes could be witnessed at all stages of Hindenburg's week-long visit, and the political climate became ever more polarized. The Reichswehr that was in charge of upholding the state of siege was reluctant to intervene.[23]

On 14 November 3,000–4,000 demonstrators, mostly from nationalist student groups, surrounded and stopped Hindenburg's car on the central Charlottenburger Chaussee. They expressed their outrage at their 'heroic' Field Marshal having been summoned to Berlin like a 'stupid boy', cheered the *Kaiserreich*, and condemned the investigation committee, the November revolution, and the 'Jewish government'.[24] That night, nationalists gatecrashed a republican event, once again amidst anti-Semitic shouts.[25]

Earlier that day, in front of the Reichstag not far from the right-wing student rally, German Nationalists had further rounded up large numbers of schoolchildren and encouraged them to show their veneration for Hindenburg. Despite the state of siege, the policemen present did not intervene in either of these demonstrations.[26] The presence of children lent anti-republican gatherings even more of an innocent aura and members of nationalist organizations recruited them for this purpose throughout Hindenburg's visit. They went into local schools, personally drove their young recruits to Helfferich's house, where the famous visitor was staying, while nationalist deans and teachers urged their pupils to attend the festivities, tempting them with a day off school. Many schoolboys and girls were only too happy to accept the offer of sanctioned truancy, and on the day of Hindenburg's testimony many of them accompanied his car on its way to the Reichstag. *Vorwärts* commented laconically: 'Open public demonstrations are banned at the moment, but those shorts and blonde ponytails have disarmed the state of siege.'[27]

For conservative commentators, Hindenburg's summoning suggested that the whole world had been turned on its head[28]—safely ignoring the fact that he had been summoned at Ludendorff's insistence. The idea that their hero was to be interrogated by representatives of a system they rejected plainly symbolized for them the ills of the Weimar Republic. According to the conservative *Kreuz-Zeitung*, rallying around him was based on the conviction that

> at this point the basic ideals differ from each other: patriotism and international outlook, pride and shameful self-humiliation, gratitude and spitefulness, enthusiasm for a great aim and petty party politics . . . Just as fire and water do not merge, there should be no bridge between the moral and political views of the revolutionary government and ours.[29]

Furthermore, the conservative daily admitted to deploying Hindenburg's visit to further a more current agenda. One could not condemn people for 'playing a trick on the state of siege', the paper contended.

Just as countering Hindenburg's claim of a 'stab-in-the-back' had been awkward without questioning his myth, criticizing political demonstrations camouflaged as Hindenburg-worship was a difficult task for the democrats. They reverted to stressing that the Field Marshal belonged to the whole German people and that no one was trying to diminish his public standing, and warning that he should not be torn into the party strife. 'The honouring of Hindenburg, which is in line with the feeling of the great majority of the people, should be welcomed', the *Berliner Tageblatt* opined, 'but if the organizers of these demonstrations seek to abuse Hindenburg's halo in order to cover up their reactionary activities, we are calling for criticism and defence.'[30] Using Hindenburg as a 'pretext' and engaging his reputation as the 'fire, which will bring the German nationalist soup to the boil' would not be tolerated.[31]

Right-wing agitation had, however, already succeeded to a considerable degree. Not only had Hindenburg sanctioned the 'stab-in-the-back' allegation, but nationalist demonstrators had defied the state of siege and found a public forum in Hindenburg celebrations to voice their anti-democratic and anti-Semitic views. So tense had the political climate become that on

the day of his testimony the streets leading to the Reichstag were heavily
guarded by troops and mounted police. The building itself was strongly
protected as well; barbed wire barred the entrance of the side doors, and
guards with machine guns were posted at each corner.[32]

Hindenburg's stay in Berlin marked a pivotal moment in the development
of his myth. Far from performing an integrative and stabilizing function—as
Baden's and Ebert's governments had expected it to do—his presence
now acted as a catalyst to the polarization and fragmentation of Weimar
politics already under way.[33] In November 1919 the streets of Berlin were a
gathering ground for monarchists and radical nationalists where, for the first
time, those who openly spoke out in favour of the Republic were subjected
to anti-Semitic abuse or beaten up. In response to these anti-republican
Hindenburg celebrations Philipp Scheidemann coined the famous phrase
'Der Feind steht rechts'—'The enemy is on the right'.[34] Whereas the spectre
of Bolshevism had haunted the Republic the previous year, Scheidemann
now warned that the threat from the right was much greater. Theodor
Wolff agreed that the radical right had remained remarkably quiet after
the revolution, but that its supporters now played 'the lion's awakening',
colonizing streets and town squares—a traditional domain of the left they
had hitherto avoided. This marked a decisive change in their agitational
style and tactics, the influential journalist observed, and brought about a
dangerous fusion of anti-republican and anti-Semitic slogans.[35] From the
perspective of the nationalist right the events of November 1919 marked
an act of symbolic liberation of public spaces previously dominated by the
'red mob'. This was an important chapter in the 'nationalization of the
masses' in Germany, a process that had begun in the nineteenth century
and would shape the aesthetics of politics in the 'Third Reich'.[36]

# Hindenburg for President?

Given Hindenburg's continued public veneration, calls for his nomination
as a candidate for the office of Reich President, first made public in August
1919 by the monarchist DVP, came as no surprise.[37] The DVP leadership
soon discussed the matter with Hindenburg, who was initially reluctant
to stand because of his age. Ernst von Richter and Gustav Stresemann,
however, were convinced that he could be persuaded if 'broad sections of
the people called on him'.[38] The last Chief of Wilhelm's Civil Cabinet,

Friedrich von Berg, even contacted Wilhelm II in his Dutch exile to seek the ex-Kaiser's approval.[39]

According to article 41 of the new Reich Constitution, which had come into force in August 1919, the President had to be determined by popular vote. Until these elections took place, the temporary president Friedrich Ebert, whom the National Assembly had elected on 11 February 1919, would continue to serve.[40] The republican government had reason to fear a right-wing victory in late 1919 and early 1920 and was reluctant to schedule a date, with the consequence that the opposition accused it of obstructing the democratic process in a bid for political power. Ideas to change the constitution and put parliament in charge of choosing the President, which the Weimar parties suggested, encountered strong resistance from the right.[41] When the DVP and DNVP proposed Hindenburg as a cross-party candidate for the presidency on 6 March 1920 the Weimar parties were further pushed onto the defensive. Hindenburg's candidacy had been engineered by the Reichsbürgerrat (Reich Citizen Council), an organization of representatives of the right-wing parties under the chairmanship of former Prussian Interior Minister Friedrich Wilhelm von Loebell.[42]

The public debate following the announcement of Hindenburg's candidacy offered a preview of the 1925 election campaign in some important respects. The German Nationalist tabloid *Berliner Lokalanzeiger* described Hindenburg as the embodiment of German unity, who was responding to the people's wishes by running for office. He considered standing his patriotic duty, the paper claimed. Echoing German propaganda for the war loan in 1917, which had portrayed subscribing as paying off a debt owed to Hindenburg, in 1920, the right urged the population to express its gratitude by voting for him.[43] The promoters of Hindenburg's election thus painted voting not as a democratic right but as the duty to one man. This theme of indebtedness would not only be a dominant feature of the 1925 election campaign, but also left its mark on the political battles of 1932.

The nationalist press increasingly attacked the government by arguing that it was putting off the election for fear of Hindenburg.[44] The government allegedly knew very well that Hindenburg would win and was boycotting the people's will.[45] As a result, republicans yet again found themselves in a position of having to stress their respect and admiration for the Field Marshal whilst explaining their opposition to holding an election. In the moderate Socialist tabloid *BZ am Mittag,* Jakob Frank insisted that Hindenburg deserved his glory, especially for staying on after the collapse, a service the left should not forget. They should even forgive him for sanctioning the 'stab-in-the-back' legend, Frank suggested. After endorsing the narrative of left-wing treason, however, he was no suitable President of the Republic.[46] The *Frankfurter Zeitung*, in its turn, reverted to the established rhetorical pattern of criticizing first and foremost the men behind Hindenburg's candidacy, who had allegedly tricked him into running and wanted to abuse his name for their own purposes.[47] Hindenburg was deployed as a 'mask' for Ludendorff, the paper speculated. Both themes, that of sinister figures luring Hindenburg into standing under false circumstances and that of his image being used as a mask, would re-surface in visual and narrative form in the 1925 and 1932 campaigns—illustrating the extent to which his status as a mythical figure dominated perceptions and public discourse about him throughout the Weimar period.

Focusing their critique, as usual, on the democratic left for allegedly thwarting a true Socialist revolution in 1918/19 rather than on the anti-democratic right, the Communists pointed out the democrats' own part in salvaging the Hindenburg myth after the war. The prospect of his candidacy had left republicans so helpless, the *Rote Fahne* claimed, because they themselves had 'resurrected Hindenburg's monumental status from the first days of the revolution'. The Hindenburg legend had gained 'superhuman proportions' and would 'crash down on those who had reconstructed it', the Communist daily predicted.[48] Although overtly polemical in its condemnation of the Social Democrats, the paper managed to identify the republican dilemma accurately.

In 1920, neither right-wing hopes for a Hindenburg presidency nor the *Rote Fahne*'s prophecy of republican demise were fulfilled. On 13 March, a few days after Hindenburg's candidacy had been put forward publicly, reactionary forces within the army around the East Prussian rural official Wolfgang Kapp and the Silesian General Walther von Lüttwitz (the 'father of the Free Corps') embarked on the first right-wing coup attempt of the Weimar years, the so-called Kapp-Lüttwitz coup.[49] Ludendorff had also been involved. Right-wing outrage at alleged republican attempts to deny Hindenburg the presidency had been one factor in convincing reactionary forces that the time was ripe for Weimar's violent overthrow.[50] The democratic government had to flee from Berlin, but the movement was crushed and order restored fairly quickly. This enterprise, however, ended right-wing hopes of a swift presidential election. Instead, Friedrich

Ebert was to stay in office for a full seven-year term without ever seeking the endorsement of the popular vote.[51] Although Hindenburg was not elected, the public debate about his candidacy in March 1920 once again confirmed that his myth was a powerful political weapon, which could silence critics and push democratic forces onto the defensive. Hindenburg was completely aware of his role at this time and even referred to himself as a right-wing 'bullet' in private.[52] The right would clearly remember the power of this ammunition when choosing Hindenburg as a presidential candidate in April 1925.

## Symbolic journeys

Even when Hindenburg was not visiting Berlin or contemplating running for president, he remained a public figure and a household name. In 1921, the industrialist Hugo Stinnes christened a ship built for him by the Bremen Vulcan shipyard 'Hindenburg' and many German towns simultaneously changed local street names in the Field Marshal's honour.[53] Meanwhile, the streets in front of his home in Hanover's Seelhorstraße witnessed a continuous stream of visitors hoping to catch a glimpse of their war hero. So many people rushed to Hindenburg's residence that the *Vorwärts* labelled it a 'new centre for pilgrimage'.[54] Hindenburg must have been used to the crowds since his headquarters had attracted similarly large numbers of visitors during the war, which had made him feel like a 'great rhino that one simply had to see'.[55] As a result of his iconic status in wartime, his image was so familiar that many people instantly recognized him in the street. Especially in the early years after his retirement, Hindenburg therefore avoided walking around Hanover or left very early in the morning to avoid people following him around.[56]

The press, too, continued to cover the events of his life. Above all the nationalist papers commemorated Hindenburg's birthdays and invoked him as a role model of duty and loyalty.[57] The Field Marshal also accepted the post of honorary chairman of nationalist and veterans' organizations such as the Kyffhäuser League, the Stahlhelm, and the Deutsche Ostbund, and issued public statements on matters of nationalist concern.[58]

In 1920, the Leipzig-based S. Hirzel publishing house issued Hindenburg's memoirs *Aus meinem Leben*, which gave a detailed account of Germany's military and political fortunes during the war. Hindenburg had not written the book himself, but hired Hermann Ritter Mertz von Quirnheim, a close wartime acquaintance and head of the Reichsarchiv in charge of writing the official German history of the war from October 1919, and the historian and DNVP politician Otto Hoetzsch as ghost writers of the book.[59] According to the contract drawn up by the publisher in May 1919, Hindenburg's memoirs were modelled on Bismarck's hugely successful *Gedanken und Erinnerungen*, whose third volume had been published in 1919, in the sense that Mertz and Hoetzsch's names would be mentioned neither on the cover of the book nor in the acknowledgements. The contract suggests that Hindenburg was well aware of the mythical precedent set by Bismarck and sought to emulate it in promoting his own fame.

The memoir was written in the first person, giving its readers no indication that they were not reading Hindenburg's own words but his ghost writers'.[60] It presented an apologetic account of wartime events and was clearly written to cement Hindenburg's reputation as Germany's greatest living hero. He strongly insisted that none of his actions had been motivated by the quest for fame and glory, once again feeding the idea that vanity was foreign to him and that he had done nothing to further his glorification.[61] He equally nurtured the mythical narrative by stressing his commitment to patriotic duty, the alleged driving force behind all his actions. Invoking the *Nibelungen* saga by comparing the German army to the heroic Siegfried and the home front to the treacherous Hagen, Hindenburg repeated the allegation of a 'stab-in-the-back' as the cause of German military collapse, thus popularizing the right-wing legend still further.[62]

Written in a deliberately simple style, the book was a big commercial success and went through numerous editions. In March 1920, Hindenburg himself scaled down his friend August von Cramon's expectations when telling him that the book was first and foremost '*volkstümlich*' and intended 'to have an ethical impact'.[63] This honest admission and the publisher's contract with Hindenburg's ghost writers illustrate once more that—contrary to the version presented in his memoirs—he engaged actively in furthering his cult and knew exactly how to go about it.

Hindenburg did not, however, have to rely solely on the written word to keep his myth alive and help strengthen anti-democratic sentiment in the early 1920s. Just like his stay in Berlin in November 1919, Hindenburg's month-long travels through East Prussia in the summer of 1922, during which he visited friends and his family's estate in Neudeck, and made numerous public appearances, were accompanied by political demonstrations and street violence. He had asked his acquaintance and admirer Wilhelm von Gayl to organize the visit lasting from 19 May until 16 June 1922.[64] Gayl was not only a member of the DNVP and East Prussian envoy to the Reichsrat, but also the leader of the Staatsbürgerliche Arbeitsgemeinschaft and the Ostpreußischer Heimatbund, two anti-republican organizations intent on protecting East Prussia's German identity after the province had been separated from the *Reich* by the Polish corridor.[65] The prospect of Hindenburg's visit delighted Gayl, because it would pay a great service to the 'national idea'.[66]

Both the Arbeitsgemeinschaft and the Heimatbund functioned as official hosts of public events during Hindenburg's visit, alarming local democratic politicians. Before the Field Marshal even arrived the head of the Rosenberg administration, Ferdinand Friedensburg (DDP), who would go on to become Berlin's Chief of Police, had written to both Hindenburg and Gayl to express his concern. He suggested that the local administrations should organize the visit instead.[67] Many East Prussian democrats perceived the Heimatbund as a threat, Friedensburg explained, and had the impression that 'the *Volkstümlichkeit* of the great figure of the Field Marshal was to be exploited' to further the organization's political aims. Friedensburg was by no means generally opposed to extracting political gain from the Hindenburg myth—again hinting at its appeal among republicans—but warned that one party monopolizing his image would ultimately sap its power:

> The time may come when we will need the tremendous capital inherent in the German people's stance towards Hindenburg to unite the people's community; that makes it all the more important not to waste this capital too early on petty aims.[68]

In response to such concerns, both Gayl and Elard von Oldenburg-Januschau, another of Hindenburg's old acquaintances and a DNVP Reichstag delegate involved in organizing the visit, repeatedly stressed the private nature of the enterprise and refused to change the schedule.[69] Count Dohna-Finckenstein, whom Friedensburg had also informed of his unease, was more straightforward when admitting that the nationalist parties had a comparative advantage for once and would not back down.[70] Both Friedensburg and members of the local SPD warned Gayl and Hindenburg in advance that the visit would create political tensions, that counter-demonstrations could not be avoided, and urged Hindenburg not to let his name be abused for the right-wing cause.[71] Once Hindenburg had arrived it quickly became clear that his visit was a 'German Nationalist propaganda trip'. The Wirth government reacted by banning members of the Reichswehr from attending the celebrations, because these were political acts.[72] Only military parades honouring the Field Marshal behind closed doors and without an audience were considered legal.[73]

The government's orders did not succeed in defusing political tensions; the conflicts intensified throughout Hindenburg's visit. When he arrived in Königsberg on 11 June violent clashes between the Reichswehr and left-wing demonstrators occurred. A church service had taken place, which Hindenburg attended, followed by an honorary Reichswehr parade behind closed doors. Communist counter-demonstrators, egged on by the *Rote Fahne*, tried to interrupt the enclosed celebrations with shouts and loud singing of the 'International'.[74] When the uniformed soldiers left the parade they poured into the central streets of Königsberg in close proximity to the official Hindenburg festivities of the Staatsbürgerliche Arbeitsgemeinschaft. Their presence in the vicinity of the nationalist celebrations made it seem as though the soldiers were defying orders and taking part in political demonstrations; and some soldiers probably did. As a result, the left-wing counter-demonstrators protested loudly and began to throw stones at some of the soldiers. During the ensuing fight the officers and soldiers also fired shots. Several demonstrators and onlookers were injured by gunfire or stab wounds, including women and children.[75]

Whilst such violent responses to Hindenburg's presence and the right-wing organizations' monopolization of his visit illustrate clearly that the Field Marshal's appearances had become dangerously divisive, East Prussian nationalists welcomed the sentiment the visit had stirred. For them, the 'Hindenburg Days' were an altogether uplifting affair: great public enthu-siasm accompanied every public appearance of the Field Marshal, and the local population was renewing its pledge of gratitude to Hindenburg who had 'saved' East Prussia in 1914. His car was stopped wherever he went, and whereas the Imperial colours dominated such scenes, the republican colours of black, red, and gold were mostly invisible. Hence, Hindenburg's visit strengthened the right-wing cause and refreshed the memory of the events of August 1914, which were to be emulated in the struggle for the preservation of the Germanic character of East Prussia.[76]

Crucially, Hindenburg's visit came at a time of intense public debates about rapprochement with Russia as laid out in the Treaty of Rapallo. Moreover, it coincided with the wave of political murders committed by members of the Free Corps, which plagued Germany in Weimar's early years.[77] In the summer of 1921, the USPD leader Karl Gareis and the Centre Party's Matthias Erzberger were shot. On 4 June 1922, whilst Hindenburg was travelling around East Prussia, an assassination attempt was made on the SPD's Philipp Scheidemann, then mayor of Kassel. And less than two weeks after the Field Marshal had left the province, on 24 June 1922, members of the right-wing terrorist group Organization Consul killed their most high-profile victim: Germany's Foreign Minister Walther Rathenau. The Social Democratic *Königsberger Volkszeitung* posited the existence of a link between the murder of Germany's leading diplomat and Hindenburg's visit to East Prussia. 'The inflammatory propaganda of the right-wing parties—to which the Hindenburg razzmatazz belonged—has again led to blood sacrifice', the paper observed.[78]

Whereas it would almost certainly go too far to suggest that Rathenau's murderers or Scheidemann's would-be killers were inspired by the events in East Prussia, Hindenburg's visit no doubt contributed to the amplification of political tensions and sparked violent clashes between left and right.[79] Before his arrival, various republican politicians as well as the Foreign Office had warned him repeatedly that exactly this would occur and begged him not to lend his name to the radical right-wing cause. Nonetheless, Hindenburg refused to change his plans or to postpone his trip. With hindsight, Carl Severing, the Social Democratic Prussian Interior Minister at the time, observed that although not connected directly, the timing of the assassinations had nevertheless validated with horrible clarity republican assessments of the political situation, to which Hindenburg had been privy several weeks before. Someone with political understanding and foresight, Severing argued, would have done without the help of revanchist politicians.[80] Ferdinand Friedensburg, who had also advised Hindenburg to alter the itinerary of his visit, obviously drew different—and more cynical—conclusions about the Field Marshal's understanding of politics. He warned that one should under no circumstances overestimate his character—or underestimate his intelligence, suggesting that he was convinced that Hindenburg was more than aware of the effects his visit might have.[81]

In the summer of 1922 Hindenburg, in fact, did not opt for 'dignified silence'[82] but knowingly chose to ignore well-informed republican warnings and to go ahead with his controversial visit. He thus prioritized furthering his nationalist acquaintances' cause over easing political tensions. Nor would he put pressure on his nationalist hosts in the future to avoid politically polarizing moves.[83] Merely two months after the events in East Prussia, en route to his annual summer hunt in the Bavarian town of Dietramszell, Hindenburg visited the nationalist politician Gustav von Kahr in Munich, an advocate of Bavarian separatism. At this time the Bavarian capital was an 'Eldorado for extreme right organizations and leading personalities of right-wing radicalism'.[84] The divisive side-effects of Hindenburg's public appearances were visible once more.[85] The government envoy reported back to Berlin:

> The streets were so packed that one could hardly get through; there were blue and white [the Bavarian flag] and black, white, and red flags everywhere, Social Democrats and Jews were insulted and sometimes even beaten up. The Field Marshal himself behaved rather quietly. But he was steered by Kahr . . . and Ludendorff, who both used the occasion to further their own popularity by bathing in Hindenburg's glory.[86]

Even if stressing that such visits were private affairs, Hindenburg's presence always had political connotations. Anti-democratic politicians used it successfully to promote their anti-republican cause and often clashed violently with their left-wing counterparts. Although broad sections of German society subscribed to the Hindenburg myth after the war, Hindenburg's willingness to act as a vehicle of right-wing agitation after 1919 meant that his predominantly stabilizing and unifying role came under threat.

## Commemorating Tannenberg

Although the Battle of Tannenberg had largely served an integrative function in 1914, commemorations of the battle in the Weimar years also became increasingly politically divisive. In 1919, Wilhelm von Gayl and the Social Democratic *Oberpräsident* August Winnig jointly promoted the commemorations in Hohenstein. A year later, Southern East Prussians and West Prussians would vote in a plebiscite on the future of Masuria and the north-eastern parts of Western Prussia as either Polish or German. In the run-up to the vote German politicians across party lines promoted pro-German festivities.[87] Reminding local Germans of the Slavonic threat of August 1914 was obviously a tool Social Democrats were happy to use as well.[88] Nationalist organizations also staged commemorations in the Berlin sports stadium, in Königsberg, and in Potsdam. Both in 1919 and 1920 these passed relatively quietly.[89]

Once the joint goal of securing the provinces' allegiance to the Reich had been realized (on 11 July 1920 the local population had overwhelmingly voted to remain German[90]) the memory of Tannenberg became ever more caught up in the nationalist struggle against the 'war guilt lie' and the 'shameful peace' of Versailles—predominantly right-wing agendas.[91] In 1921, violence accompanied the commemorations in various towns. In Insterburg fights broke out during Socialist counter-demonstrations and in Potsdam two workers were killed during a violent confrontation with German Nationalist youth groups.[92] The atmosphere during the commemoration in Königsberg was equally tense. Gayl's Staatsbürgerliche Vereinigung hosted the celebrations and Erich Ludendorff's attendance provoked Socialist counter-demonstrations and street violence.[93]

Naturally, the tenth anniversary of the battle in August 1924 witnessed the largest commemorative festivities to that day. A committee for the construction of a central Tannenberg Memorial had already been set up in 1919, and 31 August 1924 had been chosen as the date for the laying of the foundation stone.[94] At this point, no central memorial commemorating the First World War existed in Germany.[95] Building the vast Tannenberg Memorial—an enormous structure modelled on Stonehenge and the Italian Castel del Monte[96]—was therefore highly symbolic and entailed the possibility that the right would succeed in monopolizing German war memory. Because the construction was to be financed entirely from private donations the Berlin government had little say in its design.[97]

Hindenburg's presence on the battlefield near Hohenstein on 31 August was a foregone conclusion. Up to 50,000 people attended the celebrations surrounding his laying of the foundation stone—for the most part members of nationalist organizations.[98] His presence had helped to publicize the event enormously. The Field Marshal himself once again stayed in East Prussia for a whole month and Gayl organized the visit a second time.[99] Right-wing organizations, including the Stahlhelm and the Staatsbürgerliche Vereinigung, staged commemorative events in Königsberg throughout the week before the official ceremony and Hindenburg attended most of them.[100]

The celebrations in the town hall of Königsberg in late August were as much a commemoration of Tannenberg as a celebration of Hindenburg, the honorary guest. Their content illustrated that the memory of the battle was clearly bound up with a more current political agenda. The speech given by Friedrich von Berg, the head of the Deutsche Adelsgenossenschaft, the organization of Germany's toppled aristocracy, highlighted the extent to which the memory of Tannenberg was bound up with nationalist attempts to revise the Treaty of Versailles:

> One looks over to our German brothers in Memel, Soldau, Western Prussia and Posen—there might be borders now, but German hearts cannot be separated. And one looks to the west where a wound stings: the enemy on our soil . . . The memory of the events 10 years ago should strengthen us and give us hope . . . Free us, God![101]

Similarly, an event staged by nationalist students' organizations two days later was characterized by the familiar combination of commemorative practice, Hindenburg-worship, and political rally. The speeches given in the presence of the mythical Field Marshal highlighted the interconnectedness of the narratives surrounding German innocence at the outbreak of war, the spirit of 1914, and the 'stab-in-the-back'. As Wilhelm von Gayl opined:

> In August 1914 we were a people who rose to the protection of hearth and home, unified and with a pure heart; a people who will never understand why the world thinks it has earned the right to blame us for the outbreak of war when all we wanted was to protect our borders against onslaught, bloodshed and hardship.[102]

Germany had only lost because 'the German had beaten the German', according to Hindenburg's host. Now the people faced another 'Tannenberg of gigantic proportions' to be fought against the enemy within. The nationalist papers, too, hailed the commemoration of Tannenberg as a 'guide to a better future', and, in a bid to national resurgence, as a reminder that 'even a small group of heroes could achieve their aims against an overwhelming foreign power'.[103] Equally, when Hindenburg delivered the first hammer blow to the memorial's foundation stone at the central commemorative site on 31 August, he invoked the battle as 'an example for coming generations'.[104] It was no co-incidence that as President he would choose the opening of the memorial in September 1927 as the launch-pad for his public fight against the 'war guilt lie'.

\* \* \*

Salvaging the Hindenburg myth after the revolution turned out to be a heavy burden for the young Republic in its crisis years. Especially the interconnectedness of the Hindenburg narrative with the 'stab-in-the-back' meant that the extreme right increasingly defined his myth. As early as November 1919, anti-republicans discovered Hindenburg-worship as a vital resource of anti-republican agitation. The events in Berlin guaranteed the national breakthrough of the 'stab-in-the-back' and proved to be pivotal in the nationalization of Germany's masses—the Republic was now increasingly under siege. The announcement of his presidential candidacy in 1920, the events during his visits to East Prussia and Munich in 1922, and the Tannenberg festivities of 1924 consolidated this political pattern. The pro-republican parties that had benefited from the Field Marshal's integrative role in 1918/19, and had also subscribed to many narrative strands of his myth, found themselves faced with the impossible task of defying attacks on democracy dressed up as innocent hero-worship of Hindenburg. This dilemma left them increasingly defenceless, especially since many of them, such as Ferdinand Friedensburg, did not reject deploying the Hindenburg myth for political purposes outright, but were simply opposed to its anti-republican utilization.

The early years of Weimar saw a regrouping and intensified mobilization of the militant right. These were the days of political murders, waxing inflation, increasing party political polarization, coup attempts of both left and right—the Kapp-Lüttwitz Putsch and Hitler's 'Beerhall Coup' on the right and the uprisings in Thuringia and Saxony on the left—and separatist movements. In this political context the Hindenburg myth was a factor in shifting the political climate considerably to the right and in intensifying the polarization of German politics. Despite repeated warnings, Hindenburg did nothing to avert this course. On the contrary, he consciously spread anti-republican ideas not only in his statements and speeches, but also in his populist memoirs published in 1920.

Although Hindenburg's presence in the media had naturally diminished since his time of active service, he remained a very public figure after 1919. In 1925, therefore, his myth did not have to be revived. It had been firmly established as a vital component and political weapon in the right-wing struggle against the Weimar 'system' and the Treaty of Versailles. The announcement of his candidacy for the presidency in April 1925 was thus the logical outcome of a right-wing strategy rehearsed since 1919.

# 4

# Electing 'the Saviour'

Although Friedrich Ebert's term would have come to its natural end on 30 June 1925, the German public was almost unprepared for an electoral battle when Weimar's first President died suddenly on 28 February 1925.[1] Ebert had served nearly a full seven-year stint in office without ever seeking the endorsement of the popular vote. Yet, by 1925 only scant preparations had been made for choosing his successor. The Weimar constitution granted the President far-reaching constitutional powers such as dissolving the Reichstag, the appointment of the government (Article 53), as well as the Supreme Command of the Armed Forces (Article 47). Most importantly, Article 48 gave the office-holder the authority to circumvent parliament and govern by emergency decree, thus effectively preserving some of the authoritarianism of the Bismarckian Empire in a republican framework.[2]

The parties of the right regarded the presidency as key to the eventual foundation of a more authoritarian system of government. After the two failed right-wing coup d'état attempts of 1920 and 1923 and the de-radicalization of the electorate evident in the national elections of December 1924, the right had committed itself to the quasi-legal course of altering the political system from within rather than by means of a violent overthrow. The presidency was a crucial component of this new strategy.[3]

Just as in 1920, when Hindenburg's candidacy had first been announced, the Reichsbürgerrat, now chaired by the former Prussian Interior Minister Friedrich Wilhelm von Loebell, sought to find a suitable supra-party candidate who would capture the presidency for the conservative bourgeoisie.[4] Discussions for a joint nomination of all the bourgeois parties of the right represented in the so-called Reichsblock began on 5 March. The initial consideration of Defence Minister Otto Gessler, who would also be acceptable to the liberals of the DDP, was dropped after Stresemann's intervention. The Foreign Minister was anxious about the impact the election of a military figure would have on the Allies—especially the French—at a crucial time before the negotiations about the Treaty of Locarno had been concluded.[5]

Eventually, the DNVP, DVP, and the co-ordinating council of the 'Patriotic Organizations' (Vereinigte Vaterländische Verbände) agreed on putting forward the DVP's Karl Jarres, lord mayor of Duisburg. Hindenburg, whose name had also been mentioned by German National politicians from Hanover, gave his public backing to boost Jarres's candidacy.[6] Jarres, however, was unlikely to be endorsed by the Catholic Centre and the agrarian Catholic Bavarian People's Party (BVP), which deemed him both anticlerical and too closely tied to heavy industry.[7] Jarres therefore had little chance of achieving the absolute majority necessary for election on the first ballot on 29 March.

The Weimar parties failed to agree on a common candidate in the first round. The SPD nominated Prussian Minister President Otto Braun and the Centre put forward the former Chancellor Wilhelm Marx. The DDP ran its own candidate, Willy Hellpach, as did the BVP with Heinrich Held. The Communists proposed their party leader, Ernst Thälmann. On the extreme right, Erich Ludendorff ran as the Nazi Party's nominee.

With 38.8% of the popular vote, Jarres came first on 29 March 1925, but failed to obtain the absolute majority on which victory depended. Furthermore, the three Weimar parties had together gained 49.2% of the vote, compared to 43.7% for all the parties to their right.[8] A Jarres victory in the second round, in which a relative majority sufficed for victory, thus seemed highly unlikely.

In early April, the Weimar parties' decision to propose Wilhelm Marx as their joint candidate for the second round of voting exerted strong pressure on the Reichsblock to find a viable candidate in their own ranks. Due to Jarres's limited prospects, the right-wing parties now began to search for a candidate who was, above all, electable. Turning towards Hindenburg in this situation was consistent with the nationalist right's reliance on his popular appeal in previous years. The Field Marshal had already been a natural candidate in 1920 and had agreed to stand at the time. Furthermore, his public appearances since 1919 had firmly established him as a galvanizing figure for the anti-republican course. Initially, however, Hindenburg, was hesitant. In a letter to his friend August von Cramon written two days before the first ballot, he stressed that he was 'boundlessly displeased' at the prospect of taking over the presidency. Filling a post that he still insisted belonged to 'my Kaiser' went against his core beliefs. 'Furthermore I would only reluctantly want to live under a roof decorated with the black, red, and gold flag', Hindenburg explained and emphasized that, at the age of 77, he was not sure whether he would even survive a whole term. He therefore considered himself 'summa summarum . . . unsuitable' for the position. Whilst insisting that he did not intend to run, Hindenburg nevertheless concluded his letter with what read like a list of prerequisites for changing his mind:

> Under all these circumstances I could not even easily accept the post if *all* reasonable people saw . . . [my candidacy] as the *only* way of salvaging the Fatherland, furthermore if his Majesty agreed, if the Entente definitely were not to cause problems for the Fatherland, and if I could be guaranteed not to be generally embarrassed by failure in the elections.[9]

Granting him a peaceful death in Hanover was to be the expression of Germany's gratitude for Tannenberg and the 'martyrdom of 9 November 1918'. The letter was read out in a meeting of the VVV so that Hindenburg's personal reservations and implicit demands were known among the Reichsblock leadership.[10] Hindenburg continued to have qualms—not least because he feared for his mythical standing in the event of defeat—after the first ballot had shown that a Jarres victory on 26 April was improbable. As he explained in another confidential letter to Cramon:

> Regarding my presidency I think it is still too early at this time. We are not ready yet, the result will be that my name will be dragged through the dirt by the enemy press and that the German people will therefore lose the trust in their last pillar.[11]

Fully aware of the function of his myth, Hindenburg was hesitant to put his reputation on the line and risk public embarrassment. Equally, when the DNVP's Walter von Keudell and Admiral Alfred von Tirpitz arrived at Hindenburg's home in Hanover on 7 April to persuade him to run, his son Oskar informed them that his father would reject the nomination, because he was worried about losing his fame and credentials as Field Marshal.[12] When the two men assured Hindenburg that Jarres was ready to retract his candidacy if he ran and confirmed that a broad coalition of right-wing parties would back his nomination, however, he laid his reservations to rest. Hindenburg's nomination was announced the next day.[13]

The support for Hindenburg's candidacy had not been unanimous within the Reichsblock.[14] Although the DVP had been the chief promoter of Hindenburg's nomination in 1919/20, with party leader Stresemann as Foreign Minister, it now feared international repercussions—the withdrawal of foreign loans and renewed German isolation—if a military figure were elected.[15] Not everyone within the DNVP was thrilled by the prospect of Hindenburg's election either. Even a staunch Hindenburg devotee like Gayl feared that the nomination was an irrational choice. Those who had backed Hindenburg in the Loebell committee had done so for purely 'emotive reasons', he observed.[16] Franz Seldte, the leader of the right-wing veterans' organization Stahlhelm, largely agreed with Gayl's assessment and pushed for a second Jarres ticket. In a confidential circular to all local Stahlhelm leaders, he argued that the nomination of the Field Marshal distorted the purpose of the election. All nationalist veterans were drawn to Hindenburg's name, he explained, but a simple right-wing victory was not the only concern:

> There is no doubt that millions of voters voting for Hindenburg on 26 April will immediately return to their traditional party and interest affiliations after the election. The election result will not be a verdict on the strength of the national movement, but will only be a sign of how broad and great Hindenburg's veneration is amongst the largest sections of society.[17]

If the elections were to turn into a demonstration of nationalist strength, the right-wing parties would have to be able to push through *any* candidate, Seldte maintained.

As we can see, Hindenburg's mythical status was a key factor in the Reichsblock's discussions and calculations. Whilst Seldte and others feared that it threatened to eclipse the right-wing cause, it provided the right with one clear advantage: Hindenburg's appeal would broaden the Reichsblock's base considerably. In addition to the parties backing Jarres in the first round, the BVP, the Economic Party (WP), and the Nazis rallied behind Hindenburg's candidacy on the second ballot. Moreover, his allure promised to mobilize traditional non-voters and possibly even support from republicans. The prospect of actually capturing the presidency persuaded the Reichsblock to gloss over its internal differences and put on a united front. Seldte urged all recipients of his circular to keep it secret and to project an image of national bourgeois unity in public.[18] Stresemann, in his turn, published an article in the daily *Die Zeit*, emphasizing his personal endorsement of Hindenburg. According to the Foreign Minister the DVP supported him without reservations and expected the parties of the right to tone down their political differences.[19] Hindenburg's nomination thus represented a considerable change in right–wing tactics. Rather than capturing the presidency for its political power, the focus had now shifted to winning the symbolic post come what may.[20]

## Campaigning for Hindenburg

In the weeks leading up to polling day on 26 April, Germany witnessed a fierce, modern, and strongly personalized election campaign of unprecedented proportions. The campaign first and foremost unfolded in the national and local press, which reported little else, as well as in the streets of the big urban centres, most notably Berlin, where supporters of both political camps took to the streets.

Along with the general strategic shift of the Reichsblock, many of the themes of previous Reichstag election contests, such as the question of 'monarchy versus republic', were toned down. Instead, the campaign slogans were tailor-made for Hindenburg. The DNVP's Otto von Feldmann, four other members of the parties represented in the Reichsblock, and Otto Kriegk of the journal *Deutschen-Spiegel*, took up headquarters in Hanover and oversaw the national campaign from there.[21] Addressing Hindenburg's fears of being 'dragged through the dirt by the enemy press' they ran a defensive campaign that focused on protecting the Field Marshal against potential republican attacks.[22]

The Reichsblock's emphasis was on bourgeois unity. Whilst local party officials played only a minor role in the campaign itself the Reichsblock leadership was anxious to give the impression that municipal notables and chairmen of recreational clubs presided over proceedings.[23] Hence members of choirs, athletic clubs, youth groups, nationalist societies, and women's organizations often staffed pro-Hindenburg rallies.[24] By pushing such ostentatiously apolitical societies into the fore, the Reichsblock suggested that a broad and cohesive community of Germans reminiscent of the spirit of unity that had allegedly accompanied the outbreak of war in 1914 carried Hindenburg's candidacy. His cross-party nomination was presented as an antithesis to Weimar's parliamentary bickering and social discord. Carefully suppressing the political bargaining that had preceded his nomination, the right portrayed Hindenburg as a symbol of national unity towering above the party strife, a 'man who leans neither left nor right, not towards the monarchy and not towards the Republic, but only knows his duty to serve the state and the people'.[25] In emphasizing the theme of national unity the right-wing campaign could build upon the Hindenburg myth. The motifs of loyalty, duty, and sacrifice that also lay at the myth's core featured equally prominently. As in 1920, casting a vote for Hindenburg did not appear as exercising a democratic right, but as settling a debt, as the fulfilment of duty and the expression of loyalty to one man.[26] In the words of *Düsseldorfer Nachrichten*, because the 'old Field Marshal is sacrificing the serenity of old age for the German people, the German people will know how to thank him'.[27] Hindenburg himself fed this rhetoric in his private letters when stressing that he ran out of a 'sense of duty' and described his candidacy as 'the greatest sacrifice of his life'.[28]

Nationalist election material equally hailed Hindenburg as the antithesis of the political system of Weimar Germany with all its perceived shortcomings. His election would bring about 'the Tannenberg of the German spirit'; he would set an educational example for young Germans to overcome the religious, political, and social fragmentation of the people.[29] Not voting for the 'national hero' would be 'unpatriotic' and a 'miserable act' resulting in the self-inflicted exclusion from the *Volksgemeinschaft*, the people's community.[30] Reichsblock headquarters in Berlin and Hanover issued direct appeals to the various groups of 'patriotically minded' ('vaterländisch gesinnte') Germans and disseminated these throughout the country via the major papers of the right.[31] Agrarians, Catholics, nationalist workers, and habitual non-voters were targeted directly. Brochures entitled 'Why Hindenburg' listed recurrent themes of republican criticism against his candidacy, such as his age, his monarchist and militarist convictions, and his political inexperience, along with guidelines on how to counter these.[32] Concerns about Hindenburg's age were dispersed by invoking the memory of other 'great' historical personalities, who had made an impact in the late stages of their lives—Michelangelo, Wilhelm I, Marshal Blücher, Marshal MacMahon, and Goethe.[33] Meanwhile, the women's supplements of nationalist papers wooed female voters with articles on Hindenburg's social record and with poems such as 'What a man', stressing his masculinity and fatherly attributes.[34]

In spite of the campaign's rhetoric of national unity, the events unfolding in the streets of German cities prior to 26 April presented a different picture. Although conditions had calmed since the high tide of political violence in Weimar's early years, the street was still a contested space. The Reichsblock hosted numerous street rallies, and many squares in small towns and urban centres—traditionally a domain of the left—were taken over by nationalist Germans.[35] Supporters of all camps showed their political allegiance by displaying the Imperial, the republican or the communist colours in the windows of their houses and on their balconies. This 'war of the flags' let emotions run high, especially in urban areas, where the rival camps campaigned from the back of decorated election lorries driven through the streets.[36]

On election Sunday itself, Hindenburg's supporters and their adversaries clashed violently in many German towns. In Dortmund a right-wing supporter was shot dead and numerous people were injured in a gun battle between members of the republican veterans' organization Reichsbanner and their Communist rivals. In Erfurt another republican veteran was stabbed, and in Karlsruhe two people died from injuries sustained in street fights. Similar scenes occurred in Hamburg and Mannheim.[37]

While his supporters battled it out in the country's streets and the campaign unfolded in German newspapers, Hindenburg remained in Hanover. He had rejected the Reichsblock's idea of appearing at rallies in Munich and Berlin with the characteristic reply, 'I do not talk and I do not travel.'[38] As opposed to the Volksblock's Wilhelm Marx, who toured the country and spoke to mass audiences on several occasions, the Hindenburg campaign did not rely on such tactics—the Field Marshal needed no introduction.[39] He merely appeared twice during the campaign and both times in front of selected audiences in Hanover. He gave a speech in the town hall on 19 April and an interview to foreign journalists intended to bolster his reputation abroad.[40]

Instead of facing his potential voters in person by hitting the campaign trail, Hindenburg communicated with the electorate by other means—and on a truly mass scale. At 8 p.m. on 24 April 1925—less than two full days before polls opened—he made German broadcasting history.[41] Radio had been introduced two years earlier, but the speech he gave during the so-called *Reichssendung* that day was the first programme broadcast throughout Germany by hooking up various stations.[42] At this stage roughly one million Germans owned a radio and because several family members usually shared a transmitter Hindenburg's speech reached millions of people—a much greater audience than he could have ever reached at mass rallies.[43]

Nevertheless, the Reichsblock did not just rely on the written word and propaganda on the airwaves to promote its candidate; visual campaign aids perhaps played an even more important role. On cloudy nights, a large electric torchlight projected Hindenburg's name into Berlin's sky.[44] Furthermore, the *Kaiserreich*'s 'glorious' past was evoked in various media to foster attachment to a man who was promoted as the embodiment of the idea of the *Reich* and the 'good old days'.[45] A non-fictional film on the commemoration of Tannenberg the previous year was screened at several Reichsblock rallies, at cinemas, and on public squares across the country.[46] Ufa, Germany's biggest film company, showed several films invoking the virtues of recent German history in its film theatres in the run-up to 26 April—among them the highly successful Fridericus films.[47]

Moreover, in the vein of the war loan campaign of autumn 1917, when the Field Marshal's picture had covered most German advertising columns and garden fences, the entire country was flooded with Hindenburg's image. In Berlin, Reichsblock activists drove an open lorry through the streets of Berlin carrying a gigantic plaster sculpture of Hindenburg's iconic head.[48] They further distributed to German schools small flags in the Imperial colours adorned with Hindenburg's picture.[49] Equally, the major election campaign posters featured images of Hindenburg's head and a short slogan, and so resembled the war loan posters of 1917. The most famous poster of 1925, which decorated many of the Reichsblock's election vehicles, showed a drawing of the Field Marshal's face looking back at the observer with an adamant expression.

Its artistic style lent it the impression of being carved in stone and thus invoked the Field Marshal as a living memorial. It also played on the theme of Hindenburg as a 'rock', once more likening the Field Marshal to matter that resisted the ravages of time. Next to his iconic head on the poster's white background a caption in handwritten *Sütterlin* read 'The Saviour'. Hindenburg's name appeared nowhere on the poster—seven years after the armistice, at a time when wartime memorabilia could still be found in many households, this simple poster was sufficient to communicate the Reichsblock's message: 'hope and trust would return after many years of bitter disappointment, and...the people's hero would save the Fatherland for the second time'.[50] So omnipresent was

Fig. 3. Photograph of a *Reichsblock* election car with Imperial flags and a poster hailing Hindenburg as 'The Saviour' (1925).

the poster that the left-wing weekly *Die Weltbühne* would blame it for the political seduction of what it poignantly termed the 'Hindenburgeoisie':

> For weeks on end the reactionary saviour's face lured victims on every street corner. For weeks on end there was the saccharin-sweet sentimentality of the Hindenburgeoisie, which is at home in all classes and races of an immature people.[51]

## Campaigning against Hindenburg

The republican parties' approach to Hindenburg's candidacy in 1925 was precarious. The democratic left had already been quite helpless in the face of political agitation associated with Hindenburg's name in previous years. Until 1925 this agitation had at least been disguised as inconspicuous hero-worship. Now, however, Hindenburg was openly running for the opposite political camp. Faced with the prospect of running against a man whom countless republicans had also admired for his leadership during the war and its aftermath, the republican Volksblock opted for a two-tier approach: speaking out against Hindenburg's candidacy while simultaneously stressing republican admiration for him. The left's adoption of this ambiguous strategy clearly points to Hindenburg's popular base in 1925. Especially liberal bourgeois commentators close to the DDP and Catholic campaigners of the Centre Party went to great lengths to stress their respect for the Field Marshal and often targeted the 'men behind Hindenburg's candidacy' with the more severe criticism.[52] A leader by Theodor Wolff published on Easter Sunday exemplified this kind of liberal manoeuvring:

> We do not blame old Hindenburg...The great majority of the German people will reject moving Hindenburg from his withdrawn life to the highest office...and they will reject it precisely because they respect his personality and his white hair...We do not blame the old man. He does not and cannot see that his candidacy plays into the hands of Germany's worst enemies.[53]

In a similar vein the Catholic *Germania* ran a front-page article under the headline 'Poor Hindenburg', which mourned the fact that the Field Marshal's retirement had been disturbed, again focusing its analysis on

the sinister forces behind his nomination.[54] *Vorwärts*'s first response to the
announcement of Hindenburg's nomination was almost equally confused.
Hindenburg did not know what was going on around him, the paper insisted
on 9 April, and consequently 'our fight is not against him. It is against
the irresponsible schemers and demagogues [behind his candidacy].'[55] The
paper further zoomed in on the right-wing 'schemers' in a cartoon named
'The people's maltreated hero', which depicted a dozing Hindenburg in
his home in Hanover. After initially declining to run for president he is
shaken and then beaten up by Tirpitz and others and finally coerced into
compliance.[56]

A Volksblock campaign poster equally illustrated the idea that Hindenburg's reputation was being used as a masquerade by dangerous political
string-pullers, a motif already championed in 1920. It pictured several
men—a Nazi, an aristocrat, a Bavarian reactionary with a tuft of hair from
a chamois, and a soldier wearing a *Pickelhaube*—armed with pistols and
daggers carrying a giant Hindenburg mask in front of them as a shield.[57]
Given that Hindenburg had already agreed to run in 1920 and had issued
a detailed set of demands prior to accepting his nomination in 1925, such
republican commentary was, of course, far from accurate. Nevertheless,
such interpretations of the genesis of Hindenburg's candidacy proved to
be surprisingly long-lived and offered a way out of attacking the venerated
Field Marshal more openly.

Even Hindenburg's republican competitor Wilhelm Marx felt the need
to highlight his admiration for the Field Marshal in many of his campaign
speeches and invoked Hindenburg's 'unforgettable military victories' on
a campaign trip to East Prussia.[58] DDP leaflets similarly appropriated the
rhetoric of indebtedness and gratitude of the pro-Hindenburg campaign.
One read 'For the Fatherland's sake and for Hindenburg's sake vote
Marx'.[59] Another one used a quotation from the Field Marshal: ' "Those
few years I have left to live after the war I want to spend quietly",
said Hindenburg. Grant him his wish—vote Marx.'[60] Liberal democratic
campaigners obviously feared that their own followers were responsive to
the Reichsblock's appeals to people's emotional bond with Hindenburg
and therefore attempted to turn such notions of gratitude upside down.
According to the DDP true Hindenburg devotees knew what was best for
their hero and voted for Marx.[61] The *Rote Fahne* mocked these tactics by
suggesting that the motto of the republican campaign might as well be 'He
who loves Hindenburg, votes for Marx.'[62] The Communists themselves

labelled Hindenburg a 'mass slaughterer' and ridiculed him as the 'General of Defeat'.[63] Communist attacks on Wilhelm Marx, the 'agent of Capitalism', however, were equally fierce. Both candidates appeared as two sides of the same coin in Communist rhetoric.[64]

Driven by the fear of alienating a substantial part of their own electorate, the parties of the republican left, on the whole, tried to depict the dangerous consequences of a Hindenburg victory while endorsing much of the Hindenburg myth. While the majority of commentators would not recognize the downside of this strategy until after the right had succeeded, some on the left began to warn against its pitfalls before the second ballot. Heinz Pol spelled out the paradoxical nature of republican efforts to snatch victory from Hindenburg without more forward criticism of his glorification under the headline 'S.O.S.'.[65] Eduard Bernstein, one of the SPD's most eminent theoreticians also condemned the republican election strategy of 'Not a single word against Hindenburg' as fateful. Republicans ought not to remain mute towards the 'militarist Hindenburg cult', because the Field Marshal was now a political opponent, he warned.[66] The Reichsbanner's Hermann Schützinger, who had published critical pieces on hero-worship in socialist journals for some time, equally attempted a more critical assessment of the nationalist candidate in the pages of *Vorwärts*. Republicans had shied away from a thorough re-assessment of the Field Marshal's achievements, he admitted, but it was now time to portray Hindenburg truthfully by 'cutting across the artificial fog of the former War Press Office and the blue mist of new-German hero worship'.[67]

Theirs remained relatively isolated voices, however. Republican campaigners and commentators largely played according to the Reichsblock's rules by accepting the premise of Hindenburg's heroism. The Volksblock feebly offered its voters a way out of the dilemma by arguing that they could show their devotion by letting Hindenburg return to peaceful retirement. Republican strategists had clearly recognized that Hindenburg's mythical allure was the Reichsblock's biggest electoral asset. But they still made only half-hearted attempts at debunking it and could not offer a narrative with similarly strong appeal. The warning voices came too late and offered too little. More than a decade of widespread Hindenburg worship, which many republicans—especially among the liberal bourgeoisie and within German Catholicism—had endorsed, could not be annulled within a matter of weeks.

## Hindenburg's victory

In the evening of 26 April the right-wing Scherl and liberal Ullstein and Mosse publishing houses projected the election results onto giant screens set up on public buildings and squares in Berlin. Berliners stayed up long into the night to watch the latest results, offering a 1920s cinematic preview of 'live' election coverage.[68] The results they saw vindicated the Reichsblock's calculations. Hindenburg was voted German Reich President with a majority of 900,000 votes over his chief opponent Marx.[69]

Although Hindenburg did not reach an absolute majority, he was still considerably more successful than his right-wing predecessor. The turnout in the second round was substantially higher than in the first; nearly 9% of the electorate who had abstained on the first ballot cast their vote on 26 April. Whilst the actual Volksblock results remained relatively stable, Hindenburg managed to gain nearly five million votes more than Jarres had. Detailed analyses of voter coalitions have shown that Hindenburg scored highest in Protestant agrarian areas, which were traditional strongholds of the right-wing parties. Almost all of Jarres's supporters of the first round seem to have supported the joint second-ballot candidate Hindenburg.

However, there was also a substantial gain in predominantly Catholic areas. The Catholic Hindenburg vote can mostly be attributed to the BVP's support—about half a million former Held supporters switched to

Table 1: Election results of 29 March and 26 April 1925

|  | 1st Ballot (29 March 1925) | | 2nd Ballot (26 April 1925) | |
| --- | --- | --- | --- | --- |
| Eligible voters | 39,266,138 | | 39,414,316 | |
| Ballots cast | 27,016,760 | | 30,567,874 | |
| Turnout | 68.9% | | 77.6% | |
| Jarres | 10,416,658 | (38.8%) | — | — |
| Held | 1,007,450 | (3.7%) | — | — |
| Ludendorff | 285,793 | (1.1%) | — | — |
| Braun | 7,802,497 | (29.0%) | — | — |
| Marx | 3,887,734 | (14.5%) | 13,751,605 | (45.3%) |
| Hellpach | 1,569,398 | (5.8%) | — | — |
| Thälmann | 1,871,815 | (7.0%) | 1,931,151 | (6.4%) |
| Hindenburg | — | — | 14,655,641 | (48.3%) |

Source: Falter, Jürgen W. et al (eds.), *Wahlen und Abstimmungen in der Weimarer Republik: Materialien zum Wahlverhalten 1919–1933* (Munich, 1986), 46.

Hindenburg on the second ballot.[70] But Catholic support for Hindenburg did not come solely from Bavaria. Analyses of the presidential election results in some Catholic districts of the Rhineland compared to the results of the 1924 Reichstag elections suggest that a considerable number of Centre voters also opted for Hindenburg in 1925. As many as 400,000 Centre voters defected on the second ballot—a relatively large number bearing in mind that Marx was the Centre's own candidate and that Hindenburg's leading margin was less than a million.[71] Hindenburg seemingly attracted Catholics suspicious of Marx's alliance with the anticlerical and anti-monarchist SPD and who therefore favoured the Prussian Protestant over their own party's candidate. Many prominent members of the BVP and Centre Party felt that Hindenburg's conservative politics, his religiosity, impartiality, and patriotism united him with Catholics across the board.[72] The Silesian Centre Party politician Count Hans von Praschma had already warned Marx in early April that many Catholics were still monarchist at heart and would find it difficult to stomach co-operation with the SPD. He went on to predict that Catholics would mostly vote for Hindenburg or abstain altogether.[73]

Whilst Social Democratic voters were mostly immune to Hindenburg's electoral appeal in 1925, women and traditional non-voters bore an extraordinarily large share of Hindenburg votes. Out of the 3.5 million new voters drawn to the polls on 26 April, 3 million voted for the Reichsblock candidate.[74] It is therefore fair to suggest that Hindenburg's name mobilized significant parts of the population otherwise relatively indifferent towards politics. The nationalist emphasis on duty and loyalty to the Field Marshal and the highly personalized campaign often directly aimed at non-voters seem to have been remarkably successful with these groups. Not least the extraordinarily high numbers of votes cast for Hindenburg in East Prussia—more than two thirds of East Prussians supported the 'Victor of Tannenberg'[75]—suggests that the emotional appeal of the Hindenburg myth was a strong influence on the voters' decision-making process. In the province Hindenburg had allegedly saved once before the themes of gratitude and paying off a debt obviously carried special resonance.

A substantial number of women equally responded to the emotive promises of Hindenburg's image as a saviour. The Berlin correspondent of Northcliff's *Evening World* interviewed a number of female Hindenburg supporters about their reasons for casting their votes for Hindenburg.

'Undiminished popularity behind a bemedaled uniform' turned out to be one of the main factors. Others explained that they believed 'Hindenburg would valorize fortunes lost during the inflation period and "bring good times" '.[76] Frau Gramm from Berlin, an 'ordinary, simple woman' in her own words, argued along similar lines in a letter to Karl Jarres's wife, Freia: 'I have also lost everything, but our Hindenburg will bring about the revaluation of mortgages and then we will be better off.'[77]

Nevertheless, the evidence of women's emotive responses to the Hindenburg campaign and the extent of the women's vote need to be contextualized. Women were generally more prone to voting for conservative parties or those with confessional affiliations in the Weimar years.[78] Although the figures available for the second ballot in 1925 show clearly that the overall share of women voting for Hindenburg was roughly 3.6% higher than that of men's votes, the same is true for Jarres's result on the first ballot. The share of women's votes for Jarres on 29 March had also been proportionately higher than of men's votes. If anything, the ratio of male to female votes on the first ballot showed that an even slightly higher proportion of women had voted for Jarres than for Hindenburg, with over 4% more women than men supporting Jarres in March.[79] The Marx vote however, was split evenly between men and women.[80] Whereas it is thus true that women voted for Hindenburg in higher numbers than men, and that of the new voters who turned out on 26 April a disproportionately large number were female, this result was not out of line with overall female voting patterns during this period, especially compared to Jarres's result of 29 March.

Male republican commentators, however, quickly sought the explanation for Hindenburg's victory in female 'irrationality' and 'immaturity'.[81] *Germania* labelled Hindenburg's election a 'victory of emotion' for which youths and women were to blame.[82] A frustrated Alfons Steiniger even raged against female suffrage in general in the pages of the *Weltbühne*:

> The Republic—as usual—had not considered making use of its experiences to avoid the uneducated, novel-infested, pathetic-pompous, narrow-minded, but big-hearted German womenfolk by changing...article 22 [granting suffrage to men and women] of the constitution.[83]

Instead of thoroughly assessing why the republican parties—which had, after all, been responsible for the introduction of female suffrage—often failed to reach women, or why so many female *and* male voters had been drawn to Hindenburg on 26 April, it was easier to argue that women had simply got it wrong.

In fact, a variety of factors contributed to right-wing victory in 1925. The BVP's decision to turn away from its sister party, the Centre, by backing the Reichsblock and the Communists' decision to uphold Ernst Thälmann's nomination on the second ballot were both highly significant. Some contemporary observers and historians have also pointed to deep-seated monarchist sentiment as a reason for Hindenburg's victory. Allegedly, his election was a vote for the restoration of the monarchy.[84] The *Weltbühne's* Kurt Hiller, for instance, was convinced that Hindenburg's victory was the result of Germany's 'moustache mentality and sentimentality'.[85] Close to despair, the chronicler Count Harry Kessler agreed:

> All the philistines are delighted about Hindenburg. He is the god of all those who long for the return of philistinism and the glorious time when it was only necessary to make money and accompany a decent digestion with a pious upward glance. They are waiting for Hindenburg to 'consolidate' conditions, meaning adjustment to Philistine standards. Farewell progress, farewell vision of a new world which was to be humanity's conscience money for the criminal war.[86]

In spite of some Centre Party voters giving in to their monarchist convictions and switching to Hindenburg on the second ballot, however, the Hindenburg electorate cannot be regarded a 'resolutely conservative, anti-republican, and basically monarchist body, which longed for a future guided by Wilhelmine values'.[87] The catchphrase of the *Ersatzkaiser* Hindenburg—the 'surrogate monarch'—should not be taken to mean that only 'the romantic yearning for past glory and greatness' motivated voters.[88] Under their own steam the parties advocating a return to the monarchy—above all the DNVP—had not even come close to mobilizing a majority in the previous Reichstag elections or indeed in the first round of the presidential contest of 1925. They depended on Hindenburg's magnetism to capture the presidency. And this magnetism was based on much more than his monarchist credentials since 1914. Therefore, as the influential liberal publicist Ernst Feder opined in the *Berliner Tageblatt* 'It is not a political idea that has won, but the nimbus of a name'.[89] The *Frankfurter Zeitung* concurred self-critically that it had been one of the left's 'gravest mistakes to let the Hindenburg legend stay alive ... This omission ... has now taken its toll.'[90]

The critical mass of voters did not primarily respond to a particular policy programme in 1925, but to Hindenburg's image as a potential 'saviour' promising to restore social stability. The right may have hailed its victory as the 'morning glory of a new moral era', but even the *Deutsche Tageszeitung* conceded that Hindenburg's triumph had 'largely involved the heart'.[91] The Stahlhelm leadership had therefore been correct in assuming that the Field Marshal's victory would first and foremost represent a verdict on his personal standing and not a wholehearted endorsement of the anti-republican course.[92] The years of near-civil war, hyperinflation, and perceived international humiliation had taken their toll. At a time when the parliamentary system seemingly failed to meet expectations of economic, social, and political stability, voters responded to Hindenburg, 'the saviour', who, in the words of Frau Gramm, would bring 'better times'. Voting for Hindenburg in 1925 was thus the political expression of a coping strategy rehearsed during the years of wartime deprivation—opting to trust Hindenburg 'to sort it out' because there hardly seemed to be viable alternatives.

## The 'saviour' cometh to Berlin

A few weeks after the election, Berliners welcomed the President-elect in the capital. Hindenburg was to take his oath on the constitution at his inaugural ceremony in the Reichstag on 12 May and arrived by special train from Hanover the previous day.[93] The events around his arrival on 11 May left plenty of room for popular participation. He was welcomed by a government delegation at Heerstraße station in Charlottenburg before being driven through the broad boulevards of Berlin to the Reich Chancellor's residence in an open car. Along the streets leading to central Berlin—Heerstraße itself, Kaiserdamm, Bismarckstraße, and Charlottenburger Chaussee (today's 'Straße des 17. Juni')—numerous nationalist clubs and associations had been invited to greet Hindenburg upon his arrival. By 9 May, 200,000 members of various organizations, including local groups of the DNVP, nationalist workers' and women's associations, the Bismarck Youth, and shooting, skittle, and athletic clubs, had announced their participation.[94] The bulk of the crowds gathered along the (fittingly named) Kaiserdamm and Bismarckstraße in Charlottenburg on the day.[95]

En route police motorcycles surrounded Hindenburg's open car and aeroplanes trailed streamers and showered the audience with flowers. Many local residents had covered their houses with the Imperial flag.[96] To emphasize the republican nature of the festivities and to counter the ubiquity of the Imperial colours displayed by the audience, Hindenburg's car was bedecked with the black, red, and gold colours of Weimar. Furthermore, musical instruments had been banned to avoid the whole event being drowned out by the sounds of military marches.[97] Years later, Reich Chancellor Hans Luther who had travelled in Hindenburg's car still remembered people's cheers and ovations as 'indescribably' loud. 'People had been standing there since the early morning and especially the female audience's beaming eyes were enraptured by Hindenburg's imposing and militarily toned figure', he reminisced.[98] The Red Cross frequently had to drag women from the crowd who were so overwhelmed by the sight of their future President that they had fainted.[99] The *Rote Fahne* relayed this spectacle in mocking tone:

> Hysterical old spinsters waved about their flags whilst the motorcade raced pass. The noses of a few fat men with tufts of chamois hair on their little hats had even more of a red glow than before. Their even fatter spouses' bosoms began to tremble, then 'He' arrived.[100]

The festivities did not end after Hindenburg reached the Reich Chancellery. Thousands of members of nationalist associations who had lined the streets all afternoon now gathered outside taverns off Kurfürstendamm, along with the marching bands that had been banned from the official celebrations.[101] In Nuremberg, patriotic organizations staged a torchlight procession through the city centre to mark Hindenburg's inauguration and in Bremen many local residents enshrined their windows with candles and pictures of the Field Marshal.[102] On 11 May, the emphasis was on popular celebration and the festivities were a 'rallying point for an otherwise fragmented bourgeoisie'.[103]

Social Democrats and Communists tried to disrupt right-wing celebrations, but did not succeed. Berlin's SPD leadership had secretly urged party members to put up Hindenburg caricatures in public places during the night of 11 May.[104] KPD leaflets also appealed to Communists to demonstrate against his arrival, but the police had seized many of these.[105] Only

5,000 to 10,000 people—as opposed to the 200,000 or more Hindenburg devotees—participated in counter-demonstrations in the afternoon and early evening of 11 May.[106] For the most part there was no denying that the events in the streets of the capital and elsewhere were first and foremost a bourgeois nationalist affair.

When Hindenburg was officially inaugurated as Weimar's second President in the Reichstag on 12 May, several thousand people again gathered on the Königsplatz to catch a glimpse of the new President and to listen to the military music played.[107] All Prussian schools received orders to suspend classes and host celebrations teaching children 'the special significance of the events'. Schools in all other German *Länder* were encouraged to follow suit, and German radio stations broadcast a special programme to the sounds of Beethoven's *Die Himmel rühmen des Ewigen Ehre*.[108]

As a last resort of desperate optimism, republican commentators tried to convince themselves that Hindenburg's oath on the constitution would herald democratic consolidation. The promise of his Reichstag speech to serve the whole people, and not simply the interests of the groups that had orchestrated his victory, was interpreted as a republican success.[109] According to *Vorwärts* Hindenburg had sounded like a true republican on 12 May.[110] Observing the Field Marshal standing in the Reichstag amidst the Weimar colours, Count Harry Kessler momentarily hoped that some of Hindenburg's 'veneration would rub off on' the parliamentary system and would 'turn out to be quite useful for the Republic'.[111]

Different political groups thus invested fundamentally different hopes in the new President. Whilst many on the right wished he would immediately set about turning Germany into a more authoritarian state, republicans could do nothing but hope that he would keep his oath to safeguard the democratic constitution. Over the next decade, at different moments, Hindenburg would disappoint the expectations of both camps.

* * *

In 1925, the Reichsblock managed to translate Hindenburg's mythical reputation into real political capital. Since 1919, the Field Marshal's veneration had proven to be a highly effective weapon in the right-wing struggle against the Weimar Republic. Now his mythical allure had helped him capture, of all things, the highest republican office. Hindenburg's unrelentingly broad appeal did not just galvanize anti-republicans; left-wing reluctance to attack

Germany's most venerated figure substantially weakened and confused the republican campaign. This reluctance was the result of over a decade of extensive Hindenburg worship that had also penetrated republican circles.

In the following years, it seemed as though Count Kessler's hopes might indeed be vindicated. Hindenburg's first years in office coincided with a relatively stable period in Weimar's history, giving at least the impression that some of the fragmented groups of German society had moved closer together—this was, after all, the first time republicans and nationalists honoured a common symbol. The two camps supported the President for fundamentally different reasons, however, and the next presidential contest—fought with inverted fronts in 1932—would show that German politics was at least as polarized as it had been in 1925.

# 5

## Buying the icon*

In 1929, four years after Hindenburg's election, *Der Eiserne Hindenburg in Krieg und Frieden (The Iron Hindenburg in War and Peace)*, a silent non-fictional film, opened in German cinemas. Its title was reminiscent of the 'Iron Chancellor', Bismarck, who served as a mythical role model for Hindenburg, and of the 'Iron Hindenburg' nailing statue erected in central Berlin in 1915. The producers wanted to educate their audience about how 'deeply intertwined the German people's fate' had been, and continued to be, with the President's life.[1] Split into consecutive acts, the film portrayed Hindenburg's life as following an inner logic—from his early career in the Prussian army to the battle of Tannenberg in 1914, his leadership during the First World War, and finally his presidency. Hindenburg's inauguration on 12 May 1925 thus appeared as the pinnacle of a lifelong service to the German people and represented the special bond that allegedly existed between him and the public at large—a bond the film expressed through countless images of large crowds (some staged, others genuine) cheering the aged Hindenburg on his seventieth and eightieth birthdays, at his inauguration, and during his official travels.

By depicting at length Hindenburg studying military maps, the film placed great emphasis on his ingenious strategic planning in the run-up to Tannenberg that had supposedly saved the entire German home front from occupation—a fate the film alluded to in images of material destruction and dead livestock. That the 'saviour' had not managed to deliver victory in the end did not get in the way of the film's narrative: the subtitles explained military defeat with the 'inhumane' British naval blockade, the sailors' mutinies and revolution in Germany in November 1918. To re-inforce the by then well-known message of a 'stab-in-the-back' of the German army by treacherous elements at home, *The Iron Hindenburg* re-enacted scenes of revolutionary fighting in the streets of Berlin in 1918/19 under the incendiary headline 'The Red Terror'. It depicted the loss of territory inflicted on Germany by the Treaty of Versailles in no less sensationalist terms—a map of the German Empire from which giant, greedy hands tear chunks off in east and west is one of the film's most memorable sequences.

Such cultural manifestations of the Hindenburg myth were clearly on the upsurge during his presidency. With its selective plotline, tendentious subtitles and ground-breaking special effects, the film sought to drive home the message that Hindenburg's leadership was Germany's calling, and that only the political 'saviour' himself could rescue the country from a return to the years of post-war domestic strife.

Whilst he had been a political symbol in retirement—albeit an active one—prior to 1925, the Field Marshal-turned-President would become *the* most visible public figure in the second half of the 1920s. During this time, the Hindenburg myth was as much a cultural as it was a political phenomenon, which did not just occupy those engaged in German politics, but penetrated much broader sections of society in its myriad forms: a massive readership of Hindenburg books and special Hindenburg issues of the illustrated press existed, as did a receptive audience for Hindenburg films and his speeches on the radio. Equally, the purchase decisions of consumers were animated by the use of Hindenburg's name or image in modern commercial advertising.

Just as Hindenburg's extraordinary popularity between 1914 and 1918 cannot be explained solely by his military rank, his iconic status after 1925 did not rest exclusively on the presidency's radiance. Friedrich Ebert had not been pictured as frequently in the illustrated press and in films, for instance, and had not received nearly as many letters from ordinary Germans (so-called *Eingaben*) as Weimar's second president.[2] Hindenburg brought his mythical veneration into office, thereby fuelling audiences' appetites. Holding the presidency, in its turn, provided Hindenburg with an effective public platform, widening the scope of his media presence significantly, which ultimately made his myth a broader and more enduring phenomenon. Furthermore, the new media of film and radio, the ever-expanding illustrated press, and image-based advertisements, vastly extended the myth's cultural purchase when compared to the personality cults of the Wilhelmine period—for instance, those of Kaiser Wilhelm II or Bismarck. The dissemination of the Hindenburg myth via these new mass media did not just define its extraordinary scope, but also blurred the boundaries between cultural entertainment and propagandistic politics.[3]

## The celluloid myth

The somewhat nostalgic notion of 'Weimar Culture' being synonymous with the 'Golden Twenties' has long since been revised. The Expressionists, the *Bauhaus*, *Neue Sachlichkeit*, and Fritz Lang's *Metropolis* may still be admired for their artistic quality, but they were not emblematic of interwar German cultural practice.[4] The great majority of films made between 1918 and 1933 were not modern, avant-garde pieces, but non-fictional formats or 'documentaries', often targeting a mass audience and produced with an educational purpose in mind.[5] *The Iron Hindenburg* was thus a typical creation of a period in which film increasingly ascribed meaning to the unprecedented experience of the First World War. While Ebert, his predecessor as President, had hardly appeared in films, Hindenburg—*the hero of wartime Germany*—featured prominently in this new genre.[6]

The Field Marshal had already appeared on German cinema screens in the silent propaganda films of wartime produced to mobilize and entertain cinema audiences at home and at the front. Many of these wartime images were now being recycled in more modern and technologically advanced films such as *The Iron Hindenburg*, with the aim of lending an air of authenticity to 'documentaries' with a clear anti-republican bias.[7]

The film premiere took place at the Primus-Palast, one of Berlin's newest and largest cinema palaces, with over 1,000 seats. Whilst such venues catered predominantly to wealthier, bourgeois cinema audiences in big urban centres, cinema-going was by no means a leisure activity consigned to the upper echelons of German society in the late 1920s.[8] By 1930, 5,000 cinemas with a total number of 2 million seats had been built in Germany and in spite of the crippling effects of economic crisis, 4.5 million Germans still went to the cinema every week in 1932.[9] Although the socially levelling effects of the cinema experience should not be exaggerated, film clearly provided popular entertainment for a mass audience.[10]

*The Iron Hindenburg*'s key messages—that Hindenburg's leadership was Germany's destiny and that he had saved the country from the Russians, from post-war domestic strife and from prolonged international humiliation—clearly perpetuated some of the central themes of the Hindenburg

myth. And yet, the President and his staff observed the documentary's production with an eagle eye. They sought to make sure that it was completely
in line with their officially sanctioned version of events and would not
even implicitly threaten Hindenburg's reputation. Consequently, the Berlin Board of Film Classification had to inform the film's producer Johannes
Häussler that one line in particular had offended Hindenburg personally.
In a section on the end of the war, the subtitles had quoted him as saying:
'I am dead tired, but as long as this old body is still good for something,
I'll stand up until I collapse.' The President obviously considered the new
medium too powerful to tolerate such blatant allusions to his physical
frailty. Häussler, a former member of the Free Corps, was only too happy
to co-operate: the contentious scene was swiftly removed from the film.[11]

Whilst the impact of these cinematic images on viewers is difficult to
measure, the shared visual language of Hindenburg films shows the extent
to which his myth was a common cultural currency. *Einer für Alle!* (*One for
All!*), a talkie directed by Kurt Wessel and Heinrich Roellenbleg in 1932
to promote Hindenburg's re-election, equally reminded viewers of his
seminal heroic act—victory at Tannenberg.[12] *One for All!*—a title clearly
playing on the appeal of the *Volksgemeinschaft*—depicted the invading
Russian troops of August 1914 as a massive wave rolling over a map of
East Prussia thus lending visual expression to a key paradigm of wartime.
A giant shadow in the shape of Hindenburg's iconic square head was then
shown approaching from the west. After bold letters herald 'Tannenberg!'
and proclaim 'Victory! Victory! Victory!', dark clouds retreat from the map
of East Prussia back towards Russian territory. Even with such limited
special effects, the film conveyed mythical meaning effectively. It portrayed
Hindenburg as a larger-than-life figure (the colossal shadow) who single-
handedly saved the German population from dangerous and inhuman (giant
wave, dark clouds) Russian forces.

The events of August 1914 were also the subject of a feature film:
*Tannenberg*, which opened simultaneously at Berlin's Primus and Titania-
Palast in September 1932.[13] Directed by the former officer Heinz Paul,
*Tannenberg* was part of a wider trend towards films glorifying the Prussian
past, which enjoyed tremendous commercial success in the 1920s.[14] With no
less than six war films, Paul was one of Weimar's most prolific filmmakers,
but he has only recently received scholarly attention. Most of Paul's efforts
can be read as a German nationalist response to pacifist works such as Lewis
Milestone's cinematic adaptation of *All Quiet on the Western Front*.[15]

Shooting *Tannenberg* was a project of huge proportions costing half a million Reichsmark and involving 8,000 people.[16] The Zurich-based production company Praesensfilm GmbH promoted it as a 'documentary on the historic battle' although it included many fictional elements.[17] It portrayed the events of 1914 on two levels. First, it re-enacted the political and military events with German actors playing the main protagonists. Second, there was a more individualized storyline surrounding the fictional character Rittmeister von Arndt, the owner of an East Prussian estate.[18] These two interpretative frameworks allowed Paul to portray Tannenberg both as a battle of historical proportions—the work of 'great men'—and as a human tragedy affecting the lives of ordinary East Prussians. Small children crying for their mothers and asking with innocent eyes whether the 'Cossacks really eat dogs' were as much part of the film as Hindenburg and Ludendorff studying military maps. By splitting the plot along these lines, the film could invoke the battle as an example of German heroism and military success, while simultaneously letting the cinema audience re-live the sense of threat and fear of occupation experienced by the German public in August 1914. Protecting Germany's 'innocence', alleviating individual suffering, German self-defence, anti-Slavism, and military bravery—the battle's most important mythical ingredients—thus all featured simultaneously in Paul's 1932 production.

Naturally, the film was a powerful reminder of the roots of Hindenburg's adulation. And yet, the presidential bureau and the Interior Ministry called for far-reaching censorship on the basis of Karl Koerner's impersonation not 'doing justice to the Reich President's historical personality'.[19] Both Hindenburg and his influential right-hand man, State Secretary Otto Meissner, preferred a film version in which Hindenburg was a peripheral figure to one in which he was not portrayed heroically enough—perhaps suggesting that the Field Marshal's definitive role at Tannenberg was so firmly established in collective memory that reminding the film's audience was not imperative.

The *Reichlichtspielgesetz* of 1920 covered the use of people's images in films or film adverts.[20] On the basis of the new law all films had to be approved by a board of censors prior to their release. According to §1, films could be banned if they posed a threat to public order and security, hurt religious feeling, or damaged Germany's reputation abroad.[21] Although there was no orchestrated political censorship of German films in the Weimar period, the *Reichlichtspielgesetz* provided a sufficient basis for the suppression of films for political reasons.[22] Ernst Seeger, who had taken over the German Board of Film Classification in March 1924, contributed decisively to the politicization of film censorship in Germany. He helped to create a climate in which socially critical, pacifist, and republican films were increasingly suppressed, while military 'documentaries', feature films glorifying the Prussian past and the war, as well as *Heimat* films could usually be shown.[23]

*Tannenberg* was not banned outright on the basis of the original 1920 law, but Paul was instead ordered to cut several scenes following a new passage introduced into the *Reichlichtspielgesetz* by emergency decree after the political upheavals surrounding *All Quiet on the Western Front*. According to this 'Lex Remarque' of 6 October 1931, films could now be wholly or partially censored if they 'threatened vital interests of the state'.[24] The revised law extended the power of Seeger's organization to anticipate how the audience would perceive a film and what political influence this would wield. With regard to *Tannenberg*, the censor decided that most scenes with Hindenburg had to be cut, because Koerner allegedly played him in an inappropriate way and due to the potential effect this might have on audiences.[25] Because the actor's performance was vaguely 'distorting' and 'degrading', the Board argued that *Tannenberg* constituted the 'threatening of vital interests of the state represented by the serving President, who was elected by the whole people'.[26]

This decision was striking; it implied that Hindenburg—or more importantly his myth—was a vital pillar of German political stability. By the autumn of 1932, the successive governments of Heinrich Brüning and Franz von Papen had lacked a parliamentary majority for over two years and had functioned only by relying on presidential decrees.[27] The writings of political and legal philosophers, such as Carl Schmitt, who advocated circumscribing parliamentary democracy to establish greater presidential authority and who considered the President the 'guardian of the constitution', had become increasingly influential.[28] In this political climate the Film Board regarded protecting Hindenburg's authority as crucial. Safeguarding Hindenburg's portrayal as heroic was interpreted as a 'vital interest of the state'. The censorship proceedings against Paul's film therefore not only illustrate to what extent the Hindenburg myth, which had originated at Tannenberg, fed his authority as President, but also the extent to which even agencies not by definition in charge of mythmaking—and not subject to Hindenburg's direct control—considered this state of affairs a given.

## Speaking on the wireless

In April 1925 Hindenburg had made German broadcasting history when his
speech during the election campaign had been broadcast nationally. It was
the initial shared listening experience of millions of people, transmitting the
voice of the man whose image had been so ubiquitous for over a decade into
the privacy of German homes for the very first time. At this stage roughly
one million Germans owned a radio.[29] By late 1932, 4.2 million German
households were equipped with the modern technology. Considering that
several family members normally used one radio, up to 11 million people
regularly listened to the wireless in the Republic's final year.[30]

The German government had been concerned about potential misuse of
this new instrument of mass communication and had regulated the airwaves
from the very beginning. Radio programming was centrally organized and
state-supervised and was explicitly meant to be apolitical.[31] Such state-
censorship was not strictly non-partisan, however. Even if radio played
no major role in any of the Reichstag election campaigns, it featured
prominently in the presidential contests of 1925 and 1932.[32] Whereas
Hindenburg, as well as the republican candidate Wilhelm Marx, had been
allowed to broadcast their speeches in the run-up to the second round of
voting in 1925, the Communist Party leader and presidential candidate Ernst
Thälmann had been excluded from using the new medium. In the 1932
campaign the pro-Hindenburg bias would be even more obvious: neither
of the serving President's main opponents was allowed to broadcast election
speeches.[33] Hindenburg, on the other hand, was given extensive airtime on
10 March 1932 to transmit a lengthy speech outlining his decision to run
again and calling on the German people to unify at a time of economic
hardship and general crisis.[34] On previous occasions, Hindenburg had also
addressed people directly in their living rooms as a kind of national father
figure. The *New York Times*, which reported regularly on the development
of German broadcasting in the 1920s and 1930s, noted in 1930 that
Hindenburg's spoken words possessed the faculty of awakening hope and
faith in German listeners, especially at times of national calamity:

> Reacting against the dark days and pessimism which hang over the Fatherland
> now, the nation wants to hear the venerable old Field Marshal's 'reassuring
> and fatherly voice' telling people their troubles are not unnoticed in the
> Presidential palace.[35]

Because the government showed no willingness to relinquish its central control of the radio and because Hindenburg's 'fatherly voice' dominated the airwaves, communist activists came up with a creative way of appropriating the medium in late 1931. To mark the New Year, Hindenburg gave a speech in the evening of 31 December 1931.[36] Just as in 1925 and 1932, his speech was broadcast nationwide. Not just German radio listeners were to hear the Reich President's words; because he was expected to make statements on the direction of foreign policy and on reparations, his statement aroused great interest abroad. The speech, which Hindenburg read out in a rather monotonous and stilted fashion, was broadcast on all of the USA's 200 radio channels, as well as to listeners in Great Britain, Austria, Switzerland, and Denmark.[37] Just at the moment when Hindenburg likened Germany's position of 1931/32 to the events at Tannenberg in 1914, and called on all Germans to 'stand together loyally and united in fate' to master all coming hardship, the broadcast was suddenly interrupted. An unidentifiable male voice shouting 'Red Front', 'Long live the Soviet Union', 'Down with the Emergency Decrees', and calling for mass strike action was audible as Hindenburg's voice faded into the background.[38]

As the subsequent investigation by the Berlin police uncovered, three communist workers, one of them a former radio technician, had dug up the radio cable leading to the main transmitter in Königswusterhausen near Berlin, had cut open the lead mantling, removed the isolation material, and had attached their own microphone to the single cable broadcasting Hindenburg's speech.[39] Manuals on the home production of transmitters circulated widely in the Weimar years and by orchestrating interruptions of official broadcasts the Arbeiter-Radio-Bewegung (Workers' Radio Movement) had frequently sought to influence the medium from the receivers' side.[40] Knowing that a mass of listeners was hanging on Hindenburg's words, the three Berlin communists had chosen their moment in true agitprop style. Although the radio technicians in charge had immediately moved the Hindenburg broadcast to a secure line, and although the communist interruptions had only been audible in Berlin, the press coverage of the event and the police investigation over the next few weeks magnified the attention the stunt received—with the result that even the foreign press reported the incident widely.[41]

This communist agitprop feat remained exceptional, however, and did not undermine Hindenburg's presence on the radio in the long term.[42] Because of the biased regulation of interwar radio, Hindenburg, whose

limited oratorical skills would have made him an improbable broadcasting
star in a more competitive radio market, was able to put his stamp on
the new medium between 1925 and 1933. Considering that the different
German broadcasting stations were quite autonomous, especially predating
the establishment of a national station in 1930, with radio programming
differing substantially from region to region, the fact that his speeches
mobilized a national audience from the outset was crucial.[43] The hegemony
of his voice on German radio—a medium symbolic for mobilizing national
fantasy—fostered his status as a symbol of Weimar. Hindenburg's speeches
on the wireless did, of course, not create the cult. They did, however,
make for a sense of immediacy and contact on a truly mass scale.

## Home stories and popular novels

The upsurge in nationalist films glorifying the war experience from the
mid-1920s had its literary equivalent in the publication of front novels that
appeared in two waves in the early and late 1920s. The mass popularity of
these books is a phenomenon that is central to judging Weimar Germany's
literary scene. For every anti-war novel by Erich Maria Remarque or
Ludwig Renn there were huge book sales of nationalist writers such as
Ernst Jünger, Hans Grimm, Hans Zöberlein, and Josef Magnus Wehner.[44]
Authors like Wehner composed their works specifically to counter the
negative image of war put forward in pacifist works and often invoked
myth as an escape from rationalism.[45]

Werner Beumelburg, a former soldier and officer who had worked as
a journalist for the national liberal *Deutsche Allgemeine Zeitung* in the early
1920s, was one of the most prolific representatives of this new literary genre.
He dealt with his experiences at Verdun in several books, especially in
his front novel *Gruppe Bosemüller*, published in 1930, which was marketed
as a nationalist equivalent of Remarque and became a bestseller.[46] The
previous year Beumelburg had published a thematic and chronological
predecessor: *Sperrfeuer um Deutschland*, a pseudo-historical novel offering
a bird's eye view of Germany's wartime experiences, which appeared
adorned with the President's foreword.[47] All of Beumelburg's works were
published by the Oldenburg-based military publisher Stalling which had
also been commissioned by the Reichsarchiv to publish the 40-volume
series *Schlachten des Weltkrieges*, a semi-official and popularly written history

of the battles of the First World War with a nationalist conservative bias. Stalling further distributed the equally popular multi-volume series *Erinnerungsblätter deutscher Regimente*.[48]

In order to secure Hindenburg's endorsement of Beumelburg's novel, Gerhard Stalling sent a copy to the President's office explicitly inviting criticism and change requests.[49] Hindenburg and Meissner did not pass up the chance of putting their own spin on a novel including a lengthy passage on Tannenberg, which was to be promoted heavily, eventually selling over 300,000 copies.[50] Meissner, Under-Secretary of State Heinrich Doehle, and Hindenburg himself all read Beumelburg's manuscript and insisted on detailed changes. Hindenburg was keen on altering a chapter dealing with the Kaiser's abdication so that the details would be in line with the version of the events of 9 November 1918 he had sanctioned in 1919. Meissner, on the other hand, was eager to change Beumelburg's account of the events at Tannenberg, but allegedly did not discuss his concerns with the President.[51] Reading the manuscript, the State Secretary had gained the impression that Ludendorff featured too prominently on its pages. Consequently he insisted to Stalling that Hindenburg had been Tannenberg's true architect.[52] Eventually, Stalling and Beumelburg agreed to the exact wording of all the changes proposed: 'Hinter Ludendorff's Stirn arbeiten die Gedanken' was simply substituted with 'Hinter Hindenburgs Stirn arbeiten die Gedanken' and a passage on Ludendorff's nerves and Hindenburg's calmness and leadership during crucial moments of the battle was inserted into the text, thus re-iterating one of the central components of his myth.[53] The publisher, who was keen to secure Hindenburg's foreword to the novel as a marketing tool, readily complied with the demands. Just as in the case of Heinz Paul's cinematic adaptation of Tannenberg, the President exercised image control even over a popular genre by definition conducive to his veneration.

Numerous large-size illustrated books with a nationalist-conservative bias further enhanced Hindenburg's media presence. Paul Lindenberg's *Hindenburg-Denkmal für das deutsche Volk*, which went through nine editions in the 'patriotic publishing house' C. H. Weller between 1922 and 1935 and sold up to 145,000 copies, was one such example.[54] Two-thirds of the articles published by the former war correspondent Lindenberg were on Hindenburg's military career.

The expanding illustrated press, too, was a platform on which Hindenburg's image was shaped and from which his fame was spread, even if he did not have a separate press office.[55] By the 1920s tabloids, broadsheets, and party political papers used a growing number of images and published photo-illustrated weekly supplements.[56] Illustrated papers, such as Scherl's *Die Woche* and Ullstein's *Berliner Illustrirte Zeitung* (*BIZ*), offered popular entertainment ranging from reports on exotic foreign countries, sensationalist crime stories to coverage of sports and film celebrities.[57] Hindenburg's numerous public appearances, the staged celebrations with their parades and gathering crowds, and his frequent travels, made interesting visual fare, and turned the President into an ideal subject for the new medium. His iconic image and the success of Hindenburg adverts, books, and films provided ample evidence for the near-insatiable consumer demand for all things Hindenburg-related. Consequently, the President was the undisputed star of the genre after 1925; no other politician was pictured as frequently in the major illustrated weeklies. Friedrich Ebert's fiftieth birthday in 1921, for instance, had not received much publicity at all. The near-regal coverage of Hindenburg's eightieth birthday, on the other hand, exemplified his visual dominance: the main illustrated papers sold at Germany's newsstands featured the iconic birthday boy on their covers.[58]

Despite their supposedly apolitical stance, the political affiliations of the illustrated papers' respective publishing houses influenced their news coverage. The conservative, Hugenberg-owned *Die Woche*, for instance, put more emphasis on Hindenburg's career as a soldier and showed him more often in military uniform than a publication like Ullstein's *Berliner Illustrirte*, which placed more visual and textual emphasis on Hindenburg's republican role.[59] The 1927 Hindenburg remembrance issue of *Die Woche*, for instance, included several articles on his military life—*Der Kadett, Mein Leutnant Hindenburg, Kamerad Hindenburg*, and *Der General*.[60] At the same time, however, even the Scherl weekly showed Hindenburg in civilian clothes both on the front page of the birthday issue and on the official birthday photograph for the paper.[61] Whereas Ebert had shied away from such formats to popularize himself, both Scherl's and Ullstein's illustrated publications printed a large number of human-interest stories on Hindenburg: *Hindenburg als Jäger* and *Erinnerungen an Frau von Hindenburg*, focusing on his leisure activities and family life, were typical formats, as was *Ein Arbeitstag des Reichspräsidenten*, summing up a typical day for the President with photographs of Hindenburg's office and public appearances.[62] The differences in the presentational style of the illustrated papers were rather subtle, given the deep political polarization of Weimar's broadsheet and tabloid press. Even the Nazi press, whose articles stressed his military role relentlessly, would feature pictures of Hindenburg in civilian clothes surprisingly often.[63] This coverage not only formed a substantial part of the President's media presence, but extended and diversified the readership profile of Hindenburg stories, reaching white-collar workers and low ranking civil servants, who may not have taken as active an interest in the coverage of Hindenburg's political decisions in the party political papers, and thus rooting his myth more deeply in Weimar German society.[64]

## Branding Hindenburg

During the First World War, advertising specialists had introduced visual elements into German war propaganda, most notably into the war loan campaigns. Lucian Bernhard and Louis Oppenheim, who had both made a name for themselves as *Gebrauchsgraphiker* prior to 1914, were even employed by the Reichsbank.[65] Hence, the visual styles of German advertising and of political propaganda posters and postcards were strongly linked from the outset. Oppenheim, for instance, who continued to work as a prominent advertising agent in the 1920s, had also created one of the famous Hindenburg war loan posters of 1917—an image emulated widely during the Weimar years, although using heads on elections posters was surprisingly rare in the 1920s.[66] This human interconnectedness between war propaganda and commercial design may serve to explain why Hindenburg's image lent itself so readily to its utilization in advertising—advertising specialists had coined its iconography in the first place.

More sophisticated strategies of consumer targeting had only gradually established themselves in the 1920s. By introducing visuals, advertisers no longer had to rely on appealing to consumers' rational choice but could appeal to their emotions on a connotative level.[67] A new breed of advertising specialists educated at German universities regarded consumers as guidable by playing on their fears, desires, and yearning for elevated social status.[68] Rather than applying American advertising techniques without modifications, German specialists recognized that their chances of success were improved by using familiar codes and a culturally established visual language.[69] Learning how to decode images is a gradual process. Crucially, German consumers had received much of this visual training during the First World War. Consequently, visual depictions of Hindenburg simply featuring his square head, small eyes, stoical features, and grand moustache—representing stalwartness and determination—did not just work well in the election campaigns of 1925 and 1932, but were also constantly recycled in the illustrated press and, more specifically, to market commercial products. The continuity of the Hindenburg iconography was not entirely coincidental. When official painters or sculptors departed from traditional depictions of Hindenburg, his office sometimes intervened. In 1932, for instance, Meissner rebuked the sculptor Rudolf Stocker for his Hindenburg bust. The facial expression was not 'determined' and 'masculine' enough; as a result Hindenburg appeared 'too gentle', Meissner informed the artist. He duly sent over a few 'especially felicitous photographs' of the President so that Stocker would alter his design accordingly.[70] As a result of this—somewhat imposed—visual continuity, Weimar advertisers could tap into the huge resource of connotations Hindenburg's image offered and could profit immensely from associating their (often random) products with the 'determined' and 'masculine' embodiment of German wartime virtues and heroism. Hindenburg became one of Germany's first true advertising icons—selling anything from cars to liver sausage—preceding a development that was to become one of the defining features of affluent Western societies after the Second World War.[71]

The 'Hindenburg' brand worked on a variety of levels and was invoked to promote products of all kinds. Some of the most prominent Hindenburg adverts targeted members of the middle classes who aspired to bettering themselves socially.[72] Germany's largest car manufacturer Opel, for example, placed a full-page advert into the 'Hindenburg' birthday issue of the illustrated Scherl weekly *Die Woche* in 1927. The advert featured the President being driven past a parade of cheering onlookers in an open car—of course an Opel.[73]

This advert took on the 'Hindenburg' brand in a number of ways: on one level it simply used the recognition value of his name and image to promote the Opel brand. But it was also more sophisticated than that in aiming at a specific target audience—both the fact that it was placed in the special birthday issue of a nationalist Scherl publication and its particular design made it all the more powerful and effective. The image not only depicted nationalist Hindenburg devotees, clearly recognizable by the Imperial flags they carried and their uniforms, but stylized the Opel literally as a vehicle of Hindenburg worship—a technique obviously intended to resonate with the President's following. In a much less obvious

Fig. 4. 'Reich President v. Hirdenburg in the new Opel car' (1927).

way, the advertisement also suggested that being the owner of an Opel carried high social prestige.[74] 'Buy an Opel and be admired' was the subtext here. And who could symbolize social prestige more successfully than the mythical Hindenburg, whose birthday in 1927 was marked by national festivities on a regal scale?

That the 'Hindenburg' brand was a useful marketing asset for upmarket consumer goods was further illustrated by the adverts placed by Hessian wine merchant Baron von Linstow. The company offered various brands of sparkling wine and champagne, which were all named after the President—*Hindenburg-Gold, Hindenburg-Silber*, and *Hindenburg-Jubiläums-Sekt*.[75] This branding was highly successful, not least demonstrated by the fact that the German Association of Sparkling Wine Producers filed a complaint about Linstow's 'unfair comparative advantage'.[76] Linstow had apparently passed himself off as the only legitimate producer of 'Hindenburg' champagne and suggested that Hindenburg fully endorsed his products. Hindenburg had allegedly figured as a kind of product tester. As we can see, the huge amount of public trust invested in his personality, and therefore in his judgement, was not just important political capital, but could also be turned into commercial gain.

The President, however, had only limited means at his disposal when it came to combating advertisements using his name or image. A first legal step had been made when the right to one's own image had been introduced into German law by the *Kunsturheberrecht* of 9 January 1907—a response to the publication of images of Bismarck on his deathbed. Drawing the legal boundaries of the new medium of photography, the 1907 law stated that pictures of private citizens could only be published with their consent. The protection of *Personen der Zeitgeschichte*, public persons, was, however, excluded from the law according to §23. Hence, images of Hindenburg—a public person sui generis—were not legally protected. Anyone could publish his photographs or painted images, even for commercial gain, without being prosecuted or liable to pay a fee; the 'Hindenburg' brand was essentially free. The only basis on which adverts could be banned was the 1909 law concerning the combating of unfair competition. It included a 'decency clause' according to which advertising should not breach moral standards.[77] Hence, if sparkling wine producer Linstow gave the impression that his brand had Hindenburg's exclusive endorsement and no such specific backing had been given, his adverts could be legally pursued on the basis of breaching proper manners ('die guten Sitten').[78]

German companies were surprisingly creative when it came to securing Hindenburg's endorsement for their products. The particular case of optician Brennecke suggests that the 'Hindenburg' brand was in fact so valuable that even forgery seemed like a legitimate means to gain access to it. By 1928 Brennecke's rival, the Stuttgart-based optician Metzler, had been producing and distributing a special glasses frame under the name *Hindenburgbrille* ('Hindenburg Spectacles') for some time. Hindenburg had even personally agreed to Metzler having his Hindenburg frame registered as a trademark.[79] Metzler's Hindenburg model had been a huge success:

> The Hindenburg Spectacles have quite literally conquered the world, a fact which is of course a true thorn in our rival companies' side. Because our spectacles are linked to Hindenburg's sacrosanct name, the competition obviously does not dare to fight our model

the optician informed State Secretary Meissner.[80] Metzler's rival Brennecke consequently employed rather unconventional methods in his quest for the 'Hindenburg' brand: when his business delivered one of optician Metzler's 'Hindenburg Spectacles' to the President's office, Brennecke suggested that it had in fact been one of his very own models, the *Rolandbrille*, which the President had requested. To back up his claim of Hindenburg's change in preference, Brennecke began advertising with a photograph of Hindenburg at his desk, into which his *Rolandbrille* had been drawn in. The President took offence at this incident not because both companies had used his name or image, but because the photograph had been fiddled with. The forgery had not been authorized and therefore constituted a breach of proper manners and so could be pursued under the unfair competition law of 1909.[81]

Whereas there is plenty of evidence to show that Hindenburg exercised image-control, he did not intervene generally to stop commercial activities employing his name.[82] He not only lacked the legal powers to do so, but there is also no indication that he would have pursued a more rigid course had the legal framework been different. His staff only ever tried to stop specific adverts after they had received complaints, but did not actively pursue banning the 'Hindenburg' brand. In the optician's case, the President even gave his consent to the *Hindenburgbrille* being registered as a trademark, thus effectively handing control over the brand to someone else.[83] As we can see, Hindenburg did not consider his name or image being used as a brand as a threat to his own myth.

If anything, Hindenburg's attitude towards advertising reveals how relatively limited his attempts to control his own image were, especially when compared to the Nazis' later endeavours. He neither objected to his image being used as an advertising tool in general nor to its use to market specific products. He did not fear that his image would be cheapened or sold out by commercial use. Being invoked to promote spectacles and cough medication clearly implied that Hindenburg was an old man with frail health. Whilst he avoided wearing glasses at official state receptions by having his speeches printed in exceptionally large letters, Hindenburg did not seem to mind that advertisements for spectacles publicized his failing eyesight.[84] He had objected to being described as old and fragile in the film *The Iron Hindenburg*, but he did not recognize a similar message implicit in adverts for pharmaceuticals. Tolerating advertisers' allusions to his age and feeble health was a far cry from attempts by dictators such as Mussolini or Hitler to exercise total control over their images—not least by avoiding being seen as physically weak.[85]

By contrast, the Nazis considered the power of advertising a threat to the potency of their own ideology. The party was keen to remain in control of its symbols, such as the swastika or brown shirts, and regarded their deployment in advertising as undermining and degrading the goals of the Nazi movement.[86] This realization had, however, been the result of a more long-term process. Their ban on the use of Nazi symbols and Hitler's image in advertising of 19 May 1933 was partly a reaction to the wave of Hindenburg adverts, which had flooded Germany in previous years. After the Nazi seizure of power in January 1933, German businesses had increasingly begun to use Hitler's image, and often the President's *and* Chancellor's image in combination.[87]

Merely three weeks before the ban on advertising with Nazi symbols was put in place, the District Leader of Propaganda of Greater Berlin, Walter Schulze-Wechsungen, had written to Goebbels's newly-established Ministry of Propaganda complaining about an advertisement placed by an oil company from Bremen, which praised a particular 'Hindenburg' lubricant. According to Schulze-Wechsungen people were offended by the abuse of Hindenburg's name for the promotion of lubricant and he urged the Propaganda Ministry to 'adopt appropriate measures' to suppress this kind of commercial advertising in Germany.[88]

**Fig. 5.** An advertisement for brandy featuring Hindenburg and Hitler before the Nazi ban on using their images in May 1933.

It took some time before this 'battle against kitsch' was ultimately won.[89] In May 1934 the Nazi leadership finally introduced a new law intended to clarify the legal situation once and for all. In a crucial passage it stated that images of living persons from public or political life, their famous quotations, and habits could only be used with their explicit consent.[90] The Nazis thus ensured that the Hitler myth, which they rightly held to be a crucial pillar of their rule, would not be 'sold out' or cheapened by its commercialization. Hindenburg, on the other hand, had been more or less oblivious to such implications, turning the 'Hindenburg' brand into a profitable commodity that German companies used extensively to their advantage.

* * *

The portrayal of Hindenburg as an image-oblivious public figure has to be revised further. In fact, he sought to control the image he projected to a considerable degree. Whilst much of the Hindenburg worship was spontaneous—or appropriated strategically by businesses, publishers, and the film industry for commercial purposes—and not controlled by a single agent, the cases discussed here highlight his considerable efforts to safeguard his myth from the top down. Commercial advertising was an exceptional case, because Hindenburg did not seemingly recognize its broader implications. The legal situation did not give him much control over the use of his image for commercial purposes and he did not seek to extend his control—a condition the Nazis quickly altered in 1933. When he did have control or when those engaged in the cultural sector were willing to co-operate, however, Hindenburg readily intervened. Not least the cases of Paul's *Tannenberg* and Beumelburg's *Sperrfeuer um Deutschland* show beyond doubt that Hindenburg and his staff recognized the significance of film and popular fiction and were keen on guarding his mythical reputation in both genres.

Much of the political campaigning—and also the branding of Hindenburg—relied on the iconography shaped during the First World War. The successful use of his image in the new media built on the power of the existing myth—it did not create it. These new media did, however, contribute decisively to the scope and endurance of the Hindenburg myth and turned it into much more than a political fashion.

Hindenburg's iconic status does not just help to explain some of the intricacies of his political career, but also hints at the existence of common symbolic ground in German society despite its undeniably entrenched political divisions—an aspect often overlooked by scholars who stress party political fragmentation in Weimar or emphasize the iconoclasm of the republican avant-garde.[91] Hindenburg's omnipresence in the modern mass media of film, radio, the illustrated press, and in a new advertising market meant that his myth escaped strict political dividing lines. Films such as *The Iron Hindenburg* and *Tannenberg*, as well as Beumelburg's novels, of course, appealed first and foremost to those nurturing nostalgia for the Wilhelmine Empire. Readers of the Hugenberg-owned *Die Woche*, however, were frequently confronted with images underlining Hindenburg's republican role, and those who preferred the pro-republican *BIZ*, in their turn, regularly faced coverage of near-regal Hindenburg celebrations and could not escape visual allusions to the President's military career. Similarly, Hindenburg's radio broadcasts represented shared listening experiences for millions of Germans. People's attitudes towards him were therefore not just shaped by the news coverage of the party political papers; the Hindenburg myth also played into their leisure time and penetrated the sanctuary of their homes. Republicans, too, were exposed to—and sometimes shaped—Hindenburg's iconic status across various media for two decades. This had real political consequences, which, in the end, neither the SPD nor Joseph Goebbels would be able to ignore. Hindenburg's status as a national icon had confused the republican campaign against him during the presidential elections of 1925 and would make republicans more willing to support his re-election as a bulwark against Hitler in 1932. His mythical presence across various mass media in the 1920s and early 1930s smudged the lines between left and right and blurred the boundaries between cultural entertainment and propagandistic politics. In short, Hindenburg was a popular icon of Weimar Germany.

# 6

# Hollow unity

In April 1926, Carl von Ossietzky, the editor of *Die Weltbühne*, reviewed a curious new phenomenon of German political life—the republican 'Hindenburg Legend'. There was an old 'Hindenburg-Legend', Ossietzky argued, according to which the General had planned Tannenberg in advance and had exhibited true military genius in 1914. One year after his inauguration, however, the bourgeois republican press was weaving new wreaths around his head. According to this blossoming republican 'narrative' the President was a superior and gentle head of state, tactful and able to distinguish good from evil. Republicans had come to regard him as a cornerstone of Weimar politics, Ossietzky opined.[1]

This striking analysis was no polemical reflection of Ossietzky's growing frustration with republican politics, but a rather acute political observation.[2] Hindenburg's election in 1925 had come in the wake of a period of 'relative stabilization' of German politics and society.[3] The country may have witnessed four different governments within a single parliament between December 1924 and May 1928, and fought over issues of huge symbolic importance, such as the colours of the national flag, but the second half of the 1920s still heralded a significant improvement. Compared to the deep-seated sense of insecurity created by the political violence and hyperinflation of Weimar's early years, and in contrast to the near-civil war atmosphere and record levels of unemployment between 1930 and 1933, the Republic's middle years seemed reasonably stable and peaceful.

Hindenburg endeared himself to republicans not least by backing Stresemann's reconciliatory foreign policy aimed at easing international tensions and helping Germany to re-gain some of its sovereignty on the international stage. In late 1925, a mere half year after his inauguration, Germany became a signatory to the Treaty of Locarno, which marked a significant step in the *Reich*'s return to the concert of European powers. By signing the treaty, Germany accepted the status quo concerning its western borders whilst leaving territorial revision in the east through negotiation open as an option.[4] Whereas Locarno was hugely unpopular among the far right, who denounced it as 'another Versailles', Hindenburg's backing complicated their opposition considerably. 'It will be impossible to convince the people that Germany must be saved from its saviour', the pacifist journalist Hellmut von Gerlach—an advocate of Locarno—informed the Carnegie Foundation in New York with relief.[5]

The following year—and despite strong personal reservations—Hindenburg gave his consent to Germany's entry into the League of Nations, an institution German Nationalists despised.[6] The President had rejected their repeated attempts to sway him towards a more revisionist foreign policy.[7] Furthermore, he shunned several right-wing candidates for the post of State Secretary in the presidential bureau, which the right saw as key to exerting political influence in the Republic, and kept on Ebert's right-hand man, Otto Meissner, instead.[8] Although Meissner—a DDP member until 1926—would move considerably to the right in the years to come, assuming a political role that went far beyond the tasks of a civil servant, and would even continue to serve under Hitler, in 1925, republicans considered his retention as evidence of Hindenburg's constitutional loyalty and willingness to remain aloof from right-wing influence.[9] That Hindenburg disappointed his erstwhile opponents in a positive sense—by not setting out to implement an openly authoritarian system immediately after taking office—is crucial for explaining the republican eulogies that so perturbed Ossietzky.[10]

It was tempting to see the embryonic political stability of the mid-1920s, which, in fact, coincided with rather than resulted from Hindenburg's inauguration, as his personal achievement. The political recovery 'not least seemed to be founded in the tranquil, confidence-building security originating from the President's house', Ferdinand Friedensburg observed.[11] Such sentiments were not entirely new. Portraying Hindenburg as a 'refuge', and emphasizing the importance of his tranquillity, built upon an older component of his mythical narrative which had obtruded during the war and in its aftermath—that of a 'rock in the ocean' providing stability during times of chaos and insecurity.[12] Because pro-republicans in particular had subscribed to this layer of the Hindenburg myth, it was easy to interpret the apparent easing of political tensions after 1925 in a similar framework. By 1927, even a staunchly republican organization like the Social Democratic veterans' league Reichsbanner promoted Hindenburg's democratic credentials and openly claimed ownership of the Hindenburg myth.[13]

Nevertheless, Hindenburg's new republican clothes so admired by democrats could not disguise his anti-democratic convictions entirely. The right may have been ever more disappointed with the President's lack of initiative in overhauling the Weimar constitution, but he nevertheless continued to lend his weight to numerous right-wing causes, especially those of symbolic importance.[14] Throughout his presidency he bestowed legitimacy upon the anti-republican cause by remaining an honorary member of one of the most explicitly anti-democratic organizations of the Weimar years: the Stahlhelm. Ignoring all requests from the Interior Ministry to resign from this nationalist veterans' league, the President thus publicly endorsed an organization that openly advocated the overthrow of the very order he represented and had vowed to safeguard.[15]

Furthermore, in 1926 Hindenburg became embroiled in controversy over the treatment of the former German Princes. In a rare moment of left unity, the SPD and KPD and their veterans' organizations had campaigned for a national referendum on the expropriation of the Princes' property, to be held on 20 June 1926.[16] Although Hindenburg did not denounce the referendum in his capacity as President, in a letter to Friedrich Wilhelm von Loebell he noted that he 'privately' hoped for its failure.[17] The letter, which was published in the *Deutschen-Spiegel*, aroused strong criticism from the far left.[18] Paul Levi, of the SPD's Marxist wing, raged that it 'bordered on an attempted coup d'état'. It was time for the *Vorwärts* and the bourgeois parties to stop twiddling their thumbs, he opined.[19] The mainstream left, meanwhile, was too enamoured with Hindenburg's republican correctness to condemn the letter forcefully. 'Monarchical schemers' who had 'abused' 'Hindenburg's naivety' were solely to blame for its publication, Hellmut von Gerlach, amongst others, was convinced.[20] Levi, in his turn, was unimpressed by such republican blame-shifting. 'The feeling of monarchical timidity runs deep amongst contemporary republicans', he noted with resignation.[21]

In September 1927, Hindenburg gave German Nationalists further reason to hope that he was still on their side by endorsing one of their most important symbolic causes—the refutation of German war guilt as laid out in the Treaty of Versailles. His speech at the unveiling ceremony of the Tannenberg Memorial on 18 September 1927 illustrated once more that his myth was a keystone in Weimar's politics of memory.[22] In the most frequently cited passage of his speech, he established a direct connection between the new commemorative site, the battle of August 1914, and the Treaty of Versailles:

> The Tannenberg National Memorial is first and foremost dedicated to the memory of those who gave their lives for the liberation of the homeland. Their memory . . . obliges me to declare solemnly at this site: all sections of the German people unanimously reject the accusation that Germany was guilty of unleashing the greatest of all wars! It was not envy, hatred, or the will to conquer that made us spring to arms. In fact, war was the last resort to defend ourselves against a world of enemies, resulting in the German people's endurance of great sacrifice . . .[23]

Hindenburg's Tannenberg credentials made him the ideal witness for the prosecution against alleged German war guilt—after all, how could a people who had experienced weeks of supposedly brutal Russian occupation and had defended themselves so heroically at Tannenberg have been guilty of unleashing war? By adding the weight of his authority to the nationalist narrative of the 'stab-in-the-back' in 1919, Hindenburg had already contributed decisively to codifying German war memory; now he was taking a firm stand on the so-called 'war guilt lie'. His intervention gave fresh impetus to the campaign against the accusation (and thus against the continued payment of reparations) and received a great amount of public attention both within Germany and abroad.[24] The fight against the 'war guilt lie' and the promotion of the stab-in-the-back legend were decisive factors in hindering the establishment of a democratic consensus in Weimar Germany and contributed in no small measure to its downfall.[25] That Hindenburg—in his capacity as the republican head of state—was the patron saint of both narratives was decisive. In September 1927, he implicitly called into question the Republic's legitimacy and gave an incentive to nationalist forces to continue the fight against its existence.

In spite of Hindenburg's endorsements of various anti-republican issues, the first years of his presidency were a time of increasingly overlapping open republican and anti-republican Hindenburg worship.[26] Whilst the right had to stomach a series of disappointments, especially in the realm of foreign policy, Hindenburg still sided with them particularly when it came to political symbolism. Republicans, on the other hand, were so positively surprised by Hindenburg's constitutional stance that they were willing to forgive him what seemed like no more than anti-republican glitches. As

Ferdinand Friedensburg, himself a critic of Hindenburg's character, noted about republican attitudes in the mid-1920s:

> The legendary figure of the old military commander had such allure that even otherwise clearly democratically inclined people were not capable of reasoned judgement. They believed that they were dealing with a man of perhaps limited intellectual strength, but whose character...guaranteed selflessness, loyalty and honesty in simple clarity and steadfastness.[27]

## 2  October 1927—Hindenburg's eightieth birthday

No other event during his first term exemplified the popular scope of Hindenburg worship as clearly as the public celebrations and eulogies on 2 October 1927, Hindenburg's eightieth birthday. 'We honour ourselves when we honour him. His personality embodies our national aspirations and holy will,' wrote the mouthpiece of German big business, *Berliner Börsen-Zeitung*.[28] Former Reich Chancellor Hans Luther extolled the same sentiment in a special tribute issue of *Die Woche*:

> A people needs times for rejoicing. Even those whom fate has struck with the death of the bread-winner, with losing their work, with the obliteration of their savings through war and inflation also long for a little bit of joy. ...And a people needs to have faith in itself...And now one can say that the German people has found itself again in Hindenburg's name.[29]

In 1927, just as he had done in wartime, Hindenburg appeared as the embodiment of Germany itself.

Similar sentiments could be found in the journal of the Reichszentrale für Heimatdienst (RfH), the government's press and education department.[30] The October issue of *Der Heimatdienst* was adorned with a printed wood-carving of Hindenburg's chiselled and rectangular head and included articles by various public figures from different sides of the political spectrum— Hindenburg's opponent of 1925 Centre Party Chancellor Wilhelm Marx, Tannenberg memorial architect Johannes Krüger, the DVP's ex-presidential candidate Karl Jarres, and SPD politician Gustav Noske among them.[31]

Noske, who, as a member of the Council of the People's Repres-entatives and Secretary of Defence from 1919 to 1920, had acquired notoriety for his role in suppressing the radical left-wing uprisings after the revolution, took a line that differed from Luther's praise but was no less hagiographic. The extent of Hindenburg's personal contribution to Tannenberg had never been an important issue for Social Democrats, Noske explained. From the SPD's viewpoint, Hindenburg's decision to stay in office after the revolution was at least as laudable as his role at Tannenberg:

> It was merely a gesture and yet served as an imperturbable dam that restrained and held back the floods which could otherwise have had a devastating effect...Hindenburg at the head of the Supreme Command of the army flooding home was for officers and men, and no less for millions of people at home, a reassurance whose importance cannot be measured...Even if his function was only that of a towering symbol, his decision to stay in office remains a deed of great impact, facilitating the quiet development of things.

Noske's take on Hindenburg's role differed substantially from right-wing—or even bourgeois republican—eulogies. Instead of arguing that the General had saved Germany in 1914, he emphasized the positive function his myth had performed in German politics. For Noske, who belonged to the SPD's right wing, Hindenburg's symbolic role as an 'imperturbable dam' after the revolution and armistice was the true substance of his historical greatness. He had prevented chaos and facilitated the return to tranquillity—Noske's major preoccupation in 1918/19.[32] The SPD politician thus uncovered a layer of the Hindenburg myth that was essentially Social Democratic—and spelt out its function in no uncertain terms. This tribute, published in an official government periodical alongside bourgeois praise of Hindenburg clearly reflects the polyvalence of the Hindenburg myth in 1927.[33] Far from being a clear-cut icon of Weimar's anti-republican right, the President appealed to a much broader political base—and had done so at various moments since 1914.

Hindenburg's alleged non-partisanship and popular appeal, mirrored in the press eulogies, were also on display during the public birthday celebrations. The scale and layout of the festivities, which the presidential bureau and the Chancellery (then under Marx's leadership) planned in meticulous detail, were intended to turn 2 October into a popular holiday. The participation of 'ordinary' citizens was key.[34]

The main events of 2 October evolved around a giant festival in the sports stadium in Berlin's Grunewald district. The 8 km route leading from the Presidential Palais to the stadium, along which Hindenburg was driven in an open car, was lined with members of (first and foremost nationalist) organizations that Berlin police had given special permission to participate. No fewer than 200,000 people watched and cheered Hindenburg's motorcade on its way to and from the stadium. The Kyffhäuser League alone sent a delegation of 80,000–100,000 war veterans.[35]

In contrast to the inaugural festivities of May 1925, when police regulations had been far more restrictive for fear of violent clashes, participants were now allowed to carry musical instruments and flags. The marching bands with their colourful banners remained in the streets long after the motorcade had gone and blared out military music and songs such as the specially composed *Hindenburglied*.[36] The popular scope and audience involvement on 2 October differed equally from the monarchical splendour of Wilhelmine ritual and the pragmatic, unemotional style of Ebert's public appearances.[37] Reich Chancellor Marx, who joined the President in his car on the day, described the experience as among the most beautiful of his Chancellorship. Years later he would still remember vividly the 'hurricane of cries' and reminisce about how they had been overwhelmed by all the flowers thrown at them. Hindenburg and Marx, the former political rivals, even shared jokes about the corpulent women who had thrown their bouquets with exceptional fervour.[38]

Only one thousand adult guests were invited to attend the official celebration at the sports stadium. Instead, 40,000 schoolchildren—about 5,000 of whom were members of various choirs and arranged themselves in symmetric formations at the centre—made up the crowd. The stonemason Otto Hitzberger and the Werkbund's Bruno Paul were in charge of the stadium's decorations. Paul was familiar with the Hindenburg iconography as he had designed a Hindenburg war loan poster in 1917. Hitzberger, in his turn, would be asked to design the President's coffin in 1934.[39] As we can see, some of the same people were in charge of shaping visual manifestations of the Hindenburg myth from *Kaiserreich* to 'Third Reich', creating a comforting visual continuity.

The children who attended on 2 October had all applied voluntarily. Berlin's police actually received twice as many applications from across Germany as the number the stadium could legally hold: 80,000 in total.[40] The young were not motivated by the prospect of time off school; 2 October 1927 was, in fact, a Sunday. Celebrations were also staged in schools on the Friday before or the Monday after the event, providing ample opportunity to pay tribute to Hindenburg.[41] But given the portrayal of Hindenburg's heroic character in contemporary school classes, many young

Fig. 6. Hindenburg during the celebration of his eightieth birthday at Berlin's sport stadium (1927).

Germans were eager to attend. While the dynastic emphasis characteristic of Wilhelmine history teaching was slowly disappearing from Weimar's school textbooks, there was still an overwhelming focus on the role of 'great men', often entering the realm of personality cult.[42] The official government guidelines on the composition of history school textbooks, in fact, actively encouraged hero worship as a pedagogical ideal both in elementary and secondary schools.[43]

Hindenburg featured more prominently in Weimar school textbooks than almost any other historical figure, rivalled perhaps only by Bismarck.[44] Accounts of the First World War did not centre on the Supreme Warlord, Wilhelm II, but often revolved around Hindenburg's actions at Tannenberg and his leadership after 1916. Some books were explicitly based on Hindenburg's tendentious memoirs.[45] Arnold Reimann's *Heldenbuch*, used in German secondary schools from the mid-1920s, constructed its entire chapter on the First World War around Hindenburg's wartime heroism. He appeared as 'the saviour' and the 'nation's hope', whose final victory was thwarted by domestic conspiracy and treason.[46] During the war, German pupils learned, Hindenburg had

> floated above the ensemble ['dem Ganzen'], he was above the confusing impressions of the day; he set the goals, considered, permitted and quashed, improved and amended, balanced . . . His name resounded throughout the land[47]

—an account that also sat neatly with Hindenburg's presidential role since 1925. The widely-taught book by the pro-republican author Franz Schnabel equally labelled Hindenburg 'the liberator' who deserved praise for his accomplishments as a strategist and reminded school children of alleged Russian atrocities in 1914.[48]

The celebrations of 2 October 1927 were limited neither to young Germany nor to Berlin, however. The events in the Berlin stadium were also broadcast on the radio. A newspaper from Königsberg reported that the speeches and songs had sounded so overwhelming 'in one's own home that one was swept along by the enthusiasm gripping the thousand-strong mass hundreds of kilometres away like an electric shock'.[49] But far from simply staying glued to the radio, particularly bourgeois Germans participated in festivities to a degree not seen again in German provinces until 1933.[50] Large-scale celebrations were staged in numerous German stadiums and countless towns witnessed torchlight processions in the evening of 1 or

2 October.[51] In Düsseldorf 30,000 people visited the local sports arena above which fireworks drew Hindenburg's iconic head in the sky.[52] In addition, the German National Committee for Physical Exercise hosted so-called 'Hindenburg Games', allowing ordinary Germans across the country to pay tribute during 'Hindenburg Regattas' or 'Hindenburg Runs'.[53] In the northern German town of Rothenburg, local gymnasts assembled themselves in large human pyramids, upon which they hung photographs of the President.[54] The games were a tremendous success, with over 51,000 'Hindenburg certificates' and 29,200 Hindenburg pictures being awarded as prizes for participants across Germany.[55]

The extensive festivities and competitions surrounding 2 October were complemented by yet another large-scale event. Just as the seventieth birthday had been used to promote subscription to the war loan, so a 'Hindenburg Donation' accompanied Hindenburg's eightieth birthday. Giving money was once more phrased in emotive terms: Hindenburg deserved the population's gratitude and asked for a financial contribution as a 'birthday present' for German war veterans and widows.[56] In an appeal that could just as well have been published in 1917, the DNVP called on the German people to prove that they were 'worthy of Hindenburg' by giving generously.[57]

The presidential bureau stressed the non-partisan nature and apolitical character of the enterprise relentlessly—no doubt in order to bolster Hindenburg's cross-party appeal and mythical standing, of which impartiality was a key ingredient. Loebell had originally come up with the idea—probably with the 'Bismarck Donation' of 1885 in mind as a role model—but Meissner quickly made the plan his own and used it to reject other offers of 'expensive and raucous celebrations, which can easily take on a political character'.[58] The funding drive was a perfect opportunity to portray the President as a charitable and modest head of state, who was not keen on standing in the limelight.

Oskar Karstedt, in charge of the donation, ensured that different political parties issued their respective appeals on the same day and managed to win the support of rival veterans' organizations, among them the right-wing—and anti-Semitic—Stahlhelm as well as the Reichsbund jüdischer Frontsoldaten.[59] Raising 7.1 million Reichsmark, the bulk of which had come from German big business and industry, the Hindenburg Donation was no overwhelming success. Straightened economic circumstances along with that summer's flood disaster in East Germany limited its impact.

Furthermore, the 'League for the Construction of the Tannenberg Memorial' had raised funds at the same time, as had the so-called *Hindenburg Dank*, a right-wing drive to collect money for the purchase of Hindenburg's family estate in Neudeck, East Prussia, which had provided competition. And yet, 'ordinary Germans' contributed 13% of the sum in small donations.[60]

There was also no escaping the campaign in the weeks and months leading up to 2 October. The donation was promoted in the papers, in cinemas, and on the radio, and 200,000 illustrated posters were put around the country.[61] Street vendors sold 160,000 copies of an illustrated Hindenburg book on behalf of the campaign.[62] Furthermore, commercial publishers and entrepreneurs cashed in on the charitable spirit to get rid of the remainder of their stocks of Hindenburg products, pretending to donate a share of their profits.[63] In October 1927, Germany was thus flooded with Hindenburg's iconic image and numerous Hindenburg-related products on a scale comparable perhaps only to his visual ubiquity in wartime.

Despite the stage-management of the festivities' bipartisan veneer, however, the extent to which they truly rested on popular unity is questionable. On the one hand, 2 October 1927 was a rare moment of political cohesion—both the right and the moderate left willingly displayed their admiration for the same public figure. The *Berliner Börsen-Zeitung*, for instance, was convinced that the crowds of 2 October were representative of Germany's 'masses' and that no individual political or social group had dominated—a striking observation given Weimar's political and social fragmentation.[64] Other observers, however, looked beyond such surface impressions and noted evidence of Germany's polarized political culture. In the wealthier neighbourhoods of west and south west Berlin, for instance, the Imperial German flag was the most visible on 2 October. In the working-class districts of north and east Berlin, by contrast, left-wingers voiced their disapproval of the celebrations by raising red flags. Only on public buildings in the centre of the capital did the republican colours really dominate—a clear sign of people's differing allegiances.[65]

Count Rüdiger von der Goltz, the radical nationalist leader of the VVV, also noted the political division along symbolic lines in his essay 'Reverberations of the Hindenburg Days'.[66] He had been pleasantly surprised by the nature and scope of the official celebrations and yet, he claimed, the appearance of unity had been misleading, because '[t]he urban landscape showed the split among our people'. According to the anti-Semite Goltz, the names of private citizens raising the colours of Weimar usually gave away their 'un-German parentage'. 'Two Germanies', Goltz concluded. 'One must not delude oneself. And the third, Red Germany, had not raised any flags at all. Three Germanies.' As such spiteful commentaries show, the 'Hindenburg Donation' may have included Jewish veterans, but the nationalist right had certainly not altered its views about them.

Nor were Goltz's observations about the passivity of 'Red Germany' entirely accurate. Communists and left-wing Social Democrats in fact used the occasion to attack Hindenburg and his republican eulogists. Celebrations were inappropriate, Paul Levi argued, because one should rather pay tribute to war widows and orphans. 'And no joyful hymns sound from the chambers of those left behind or from the graves of the dead', he remarked.[67] Hindenburg's dictum that the war 'suited him like a health spa' was invoked particularly frequently by the far left to expose the President's inhuman aloofness.[68]

Communist activists also voiced their dissent in the streets. Although counter-demonstrations had not been given police permission, the KPD and its veterans' league planned elaborate agitprop stunts for the 'Hindenburg Days' in Berlin. They distributed leaflets, hosted 'comrade evenings' with speeches and discussions, and urged party members to raise banners in public places to create 'Anti-Hindenburg-Razzmatazz'.[69] More original agitprop acts appropriated the style of bourgeois Hindenburg worship—'flying agitprop squads' lined the festive streets with medals made of beer mats or tin cans, or held up sticks with swedes carved with letters that, put next to each other, made up anti-Hindenburg slogans such as 'Cheers to Hindenburg, Hold out, Shut up'.[70] Moreover, many Communist slogans and leaflets were sarcastically phrased as if in praise of Hindenburg. A leaflet styled as an open letter to Hindenburg at first glance congratulated the President, but then went on:

> Deeply moved, we remember the days when you sent us to the delightful spa of steel (*Stahlbadekur*). With frozen gratitude, Your Excellency, our hands, insofar as they have not been shot or mutilated, embrace yours, which under God's protection have luckily been preserved. And so we join in the general hurrah, even if it may sound a little croaky because of our tubercular lungs.[71]

Appropriating mythical rhetoric to contrast the heroic memory of the war embodied by Hindenburg with the real suffering of its victims was a powerful means of dissent, which mirrored the extent to which his myth dominated Weimar discourse. Only by resorting to quasi-mythical language themselves could radical left-wingers lay bare the—in their eyes—increasingly absurd personality cult surrounding Weimar's second President.

Even when one leaves aside the radical left, which had never subscribed to the Hindenburg myth and never would, however, the joint celebrations of republicans and anti-republicans around 2 October 1927 could not hide the fact that the wide political gulf between these groups could not be bridged. In this period of relative stabilization, the unity shown on Hindenburg's birthday was equally relative. Hindenburg's first years in office had not so much endeared the Republic to anti-republicans as they had endeared the new President to republican politicians and journalists. The President's eightieth birthday was thus a 'bogus-victory' for the Republic, but a significant success for the Hindenburg myth, whose base of support had broadened considerably since 1925.[72]

## Field Marshal vs. Reich President

Whilst republican and right-wing anti-republican devotion to Hindenburg momentarily coincided in October 1927, the following years saw the slow inversion of political fronts. In spite of their palpable disappointment with the President's constitutional stance, the nationalist right had held back open criticism during his first years in office.[73] The Pan-German leader Heinrich Claß would be the first to unravel this consensus. In 1927, the League had participated in the birthday festivities, but less than a year later, on 8 September 1928, Claß declared his opposition to Hindenburg's politics in a deliberately strongly worded speech in the Saxon town of Plauen.[74] The appointment of the Social Democrat Hermann Müller as Reich Chancellor in June had finally persuaded Claß that the time had come for the nationalist fight against the Republic to include the President. 'Everything has become worse since the day Hindenburg took office', Claß explained.[75] Many republican commentators saw the Pan-German attack as evidence that Hindenburg had indeed switched sides.[76] More moderate conservatives, on the other hand, considered it a 'regrettable' lapse.[77] The Plauen speech was a precursor for what was to become the defining strategy of right-wing anti-republican attacks on Hindenburg: the rhetorical separation of Field Marshal and Reich President.

The latter half of 1929 and the early months of 1930 were defined by public debates over the ratification of a new international treaty on the payment of German reparations agreed at The Hague in August 1929. The new agreement was based on a plan devised by the American financial expert Owen D. Young. It foresaw the payment of reparations for another 59 years, but also made provisions for an early withdrawal of French troops from the Rhineland (by June 1930), and promised to place the Reichsbank and Reichswehr back under full German control; it thus represented a revision of the Versailles Treaty and a decisive step towards full German sovereignty.[78] The right-wing parties were nevertheless outraged at the prospect of the treaty's ratification. Regarding it as a 'Treaty of Enslavement' that would subjugate future generations of Germans, the DNVP, the Nazis, the Pan-Germans, and the Stahlhelm sought a national referendum to overturn what everyone called the Young Plan.[79] The German population was called upon to vote for what they grandly named the 'Law against the Enslavement of the German People' or 'Freedom Law' in a referendum on 22 December 1929. Not only did the envisaged law entail the rejection of the Young Plan, but it also included the retraction of the war guilt clause and the liberation of all German territory still under foreign occupation, and threatened prison sentences for those politicians who signed treaties with foreign powers designed to 'enslave' the Germans.[80] The right-wing campaign was a fight against the Republic by proxy, and its real importance lay in the combined efforts of the disparate right-wing groups that rallied around a common goal for the first time.[81] The plebiscite itself was far from successful, however. Only 13.8% of voters voted in favour of the 'Freedom Law' in December 1929; over 50% would have been necessary. After stormy debates the Reichstag finally passed the treaty on 12 March 1930. Hindenburg's signature on 13 March 1930 made it legally binding.[82]

Republicans were thrilled by Hindenburg's signature. He was no longer a 'Reich President for the Rich', but had crossed the divide and sided with the poor, *Vorwärts* was convinced.[83] Other republican papers opined that the signature confirmed that Hindenburg 'hovered above the parties' and that his name was no longer a 'name of war' but a 'name of peace'.[84] Georg Bernhard's assessment in the *Vossische Zeitung*, meanwhile, clearly reflected the fact that the political configurations had changed profoundly since 1925. Opposing Hindenburg's candidacy had been a republican right, he opined, and welcoming the new President in May 1925 had been a republican duty. But expressing gratitude for Hindenburg's signature was now 'a heartfelt desire'.[85] The *Frankfurter Zeitung* went even one step further when stating that more reasonable conservative forces had rendered outstanding services to the Republic by nominating their 'best man' in 1925. 'It was good that the right and not the left won the presidential elections'.[86] This candid admission by arguably the most prestigious republican newspaper shows with striking clarity how much the Hindenburg myth crossed Weimar's deep political fault-lines—albeit without ever actually endearing his different devotees to each other.

For many of his supporters of 1925, however, his endorsement of the Young Plan was the most controversial decision of Hindenburg's presidency. His signature lay at the heart of the right-wing public debate before and after 13 March 1930 and reached a further climax when Hindenburg also signed the second treaty devised at The Hague, the so-called 'Polish Liquidation Agreement' concerning the former property of Germans on what was now Polish territory and the rights of the German minority in Poland.[87] Hindenburg released a detailed explanation for his decision, which the Reichstag subsequently voted to publicize and put up in public places in the hope that his reasons would convince even broader sections of the population of the treaty's merit. It had been a difficult decision, Hindenburg explained, but he was now convinced that the Young Plan was a significant step in the right direction. He had received many letters urging him personally 'not to blacken the military leader's name by backing the treaty', but he had learned not to think of himself and to do his duty. Now it was time for all Germans to leave their divisions behind and to unify.[88]

As a result, more moderate right-wingers, most notably the Westarp wing of the DNVP, separated their criticism of the Young Plan from their verdict on the President. The *Kreuz-Zeitung* declared that it would never accept the treaty, regardless of whether Hindenburg had signed it or not, but would refrain from attacking him personally.[89] The mouthpiece of East Elbian conservative agrarian interests, *Deutsche Tageszeitung*, followed a similar line. Whilst the paper condemned the grand coalition government for the treaty, it exonerated Hindenburg personally and was pacified by his promise to start a large-scale subsidy programme for eastern German farmers and landowners—the so-called *Osthilfe*—as compensation. Some might have preferred the President's resignation rather than see his 'historical name' tainted, but in order to bring about Germany's resurrection, the paper explained, Hindenburg was still 'indispensable'.[90]

Count Kuno von Westarp, who had resigned as leader of the DNVP's Reichstag party in December 1929 and who would leave the party for good a few months later as a result of a disagreement with Alfred Hugenberg to found the Conservative People's Party, warned that a debate on Hindenburg's acceptance of the Young Plan would ultimately develop into a debate on his general standing, too. This had to be avoided at all costs, he urged. Hindenburg did probably not really believe in the treaty, Westarp opined, but had seen no alternative after the failure of the referendum.[91]

Not all right-wing commentators let Hindenburg off so lightly, however. For some, 13 March 1930 was the breaking point. Heinrich Claß, for instance, launched his most forceful assault on the President yet. He was in the office of the Pan-German *Deutsche Zeitung* when the news of Hindenburg's signature reached him and immediately penned an article entitled 'Farewell'. He also made arrangements for the front page of the next edition to be published with a black ribbon.[92] Hindenburg's presidency had been a continuously worsening 'martyrdom' for his old admirers, Claß explained:

> We do not think that any merit is too great to be offset by guilt. This is the case ... regarding the Reich President. The admiration, the veneration and the love that the Field Marshal had earned for his unforgettable deeds ... have been called into question through his behaviour at the head of the Reich. Today, as far as Germans with an untainted national feeling are concerned, he has completely gambled away the near-inexhaustible trust in him. We will not forget the deeds of Hindenburg, the military leader ... But we have to announce that Hindenburg, the Reich President, we recognize as our political enemy ... On this note we bid farewell to the Victor of Tannenberg.[93]

The article's content and the front page's design as an obituary encapsulated the degree to which Hindenburg's mythical veneration was part of the public debate.[94] Such a retreat to fantasy would have been almost comic, if myths had not been so potent in Weimar Germany. By announcing the Pan-German farewell to the President whilst vowing not to forget Hindenburg's accomplishments as a military leader, Claß followed the rhetorical separation between Field Marshal and Reich President he had championed since 1928—albeit now much more unforgiving in his condemnation. Although this symbolic obituary exemplified a pivotal moment in radical right-wing attitudes towards Hindenburg, it would not remain the final verdict. Claß left a back door open—if Hindenburg somehow lived up to his wartime credentials again, the President could once again become the rightful bearer of his own myth. It was this discursive separation between Field Marshal and Reich President that would enable the radical right to return to the flock of Hindenburg devotees with ease once he had appointed the Papen cabinet in June 1932. And it is against the background of this rhetorical ploy that the inversion of political fronts between 1925 and 1932 has to be understood. Although nationalist Germans may have come close, they did not bid farewell to the Hindenburg myth irreversibly, especially not the less radical conservatives represented by Westarp. They would later be able to peel away the unwelcome layers of the narrative—Hindenburg's alleged contribution to republican consolidation in 1918/19 and after 1925 highlighted by Weimar democrats—to reveal what lay at the core in their eyes: the trusted Victor of Tannenberg who had embodied German virtues during wartime.

## Hindenburg vs. Goebbels

Towards the end of the 1920s, the Nazi party, which had gained entry into the circles of the respectable right as a result of the joint campaign against the Young Plan, began to deploy the established techniques of both left and right in dealing with the Hindenburg myth as a political force.[95] During the Nazi campaign for the 'Freedom Law', Joseph Goebbels repeatedly accused republicans of hiding behind Hindenburg's larger than life status—an accusation that republicans had also levelled at the nationalist right in 1925. According to Hitler's chief propagandist, Hindenburg's reputation was being engaged as a 'backdrop', a 'protective shield', and an 'amulet' in order to ward off criticism of the Young Plan.[96] Furthermore, he appropriated the strategy of separating Field Marshal and President deployed by Claß. On 29 December 1929, Goebbels published an article and a cartoon in his Berlin daily *Der Angriff*, which would lead Hindenburg to sue for libel. The cartoon depicted the President watching inertly while the German people were 'enslaved' for sixty years. The caption ran 'And the Saviour watches'. Under the headline 'Hindenburg, are you still alive?' Goebbels's accompanying editorial suggested that Hindenburg had died without anyone taking notice.[97] Whilst Claß's later obituary notice would symbolically bury Pan-German allegiances to Hindenburg, Goebbels insinuated that the true Hindenburg—the 'Victor of Tannenberg'—was already dead and that the republican head of state was someone else entirely.

The libel trial that followed provided an enormous—and highly wel-come—opportunity for Goebbels to generate publicity for the Nazi party.[98] At the trial in Berlin on 31 May 1930, he was sentenced to a fine of 800 Reichsmark—a far more lenient sentence than the nine months' impris-onment the Communist editor Arnim Hauswirth had been handed down for a similar offence a few years earlier.[99] Goebbels himself was given time to make extensive speeches in his defence in the courtroom. He stressed relentlessly that he had never intended to attack Hindenburg personally or to question his authority. He had not wanted to criticize Hindenburg in his capacity as Field Marshal and hero of the First World War, but had merely aimed at the President's stance towards the Young Plan.[100] His defence thus largely rested on the idea that the Reich President and the memory of the Field Marshal could be justifiably divided. Imposing a comparatively small fine, Judge Schmitz was seemingly won over by this reasoning: the verdict certified that Goebbels had been led not by dishonourable motives but patriotic concerns.[101] Naturally, the guilty party was thrilled: 'Marvellous propaganda for us . . . Victory all the way', the future Propaganda Minister noted in his diary.[102]

When Hindenburg realized that his attempt to safeguard his mythical image by suing for libel had backfired, he entered negotiations to come to a settlement that could yet yield his desired result. Hindenburg agreed to retract his complaint if Goebbels issued a statement emphasizing that he still recognized the President's historical merit. After detailed negotiations between Meissner and Goebbels's young lawyer Count Rüdiger von der Goltz, the son of the leader of the Patriotic Leagues, they reached agreement on the wording of the statement to be published in Der Angriff: Goebbels would stress that the cartoon and the article had been intended as current political criticism and that Hindenburg's wartime heroism was beyond reproach.[103] As long as his wartime credentials were left intact Hindenburg could evidently live with being affronted.

Because the state prosecutor had appealed against the verdict of 31 May, the President could not stop a second trial being scheduled for 14 August 1930. He did, however, send Goebbels a letter confirming that he personally regarded the matter as closed.[104] When Goebbels produced this letter to great surprise at the second hearing—neither the accused nor the President had notified the prosecutor or judge in advance—it was obvious he would be acquitted.[105] Hindenburg had thus aided the Nazis' chief propagandist in exploiting the trial as yet another propaganda coup.[106] Just like his manifold interventions in the cultural realm, Hindenburg's libel action had clearly been motivated by concerns over his public image.[107] His readiness to negotiate an amicable settlement and failure to inform the prosecutor of the discussions, however, meant that Goebbels's surprise coup during the second hearing—producing Hindenburg's reconciliatory letter—furthered the impression of a clear Nazi victory, which undoubtedly enhanced the party's image of respectability. Hindenburg thus prioritized protecting his wartime myth over condemning Nazi publicity methods and over not granting Goebbels unwarranted attention. Hence, the 'Hindenburg vs. Goebbels' episode is further cause to question the notion that Hindenburg did not worry about his reputation.

* * *

After the ratification of the Young Plan, the main bracket holding together the grand coalition had disappeared. Hindenburg had long sought behind closed doors to remove the SPD from government and to appoint an essentially anti-parliamentarian and anti-Marxist cabinet.[108] After Reich Chancellor Müller's fall in late March 1930, Heinrich Brüning of the Centre Party formed the first so-called 'presidential cabinet'. Without a parliamentary majority, it relied solely on Hindenburg's powers of emergency decree. The onset of the era of the presidential cabinets was a qualitative leap towards turning the Weimar Republic into a semi-authoritarian system of government.[109] Especially the events of July 1930, when Hindenburg for the first time dissolved the Reichstag after it had overturned one of his emergency decrees, made it clear that the presidential cabinet marked a new departure in constitutional terms.[110] Hindenburg had effectively wrested power from parliament.

His ever-growing political influence and increasingly open unconstitutional stance after March 1930 should have squashed the notions of Hindenburg as a guardian of democracy and protector of republicanism that bourgeois republicans and Social Democrats had conceived after 1925. But in the light of a fragmented Reichstag and a lack of political alternatives—and given that Hindenburg had sided with republicans over the Young Plan as late as March 1930—the image of an 'imperturbable dam' whose presence would prevent the collapse of the democratic state proved durable.

After the Nazi party had gained phenomenally in the Reichstag elections of September 1930, making it the second largest party with 18.3% of the vote, the SPD's fight against fascism became its top priority. To this end—and in order to maintain Otto Braun's 'Weimar coalition' in Prussia—the SPD decided not to back motions of no confidence in the Reichstag and to tolerate Brüning's government as a lesser evil. Supporting Hindenburg's re-election as a bulwark against Nazism would be a vital component of this strategy of toleration.[111]

Hindenburg's first term in office had thus witnessed profound changes in attitude among his followers and former opponents. Although he owed his victory of 1925 first and foremost to the moderate to radical right, radical right-wingers, such as Claß and Goebbels, had temporarily turned their back on the President by 1930 while republicans had begun to sing his praise. This striking inversion of fronts had not happened overnight. There was a considerable, if momentary, overlap of republican and anti-republican worship, most evident on 2 October 1927 when the festivities were carried by strong popular participation. The outward harmony on Hindenburg's eightieth birthday, however, did not strengthen the Republic for good; the unity, in fact, sounded hollow.

That the Hindenburg myth nevertheless proved polyvalent enough in this era of political polarization to attract a diverse band of followers ranging from right-wing Social Democrats like Gustav Noske to the NSDAP's Joseph Goebbels (who still claimed to believe so fervently in Hindenburg's wartime heroism) is highly significant. Only when charting the mythical narrative as a phenomenon with different layers appealing to different groups—military heroism, victory over foreign occupiers, and strong leadership on the one hand, and trustworthiness, tranquillity, and the prevention of chaos on the other—can we begin to understand its incommensurably broad and enduring appeal. The myth's multi-layered nature meant that the radical right could peel off Hindenburg's republican coating with ease once he sided more openly with their political aims from mid-1932. It would also make republicans less perceptive when it came to recognizing—and holding the President accountable for—the quiet constitutional takeover after 1930, and it would lead in no small measure to Hindenburg's re-election as the saviour of the Republic in 1932.

# 7

# The 'inverted fronts' of 1932

In the spring of 1931, Heinrich Claß made a striking prediction about the political configurations of a future presidential contest. Compared to 1925, Germans would witness 'inverted fronts... —a truly harrowing and deeply painful chapter of German tragedy'.[1]

The events of the following spring vindicated the Pan-German leader's judgement. The two rounds of Weimar's second presidential elections of 13 March and 10 April 1932 were indeed fought with 'inverted fronts'. The SPD, the Centre Party, and the Deutsche Staatspartei (the DDP's successor organization)—Hindenburg' opponents in 1925—joined ranks to bring about his re-election. Neither the leadership of the DNVP, nor that of the Stahlhelm, the Pan-Germans, the National Rural League (Reichslandbund), Germany's largest and most influential agrarian interest organization, nor the Patriotic Leagues—all chief campaigners for Hindenburg in 1925—backed his nomination.[2] Only two noteworthy parties, BVP and DVP, backed Hindenburg both in 1925 and 1932. The small Hanoverians, the WP, and the Young German Order, which had already campaigned for Hindenburg seven years earlier, also did so again in 1932.[3] In addition, the right-wing Protestant party Christian Social People's Service, composed of former German Nationals who had split from the DNVP when Hugenberg took over, campaigned fervently on his behalf.[4]

At first glance, the results of 13 March and 10 April 1932 were clear: Hindenburg beat Hitler decisively in both rounds. On 13 March, Hindenburg even came close to gaining the overall majority necessary for an early victory. Although the turnout was slightly lower in the second round, Hindenburg increased his votes by more than 700,000—most of these seem to have come from the Stahlhelm's second-in-line Theodor Duesterberg, who withdrew from the race after the first ballot.[5] Whilst a considerable number of Duesterberg supporters abstained in the second round, the

Table 2: The election results of 13 March and 10 April 1932

|                | 1st Ballot (13 March 1932) |          | 2nd Ballot (10 April 1932) |          |
| -------------- | -------------------------- | -------- | -------------------------- | -------- |
| Ballots cast   | 37,648,317                 |          | 36,490,761                 |          |
| Turnout        | 86.2%                      |          | 83.5%                      |          |
| Hindenburg     | 18,651,497                 | (49.5%)  | 19,359,983                 | (53.0%)  |
| Hitler         | 11,339,446                 | (30.1%)  | 13,418,547                 | (36.8%)  |
| Thälmann       | 4,983,341                  | (13.2%)  | 3,706,759                  | (10.2%)  |
| Duesterberg    | 2,557,729                  | (6.8%)   | –                          | –        |
| Winter         | 111,423                    | (0.3%)   | –                          | –        |

*Source*: Falter, Jürgen W. et al. (eds.), *Wahlen und Abstimmungen in der Weimarer Republik: Materialien zum Wahlverhalten 1919–1933* (Munich, 1986), 46.

majority—roughly 1.5 million—backed Hitler.[6] The Nazi leader was, in fact, able to increase his votes by more than 2 million between the first and second ballot. The remaining 600,000–700,000 or so additional Hitler votes came from disaffected KPD supporters.[7]

Supporters of the SPD, the Catholic Centre, and the BVP voted for Hindenburg in record numbers. Hindenburg won an absolute majority in southern Germany, in Westphalia, and in the Rhineland. Proportionately, he fared best in Lower Bavaria: 72.3% voted for him there.[8] In Protestant, predominantly agrarian areas where Hindenburg had been strongest in 1925, Hitler was disproportionately successful and Hindenburg gained less than average results. Women, furthermore, voted for Hindenburg in even greater proportions in 1932 than they had done in 1925. On 13 March only 44.2% of men, but 51.6% of women backed the serving President; on 10 April these figures rose to 48.7% and 56% respectively.[9] This distribution of votes along gender lines can partly be explained by the fact that Catholic women tended to follow the official party line of BVP and Centre more obediently than men, but it is also likely that within the nationalist bourgeoisie Hindenburg fared better among women, who were repelled by Nazi violence and who feared a new war in the event of a Hitler victory.[10]

Although the Nazis did not win, their 30.1% of 13 March and 36.8% of 10 April represented significant increases from their 18.3% in the previous national election.[11] Moreover, according to the most recent statistics, half of the 14.7 million Germans who had voted for Hindenburg in 1925 voted for Hitler in March 1932.[12] Assuming that all of Duesterberg's 2.5 million voters of 13 March had voted for Hindenburg in 1925, less than a third of those who had once voted for Hindenburg did so again in the first round in 1932.[13] Considering that the SPD, Centre, BVP, and Staatspartei had jointly polled only 15 million in the previous Reichstag election, however, Hindenburg's victory cannot have been entirely the result of support from his one-time democratic opponents. In the northern German constituency of Mecklenburg-Strelitz, where local elections took place on the same day as the presidential contest, for instance, many of those who voted for Hindenburg cast their ballots for the NSDAP or the DNVP in the local contest, suggesting that far from all supporters of these parties were immune to Hindenburg's appeal.[14] All in all, at least 3.5 million of Hindenburg's votes of 13 March must have come from first-time voters, from the moderate right, or more loyal long-term followers. On 10 April they even amounted to over 4 million.[15]

Nevertheless, a 'reversal of voter coalitions' took place between 1925 and 1932—Hindenburg's one-time supporters now made up the core of the Nazis' following.[16] Apart from establishing these raw electoral statistics, however, the 1932 presidential elections—and especially the pro-Hindenburg campaigns—have received surprisingly scant attention. The events are usually treated as an episode in the Nazis' rise to power.[17] The historiographical focus has been on the Nazi propaganda campaign, the split between Hugenberg and Hitler,[18] and the breakthrough of the 'Führer cult'.[19] Scholarship on the Hindenburg campaign has focused either on Hindenburg's relationship with Brüning[20] or on the organizational structure of the Hindenburg campaign.[21] Its style and content, on the other hand, have not been analysed in any further depth.[22] A closer look at the campaign, however, is important to sketch what motivated voters' choices in the early spring of 1932—a notoriously difficult endeavour for want of opinion polls. The fact that so many of Hindenburg's former supporters defected can all too easily lead to the conclusion that his myth was dead in 1932, that it 'sounded hollow' or had to be re-created from scratch.[23] Had republicans, especially the SPD, supported the serving President only as the 'lesser of two evils' and had the right thoroughly turned against him, one would have expected a complete absence of mythical rhetoric from the campaign.[24] Strikingly, however, the Hindenburg myth was not only at the heart of the pro-Hindenburg campaign but also a central feature of the debates raging within the nationalist organizations, a fact which merits a re-examination of notions of clear-cut republican pragmatism and whole-hearted nationalist disaffection in 1932.[25]

# The genesis of Hindenburg's second candidacy

Hindenburg's seven-year term was due to end in April 1932. The possibility of adjourning the election and granting him a second term or appointing him for life by parliamentary vote had been debated since the previous year. The discussion was nudged by moderate conservatives, such as Artur Mahraun of the Young German Order and Count Kuno von Westarp.[26] Keen on avoiding a bitter electoral contest at a time of economic crisis—in February 1932, a record number of 6.1 million Germans were unemployed[27]—and near civil war, Centre Party Chancellor Brüning, whose party had nominated Wilhelm Marx in the 1925 elections, but whose government Hindenburg had supported with emergency decrees since 1930, made the plan of appointing the aged President for life his own.[28] Hindenburg had declared in early January that he would only tolerate communist opposition and expected an election committee as far to the right as possible.[29] Alfred Hugenberg and Adolf Hitler, the self-proclaimed leaders of the 'national opposition'—whose support was crucial to the success of Brüning's endeavour—however, were reluctant to co-operate with the Chancellor.[30] They had been bent on bringing his government down for some time. On 11 and 12 January 1932 respectively they informed him of their final denial of support.[31] An election had now become unavoidable.

The cross-bench mayor of Berlin, Heinrich Sahm, had begun to put together a supra-party re-election committee in January and, after receiving the official go-ahead, set a press campaign in motion.[32] Because Hindenburg would not agree to being nominated by a political party, he needed the signatures of 20,000 eligible voters to secure his nomination. Sahm urged all newspapers to display official lists people could sign in their salesrooms in early February. The appeal mobilized considerable public support—three million signatures in just four days.[33] In a separate move, Westarp convinced 430 prominent conservative figures—many of them retired officers, civil servants, theologians, and business leaders—who had backed the Field Marshal in 1925 to sign a statement of renewed support.[34] Despite the republican parties' leading role in promoting the re-election, the appearance of a supra-party candidacy—vital to Hindenburg's agreeing to run—was therefore upheld. To reinforce this message of non-partisanship, the Sahm Committee was dissolved. In its stead the 'United Hindenburg Committees' took up their headquarters at Berlin's upmarket Hotel Continental under the chairmanship of the industrialist Carl Duisberg, a man with an impeccable conservative record; Sahm moved to the background and, to keep nationalist voters on side, the SPD was encouraged to 'march separately' during the campaign.[35]

On 15 February 1932, with all prerequisites for a supra-party campaign in place, the 84-year-old President decided that he was willing to face the public vote on 13 March. In the vein of his long-term rhetoric highlighting his commitment to dutiful service, Hindenburg announced the next day that it would have been irresponsible to 'leave his post' at a difficult time. He considered running his 'patriotic duty'.[36]

## 'The most loyal opposition'

Whilst republicans and moderate conservatives rallied around the President, his decision to stand was deeply controversial among many of his former voters. Naturally, Hindenburg was disappointed with their defection. His son Oskar and Otto Meissner helped him to draft a statement he sent to some of his old acquaintances who had voiced unease about his candidacy, among them retired war hero August von Mackensen and General Karl von Einem.[37] Hindenburg accused the Nazis of attempted blackmail and insisted that he was not the SPD's candidate. He also expressed his disappointment with the Stahlhelm in no uncertain terms. The organization's behaviour had nothing to do with his personal understanding of 'loyalty', he complained bitterly. Styling himself as a martyr in the vein of Jesus, he declared melodramatically that he would prefer 'the Passion of personal attacks' to forcing Germany down the 'Passion of civil war'.[38]

In response to this explanation, Einem urged Hindenburg to understand the Stahlhelm's campaign for Duesterberg as an expression of the 'most loyal opposition' ('allertreueste Opposition'), a 'tragic duty of conscience'.[39] This ambiguous stance towards their revered hero of Tannenberg was emblematic for many of Hindenburg's former followers. Unable to support the President, a result of his sanctioning of Brüning's politics and his co-operation with the treacherous 'November criminals' of the SPD, they ran a rival candidate. But they still felt a deep-seated sense of loyalty towards the 'Victor of Tannenberg', which was not easily destructible.

Those representatives of nationalist organizations who chose to support Hindenburg often faced heated reactions from ordinary members. Friedrich von Berg, Wilhelm II's last Chief of the Civil Cabinet, who had issued a public statement of support for Hindenburg, was forced to resign after 12 years as leader of the Deutsche Adelsgenossenschaft (DAG) following extensive internal protests against his decision.[40] Other members of the 17,000-strong organization had sided with Berg. In East Prussia, several women's organizations affiliated with the DAG and the DNVP signed a pro-Hindenburg appeal in defiance of their male counterparts.[41] The nomination was similarly controversial within the bourgeois conservative DVP. Although it avoided open co-operation with the SPD, some local leaders and many ordinary members left the already-weakened party as a consequence of its pro-Hindenburg stance.[42]

Within Germany's largest veterans' organization, the Kyffhäuser League, responses were particularly impassioned.[43] Its leader, the retired General Rudolf von Horn, had issued a public statement of support for Hindenburg in the organization's newspaper. Whilst insisting on the League's 'apolitical' character, Horn concluded with a clear pro-Hindenburg appeal: 'Let us old soldiers place in our revered honorary president the trust he deserves and display the loyalty he has shown us. Let us not abandon our Hindenburg!'[44]

Following a heated internal debate, Horn was forced to clarify his stance soon afterwards. The President had demanded to know whether the old soldiers would remain loyal to him, and giving such a pledge of loyalty was self-evident, he argued. Horn did not believe in the merit of the 'most loyal opposition'. It was impossible to pledge loyalty on the one hand and to support another candidate on the other, he declared in a leaflet distributed to all members.[45]

Horn's explanations did not manage to appease all veterans. Over several weeks he had to endure harsh personal attacks and was eventually forced to give up his post.[46] Many of the League's members had written to him or bombarded their local veterans' organizations with letters and phone calls as soon as the first rumours of a pro-Hindenburg appeal appeared in the press. Many resigned.[47] Whilst some simply bemoaned procedural technicalities, many letter writers reflected on their feelings for Hindenburg. These avowals of support and dissent are important sources to understand what motivated right-wing voters in 1932.[48] Tackling the complicated issue of loyalty towards Germany's most venerated war hero, one Dr Gruhl from Dresden opined: 'Loyalty is purely an emotional feeling, which is no good as a basis for politics', and a retired Captain Lieutenant from Falkenau complained that Hindenburg had committed a 'breach of trust' by co-operating with the left.[49] Berlin-based Kurt Zoepke went further when invoking the spectre of alleged left-wing treason in 1918/19 in accusing Horn of having 'stabbed the national front in the back'.[50]

For many veterans, taking a stance against the mythical Hindenburg was not as straightforward, however.[51] They often reverted to separating the 'Field Marshal' and 'Reich President'—thereby appropriating a technique championed by Claß and Goebbels since the late 1920s, a technique which also lay at the heart of the right-wing campaigns in 1932. A veteran from Heidelberg explained that although he had taken part in the celebrations of Hindenburg's eightieth birthday in Berlin in 1927 and had campaigned at numerous pro-Hindenburg rallies in 1925, he was convinced that the President did not represent the veterans' interests. Field Marshal Hindenburg was the Kyffhäuser League's honorary President, not Reich President Hindenburg, he argued.[52] In the same vein, another veteran from Berlin wrote:

> As an old front fighter who faced the bullets at Tannenberg and in other battles I tell you this, and I do not stand alone: 'Respect for the character of Field Marshal von Hindenburg, but not a single vote for Reich President von Hindenburg!'[53]

Horst Vollmers from Berlin had even stronger qualms. 'Deep in his soul' he 'thoroughly regretted' not being able to remain loyal to 'the man who saved our German Fatherland from the Russians during the war'. He had always admired Hindenburg, but the President had now deserted him.[54]

Paul Puls from Western Prignitz was more forthcoming in his praise for chairman Horn. 'It is our holy duty not to let our Hindenburg down', he wrote and attached a text hailing the Reich President as the 'leader now and forever'.[55] A retired officer from Bavaria was equally supportive. He had spoken to numerous of his Bavarian comrades, most of whom had expressed their regret at the failure of the German officer corps and the old soldiers to unite behind their Field Marshal. Hindenburg was generally regarded very favourably in Southern Germany, he reported.[56] Ordinary members of the Kyffhäuser, in fact, reacted strongly not only to Horn's support for Hindenburg, but also voiced their disapproval of hostility towards Horn. Some members still utterly devoted to Hindenburg even chose to resign from the League.[57] Joachim Tiburtius from Berlin, for instance, accused the rival Stahlhelm of betrayal. Hindenburg had been loyal to the organization and had protected it against many attacks for seven years, an expression of loyalty now repaid by running a rival candidate, he opined.[58]

Some of the reactions to a speech Hindenburg broadcast on national radio on 10 March 1932, outlining his reasons for running again and urging all Germans to unite, equally reflect the resonance his myth still had among many of his ordinary followers. Kurt Hilbert, a teacher from a small village near Halle, reported how he and twenty or so of his neighbours had gathered in his living room to listen to the wireless; it had been a true 'happening' in their eyes, he wrote in a letter to Hindenburg immediately after the broadcast. There was still such a thing as 'German loyalty', he assured the President, and promised that all listeners of that evening would remain faithful to him just as he had been faithful to them all this time. People in remote villages were grateful for Hindenburg's 'sacrifices', Hilbert pledged. The whole event so moved him that he had to cancel his plans for the rest of the evening.[59] Hindenburg's speech had a similarly strong effect on Ellinor Elbertshagen from Berlin. She also sent a letter that same night. She described how she had been sitting in front of a picture of Hindenburg whilst listening to his speech, condemning those parts of the German people she felt had brought shame on themselves for breaching their loyalty to the President. She in her turn would always remain loyal to Hindenburg, she pledged. 'Hindenburg remains Germany's saviour', Elbertshagen wrote and, putting the quasi-religious aspect of her devotion onto paper—thereby echoing Hindenburg's own references to his martyrdom—went on: '2,000 years ago the saviour was also crucified, but he still succeeded.'[60]

As we can see, the theme of 'loyalty' was far from absent from the 1932 campaign. Hindenburg's mythical veneration still shaped perceptions to a large extent. Voting, for many, did not mean exercising a democratic right, but became an expression of loyalty or treachery. Just as a truly devout person would not question her religious beliefs in the event of a tragedy, devotees like Ellinor Elbertshagen would never have questioned Hindenburg's authority. Even those who turned their backs on Hindenburg, however, often did so reluctantly and amidst crises of conscience.

## Campaigning against Hindenburg

This double-edged stance of the 'most loyal opposition' was mirrored throughout the campaign of DNVP and Stahlhelm. Unwilling to support Hitler because of inner rivalries within the Harzburg Front, the Stahlhelm had nominated Duesterberg in the hope that his candidacy would enable the organization to tip the scales towards Hindenburg or Hitler in a likely second round.[61] The organization, however, promised a 'chivalrous fight' against Hindenburg, 'the symbol of a great and glorious past, which we wish to preserve for the future.'[62] The chief editor of the *Fränkischer Kurier*, which had supported Hindenburg in 1925 but now backed Duesterberg, invoked the 'crises of conscience' many of his readers faced in an article and in a letter to the presidential bureau:

> Do you think that the decision has been easy for even one of us...to defy our obedience to your name, whose sound we followed faithfully and blindly without regret into the drumfire of the greatest of all wars? Days of most severe internal agony lie behind us...We have only managed in the knowledge that the name Hindenburg in terms of this candidacy is separate from the Hindenburg idea. Our farewell to the Reich President is accompanied by the slogan 'Long live the Field Marshal'.[63]

Clarifying their stance towards Hindenburg—and trying to square their continued veneration with running a rival candidate—dominated the anti-Hindenburg campaigns of the nationalist organizations. The Hugenberg press and the Stahlhelm newspaper constantly stressed that the fight against the despicable 'system' was the top nationalist priority. They regretted the decision, but personal feelings of loyalty could only be of secondary concern, articles insisted.[64] The omnipresence of this theme suggests that the DNVP and Stahlhelm believed that a considerable number of Hindenburg's long-term supporters still harboured feelings of great admiration and indebtedness. In East Prussia, where feelings of gratitude towards the 'Hero of Tannenberg' were rooted deeply, the conservative *Ostpreußische Zeitung* published a front-page article entirely concerned with the meaning of 'duty' to ease its readers' conscience. The national opposition fulfilled a 'necessary duty' by rejecting Hindenburg's candidacy. Whilst honouring the 'historical figure of the Field Marshal', the article stated that Hindenburg's course (of supporting Brüning) was wrong and that people's primary duty was to the nation.[65] The press affiliated to the influential National

Rural League followed a similar line. The association admired Hindenburg as much as in 1925, an Upper Silesian paper argued, and was loyal to him as a military leader and 'German man', but unable to follow him as President.[66]

Whereas DNVP and Stahlhelm relied first and foremost on Hugenberg's press empire to promote Duesterberg's candidacy, the Nazis sought to lead Hitler to victory by other means. The party leadership hoped that Hitler would triumph over Hindenburg as early as the first round of voting.[67] Although the effectiveness of the Nazi propaganda campaign should not be exaggerated, they did launch a massive media crusade; the whole country was saturated with pamphlets, rallies, and theatrically orchestrated appearances of Nazi leaders. No fewer than 30,000 party-sponsored meetings took place throughout the Reich and 8 million Nazi leaflets were distributed.[68]

Since the presidency could only be won by a broad-based electoral breakthrough, Hindenburg's lasting veneration in the moderate right-wing constituencies in which Hitler hoped to gain ground was a crucial factor Nazi campaign strategists had to take into account. Harsh personal attacks against him were unlikely to resonate. A confidential memorandum Goebbels sent to all local party leaders in early February therefore stressed that the main thrust of the campaign should be aimed at the Weimar 'system'. At all party gatherings the presidential race was to be portrayed as an existential struggle of the German *Volk*. The joint 'bourgeois-social democratic' candidate—simply labelled as 'y' in the circular, because Hindenburg's candidacy had not been announced officially at the time it was written—was the enemy, Goebbels stated. The Nazis' fight was

> not to be directed against the personality of y, but rather against the system he represents. This system has to be fought most vigorously with all means available, whereas the personality of y should only be mentioned in the second instance.[69]

Not quite the 'most loyal opposition', but still a strikingly tame approach considering the party's traditional ruthlessness in dealing with political opponents and their attacks on Theodor Duesterberg as a 'half-Jew'.[70] Local party leaders followed the official line. Most 'Nazi speakers emphasized the NSDAP's complete admiration for Field Marshal v. Hindenburg', a police report from northern Bavaria observed.[71]

The Nazis, in fact, recycled many elements of the republican campaign of 1925 in their quest for the presidency.[72] Attacking those allegedly 'pulling the strings' behind Hindenburg's candidacy was a strategy of both the Volksblock in 1925 and the Nazis in 1932. As Goebbels noted in his diary on 24 February: 'The system is hiding behind the towering figure of the Field Marshal!'[73] Visually, this line was evident in a cartoon printed in the Nazi magazine *Die Brennnessel* in early March. The colourful full-page caricature depicted a Jew, a Bolshevik, and a capitalist playing a game of cards in a backroom shielded from the public eye by a giant mask with Hindenburg's rectangular features—the caption underneath stating 'A dishonest game behind an honest mask'. In 1925 a republican poster, in its turn, had shown right-wingers acting under the guise of a giant Hindenburg mask. Both posters identified Hindenburg's larger-than-life reputation as a political asset that covered up more sinister machinations. Implying that Hindenburg was politically innocent, both posters condemned the exploitation of his mythical status, but not his veneration itself.

His Nazi opponents also engaged with the themes of 'loyalty' and 'duty' to Hindenburg. On 18 February, Goebbels explained his own understanding of 'duty' to the readers of *Der Angriff:* 'Duty means showing the German people what a brazen game is being played with Hindenburg. Duty means using the presidential elections for a historical reckoning with the regime of 1918.'[74] Five days later he repeated this mantra even more forcefully. No one intended to deny Hindenburg's great wartime merit, but it was important to emphasize that 'The Hindenburg of Tannenberg is a different Hindenburg to the one of the Young Plan. The former deserves our greatest admiration, the latter we will challenge.'[75] And challenge he did. In a Reichstag speech of 23 February Goebbels announced that Hindenburg was praised by the 'deserters' party', the SPD. His comments sparked such outrage among republican delegates that the debate had to be suspended. The pro-Hindenburg press was equally incensed.[76] Although this was no doubt the most forceful attack on the President during the campaign, Goebbels nevertheless stressed in a letter to Groener—and also in his diary—that he had not intended to offend Hindenburg but to criticize Brüning and the SPD.[77] Generally speaking, Nazi campaigners trod a fine line between dismissing Hindenburg's political credentials and carefully aiming not to scare off those who held him in high esteem. Hitler himself was especially careful not to overstep the line.[78]

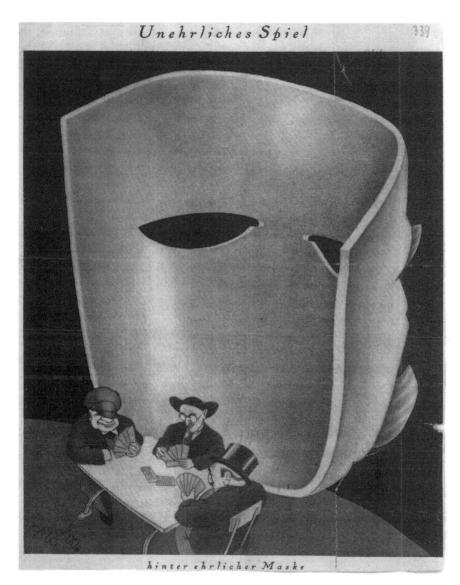

**Fig. 7.** Nazi cartoon: 'A dishonest game behind an honest mask' (1932).

The Nazi press's increasing emphasis on Hitler's experiences at the front suggests that the party's propagandists felt the need to counter Hindenburg's lasting reputation as a great military leader with an image of Hitler as an equally—or even more—heroic ordinary soldier in the hope that this would resonate with rank-and-file veterans and their families.[79] Wilhelm Weiß invoked the memory of the 'community of the front' in the *Völkischer Beobachter,* and claimed that one should respect the Field Marshal, but trust the front soldier Adolf Hitler.[80] Along similar lines, *Der Angriff* contrasted Hindenburg's Tannenberg fame with Hitler's experiences at the front. It was very convenient to invoke Tannenberg in an attempt to revive Brüning, Goebbels's daily stated. 'Not a word against the General's glory of Tannenberg, but it is no greater than the glory of the unparalleled German front soldiers.' According to Goebbels, a picture of the 'Victor of Tannenberg' could be found in a prominent place in every German parlour, but the Nazis were not to blame for the fact that the President had not been able to secure a place in the hearts of the German people, too.

> It is a fact that one cannot speak of the 'Victor of Tannenberg' when referring to the Reich President. The two concepts are a whole world apart . . . We have to leave the General of the Masurian Lakes out of it, otherwise this image, which is untouchable to us, will also be debased as emotional junk by the tabloid press.[81]

Backtracking considerably from his confrontational Reichstag speech a few days earlier, Goebbels thus salvaged the untouchable core of the Hindenburg myth while slating Hindenburg's republican role. He would not have pursued this course, had he not believed in the continued power of the mythical narrative or subscribed to it himself.[82]

Whereas the combination of attacking Hindenburg's presidential politics and praising his character overtly was a decisive feature of their campaign up to 13 March, the Nazis toned down their rhetoric even further in the second round. The emphasis was now explicitly on targeting bourgeois voters and women, who had supported Hindenburg in record numbers on the first ballot. Aggressive campaign tactics were not bound to resonate with these groups.[83] But the Nazis revised not only their campaign themes, but also their propagandistic methods, which had been fairly conventional in the first round.[84] Their defeat on 13 March, and the fact that Hindenburg had announced an 'Easter Truce' from 20 March to 3 April during which public campaigning was banned, effectively limiting the second campaign to just one week in early April, meant that they had to wage their second battle with greater force.[85] To reach as many people as possible directly, the Nazis staged Hitler's first *Deutschlandflug*—'flight over Germany'. Setting off from Munich on 3 April in a Junkers D-1720 enabled Hitler to speak at 23 mass rallies within merely seven days—compared to 12 rallies in 11 days in the first round.[86] It also provided the party press with a subject to cover extensively on a daily basis. Countering Hindenburg's long-term image as a saviour, the 'flight over Germany' and its coverage presented Hitler as a political messiah, floating above Germany just as he allegedly towered above the fray of party politics.[87]

The flight was undoubtedly a massive media event and helped to foster the Hitler cult in the long run. The Nazi presidential campaign, however, was by no means more advanced or more modern than the Hindenburg campaign. Especially the technical equipment at the Nazis' disposal was quite primitive.[88] Film played no significant role before 1933 and whilst they made extensive use of the radio after 1933—promoting a *Volksempfänger* in every home—Nazi politicians were barred from speaking on the wireless before 1933.[89] Whereas Hindenburg, Brüning, and other politicians used broadcasting quite openly as a campaign tool, Hitler was not granted access to the medium.[90] In spite of the spectacular nature of the 'flight over Germany' and the sophistication of Nazi propaganda after 1933, the presidential election campaign illustrates the fact that, in 1932, the NSDAP was not yet a propagandistic role model. Quite the reverse—the Nazis did not just generally seek inspiration in the left's propaganda, but would also copy ideas from the Hindenburg Committees in subsequent electoral contests, such as the use of loudspeaker cars.[91]

## Campaigning for Hindenburg

From the outset, the United Hindenburg Committees envisaged a highly modern campaign. A four-man working committee, consisting of the former Reich Chancellery's State Secretary Franz Kempner as well as Günther Gereke, Count Westarp, and retired Major-General Detlof von Winterfeld, was in charge of advertising for the campaign.[92] They intended not just to rely on conventional methods of voter mobilization such as posters, pamphlets, and public rallies, but also to employ the most sophisticated techniques of mass propaganda, including film and the ostentatiously apolitical radio.[93] The campaign, which altogether cost 7.5 million Reichsmark—and thus one million more than the Nazis' campaign—was financed largely from donations by prominent German industrialists, such as Carl Duisberg of the I. G. Farben, Tilo von Wilmowksy of the Krupp Empire, and Carl Friedrich von Siemens.[94]

The committee placed great emphasis on the impartial appearance of the campaign; propaganda strategists had to operate as invisibly as possible in order to project an image of a candidacy carried by the will 'of the people', Kempner wrote in a detailed memorandum on the campaign's advertising strategy.[95] He considered visual propaganda essential to Hindenburg's success: 80,000 picture posters were necessary to saturate Germany, he estimated. Additionally, a slide of Hindenburg's image was to be shown in 4–5,000 cinemas.

The actual proportions of the campaign dwarfed even Kempner's generous early estimates. In the week before 13 March, over 100,000 picture posters were put up in all parts of the country. 3 million illustrated leaflets were handed out and up to 30 airplanes dropped a further 10 million leaflets on smaller towns and villages. No fewer than 21 million leaflets had already been distributed by various means in previous weeks.[96] In Berlin, numerous advertising pillars were entirely covered with Hindenburg's image, and oversized posters featuring merely his iconic head were put up on prominently located traffic islands in the capital. Over 130 banners spanned the city's busy streets and its landmarks such as the Brandenburg Gate, which simply stated 'Vote for Hindenburg' or 'Only Hindenburg'. At night so-called miracle letters were projected onto the cloudy sky, calling on the population to cast their vote for the serving President.[97] 1,500 German cinemas showed the *Wochenschau* with moving images of Hindenburg in their daily programmes, which had been compiled by Fox and the SPD-affiliated company Emelka.[98] Furthermore, the propaganda film *Einer für Alle!* was regularly shown in over 200 cinemas throughout Germany.[99] Hindenburg's campaigners considered sound recordings of his voice and sound films especially important to counter questions concerning his frame of mind, mental ability, and physical stamina.[100] The Reich President's radio speech of 10 March 1932, in which he defied the attacks against him and stressed that his candidacy transcended party boundaries and was motivated only by his sense of duty and loyalty, was crucial in this respect.[101] In order to prevent the broadcasting of any possible slips Meissner, who took a role in the campaign so active it was irreconcilable with the duties of an 'apolitical' civil servant, made sure that Hindenburg's speech was first recorded on a gramophone record—and not broadcast live as millions of listeners were made to believe.[102]

The United Hindenburg Committees further hired 15 large cars equipped with loudspeakers and drove them through no fewer than 1,200 German towns and villages. Typically, they played a gramophone recording of a statement Hindenburg read as well as military marches. The crews handed out campaign leaflets, and carefully chosen speakers gave speeches directly catered to the local audiences from the back of their lorries.[103] According to the reports the drivers sent back to Berlin, their methods were highly effective. Within minutes of the vehicles appearing in villages, people opened their windows and quickly streamed into the streets, surrounding the cars and tearing leaflets from the crews' hands. Recordings of Hindenburg's voice proved especially effective—as soon as the gramophone record was played from the open cars even his political opponents were silenced, an allegedly average report from the campaign trail noted.[104]

The Hindenburg campaign also relied heavily on the press. Representatives of the Hindenburg Committees met regularly with newspaper editors and tried to win them over in private conversations.[105] In addition, WTB provided a *Materndienst*—a centrally run service offering ready-made articles and illustrations—free of charge.[106] Edited by Paul Steinborn, a former employee of the *Berliner Tageblatt*, this service was especially important in wooing people in the countryside and in small villages where rallies were less likely to take place and posters could not be so easily distributed. The effectiveness of this service meant that the election coverage was remarkably similar in newspapers across Germany and often emphasized events in Berlin.

To reach less educated sections of the electorate, especially those voters who did not regularly read the traditional party press, the campaign placed special emphasis on spreading Hindenburg's message in the illustrated papers. On the Sunday before the first round of voting, the Hindenburg Committees agreed a contract with many of the big publishing houses to run special Hindenburg editions with illustrated supplements. 1,187 local papers followed suit.[107] This particular ready-made page on offer from WTB was an illustrated report on a typical day for 'Hindenburg at work'. It featured pictures of the Reich President in military uniform, in civilian clothes during a morning walk with his grandchildren, and images of the traditional

Fig. 8. Photograph of a Hindenburg election car in Berlin (1932).

New Year's reception of the diplomatic corps. The accompanying text provided readers with more or less intimate knowledge—how much mail Hindenburg received every day, when he usually got up, and how much he had loved his now deceased Alsatian Rolf.[108]

Hindenburg's propagandists did not have to coin a new iconography in 1932, but could rely on the imagery employed by German propagandists and in commercial advertising since the war. Some of the same graphic designers worked for the Hindenburg campaigns of 1925 and 1932, ensuring visual continuity[109]. Just like the war loan posters of 1917 and the 'saviour' poster of 1925, the campaign posters of 1932 often featured only Hindenburg's head on a bright background with a catchy slogan such as 'Vote for our best' or 'With him'.[110] Other posters and leaflets—even those commissioned by Social Democrats—invoked the famous nailing statue of wartime Berlin. One depicted the President in monumental fashion with a military coat, his hands resting on a sword. Playing to fears of renewed hyperinflation as a consequence of the world economic crisis, the caption read 'Vote Hindenburg, the saviour of the mark.'[111] Another featured the 84-year-old as a youthful Atlas, complete with inflated muscles and loincloth.[112]

The Hindenburg Committees' Berlin headquarters also commissioned and distributed numerous brochures targeting different groups of voters.[113] For the second round, Westarp and others compiled a booklet directly aimed at former Duesterberg supporters with the title 'Hindenburg and his voters of 1925'. Only Hindenburg's candidacy cut across the social, regional, and ideological divisions that had become so deeply entrenched in Germany's national life, Westarp argued, and he praised the President's 'steadfastness and courage in the face of fire' that had served him so well at Tannenberg.[114] A brochure aimed at Catholic voters named 'To our Hindenburg' focused on the Reich President's conservative social record—images of him with his children, leaving Sunday Communion, and visiting orphans featured prominently and were intended to resonate with family-orientated Catholics.[115]

Furthermore, the propagandists stationed in Berlin distributed briefing papers for campaign speeches to local offices. Long lists provided arguments with which to counter potential Nazi lines of attack—on Hindenburg's age, on his signing of the Young Plan, his family's and employees' political affiliations, and on the Weimar parties' support for his re-election.[116] Such material frequently invoked the image of Hindenburg as a political saviour: he had freed East Prussia from the Russian threat and had liberated the

Rhineland from military occupation by means of clever diplomacy.[117] He was portrayed as the only man who could salvage Germany from otherwise certain civil war, the only German who guaranteed stability in foreign policy, and as the 'guarantor of Germany's future'.[118] Edgar Julius Jung, one of the leading young right-wing intellectuals of the 'Conservative Revolution', who had already campaigned for Hindenburg in 1925, picked up these themes in essays written during the campaign. Although of course he did not favour Hindenburg as a saviour of republicanism, he promoted him as a saviour from the 'chaos of Weimar', a 'legendary' figure who would ultimately bring about Germany's renewal.[119] Along similar lines, the Protestant nationalists of the Christian Social People's Service endorsed Hindenburg as the god-given national leader and urged their supporters to follow his calling faithfully.[120]

Reich Chancellor Brüning was especially prolific in stylizing Hindenburg as a mythical hero to whom voters owed gratitude.[121] He was a symbol of strength and unity, and every vote against him was a negation of the will to unity, Brüning argued during his speeches at the Reichstag and at other venues such as Berlin's Sportpalast and Dortmund's Westfalenhalle.[122] The DVP equally phrased its Hindenburg support in mythical language. The party's youth organization, evocatively named *Hindenburgbund* (Hindenburg League), declared that it looked up to the Reich President in admiration and would fight for him with burning hearts. Whilst emphasizing its opposition to the Brüning government, the party leadership also described Hindenburg as a national role model.[123]

Whereas the DVP, the Catholic Centre, and BVP had no reservations about casting themselves as Hindenburg's most loyal servants, the SPD press phrased much of its pro-Hindenburg campaigning in defensive and rational terms.[124] For the Social Democrats, Hindenburg was primarily the lesser of two evils, a choice necessary to guarantee the survival of Weimar democracy and to defend the republic against the fascist onslaught until the Nazis lost momentum and the economy recovered.[125] The party leadership believed that Hindenburg was the only person who could salvage the Republic.[126] In the weeks leading up to the first round of voting *Vorwärts* regularly featured bold headlines telling voters to 'Vote for Hindenburg, beat Hitler!'[127] Hammering home the point that Hindenburg was the only candidate who could accomplish this, *Vorwärts* told its readership: 'And if you don't do it out of love, do it out of hate'—hate for the 'Fascists'.[128]

The Iron Front, an anti-fascist alliance of SPD, Reichsbanner, the trade unions, associations of white-collar workers, and the Workers' Sports Organizations, also campaigned massively on Hindenburg's behalf. Since its foundation the previous December the Iron Front had been pursuing a more radical approach to political agitation than the SPD by emulating the symbolism of street politics, hitherto a domain of Nazis and Communists.[129] On 6 March 1932 the organization staged the first large-scale Hindenburg rallies across Germany. No fewer than 100,000 people attended the largest one in Berlin.[130] The diplomat and eloquent chronicler of Weimar politics, Count Harry Kessler, could not help but note his astonishment at witnessing the organization's efforts:

> Iron Front demonstration for Hindenburg in the Lustgarten. A mass of people and a forest of red flags, putting the black-red-gold colours in a distinct minority. Odd, this Red demonstration on Hindenburg's behalf. I had to think of what he said to me in 1917 in Kreuznach when David and a few other Social Democrats congratulated him on his birthday—that he was quite popular with the comrades and would soon have to acquire a red beret.[131]

Kessler's observation touched upon a key factor of the SPD's support for Hindenburg. Despite the initial reluctance of the party's left wing to vouch for him in February, the history of the SPD's co-operation with Hindenburg was, in fact, a long one.[132] His mythical initiation had rested on a defensive battle against the Social Democrats' arch-enemy, Tsarist Russia, and this, along with his co-operation during the revolution and his constitutional stance since 1925, had won over many Social Democrats. Carlo Mierendorff, for instance, a left populist and leading member of the Iron Front, was convinced that Hindenburg 'symbolized legality'.[133] As a result of such conviction, not all SPD activists resorted to entirely defensive rhetoric during the campaign. Whilst Carl Severing and Ernst Heilmann, the head of the SPD delegation in the Prussian parliament, joked privately that they could only vote for Hindenburg after downing a shot of *schnaps*, Reichstag President Paul Löbe employed language more commonly associated with nationalist Hindenburg devotees when invoking the theme of loyalty during a rally in Rostock.[134] He described Hindenburg as an upright man whose 'loyalty' over the years the Social Democrats would now repay—by voting for him in the elections.[135] This did not sound like a strictly negative consensus on the 'anti-Hitler' Hindenburg. Minister

President Otto Braun—a particularly exuberant Russophobe in 1914 and one of Hindenburg's strongest advocates in the SPD—equally opted for a more positive justification of the SPD's support for Hindenburg.[136] The Prussian politician, who was positioned on the party's right flank, did not try to hide the ideological and political differences between Hindenburg and the SPD in his *Vorwärts* article 'I vote for Hindenburg', but emphasized that the President was a man of good judgement and personally respectable and that this integrity unified the SPD with him to a large extent. Moreover, he hailed Hindenburg as the embodiment of 'continuity', of 'masculine loyalty', and 'dutiful service'. He would uphold this judgement even after 1945.[137]

Such statements show that while excluding Hitler from office was no doubt the Social Democrats' chief aim, their campaign was not conducted entirely along defensive lines, but fell back on invoking Hindenburg's mythical qualities on various occasions. Since Social Democrats had long seen in Hindenburg an 'imperturbable dam' against the forces of chaos and destruction, as Noske had phrased it in 1927, it was only a small step towards counting on him as a bulwark against Nazism. Heinrich Brüning, for one, who had to downplay his cooperation with the SPD in 1932, was convinced that the party campaigned fervently for Hindenburg's re-election as a result of their 'belief in the Hindenburg myth'.[138]

If Social Democrats were ready to resort to mythical rhetoric, this came even more naturally to the liberal bourgeoisie. Prominent left-leaning liberal journalists, such as Theodor Wolff, Julius Elbau, and Ernst Feder, employed first and foremost moral and emotional—not pragmatic—categories when discussing Hindenburg's re-election. They frequently referred to him as a 'monumental figure' and a 'symbol'.[139] Theodor Wolff, who—although he was critical of Hindenburg's conservative politics—had promoted and defended his Tannenberg glory since August 1914, again invoked the memory of the battle in glowing terms in 1932.[140] He accused the President's right-wing opponents of having committed a 'breach of loyalty', and singled out the 'abhorrent' 'apogee of ingratitude' of the East Prussian aristocracy:

> Have these gentlemen forgotten that Tannenberg is in East Prussia? Have they forgotten how, in August 1914, the East Prussian people fled from the Russian bands, how the villages burned, how the cities were bombarded, how a cry of despair went through the country, and how they themselves feared for their possessions, until Hindenburg appeared, saved East Prussia, and how, instead of a cry of despair, the gratitude to the liberator resounded?[141]

Julius Elbau, editor of the *Vossische Zeitung*, equally resorted to mythical rhetoric in an article entitled 'The Marshal of Peace'. The millions of votes cast for Hindenburg on 13 March showed the gratitude of all reasonable people for the 'deed of the leader who (...) has once again sacrificed his glory to salvage the country from civil war and self-destruction', Elbau exclaimed.[142]

This Hindenburg fervour of liberal campaigners was no aberration on their part—an inexplicable temporary clouding of their judgement by the 'banal' and 'sentimentalist' Hindenburg myth which none of their 'critical contemporaries' subscribed to.[143] These highly educated and acute republicans did not resort to the rhetoric of myth because they had lost touch with reality. Quite the reverse—because they expected their readers to respond and because they had also subscribed to layers of the mythical narrative since 1914 they invoked it effectively to promote Hindenburg's re-election. Their backing rested on belief as well as calculation.

If it had exclusively been the 'weak bracket of opposition to Hitler' that united Hindenburg's supporters in 1932, as Andreas Dorpalen, amongst others, argued, they could have chosen any other politician willing to run against the Nazi leader.[144] Only Hindenburg's public image, however, was polyvalent enough in 1932 to unite a heterogeneous political front ranging from conservative monarchists, such as Count Westarp and the young conservative intellectuals of the 'Conservative Revolution' to the Catholics of Centre and BVP, and the Social Democrats, as well as trade unionists represented in the 'Iron Front'. One person's saviour *from* Weimar might have been another's saviour *of* Weimar—but a saviour nevertheless.

\* \* \*

As a case in point, many commentators attributed Hindenburg's victory to his continued mythical veneration. With hindsight, campaign manager Günther Gereke, who would serve as Reich commissioner for job creation in Hitler's first cabinet, admitted openly to deploying the 'old Hindenburg myth' to garner electoral success.[145] The Republic had been strengthened, Hitler's 'spell' broken, and much of the Nazis' nimbus destroyed, many papers were convinced.[146] According to the DVP's *Nationalliberale Korres-pondenz* '[i]t was a victory of personality, of this great German name, of just will, and selfless service to the fatherland'.[147] With an echo of 1925, the DDP's *Demokratischer Zeitungsdienst* praised Hindenburg's victory as the 'salvation' in times of crisis and catastrophe.[148]

It was not only his supporters, however, who cited the Hindenburg myth as a reason for his victory. Carl von Ossietzky, who, sceptical of the 'lesser evil' strategy of the SPD, had backed Ernst Thälmann, equally emphasized the role of personality:[149]

> Indeed, no political thesis or programme has triumphed. Only a very famous old man has…Hindenburg has triumphed, a piece of legend, a heroic frame onto which anyone can clamp whatever colourful web of illusions he desires.[150]

Even if the future Nobel laureate underestimated the President's own role in filling this 'heroic frame', as it soon turned out, his hesitation to see in Hindenburg a vigilant and dedicated defender of the Republic was certainly justified.

The Nazi press, meanwhile, downplayed the original aim of seizing the presidency and argued that Hindenburg's victory had been a foregone conclusion. The party's gains since September 1930 were the real success, *Der Angriff* opined after the first round.[151] In the same vein, Goebbels spun the outcome of 10 April as a 'powerful victory' for Hitler and did not even mention Hindenburg in his leading article after the second ballot.[152] The Nazis had indeed achieved an important goal. The '*Führer* cult', which had hitherto been the property of a small group of die-hard supporters, achieved a breakthrough on the national stage, giving the party additional momentum for the forthcoming regional elections in Prussia and Bavaria and the Reichstag elections in July.[153]

Nevertheless, this was, above all, a symbolic success. The real victor was Hindenburg. He had been confirmed for another seven-year term, and his re-election would make him the final arbiter of Hitler. Less than a year after being elected as a bulwark against Nazism, Hindenburg would install his former rival in the Chancellery. Without the unremitting appeal of his myth in 1932, he would ultimately not have been in a position to do so.

# 8

# 'The Marshal and the Corporal . . .'

Since Brüning's formation of a presidential cabinet, orchestrated by Hindenburg and his entourage in March 1930, Germany had slowly been transformed from a parliamentary democracy into a semi-authoritarian state. Because the political parties in parliament were blocking and paralysing each other, Hindenburg was able to interpret and use his far-reaching constitutional powers extensively and rigorously. Power had thus shifted in favour of his ever-expanding authority and extra-parliamentary actors, especially the Reichswehr and bureaucracy.[1]

When Hindenburg dismissed Heinrich Brüning, his chief campaigner of the spring, in May 1932, this was in large part because of the Chancellor's failure to mobilize enough right-wing support in the presidential elections. Not least because his successor Franz von Papen could no longer count on the toleration of the SPD, Brüning's departure heralded a new phase in the dissolution of Weimar democracy.[2] The Centre Party politician Papen was considerably further to the right and sought to cement Germany's authoritarian character by means of the kind of far-reaching constitutional reforms many on the right had hoped for when Hindenburg was first elected in 1925. A significant step towards this 'new state' was achieved on 20 July 1932 when Hindenburg backed Papen's decision to dissolve the Prussian government, the last federal government comprised of the 'Weimar parties'.[3] The Social Democrat Otto Braun—who had helped to campaign for Hindenburg in the spring—was dismissed as Minister President, and Prussia was placed under executive control.[4] Hindenburg thus helped to wrest political power from those who had supported him as a guardian of parliamentary democracy a few months before. These developments did not, of course, go unnoticed among Hindenburg's democratic supporters of the spring, and initially began to sap some of the trust they had invested in him. Given the lack of political alternatives, however, republican criticism remained deliberately muted.[5]

The Reichstag elections of July 1932 made the Nazis the strongest party, with 37.4% of the vote. As a result, Hitler pursued an all-or-nothing policy, refusing to enter a cabinet unless he was made Chancellor. Hindenburg, however, declined to appoint the 'Bohemian corporal'.[6] When Hitler repeated his demands in a meeting with the President on 13 August, he was flatly rebuffed. The presidential bureau immediately published a communiqué portraying the interview as a humiliating defeat for Hitler, indicating that the President had put the Nazi leader in his place once and for all.[7] Hindenburg's reputation as a bastion against National Socialism was thus safeguarded for the time being, and the non-Nazi press overwhelmingly lauded him once more as the 'guardian of the constitution'.[8]

When Hindenburg turned 85 two months later, much of the press praised his political wisdom.[9] Only the Social Democrats felt unable to join the celebrations, because, as the *Vorwärts* explained, their long-term political opposition to Hindenburg had finally turned into 'human disappointment' after the events in Prussia in July.[10] By contrast, the *Deutsche Zeitung*, which had buried the President symbolically two years earlier now featured a framed etching of Hindenburg on its cover. Brüning's dismissal and the dissolution of the democratic government in Prussia had again endeared the President even to a radical like Claß.[11] The *Frankfurter Zeitung* meanwhile conceded that Brüning's departure had shocked many of those who had voted for Hindenburg in March and April. For most democrats this had been no reason to revise his image, however. 'The same people who reject Papen do not feel hindered from believing in Hindenburg, in spite of everything that has happened', the left-liberal daily observed. 'The people view Hindenburg as the representative of their best virtues'—simplicity, straightforwardness, and a mighty sense of duty that his 'broad-shouldered' and 'upright body' still personified.[12]

This unquestioning faith was also evident among Catholic Germans. In a joyless period of economic, political, and social crisis, the *Germania* argued, Hindenburg floated in an elevated sphere. He was 'still—and today more than ever—the refuge of the people'—a status 'not easily shaken by political activity', the paper observed.[13] Georg Schreiber, a prominent Centre Party Reichstag deputy from Westphalia, outlined this stubborn adherence to the Hindenburg myth in a brochure written soon after Brüning's dismissal.

The swiftness of the President's decision had alienated some of his voters, Schreiber admitted, but supporting the President remained the right course:

> A nation cannot afford the luxury of condemning itself to naked poverty and indefinite political disunion when it comes to recognizing its great leaders... So the name Hindenburg shall persist in its monumental greatness. We do not even think about burning what we worshipped yesterday.[14]

As we can see, for many, debunking the Hindenburg myth was not an option. His veneration clearly had its own momentum and persisted in the face of disappointment.

After their massive gains in July, the Nazis had seemingly passed their zenith in November, when they lost over two million votes in the national elections. Especially conservative middle-class Germans were repelled by Nazi violence and the socialist elements and preferred a more traditional authoritarian government.[15] The German parliamentary system, however, remained paralysed after the November elections. By the winter of 1932/33 a cabinet with a parliamentary majority had still not been formed and the Nazi leader had at least signalled his willingness to compromise regarding the composition of a possible cabinet under his leadership, so that his appointment began to look like an increasingly viable option.[16] Crucially, General Kurt von Schleicher, who had succeeded Papen in December, had not succeeded in splitting the Nazi party and forming a joint government with the Strasser wing of the NSDAP. Hindenburg and his advisers therefore increasingly believed that appointing Hitler was the only choice other than declaring a state of emergency.[17] A military dictatorship would of course not have saved German democracy at this stage, but at least it would have kept open the possibility of eventually re-establishing it. Most importantly, however, it would have avoided appointing Hitler, whose party may have lost momentum following its first setback in November.[18] Hindenburg, however, shied away from authorizing a state of emergency.[19] Instead, the President followed Papen's reasoning that even as Chancellor Hitler would be dependent on his presidential authority and could be kept in check. After much backroom politicking, Hindenburg dismissed Schleicher and, on 30 January 1933, appointed Adolf Hitler as Chancellor of Germany. In this new cabinet of 'national concentration', three Nazis were 'fenced in' by nine conservatives, but—crucially—the Nazi leader had behind him a dynamic mass party with a paramilitary wing comprising hundreds of thousands of members.[20]

Even if Hitler's appointment did not mean that Hindenburg sanctioned the type of dictatorship Nazi Germany would eventually become—not to mention the crimes committed in its name—the fact that he was not a democrat at heart and favoured Nazi rule in January 1933 was highly significant. The NSDAP had always been instinctively closer to Hindenburg than, for instance, the Social Democrats, with whom he had also cooperated—more or less reluctantly—in previous years. As much as the growing public support for the NSDAP since 1930 may have made Hitler's eventual appointment seem a foregone conclusion, the role of personality also mattered in the fall of Weimar democracy.[21]

Hindenburg had begun to dig Weimar's grave by hollowing out parliamentary democracy in the era of the presidential cabinets. Yet he—although open to including Hitler in a 'national cabinet' in a more junior role since at least the summer of 1932—had not been ready to appoint the Nazi leader as Chancellor. When that changed in January 1933, Hindenburg became an undertaker of the Republic for whose salvation many on the left and the centre had re-elected him less than a year before and whose inception his authority had helped to ease in 1918/19. That a significant number of republicans had been swayed by his allure and stubbornly clung to their beliefs even when the President had already turned his back on Weimar was a key piece of this puzzle. The Hindenburg myth was a factor in the Republic's demise that should not be underestimated.

## 30 January 1933

On 30 January 1933, the Nazis celebrated Hindenburg's 'big-hearted decision' to appoint Hitler with grand torchlight processions through central Berlin, creating enduring images of the Nazi 'seizure of power'.[22] In the evening of that Monday between 20,000 and 60,000 SA men marched past 73 Wilhelmstraße where Hindenburg watched from the first floor. The police beamed a searchlight onto his illuminated window so that the passers-by could see him observing the proceedings.[23] The scene was also filmed, and within days German cinema audiences relived the event; in the years to come the images would be recycled repeatedly in Nazi propaganda films, casting 30 January as a date of secular importance.[24]

The Nazi press highlighted Hindenburg's integral role on the day. The 'aged Field Marshal', who had appointed the 'young leader', Adolf Hitler, had 'greeted the SA pennants' on this 'historical day':

> Thousands of arms were stretched towards him, and thunderous cries of hail surged towards the walls of his palace... Hundreds of thousands of beaming eyes looked up to the illuminated windows of Wilhelmstraße where the Reich President and the new Chancellor—visibly moved—stood to receive the nation's pledge of loyalty with gratitude[25]

*Der Angriff* reported with exaggerated pathos. Hitler and Hindenburg looking out of two separate buildings was styled as a show of agreement and unity.[26]

From the outset, Nazi propagandists portrayed Hindenburg's decision to appoint the Hitler cabinet as the expression of a personal bond between the two men. Whilst engaging fervently and systematically in furthering the cult of Adolf Hitler, the Nazis never attempted to oust Hindenburg from the public stage, and Hitler himself consciously refrained from projecting his image in competition with that of Hindenburg. The polarity of these two figures—symbolized in their running against each other in the presidential elections less than a year before—was dissolved into harmonious unity after 30 January 1933.

During this first phase of Nazi rule, Nazi propaganda carefully incorporated Hindenburg into its imagery, most notably in the run-up to the parliamentary elections of 5 March.[27] In a climate of fear created by the intimidation of Communists and Social Democrats, and the unrestricted terror of the SA in the streets, the Nazis relied on several posters depicting 'The Marshal and the Corporal' together.[28] They showed sketches of Hindenburg in his Prussian Field Marshal's uniform and Hitler in brown shirt shaking hands whilst hovering above a sea of flag-bearing SA men, or cut-out photographs of Hindenburg's and Hitler's faces placed side by side, usually completed with a caption that called on the people to follow the President's example and place their trust in Hitler. Just as German companies had used Hindenburg to suggest his endorsement of a particular brand throughout the 1920s, he was now being engaged as a product tester of a different kind. The posters clearly aimed at transferring to the Nazi party some of the trust voters had previously invested in Hindenburg.

While these early posters differed in some ways considering their artistic style and imagery, they were near-identical in one important

**Fig. 9.** Nazi poster: 'Never will the Reich be destroyed if you are united and loyal' (1933).

respect: all of them showed Hindenburg to the left of Hitler and his head—or body—always as slightly elevated. Read like a text—from left to right—this clearly conveyed the notion that Hitler was Hindenburg's mythical successor and had been appointed by Hindenburg's authority. Hindenburg was also incorporated into future Nazi ceremonies so that German cinema audiences were treated to a constant flow of images of their President and Chancellor together.[29]

A week after the March elections, from which the Nazis had again emerged as the strongest party, with 43.9% of the vote, the President took part in a Volkstrauertag ceremony in Berlin's Neue Wache.[30] He appeared in military uniform whilst Hitler arrived in a long dark coat and civilian clothes. The literary scholar Victor Klemperer, who visited a cinema around this time, considered the images of the day a revelation of a kind not anticipated by Nazi propaganda.[31] As he noted in his diary—one of the most valuable records of daily life in Nazi Germany:

> Hindenburg in front of troops and SA men... When I saw him filmed about a year ago: the President... walked somewhat stiffly, but quite firmly and not at all slowly... an old but vigorous man. Today: the tiny, laborious steps of a cripple. Now I understand it all:... I am now completely certain that Hindenburg is no more than a puppet, that his hand was already being guided on 30th January.[32]

Klemperer reacted to Hitler's appointment by convincing himself that Hindenburg could not have been in his right mind, that he did not know what he was doing on 30 January 1933; guided by ill-intentioned advisers he had brought Hitler to power and was now a marionette.[33] Those in close contact with Hindenburg at this time overwhelmingly testified that—though increasingly fragile—his mental capacity did not deteriorate until shortly before his death in the summer of 1934.[34] Nevertheless, people joked that Hindenburg constantly confused his aides with Ludendorff and Hitler with Brüning, mistook the marching SA men on 30 January 1933 for Russian prisoners captured at Tannenberg, and readily signed any random piece of paper within reach.[35] These were new variations of much older interpretations of Hindenburg, which had surfaced, for instance, during the election campaigns of 1925 and 1932—of Hindenburg as a 'mask', or a 'puppet', a well-intentioned and honest old man, who was not to blame for the actions of those behind him. And just like the rumours about Hindenburg's death or illness circulating within Germany towards the end of the First World War, these political jokes mostly stopped short of vilifying the President.

At the same time and in spite of this perceived weakness, Hindenburg remained a last resort—a protective shield or lifesaver—for some of the Nazis' opponents and victims, a source of hope for resistance at the eleventh hour against the increasingly oppressive Nazi dictatorship.[36] Especially the liberal bourgeois press frequently invoked the President as the guardian of the constitutional spirit and asserted that he would never willingly break his oath.[37]

Throughout 1933 and 1934, Hindenburg's office also received numerous *Eingaben* from different organizations, many of which had campaigned for his re-election in 1932. Stressing their loyalty and veneration, figures such as Leo Löwenstein of the Jewish veterans' league Reichsbund jüdischer Frontsoldaten and Theodor Leipart of the association of German labour unions (ADGB), appealed to Hindenburg to stop the Nazi terror.[38] With the exception of his intervention to exempt Jewish war veterans from the law banning all 'non-Aryans' from the professional civil service in April 1933—a decision that should not be mistaken as evidence of his general opposition to the social exclusion of Jews—Hindenburg passed most of the other matters onto Hitler, thus helping to seal the fate of those who hoped for his protection.[39]

## The 'Day of Potsdam'

Whereas Klemperer had been disillusioned with his cinematic experience of the Volkstrauertag, Goebbels was enthused by the event he had orchestrated and—clearly warming to Hindenburg after being made Minister of Propaganda on 13 March—felt 'lucky . . . to know that this old, towering man . . . is above us'. 'Hitler and Hindenburg. Symbols of youth and of old age, which have shaken hands in these two men', he noted excitedly in his diary.[40] The scenes of 12 March were probably his source of inspiration for one of the most notorious propagandistic productions of the early years of Nazi rule—the opening of the new Reichstag after the March elections. Christened the 'Day of Potsdam' by the Nazi press, the festivities were a carefully orchestrated display of the supposed historical links between National Socialism and the Prussian past.

Because the Reichstag had been damaged in the arson attack in February, the ceremony took place at Potsdam's Garrison Church. Built during the reign of the 'Soldier King' Friedrich Wilhelm I, who was buried there along with his son, Frederick 'the Great', the church was of great symbolic significance.[41] Planned in meticulous detail by Goebbels, the ceremony was intended to 'continuously mobilize those sections of the population who had not voted for the Nazis in the March elections' and to associate Hitler's 'young Germany' with both the values of the Christian tradition and the Prusso-German military legacy.[42] Originally scheduled to take place in early April, the event was moved forward to a more symbolic date—21 March 1933, the first day of spring and the 62nd anniversary of the opening of the first German Reichstag in 1871.[43]

On the day, hundreds of thousands of visitors streamed into Potsdam, from the early hours of the morning. The whole town had been decorated with the Imperial and new swastika flags; numerous street vendors sold insignia in the new national colours, many shop owners displayed pictures of Hindenburg and Hitler in their shop windows, and banners flew across countless streets reminding passers-by of the day's official motto, the last two lines of a poem by Max von Schenkendorf written during the wars of liberation: 'Never will the *Reich* be destroyed—if you are united and loyal' ('Nimmer wird das Reich zerstöret—wenn ihr einig seid und treu').[44] After Hindenburg arrived in Potsdam his motorcade drove around the city centre and the park of Sanssouci for some time, giving masses of people the chance to catch sight of him. The *Deutsche Zeitung* conveyed the audience's sense of excitement in near-messianic terms:

> The cars are not yet in sight, but the thunderous reception is getting closer, it is becoming stronger, louder. 'Hindenburg is coming, Hindenburg is coming!' Necks are craned, nervous twitching among the masses of people. The first flags are waved, people are breathing more quickly. Then the tension is relieved like an electric shock . . . Boundless jubilations begin: 'Cheers for Hindenburg! Cheers for Hindenburg!' Again and again it resounds.[45]

When Hindenburg reached the Garrison Church, members of the SA and other nationalist organizations lined the adjacent streets. Wearing his full Field Marshal's uniform, he took their salute. Hitler, on the contrary, wore a frock coat and top hat just as he had done for the Volkstrauertag—a get-up aimed at winning over bourgeois Germany. The Nazi leader thus styled himself as the humble, obedient statesman who was to receive the great military leader's blessing.[46]

Hindenburg and Hitler were the focal point of the whole ceremony. Seated in giant armchairs below the altar, they stood up one after the other to give speeches to the gathered Reichstag delegates (with the exception of the KPD's and SPD's deputies who had been banned from the ceremony or abstained) and other official guests. The President invoked the old German values he had represented for nearly twenty years—piety, dutiful work, bravery, and patriotism—and which had allegedly defined Prussia and brought about German unification in 1871. According to Hindenburg, the new government equally represented these values.[47] Meanwhile, Hitler flaunted his newfound humility. Stressing the need for German unity on the path to resurrection, he expressed his gratitude to Hindenburg for 'blessing' the Nazi cause and acting as the 'patron of the new movement'. His blessing had 'consummated the marriage between the symbols of the old greatness and the new strength.'[48] After Hitler's speech, Hindenburg rose and entered the crypt where the Prussian Kings were buried alone, to lay wreaths at their tombs. In the words of the *Deutsche Zeitung*, this was the moment when through this 'living link' the 'great historical deeds of the two Fredericks' and the 'new Germany resurrected from darkness and deepest humiliation' 'became one'.[49]

After the wreath-laying, Hitler and Hindenburg shook hands inside the church—representing the Nazi leader's coronation and symbolizing the 'marriage' between the Prussian past and the National Socialist future, a signal not only devout Christians understood.[50] The 'Day of Potsdam' did not end there. On his way back to Berlin, Hindenburg stopped at the Palace in Charlottenburg to lay a wreath at the tomb of Wilhelm I. Jubilant crowds lined the streets along the way. When he finally reached his residence in the early afternoon, even larger crowds awaited his return.[51] The same evening, major torchlight processions were staged in the German capital and in small villages throughout the country.[52] Goebbels's ministry had done everything in its power to stimulate popular participation throughout Germany. He encouraged countless towns to host their own versions of the celebrations, including church services, torchlight processions, and jubilant bonfires, thus mobilizing considerable parts of the rural population.[53] Flags were raised on all public buildings, and all schools had to close. Shops had to shut for two hours at lunchtime to enable people to follow the extensive radio coverage.[54] Germany's national radio station would subsequently adopt the sound of the Garrison Church's bells as its new interval sign in order to keep the memory of the day alive. The UFA-Wochenschau and Deulig-Tonwoche, Germany's two newsreels, filmed the scenes and edited them at great speed; millions of German cinema-goers were thus able to witness the events of 21 March only a few days afterwards.[55] Klemperer, who visited a cinema in Dresden in late March, noted in his diary how a young soldier next to him had clapped enthusiastically whenever Hitler and Hindenburg appeared together on screen.[56] In the following weeks and months, many local communities further competed in displaying their admiration for Hindenburg and Hitler—countless trees were named after them and numerous towns conferred honorary citizenship on both men.[57]

The 'Day of Potsdam' was a great propagandistic success that convinced many more politically moderate and bourgeois Germans of the merits of Hitler's rule.[58] The ceremony's broad appeal rested on its incorporation of versatile symbols. In particular, the religious connotations of the celebrations—not just of those in Potsdam but throughout Germany—helped to endear the Nazis to a much broader coalition of social groups, first and foremost in Protestant areas, but also across Catholic Germany. The religious elements made Hitler appear as a Chancellor by grace of God, with Hindenburg acting as a kind of 'substitute bishop', who, after having appointed him in his capacity as President, now helped to bestow upon Hitler religious—and mythical—legitimacy as well.[59]

The willing participation of Hindenburg—the 'mythical memorial' as Goebbels termed him in his diary[60]—was key to making the ceremony work. The propagandistic orchestration of the 'Day of Potsdam' and its prolonged media aftermath undoubtedly helped, as Ian Kershaw put it, in 'transposing to Hitler some of the trust in Hindenburg as the embodiment of German national values'.[61] Hindenburg's public 'blessing' was integral to the Nazis, who, at this stage, had been in power for less than two months.

The ritual of national integration and inclusion staged at Potsdam was quickly followed, however, by steps towards the exclusion of those unwelcome in the new people's community.[62] The first law the Reichstag passed after Potsdam was the notorious Enabling Act, granting Hitler the power to pass laws without parliamentary approval and without having to rely on the President's powers of governing by emergency decree—thus spelling a tremendous increase in Hitler's dictatorial powers.[63] Hindenburg welcomed the Act because it lightened his workload.[64] Within just days of

'Potsdam', and with the aid of Hindenburg's mythical authority, German parliamentary democracy had thus practically ceased to exist.

## Nazifying the Hindenburg myth

The Nazis continued to include Hindenburg in their new festive calendar and to invoke his mythical authority after March 1933. He addressed Germany's youth in Berlin's Lustgarten on 1 May 1933, the 'Day of German Labour'—a newly created national holiday designed to woo workers and stress the Nazi party's Socialist credentials.[65] In August of the same year, the Nazis turned the anniversary of Hindenburg's seminal mythical moment—Tannenberg—into a powerful show of national cohesion and a condemnation of the Treaty of Versailles. On 28 August 1933, *Der Angriff* reminded its readers on its front page of 'How Hindenburg had entered the realm of world history' nineteen years earlier.[66] Furthermore, a commemoration ceremony was staged inside the Tannenberg Memorial in East Prussia on 27 August. Most high-ranking party officials and the leaders of the army and navy attended. Hindenburg, Hitler, Vice Chancellor Papen, and Hermann Göring were the last to enter the memorial through a narrow alley left open among the formations of the SA and SS.[67] The speeches by Hitler and others praised Hindenburg as a 'mythical figure' who would forever be associated with the province.[68] Taking the country's pledge of gratitude and indebtedness to new heights, Hermann Göring presented Hindenburg with the 'seigniory of Langenau and Preussenwald', which bordered on his Neudeck estate, as a 'gift of gratitude'.[69] Hindenburg—now dubbed *Der Alte vom Preussenwald*—thus once more provided a mythical link to Bismarck, one of whose many sobriquets had been *Der Alte vom Sachsenwald* after Kaiser Wilhelm I had awarded him a large stretch of territory near Hamburg.[70]

The Nazi press duly hailed the Tannenberg commemoration—and the near-simultaneous rally in support of a return of the Saarland to Germany staged at the Niederwald Memorial near Rüdesheim[71]—as a 'powerful display of a unified nation'. East and West had allegedly experienced a spirit of unity on this day—exemplified by the bond between Hindenburg and Hitler—and the experience would live on in millions.[72] The two celebrations of 27 August 1933—both endorsed by the President—served the purpose of promoting the revisionist Nazi foreign policy so vital to the movement's popularity.[73]

Furthermore, Hindenburg's backing was sought to sell Germany's withdrawal from the League of Nations to the German public a few months later. On 11 November 1933, the day before the pseudo-democratic plebiscite on the withdrawal, Hindenburg endorsed Hitler's move in a speech broadcast on national radio.[74] Hitler explicitly ordered the increasingly controlled press to report on this speech at length. Hindenburg's words were to receive more extensive coverage than Hitler's own pro-withdrawal speech given on the radio the same day.[75]

The Nazi leader had also made capital by publicizing his subservience when Hindenburg turned 86 the previous month. Soon, the President's birthday would be the only one of a politician other than Hitler the German press would be allowed to commemorate.[76] As Hindenburg had requested, no large-scale celebrations were staged on 2 October 1933, but Hitler did not pass up the chance to stress his veneration publicly and visited Hindenburg at home in Neudeck. The press duly raved about the 'close personal relationship' and 'cordial human connection', which had developed between the Field Marshal and Chancellor.[77] The emphasis, however, had shifted decisively since the previous autumn. Whereas hitherto newspaper congratulators—depending on their paper's political affiliation—had stressed Hindenburg's leadership during the war, his 'self-effacing' decision to stay on in 1918, or his integrative role after 1925, the focus of the Nazi co-ordinated press was firmly on 30 January 1933. According to the *Völkischer Beobachter*, 30 January and the subsequent unification of the nation represented the 'crowning moment of Hindenburg's life of duty and loyalty'.[78] Although articles were not subject to pre-emptive censorship, the German press had been brought into line by means of the Reichstag Fire Decree of February 1933 and the so-called *Schriftleitergesetz* of October 1933, which made newspaper editors subject to racial and political vetting. The press orders frequently issued by Reich Press Chief Otto Dietrich increased the uniformity of German press coverage.[79]

By the autumn of 1933, the narrative surrounding Hindenburg had been reconfigured and Nazified. Hindenburg's complex contribution to the development of German politics during the Weimar years was shrouded and a streamlined interpretation of his intricate role offered instead. The Nazis painted him as a National Socialist hero: a victorious military leader, a symbol from a long-gone past, who reminded Germans of their country's former greatness and their duty to work towards its resurrection—a resurrection supposedly only possible under their rule.

## The politics of death

In early June 1934, the 86-year-old Hindenburg, who had suffered from a bladder ailment for some time, retreated once more to Neudeck. His departure from Berlin and physical decline occurred at a crucial—and extremely opportune—time for Hitler, who was in the process of consolidating his rule by ridding himself of unwanted competitors. Starting on 30 June 1934, the SS and Gestapo killed around 200 members of the SA leadership and several prominent conservative politicians during the 'Night of the Long Knives'.[80] Hindenburg made his contribution to supporting the official version of an SA conspiracy by sending Hitler and Göring congratulatory telegrams expressing his 'deeply felt gratitude and genuine appreciation' of their decisive action on 2 July.[81] The telegrams were, of course, duly published.

Meanwhile, the regime's desperate opponents once more found a release valve for their anxiety in joking about the situation. Convinced that Hindenburg was on their side, their jokes portrayed the aged President as a fellow victim of Nazism: 'What is Germany's smallest concentration camp? Neudeck—it has just one prisoner: Hindenburg'.[82] The theme of Hindenburg as a prisoner of the regime would soon be picked up in anti-Nazi leaflets that the Gestapo classed as 'particularly dangerous'.[83] Another joke was that Hindenburg had vanished, that Adele Sandrock, a famous German actress with a very masculine voice, had taken over his part—after all, the saviour of 1914, 1925, and 1932 could not have sanctioned the murderous policies of June 1934.[84] But it was not 'die Sandrock' who issued the telegram; the President did so himself, although it remains unclear how much he knew about the true nature of the purge.[85] It would be the last occasion at which the Nazi party could count on the living Hindenburg's authority to sanction its increasingly violent measures.

Shortly after 9 a.m. on 2 August 1934, Hindenburg died. Hitler visited the dying man one last time on 31 July—to draw public attention to their close personal relationship and to see for himself how much time remained until the head of state and commander-in-chief would finally be out of the way.[86] Galvanized into action by his impressions from Neudeck,

Hitler began to implement a plan he had laid with Goebbels, amongst others, since the previous year.[87] Before Hindenburg had even breathed his last breath, the cabinet passed a law to take effect immediately after his death—merging the offices of President and Chancellor and thus giving Hitler all of Hindenburg's previous competences.[88]

In numerous army barracks throughout the country ceremonies had been scheduled for 2 August to commemorate the outbreak of war in 1914. Reichswehr Minister Werner von Blomberg used the occasion to make German soldiers swear an oath of unconditional allegiance to Hitler personally—a far cry from the oath to protect the constitution they had had to swear previously.[89] All of Germany's civil servants would soon have to follow suit.[90] As a Jewish civil servant, Victor Klemperer grew increasingly 'bitter and desperate' as a result of what was happening around him. A complete 'coup d'état', he noted in his diary. '[I]t all takes place in silence, drowned out by hymns to the dead Hindenburg'.[91]

Even while he was completing his 'coup d'état', Hitler continued to stress his subservience to the mythical departed. Crucially, he refused to assume the title 'Reich President' despite formally taking over the office. 'The greatness of the deceased has given the title Reich President unique meaning', an official decree explained. Hitler would therefore only be referred to as Reich Chancellor and *Führer* in the future. In addition, merging the two offices was to be sanctioned by a referendum on 19 August.[92] Even after Hindenburg's death, Hitler thus shied away from assuming Hindenburg's role too boldly in the symbolic realm—a clear illustration of the weight he ascribed to the deceased's unbroken mythical authority.

At the same time, the Nazis made sure that the Nazified narrative would be the one to last. According to the journalist Gerhard Schultze-Pfaelzer, who had assisted Hindenburg in press matters since the 1920s, the East Prussian *Oberpräsident* Erich Koch let it slip on the day of the President's passing that the Nazis would now 're-configure the Hindenburg legend the way the party needs it'. Although this account is subject to debate, Koch's alleged statement was certainly in line with how the party proceeded.[93]

The Propaganda Ministry controlled the media coverage meticulously. To create the greatest possible effect, the Reich Press Chief had banned special editions and sensationalist headlines on the President's illness prior to his death as well as any speculation on the succession.[94] Less than half an hour after Hindenburg had died, Goebbels seized the initiative and went on air to announce the news and to read out the official decree on the

period of mourning. For a record time of two weeks official Germany had
to pay its respects to the deceased.[95] No public events were to take place
on 2 or on 7 August, the day of the funeral, no music was to be played in
pubs and bars until after Hindenburg's burial, all churches had to ring their
bells for one hour each day, civil servants had to wear black ribbons for
two weeks and radio programmes would be adjusted appropriately. On the
day of the funeral, there would be a one-minute silence at all workplaces
and traffic would stop for the same amount of time.[96] Hindenburg's death
was thus not only commemorated in official services, it was also bound to
impact significantly on people's private lives for the next two weeks.

The co-ordinated press went into overdrive to cover the seminal events.
Countless special issues almost exclusively featured images of Hindenburg on their covers and many showed pictures of the President on his
deathbed.[97] All the papers recapitulated the various stages of Hindenburg's
career. The Nazi press, in particular, promoted the by then familiar theme
of Hindenburg and Hitler as an inseparable entity. An article with the
headline 'What Hindenburg meant to us' by the party's Reich Press Chief
opined audaciously that 'perhaps no one in Germany personally mourns
Hindenburg more than Hitler'.[98] The Nazi journalist Hans Schwarz van
Berk, in his turn, penned an article with a title worthy of a penny dreadful—'How Hindenburg and Hitler found each other'—which enlightened
readers about how the President had begun to refer to the Chancellor as
his 'true son' within weeks of his appointment. 'And when Hitler left
Hindenburg's death room in Neudeck, his face reflected the pain of a child
mourning its father.'[99]

## Burying the 'fatherly friend'

During the five days that passed between Hindenburg's death and his
funeral, it was nearly impossible for ordinary Germans to escape the
constant coverage of the events.[100] In the words of Victor Klemperer the
'din of the Hindenburg-Tannenberg ceremonies ... cloaks everything'.[101]
On 6 August, a parliamentary memorial service took place in Berlin, during
which Hitler spoke and which was broadcast and played in all German
factories, post offices, and other public places.[102] After the ceremony Hitler
demonstrated his new powers by taking the Reichswehr's salute on the
Reichstag's steps. The actual funeral of 7 August was arranged on an even

grander scale—and one befitting the importance of the Hindenburg myth to Nazi rule.

Hindenburg had wanted to be buried in Neudeck, but Hitler convinced the family that a grave inside the Tannenberg Memorial was more appropriate.[103] On 6 August, Hindenburg's coffin was moved from his death room and transported to Hohenstein overnight, accompanied by a torchlight procession of SS and SA.[104] Around 4,000 honorary guests were invited to follow the ceremony inside the Tannenberg Memorial—many of them members of the military, which lent the funeral the purpose of creating legitimacy for Hitler's new role as commander-in-chief.[105] The photographs of the official service, which were subsequently printed in all the major papers, clearly convey the extent to which the whole event was stage-managed. Many of the shots were taken from a top-down angle and—fulfilling the spatial ideas of the Speer-orchestrated Nuremberg party rallies—put across both the monumentality of the Tannenberg Memorial and the symmetry of the military formations inside.[106]

Hindenburg's coffin, wrapped in the *Reich* war flag, was brought onto the central square of the memorial to the sounds of Beethoven's 'Eroica', and the military chaplain Dohrmann gave the funeral speech. Hindenburg himself had chosen a passage from the Revelation of St John as the maxim of the service once again championing the theme of loyalty so central to his myth—'Be thou faithful unto death, and I will give thee a crown of life'. The speech emphasized Hindenburg's faithful personality and his allegedly self-effacing modesty accordingly, and invoked his extraordinary career, albeit emphasizing his military leadership, and the 'unforgettable image' of the 'Day of Potsdam'. His spirit would live on in the present generation and would assist in 'building the Third Reich', Dohrmann concluded.[107] Hitler's speech, which followed, sought to codify the Nazi adaptation of the Hindenburg myth once and for all. He exonerated the Field Marshal of all responsibility for military failure in 1918; Germany had been defeated for 'political reasons' alone, Hitler explained, and Hindenburg's election in 1925 had opened the door to Germany's resurrection; his burial at Tannenberg now closed a circle—the Field Marshal's body was brought back to the place where his mythical roots lay. He would continue to be inspirational, Hitler concluded:

> The German people will come to their dead hero in times of need to gain strength for their lives. And even when the last trace of his life has gone with

Fig. 10. Photograph of Hitler speaking at Hindenburg's funeral at the Tannenberg Memorial on 7 August 1934.

the wind, the name will be immortal. Deceased Field Marshal, now enter Valhalla![108]

The *Führer* thereby consigned Hindenburg to a mythical afterlife in the Germanic pantheon—a rhetorical coup not received with enthusiasm by all admirers of the pious Hindenburg, but which certainly served the Nazi purpose of twisting the cult to meet the party's own ends.[109]

Ordinary Germans were not excluded entirely from participation in the funeral. Around 120,000 people gathered to the south of the Tannenberg Memorial. Once the official part of the ceremony was over, they filed past Hindenburg's coffin in one of the memorial's towers. Up to 200,000 people seized the opportunity on 7 August alone. The tower remained open for two weeks, and countless special trains carried a steady stream of visitors to nearby Hohenstein railway station and on to the memorial from there on special buses.[110] The millions who could not make it to Hohenstein did not have to rely on newspapers and newsreels to gain a sense of the service's atmosphere, but were given an opportunity to join in as the whole burial was broadcast on every German radio station. In Berlin, groups of silent listeners gathered in front of newsagents, pubs, and on public squares, where loudspeakers had been put up especially for the occasion.[111] People's mourning seemed genuine and, despite Nazi stage-management, there was a strong element of spontaneity and voluntary participation to the way people expressed their grief—be it by gathering in front of public loudspeakers, by signing the lists of condolences, or by displaying images of Hindenburg in the windows of their homes.[112]

One did not have to believe the Nazi rhetoric of Hitler mourning his 'fatherly friend' to be genuinely shaken. Many non-Nazis who criticized the hyperbole of the funeral were repelled not by the public display of grief but by the 'detectable hypocrisy of the Nazis'.[113] The exiled novelist Thomas Mann, for instance, was put off by the 'Pompe funèbre' and Hitler's 'homage to his "fatherly friend"'.[114] In spite of rejecting the event's propagandistic exploitation and having considered Hindenburg powerless for some time, Klemperer, for one, was 'very downhearted'. 'For a long time no more than a name and yet a last counterweight, which now falls away,' he noted on 2 August. He also recorded a conversation with a local tax official in Dresden in his diary, who had told him: 'After all, Hitler had to deliver a report to him.' When Klemperer reasoned that Hitler had, in fact, been ruling alone for a long time, the man had simply replied 'That certainly—but the old gentleman was still there nevertheless.' 'Quite simple, Aryan, petty bourgeois people', Klemperer observed, 'And the man, depressed...But all this in a whisper, depressed, fearful, helpless. That is probably the voice of the German people.'[115] Klemperer had harboured hopes of an eventual Reichswehr coup to overthrow Hitler, which were crushed when the army immediately swore its voluntary oath of personal allegiance to the *Führer*.[116] The reports of the exiled Social Democratic leadership conveyed similar sentiments. Although the party had begun to turn its back on the President after July 1932, many informants now noted a mood of 'depression', a sense of 'disappointment' and 'anticlimax' in August, especially among workers.[117] To the Social Democratic writer and journalist Jochen Klepper it had equally seemed as though 'the last foothold' had disappeared with Hindenburg's demise.[118]

Many German Jews, especially the Jewish veterans of the Reichsbund jüdischer Frontsoldaten, who had striven towards national assimilation, equally mourned Hindenburg's death. Gestapo agents from different parts of the Reich noted disapprovingly that many Jews displayed Imperial flags in their windows and paid homage to Hindenburg in commemorative ceremonies.[119] After all, he had intervened once before on their behalf and with his death the last hope in further protection against the Nazi terror—albeit a minimal one—had ceased. That he had still formally been the head of state had been important psychologically—Hindenburg had represented a last barrier to Hitler achieving total power. This rather abstract sense of his presence somehow alleviating a threat was, of course, nothing new. The German population had adopted this coping strategy during wartime, when it had in no small part believed that 'Hindenburg would sort it out' one way or another. And even though he had repeatedly disappointed the hopes invested in him, this mechanism had been left largely intact until after 1933, perhaps even become more effective due to the lack of alternatives. As Thomas Mann noted in his diary with acuity: 'The German will to legends and to myths...obtrudes particularly at this time.' Hindenburg had delivered Germany to the wretched rule of Hitlerism, and yet the German people did not seem to care, the exiled writer reflected with astonishment: '[H]e is and remains the loyal Eckehart...full of monumental loyalty.'[120]

## Hindenburg's legacy

Merging the offices of Reich President and Chancellor was the final act in the Nazi 'seizure of power'.[121] After having purged those in the party's own ranks who had threatened his rule in late June, the events of 2 August 1934 gave Hitler authority over the last two institutions—except the churches— which had hitherto not been fully Nazified: the army and the presidency. With Hindenburg's death Nazi Germany thus turned into a fully-fledged dictatorship in which the last remnants of the Weimar constitution were finally overcome.

Unknown to ordinary Germans, Hindenburg had provided Hitler with even more symbolic ammunition—a political will. The document, published on 15 August 1934, included a passage from Hindenburg's memoirs appealing to the young generation to realize his hopes for German rebirth and reconstruction, followed by a passage on Nazism. He thanked providence for letting him witness Germany regain strength. 'My Chancellor Adolf Hitler and his movement', he stated, had taken a historical step towards bringing about the internal unification of the German people. Much remained to be done, but, as Hindenburg pledged,

> I part from my German people in the hope that what I longed for in 1919 and which . . . led to 30 January 1933, will grow into the complete fulfilment and accomplishment of the historic mission of our people. Reassured I can close my eyes in the firm belief in the future of our fatherland.[122]

Hindenburg's will explicitly sanctioned the Nazis' claim to historical continuity. Referring to Hitler as his Chancellor gave credence to the notion of a quasi-familial bond between the 'Marshal and the Corporal'.

A second part of the political will recommended the restoration of the monarchy. Whereas the first part of the document was addressed to Hitler and 'the German people', however, the second part, contained in a separate envelope, was addressed to Hitler personally. On 15 August 1934, Papen delivered both documents to Hitler at Berchtesgarden, who decided to publish the first part immediately.[123] The second part, by contrast, was never published. In spite of the differing accounts of this crucial document's genesis, it can be established beyond doubt that Hindenburg agreed with its content (even if it was partly drafted by others) and also decided to split the document into two parts. His was also the choice to leave the decision on the publication of his recommendation for the restoration of the monarchy up to Hitler.[124]

The published will was key in mobilizing the population for the referendum of 19 August 1934.[125] According to the *Germania*, the political will was

> Hindenburg's last 'Yes' to Germany...—a 'Yes' to Adolf Hitler and his movement, a 'Yes' to the question the German people will be asked on 19 August...No reason can be grave enough—other than secret hostility towards Germany and its future—to deny a 'Yes' to the man whom Hindenburg has chosen as the executor of his will.[126]

Hindenburg's son Oskar did his share in backing Hitler as the 'executor' in a radio speech the day before the plebiscite. His father, he told millions of listeners, had regarded Hitler as his legitimate successor.[127]

We cannot know whether invoking Hindenburg's endorsement at this stage swayed those who were not convinced of the movement's merits already. Despite the intimidation of voters and the rigging of the referendum, the outcome was not the overwhelming success the Nazis had hoped for. 89.9% voted in favour of Hitler's new powers, but 10.1% still opposed the move.[128] Many simply refused to believe that the will was real. 'But is it probable, after everything that has happened, that it is *not* forged?' Thomas Mann contemplated in his diary. 'The Reichstag fire, the Communist conspiracy, the Röhm conspiracy, one hundred muddy lies and roguery, the cheap sensationalist crime novel narrative of it all—and this testament should be real?'[129] The circumstances seemed too convenient for the Nazis, and it thus remained easier to believe in malicious manipulation than in Hindenburg's authorization of a total dictatorship. In spite of all the violent measures he had lent his name to over the previous eighteen months, and in spite of this whole-hearted endorsement of Nazi rule, once again—and in line with a 20-year-old pattern of interpretation—he was exempted from responsibility.[130]

Although Hindenburg's media presence naturally diminished after his death, the Nazis did not stop invoking his myth. On Hindenburg's birthday in October, commemorative ceremonies took place both in Berlin and at the Tannenberg Memorial. Crowds gathered in front of 73 Wilhelmstraße and thousands filed past Hindenburg's grave and many saluted it with the Nazi greeting.[131] The following August, the press was again ordered to commemorate the death and all units of the armed forces held commemorative parades.[132] Such ceremonies would be staged at the Tannenberg Memorial with a wreath laid in Hitler's name every 2 August throughout the years of Nazi rule. From 1936, the army's watchword on every 2 October—Hindenburg's birthday—was 'Hindenburg'.[133] And in imitation of 1917 and 1927, the German people were encouraged to give money to a 'Hindenburg Donation' for charitable causes before his ninetieth birthday in 1937.[134] The Nazis also continued to rely explicitly on the memory of Hindenburg to seek political legitimacy. Before the referendum on the remilitarization of the Rhineland in March 1936, the press was told to reprint Hindenburg's political will and the radio speech he had given to endorse Germany's withdrawal from the League of Nations in 1933.[135] And the introduction of military conscription on 16 March 1935—a key step in preparing Germany for war—was promoted as having been guided by 'Hindenburg's spirit'.[136]

The most widely visible manifestation of the Nazis' continued veneration of the deceased President was Zeppelin LZ129—the biggest airship of its kind—christened 'Hindenburg' in early 1936.[137] As a kind of flying ambassador of the 'Third Reich', the 'Hindenburg'—with swastikas on its tail fins—projected an image of modernity, technological achievement, and progress on its transatlantic voyages to the USA and Brazil. Domestically, it was a spectacular publicity prop. The airship appeared in Berlin during the Olympic Games of 1936 and during the election campaign in March of that year it hovered over all the major cities of the *Reich*, dropping leaflets, blasting music and Nazi campaign slogans from loudspeakers.[138] The 'Hindenburg disaster' of 6 May 1937, when its exterior varnish caught fire and the airship crashed in Lakehurst, New Jersey, killing 35 passengers and crew, naturally cast some doubt on Nazi Germany's technological achievements. The spectacular images of the burning zeppelin and the extraordinary amount of press coverage they received worldwide, however, meant that nearly three years after Hindenburg's death, his name was once more ever-present.[139]

Moreover, Hindenburg's iconic image remained a physical reality throughout Germany. In 1936, cinema audiences were treated to a documentary on Hindenburg's life—simply entitled *Hindenburg*—which continued the theme of unity between 'The Marshal and the Corporal'.[140] And not only would countless Hindenburg memorials be erected throughout the 1930s, but his head—not Hitler's—would be used unaltered on German coins throughout the Nazi years.[141] A Hindenburg stamp first issued in 1927 was re-printed and used as the first German postage stamp of the General Government of occupied Poland after 1939—perhaps to invoke Hindenburg's contribution to protecting the Germanic character of the eastern part of the *Reich* in 1914.[142]

Hindenburg's anti-Russian credentials gained at Tannenberg sat neatly with Nazi anti-Bolshevism. According to the nationalist writer Joseph Magnus Wehner, the central question arising from Hindenburg's death was whether the country would find a military commander of similar stature at a new moment of danger: 'Will Bolshevism conquer the world or will Germany halt it?' he asked in his book on Hindenburg that dedicated only 1.5 out of 108 pages to Hindenburg's republican presidency.[143] Invoking the memory of the Russian invasion of 1914—and Germany's 'liberator'—was no doubt useful in stoking up Russophobia in preparation for a future war against the Soviet Union.[144]

The largest commemoration of Hindenburg after August 1934 took place on his 88th birthday. Evidently, the Nazis did not deem one pompous funeral enough to honour their 'patron'; on 2 October 1935, Hindenburg was buried for the second time. The streets leading from Hohenstein station to the memorial site were again lined with members of the SS, and Wehrmacht soldiers in military formations had gathered inside. Hitler issued an official statement, according to which the Tannenberg Memorial should henceforth be called *Reichsehrenmal Tannenberg* thus making it Germany's official war memorial.[145] The walled and towered monument had undergone a major redesign over the previous year.[146] The once grass-covered Court of Honour had been deepened and lined with granite from all parts of Germany. The graves of the twenty unknown soldiers previously buried in the centre were moved to turn the court into a site for mass gatherings. The giant cross previously located in the centre of the square had been attached to one of the towers and an iron cross mosaic built into the floor as a replacement. The memorial had thus been Nazified and its Christian symbols marginalized. Its axis had also been transformed: the tower bearing Hindenburg's tomb and a so-called 'hall of honour' were now the focal points of the whole site.

A monumental entrance to the vault holding the coffin of Hinden-burg—and soon also that of his wife—had been added to one of the towers. The word 'Hindenburg' was inscribed into a monolith above the door, and two oversized statues of German soldiers were placed on either side of the entrance, symbolically keeping watch over their deceased

Field Marshal.[147] The German public had been closely informed about the *Führer*'s involvement in the architectural planning process. He met personally with the architects and had allegedly drawn in his own ideas for the new design on their blueprints.[148] It had supposedly also been Hitler's idea to shift the memorial's commemorative emphasis from the battle of 1914 to Hindenburg himself—to effectively turn the Tannenberg Memorial into a Hindenburg Memorial.[149]

By October 1935, the Nazification of the hitherto multi-layered Hindenburg myth was complete: from an all-encompassing symbol of German virtues, Hindenburg, who now lay buried in a shrine at the site of his seminal heroic act, had been re-cast as the Nazis' patron and military leader, his former polyvalence reduced to the shining example which would guide Hitler in a future war.

\* \* \*

The Nazis stressed Hindenburg's mythical endorsement of their rule from day one and went to great lengths to orchestrate public displays of harmonious unity between the 'Marshal and the Corporal'. Given their ruthlessness in dealing with opponents, their extensive efforts to stress this unity are striking—and explicable only if the party leaders felt genuinely attached to the man who had appointed Hitler, or if they believed they would not fare as well on a more confrontational course. The Nazis continued to accept and honour Hindenburg as a parallel symbolic authority, and his myth was a crucial—and often overlooked—tool in the process of consolidating their rule;[150] the 'seizure of power' could not be completed until Hindenburg died. If, as has been argued with reference to the 1932 presidential elections, Hindenburg had had no genuine followers in the last years of Weimar, but had been perceived entirely as the lesser of two evils by the democrats on the one hand and deserted completely by most right-wing Germans on the other, the Nazis would not have had to rely—and could not have relied—on his mythical authority to the extent that they did. Their painstaking efforts to use Hindenburg's laurels, which continued until long after his death, however, prove that they were convinced of his myth's unremitting potency.

Hindenburg did nothing to stop his veneration playing into the hands of the Nazi regime. Quite the contrary—he willingly participated in the stage-managed shows of unity with Hitler. Moreover, his political will provided the regime with invaluable symbolic ammunition after his death and sanctioned the Nazi leader's claim of being the chosen successor. The party did not even have to be as cynical as some believed they had been and forge Hindenburg's testament; the one he left was entirely sufficient. The deployment of the Hindenburg myth by a political party to further a more current political agenda was, of course, no new phenomenon. The Nazis' implementation of the strategy was just particularly bold and the ends to which they deployed it would ultimately have the most serious consequences.

Strikingly, Hindenburg remained a rallying point for opponents of the regime in spite of his complicity in the Nazi takeover. Many continued to believe in his integrity and considered him a fellow victim of the regime, or at least a senile old man who did not know what he was doing and who was being exploited. His death, and with it the end of all hopes in an army coup, left many Social Democrats, as well as Jews like Victor Klemperer, depressed and fearful of what was to come. Even if they had not been genuine Hindenburg devotees, a sense of trust in his personal integrity and his power to alter their fortunes had remained. This intangible belief that Hindenburg would 'sort things out' and would 'save' Germany had meant different things to different groups of society during the previous twenty years. Ultimately, the trust of those who had hoped, as late as 1932, that he would save the country from Nazi rule, was bitterly disappointed.

# 9

# Hindenburg after 1945

## 'Operation Body-snatch'

The clandestine proceedings taking place in the Hessian town of Marburg on 25 August 1946 marked the end of a series of events an American newspaper christened 'Operation Body-snatch': twelve years after his first burial and almost 32 years to the day since Hindenburg had shot to fame, his mortal remains and those of his wife found their third resting place in Marburg's Elizabeth Church.[1]

Hindenburg's coffin had been on a 19-month-long odyssey since late January 1945, when Hitler had ordered the body of the Nazis' 'patron' to be moved from the Tannenberg Memorial, just days before the advancing 3rd Belorussian Front captured the nearby town of Hohenstein.[2] Even with total German defeat looming ever larger, symbolic politics still mattered. The Nazi leader was determined not to let the shrine of the Defeater of the Russians, who had been so vital in bestowing legitimacy upon his rule, fall into the hand of the Soviets, who, in their turn, galvanized their troops with the prospect of extracting revenge for the humiliating defeat of the Narew Army in August 1914.[3] Retreating German units removed the coffins of the Field Marshal and his wife before blowing up the Hindenburg vault and the memorial's main towers.[4]

Whereas German refugees made their way westward on foot, the two sarcophagi were evacuated from Königsberg on a German cruiser, because Soviet forces were in the process of encircling the East Prussian capital.[5] The coffins were initially stored at Potsdam's Garrison Church—the site of the infamous propagandistic display of 21 March 1933—but soon moved secretly to a more secure location: a salt mine near the small Thuringian town of Bernterode. On 27 April, three days before Hitler would commit suicide in his Berlin bunker, American soldiers stumbled across the sealed mine and discovered not only a vast treasure hoard, including the Hohenzollern imperial jewels and other paraphernalia of former German glory, but also four caskets on which the names of the famous deceased had been written hastily in red crayon. In addition to Paul and Gertrud von Hindenburg, the two Prussian Kings Friedrich Wilhelm I and Friedrich II, previously buried in Potsdam, had been moved there.[6] Since Thuringia would be handed over to the Soviets as part of their zone of occupation, the Americans moved their discovery westward in May 1945. The four caskets ended up in Marburg, an old university town which had survived the war relatively unscathed and served as a central collection point for US war booty.

From the outset, the US military was uneasy about having the mortal remains of these symbolic German figures in its possession. Worried about the reactions of the occupied Germans, the military authorities decided at the highest level that they would rid themselves of the responsibility as quickly as possible.[7] Finding a suitable burial place was no easy task amidst post-war chaos, however. While the last remaining Hohenzollern castle in the West was located in the Swabian Alps and thus part of the French zone of occupation, Hindenburg's family had settled in the British zone, in Uelzen near Hanover. Arranging family funerals would therefore have entailed negotiations with the other Western occupying powers possibly prolonging proceedings for some time. Driven by a desire to move swiftly, the US military government opted for a local solution: they deemed Marburg's Protestant Elizabeth Church sufficiently dignified and private enough to avoid turning the burial sites into centres of potential neo-Nazi pilgrimage—a prospect the US military feared. The plans for the impending burials remained a well-guarded secret until August 1946. Not even the parish council was informed, for fear of counter-demonstrations.[8]

The Military Government not only made provisions for the re-burials to be as unobtrusive as possible, but also sought to ensure that the graves themselves would not generate unwarranted attention. Whilst the original plan to close the whole Northern choir where Hindenburg and his wife were to be buried to the public was abandoned after the local priest protested, the Military Government insisted on the coffins being sunk so deep into the church floor that their stone lids would be at ground level—and would thus not be an obvious feature.[9] This could not be realized either. When digging into the floor of the Elizabeth Church, construction workers came across the medieval foundations of an

**Fig. 11.** Photograph of the reburial of the Hindenburgs and the Prussian Kings at night-time in Marburg's Elizabeth Church (August 1946).

older church that had stood on the same site and could not go deeper. Consequently, the Hindenburg graves had to be slightly elevated after all.

In spite of these setbacks, Hindenburg's clandestine third funeral, attended only by a select few family members, representatives of the Military Government, and church officials conveyed the extent to which the Military Government was determined to make the erstwhile mythical President a *persona non grata* in post-war Germany. No official photographs were taken, but the archivist of the Elizabeth Church, Hermann Bauer, took a number of pictures of the graves' excavations. These badly lit, wiggly amateur shots of a few men standing conspiratorially around a hole in the ground in an almost dark church could not mark a starker contrast to the images of the Nazi-choreographed pomposity of Hindenburg's funerals in 1934 and 1935.

The design of the post-war graves equally differed fundamentally from the Tannenberg Memorial with its Hindenburg tower and Hall of Honour. The Hindenburg graves situated immediately to the left of the main church entrance are barely lit. Although the names of the deceased are carved into the gravestones they are almost impossible to read from the visitors' angle due to the graves' slight elevation and because the area is sealed off with a cord. They have to study the church's information brochure rather carefully to know who actually rests in front of them.[10] What is more, visitors are greeted by a large—and clearly visible—panel next to the graves that commemorates the 'victims of war and violence' (added in 1961), which clearly alludes to Hindenburg's key role in bringing the Nazis to power.


## Reinterpreting Hindenburg in the two Germanies

After the coffins had been buried in Marburg, not everyone played along with the American plans of limiting public attention. Hermann Bauer, the Elizabeth Church's archivist and US-vetted editor of the licensed *Marburger Presse*, for whom collecting information on the Hindenburg graves would become a private passion, published the first article on the burial in German on 27 August 1946.[11] He called on all residents to prove worthy of the 'honour bestowed upon them', and, although acknowledging that the Nazis had deployed Hindenburg's image to consolidate their rule, he still referred to the former President and the two Prussian Kings as 'national heroes', 'national saints', and objects of a 'national cult'. Such sentiments, which had formed a near-consensus in the 1920s and 1930s, could no longer be voiced without arousing controversy in US-occupied Germany, however. The Information Control Division, in charge of denazifying and re-educating the German public and responsible for controlling the German press, quickly reprimanded Bauer. An American official cautioned him 'that the use of such words as "Nationalkult" and "Nationalheiliger" are dangerous' and violated US re-education policy.[12] Transforming the 'inner character' of the Germans in the long-term had been one of the declared aims of the Allies since their Casablanca conference in January 1943.[13] On taking on the role of occupiers they left little doubt that constructing a post-war German democracy would be possible only if the country was to break with the past and eliminate all National Socialist and overtly militarist influences from German public life. From an American perspective there was to be no place for Hindenburg in a future West German pantheon.

The denazification trials of some of Hindenburg's former acquaintances and aides in the second half of the 1940s contributed to the slow revision of Hindenburg's image in equal measure. The authenticity of his political will played a central role in the trials of Papen, Meissner, and Oskar von Hindenburg.[14] It was the first time it became known publicly that the will had consisted of two separate parts only one of which had been released by the Nazis. The news of the suppression of the second document, calling for the restoration of the monarchy, at first seemed to confirm the rumours of Nazi foul play.[15] That the will had been no outright forgery—which many had believed—meant, however, that it was not enough for a far-reaching exoneration. As Franz Josef Schöningh, one of the founders of the left-liberal *Süddeutsche Zeitung,* opined in a front-page leader just days before Hindenburg's re-burial in Marburg, the time had finally come for the destruction of the Hindenburg 'legend'. Echoing contemporary academic discourses critical of myth, he concluded that only those who favoured blind faith in myth over a thorough study of contemporary history could still refuse to re-examine the former President.[16]

Many left-wing commentators shared Schöningh's opinion and the occupiers' unease with Hindenburg eulogists like Bauer. The Social Democrat publisher of the newly-established *Frankfurter Rundschau,* Karl Gerold, equally stressed the necessity to destroy the 'legendary wreath' that had been constructed around Hindenburg during his lifetime. A stop had to be put to the 'distorted image of the Prussian national saint', he insisted.[17] Erich Wollenberg, a well-known KPD activist in the 1920s, concurred that Hindenburg had been responsible for spreading the fatal theory of the 'stab-in-the-back' and had empowered the Nazis in his political will. He thus bore a large share of responsibility for the Second World War and the regime's crimes. Wollenberg went as far as accusing Bauer of emulating Goebbels's propaganda by trying to 'conserve the Hindenburg legend'. 'Only once this slow poison has been secreted from the German national body will a democratic Germany be able to flourish', he concluded.[18] Hermann Brill, the Chief of the State Office in Wiesbaden and a former SPD activist who had been imprisoned in Dachau, echoed Wollenberg's thoughts and argued that even the US military government had not made a clean enough break with Hindenburg. The 'privileged' burial site of the man who had appointed Hitler might interfere with the 'purification of the moral consciousness so urgently necessary' in post-war Germany, he warned.[19]

The Nazis themselves had put great effort into Nazifying the Hindenburg myth and reconfiguring 30 January 1933 as its predestined telos. When the 'Third Reich' lay in ruins, the party's emphasis on the last two years of Hindenburg's life remained intact—albeit now with negative connotations. In mainstream post-war public discourse, as well as in many of the memoirs Hindenburg's Weimar contemporaries published, he was portrayed neither as the liberator and saviour of the German people nor as a symbol of political stability. Instead, he appeared as the 'undertaker of German democracy', as Hitler's 'precursor' or *Steigbügelhalter*—a somewhat tragic figure who had helped the Nazis into power albeit with varying degrees of personal responsibility or guilt attributed to him.[20] Walther Hubatsch, for instance, wanted to exempt the aged Reich President from responsibility. Hindenburg should be judged solely on his actions before 1933 and considered tragic for 'having lived two years too long',[21] Hubatsch explained. The notion of the 'tragic' Hindenburg has turned out to be remarkably long-lived: Michael Salewski, for one, only recently described him as the 'classic tragic figure', because Hindenburg had allegedly realized too late that he had 'delivered his fatherland' to the Nazis.[22]

This volte-face was not free of apologetic tendencies. The rhetoric of 'secreting poison' and the need for moral 'purification' branded the Hindenburg myth as a substance alien to the German 'national body'. Focusing on the President's alleged shortcomings (a lack of political understanding, old age, a limited intellect) one could put off painful self-examination and avoid pinning the responsibility for Nazi crimes on Germans at large, many of whom had voted for the NSDAP before the 'seizure of power' and without whose consent numerous Nazi policies could not have been implemented. The notion of a senile Hindenburg and his small camarilla of sinister advisers 'delivering' the German people to Hitler sat neatly with the post-war paradigm of the Nazi dictatorship as an 'historical accident'. Not only Friedrich Meinecke singled out Hindenburg's 'accidental' weakness as a major factor in the destruction of Germany's first Republic.[23] In this respect, even Karl-Dietrich Bracher's monumental study of Weimar's collapse, a milestone of Weimar scholarship first published in 1955 and still unsurpassed on many levels, was a product of its time. Bracher blamed first and foremost the 'grandiose miscalculation' of Hindenburg and his small clique of 'intrigants' for Hitler's appointment, and explicitly exonerated 'the German people'.[24] At least until the 1960s, Hitler's appointment appeared as the pivotal date in West German discourse and scholarship on the 'Third Reich'. Obsessing about 30 January 1933, however, also meant being able to talk about Nazism without having to talk about genocide—a key trait of German debates on Nazism in the early years of the Federal Republic.[25]

This idea of Hindenburg being chiefly to blame for Nazi rule found expression in West German iconography as well. A photograph of Hindenburg shaking the hand of the bowing Hitler on the 'Day of Potsdam' became one of the most widely used historical images in German school textbooks, illustrated publications, and encyclopaedias. Whilst the Nazis themselves had favoured images of the ceremony highlighting popular participation, the 'handshake' blanks out the audience and focuses entirely on Hindenburg and Hitler. It thus personalizes responsibility. Because post-war observers were aware that Hitler's actions after March 1933 made a mockery of his posture as the 'humble servant', however, the image also highlights the Nazis' hypocrisy and powers of seduction. The photograph suggests that Hindenburg—symbolizing the gullibility of the (doubly) old elite—had been conned by the Nazi leadership.[26] It was thus a further variation of the theme of the sinister forces behind Hindenburg that were to blame for the old man's actions, a theme that had defined the Hindenburg myth almost from its inception. The picture's wide distribution shows that it touched a nerve in West Germany, but also means that it contributed to the longevity of notions of the Nazis' irresistible powers of seduction in its turn.[27]

Fig. 12. Photograph of Hitler and Hindenburg shaking hands outside the Garrison Church in Potsdam on 21 March 1933.

The lessons learned from Hindenburg's case, which were part of the lessons of Weimar, also had constitutional consequences. Avoiding a repetition of the mistakes and innate weaknesses of Germany's first Republic was one of the central concerns of the members of the Parlamentarischer Rat when drafting the new German constitution.[28] The Basic Law ratified in May 1949 banned key elements of mass politics. Most importantly, the Federal President would be elected not by popular vote but by representatives of the upper and lower houses (the so-called Bundesversammlung) instead. In order to curtail a 'second Hindenburg' (not 'another Ebert', who was about to be re-invented as a 'second Lincoln'[29]), the actual powers of the President were greatly reduced. In the Federal Republic the President could no longer sidestep parliament or govern by emergency decree; since 1949, he has played a largely representative role.[30]

The first West German opinion polls reflected Hindenburg's gradual departure from the mythical stage. Asked whom they perceived as the greatest German, Bismarck and Hitler continued to top people's answers in the late 1940s and early 1950s. In third place 10–14% of interviewees named other 'Emperors, military commanders, and Kings'. It is likely that Hindenburg was mentioned as part of this group but not frequently enough to merit an individual listing.[31] Instead, the German public began to invest its trust in yet another aged statesman: the first post-war Chancellor Konrad Adenauer succeeded Bismarck as the 'greatest German' in the 1960s and retained his crown only recently in a poll of over 3 million television viewers asked to name the 'best German'. Hindenburg did not even make it into the top 100.[32]

At the same time, however, there was no shortage of volunteers who, like the historian and Hindenburg campaigner of 1932, Bernhard Schwertfeger, sought to 'retrieve Hindenburg's historical honour'.[33] Former press aide Gerhard Schultze-Pfaelzer, by his own account, also tried 'to do everything . . . to prevent Hindenburg's image as a gentlemanly, kind, and wise man from going under in the foul waters of the Nazi tide.'[34] Hindenburg's family—though antagonized by the likes of Schultze-Pfaelzer, whose efforts to exonerate Hindenburg often went hand in hand with vilifying his son Oskar—also continued to work tirelessly to rescue his reputation.[35] Consequently, the only two scholars to whom they gave access to Hindenburg's personal papers were the conservative historians Walter Görlitz and Walther Hubatsch, who published a biography and an edited collection of Hindenburg's papers respectively.[36] Oskar and his wife Margarete carefully vetted both and the latter continued to assure herself that the accounts 'would match . . . [the family's] convictions' as far as possible.[37] As a result, their studies were rather hagiographic.[38]

Naturally the negative shift in West German perceptions of Hindenburg after 1945 was not an all-encompassing or straightforward affair. German memory, especially in the 1950s, was neither defined solely by the spirit of re-education nor was it crafted by left-wing journalists. There is considerable evidence to suggest that beneath official West German politics of memory there continued to be an undercurrent of Hindenburg worship among select, yet influential groups. When the conservative *Frankfurter Allgemeine Zeitung* published a series of articles critical of Hindenburg in the mid-1950s, for instance, the paper received an unusually large number of letters from its readers. Some of these were supportive, but many others complained about its attempts to 'besmirch the national nest', to 'darken' or 'obfuscate' German history. According to one of the publishers, Paul Sethe, the tone of the letters clearly conveyed the authors' 'painful agitation that one was trying to touch what was sacred to them'.[39]

The number of people visiting Hindenburg's grave in Marburg also suggests that he continued to capture people's imagination. Within two months of Hindenburg's re-burial, his grave had allegedly become a 'place of pilgrimage'.[40] In 1966, the Elizabeth Church's sexton explained that many visitors obviously still venerated the deceased President. Postcards of the graves 'sold like hot cakes', he revealed, and visitors often brought flowers, especially in the summer months, when the graves were covered with wreaths and bouquets so densely that one could hardly make out the gravestones.[41]

On the anniversary of Hindenburg's death and on his or his wife's birthday the family often held memorial services at the church, sometimes attended by members of the old veterans' organizations, such as the Kyffhäuser League.[42] More importantly, Hindenburg's grave became a site of memory for German expellee groups, a considerable force in post-war West German society: 16% of West Germans in 1950 had been expelled from Germany's former Eastern territories.[43] They were highly organized and had their own national pressure groups, the so-called Landsmannschaften, with their respective press organs and institutional structure, claiming between one and two million members by the early 1950s.[44] Many of those who laid wreaths in Marburg felt a common bond of destiny with Hindenburg, whose mortal remains had also been 'expelled' from the East and whose family had lost its property. The location of Hindenburg's post-war grave in Marburg—a town to which he had had no personal connection—seemed to symbolize the expellees' plight.

Such sentiments were not just shared by the older generation that had lived through Hindenburg's presidency. A popular biography of Hindenburg written by the young author Martin Lüders, and published by the radically right-wing Druffel publishing house in 1961, explicitly aimed at young readers and openly sought to keep Hindenburg's memory alive with reference to Germany's lost territories in the East:

> Will this coffin be lifted onto young shoulders once more and will it, after all, find its final resting place under the trees of Neudeck, as the 'old gentleman' wished? A book about Hindenburg cannot close other than with invoking his East Prussian Heimat and the unity of the German Reich.[45]

In the same vein, East and West Prussian Landsmannschaften frequently seized on the anniversaries of Tannenberg and Hindenburg's death to commemorate 'the saviour of the *Heimat*'.[46] Almost thirty years after his death, some groups still called upon Hindenburg's memory to further a more current agenda. Among some of the Landsmannschaften he has even remained a positive reference point to this day.[47]

The Elizabeth Church and local politicians did not welcome all displays of affection for the famous deceased. Particularly when Otto Ernst Remer, a former Major-General who had played a key role in suppressing the resistance plot of 20 July 1944 and had co-founded the neo-Nazi Sozialistische Reichspartei, appeared in Marburg to pay his respects to Hindenburg, locals considered the event an 'embarrassment' for the town.[48]

The somewhat impassioned reactions of local politicians to relatively minor incidents at the graves illustrated how seriously they took their efforts to safeguard the German Republic the second time round.[49] When a few young people laid a wreath and some heath shrubs on the graves of Hindenburg and the Prussian Kings in early 1947, the incident sparked a special investigation and two heated debates in the Hessian parliament, during which the Social Democratic Minister President Christian Stock vowed to fight such 'nationalist demonstrations against the Republic'.[50] The parish council and the local government were clearly determined not to let the site become a place of open anti-democratic pilgrimage. With yet another 'lesson of Weimar' in mind—the potential repercussions of issues of symbolic importance—in 1951 the parish council banned the laying of wreaths with coloured ribbons for fear of black, white, and red decorations appearing. Political speeches or demonstrations in front of the graves were banned as well.[51]

Despite such left-wing determination, however, Hindenburg also continued to be invoked by the Bundeswehr, which was eager to place itself in a positive line of German military tradition after its creation in 1955. While the Defence Ministry did not issue official guidelines on military role models acceptable for a democratic German army, its education of future officers encouraged an image of the Bundeswehr as linking up to Germany's pre-1933 military history.[52] The decision whose pictures would go up in army barracks was left up to individual commanders. Choosing an erstwhile vanquisher of the Russians as a role model was perhaps a natural choice for an army designed to withstand a potential Soviet onslaught in Europe in the era of the Cold War. An American journalist who profiled Germany's new troops for the *New York Times* in 1957 hence found Hindenburg's portrait proudly displayed on the walls of the Officers' Mess of the Mountain Division in Mittenwald near Mount Zugspitze.[53] This was no 1950s aberration: several Bundeswehr barracks, in Münster and Ulm amongst other towns, are named after Hindenburg to this day, thus contributing to keeping his memory alive in army circles and among the local populations.[54]

Although such pluralist memories doubtless continued to exist in Soviet-dominated East Germany as well, the Socialist state quickly limited the room in which these could be voiced.[55] Nostalgic accounts about their former *Heimat* by millions of expellees in East Germany—or 're-settlers' as they were termed in the GDR—were not permitted in the public realm for fear of causing frictions with the country's Eastern neighbours. Nor was military pulp fiction glorifying Wehrmacht soldiers—a popular genre in the West—acceptable as part of official memory in the GDR. Because the Battle of Tannenberg had been fought against Russian troops, Hindenburg was entirely unsuitable as a role model for East German soldiers in an era of publicly celebrated German-Soviet friendship—in spite of the undeniable influence of Wehrmacht traditions on the newly-created National People's Army after 1956.[56] The officially sanctioned historical narratives in the GDR may have only mirrored the beliefs and experiences of a tiny minority—former KPD functionaries many of whom had spent the Nazi years in Soviet exile—but they defined what could be voiced openly.[57]

A considerable number of East German historians, in particular, had been active KPD members in the 1920s.[58] The party had opposed Hindenburg as the warmongering representative of German imperialism from the outset. Placing itself in this tradition was a welcome source of legitimacy for the new Socialist state. The Communists had pursued a confrontational strategy towards Hindenburg throughout the 1920s: party leader Ernst Thälmann had run against Hindenburg in both presidential elections instead of 'choosing the lesser evil' as the rival Social Democrats had done in 1932. The SPD had thereby allegedly undermined the establishment of a united working-class front against its natural enemy, the 'Imperial Field Marshal'.[59] His helping hand in consolidating Nazi rule after 1933 had seemingly vindicated the Communists' uncompromising stance; Socialist East Germany would continue this virtuous fight against Hindenburg in the realm of memory.

Teachers and those caring for young children were urged to join in the struggle against 'reactionary', 'neo-fascist', and 'militarist' sentiments, and 'democratized' German school classes were no longer allowed to glorify royals and military figures.[60] The teaching of German history in the one-party state was streamlined and competing interpretations were muted. Official Marxist historiography understood National Socialism as the outcome of the policies of a small imperialist, monopoly capitalist, and military-bureaucratic elite.[61]

Wolfgang Ruge's Hindenburg biography, published in 1975, fittingly titled *Portrait of a Militarist* is emblematic of this approach.[62] In spite of his biographical method, Ruge, one of the GDR's leading historians, did not focus exclusively on Hindenburg's life, but on the 'fundamental ideological problems of German history, on the essence of imperialism, the role of militarism, the purpose of the state, and on the relationship between the masses of the people and their exploiters...'.[63] He accused 'bourgeois' scholars of attempting to salvage the imperialist–militarist system by arguing that a 'senile General' was the root of all evil.[64] In reality, Hindenburg had been no more than a tiny screw in a giant 'mechanism of perfect inhumanity', he argued. Only when all forms of imperialism had been defeated once and for all could Hindenburg's name be allowed to fade into obscurity. Until then the memory of his 'macabre personality' had to be preserved for posterity in order to 'make a contribution to the destruction of the system he represented'.[65]

Although such East German accounts certainly advocated a more complete break with the Hindenburg myth than their 'bourgeois' West German
counterparts, they were equally riddled with apologetic tendencies. Because East German scholarship was focused on proving the culpability of the
capitalist and militarist elites, there was not much room for acknowledging
the susceptibility of ordinary Germans to the Nazis' allure. Hindenburg
seemed to fit in perfectly: the militarist Prussian Junker with a vast estate,
whose family had faced allegations of corruption, was to be blamed for
the appointment of the Nazi leader—a narrative also exemplified in the
character of 'Dogsborough', a thinly-veiled version of Hindenburg in Bertolt Brecht's allegory of Hitler's rise to power *The Resistable Rise of Arturo
Ui*, which was performed at East Berlin's Berliner Ensemble from 1959.[66]
Emphasizing the fateful role of the 'Imperial Field Marshal' however, enabled East Germans to project the guilt for German crimes onto a select
group of men and to distance themselves accordingly. Although conceived
in very different political systems, the memory strategies in East and West
Germany overlapped to a surprisingly high degree in their self-exculpatory
thrust.[67]

East German historiography in the main underwent some surprising
transformations within the parameters of Marxist-Leninist scholarship.
From the 1970s onwards, for instance, historians re-cast the history of
Prussia in a more positive light. The restoration of the equestrian statue of
Frederick the Great in 1980, which had been removed from East Berlin's
central avenue Unter den Linden in 1950, was a visible symbol of this shift.
More approving biographies of Frederick the Great and Bismarck were
published as well.[68] East German interpretations of Germany's second Reich
President, however, never witnessed such revision. There was no room for
public Hindenburg eulogies in East Germany. On the contrary, he remained
a symbol for the pitfalls of the 'bourgeois-imperialist system'—including
the GDR's western neighbour, the Federal Republic.[69]

## Sites of past and present Hindenburg memory

Hindenburg's different standing in post-war East and West German memory
was reflected not just in academic discourse, but also in spatial terms. For
the duration of the separation of the two German states, their disparate
treatment of Germany's second President was mirrored in Berlin's most

central square.[70] Today's Platz des 18. März on the western side of Brandenburg Gate had been named Hindenburgplatz within days of his death in August 1934. From 1961 onwards the GDR's 'anti-fascist bulwark', the Berlin Wall, ran right through it. Whereas the West Berlin side of the square continued to be named Hindenburgplatz until after German re-unification, the Eastern side of the square was given its pre-1934 name Platz vor dem Brandenburger Tor in 1958.[71]

Whilst the names of prominent Nazis like Hitler, Goebbels, and Göring were often eradicated from street signs spontaneously by Red Army soldiers, the Soviet occupation authorities also issued detailed lists to local councils with the names of all those historical figures to be changed in the coming years. Hindenburg's name was included.[72] His name was replaced with those of figures more suited to a Socialist Germany. Berlin's Hindenburgbrücke, linking the districts Prenzlauer Berg and Wedding, was re-named Bösebrücke in 1948, honouring Wilhelm Böse, an anti-fascist activist murdered by the Nazis.[73] In Jena, meanwhile, the Hindenburgstraße was re-named Ernst-Thälmann-Straße to commemorate the KPD leader who had twice challenged Hindenburg to the presidency and who had been killed in Buchenwald.[74]

A denazification of street names also took place in post-war West Germany; one will search in vain for 'Hitler', 'Goebbels', or 'Göring Streets' today. The Western policy, however, did not include Hindenburg as straightforwardly. Because responsibility for West German streets has lain with individual town councils, these have been able to proceed differently since 1945: whereas Frankfurt am Main has rid itself not only of its Hindenburg- and Tannenbergstraße, but its Bismarckstraße, too, cities like Bonn, Mainz, and Saarbrücken each still have two streets commemorating Hindenburg. The small town of Dillingen in Lower Saxony holds the record with three. The district of Lichterfelde in south-western Berlin still has its broad Hindenburgdamm, and the giant causeway connecting Sylt with mainland Germany, named Hindenburgdamm in 1927, also still bears that name today. While not a single Hindenburg Street has survived in East Germany, of 209 larger West German towns and villages over 70 still feature Hindenburg Bridges, Streets, Squares, Parks, and Walls.[75] Controversy surrounding these visible traces of Hindenburg's erstwhile veneration has flared up repeatedly across the country, especially since re-unification. Left-wing party groups in local councils, such as the Greens or the PDS, have mostly been the driving force.[76] Due to the great bureaucratic complications involved in re-naming streets, however, such endeavours have rarely been crowned with success.

Similarly, attempts to revoke Hindenburg's honorary citizenship in some of the numerous towns and villages that bestowed the honour upon him during his lifetime have generated heated debates, but have for the most part failed.[77] In the run-up to the seventieth anniversary of the 'Day of Potsdam' in 2003, debates on the retraction of Hindenburg's honorary citizenship ensued in both Potsdam and Berlin.[78] According to a petition by the Green Party, the former Reich President no longer deserved to be honoured in the capital, because his political decisions had led to 'war and tyranny' and had made possible 'the murder of thousands of Berliners in extermination camps, the death of the German civilian population, and the destruction of Berlin in the Second World War'.[79] The conviction that Hindenburg was directly responsible for the Nazis' crimes could hardly be made more explicit.

The local SPD, CDU, and FDP all opposed the idea of a retraction—not because, they argued, Hindenburg should still be venerated, but because lists of honorary citizens were historical documents in their own right, which should not be altered. The Social Democratic head of Berlin's chamber of deputies and former mayor of West Berlin, Walter Momper, stressed repeatedly in an interview that although he opposed the retraction, he did not want to be seen as 'defending Hindenburg'. Deciding to oppose the Greens' initiative had not been easy, he explained, because 'after all there is no one who stands up for Hindenburg with enthusiasm'.[80]

Although Hindenburg has remained an honorary citizen of Berlin and Potsdam, Momper's statements more or less reflect the public consensus in re-unified Germany at the beginning of the twenty-first century.[81] While most German politicians and other opinion-makers would not want to be seen as Hindenburg hagiographers, his memory is no longer deemed threatening enough to warrant erasure—be it from street signs or lists of honorary citizens. Especially when compared to the somewhat impassioned public reactions to the—relatively contained—Hindenburg worship in Marburg in the late 1940s, it is clear that debates about Hindenburg have lost most of their urgency. Accordingly, most of the recent scholarly works on the Weimar Republic still refer to his popular veneration as a political factor, but do not re-visit the shrill—and partly apologetic—debates of the late 1940s and 1950s, during which Hindenburg was cast as the man who had 'delivered' the German people to Nazi rule.

The fact that a non-democrat was the elected head of state of the Republic is now generally considered one of many factors leading to Weimar's downfall.[82] Although traces of Hindenburg's former veneration remain in the public realm, he no longer has mythical status. As Rainer Blasius opined when commemorating the 90th anniversary of Tannenberg in the *Frankfurter Allgemeine Zeitung*, his name was becoming a historical admonition: 'Ninety years after the outbreak of war in 1914 there is hope that in spite of their alleged military or political victories, myths and self-declared or glorified saviours have lost their allure forever.'[83]

\* \* \*

The illustrative fate of a statue by the sculptor Hermann Hosaeus perhaps best sums up the extent to which Hindenburg has been subject to different cycles of German memory since his death. Erected by German veterans near the Kyffhäuser Memorial in Thuringia in 1938, it was encountered by Soviet soldiers or local Communists after 1945. Keen to get rid of the memorial to the 'Imperial Field Marshal', they intended to blow it up. Because the statue was made of porphyry, an exceptionally hard stone, however, they had to settle on pushing the statue over and burying it. In the 1970s, a recreation home for members of East Germany's secret police, the Stasi, was built on the site. Construction workers discovered the statue during the laying of the building's foundations and seemingly consigned it to an eternal fate underground: the statue's feet were cast in concrete and a pavilion built above. Though probably unaware of the fact, Stasi spies on vacation now enjoyed their holidays on top of Hindenburg's effigy.

In the 1990s, a resourceful West German businessman who had since bought the building and converted it into a hotel, learned about the statue buried on his property and spotted a business opportunity. Much to the dismay of some of the long-established East German villagers of Bad Frankenhausen, he decided to dig up Hindenburg in 2004. His plan to restore the statue in the hope of attracting extra guests to the Kyffhäuser Hotel aroused considerable controversy; the spectre of a resurrected Hindenburg—a possible symbol for the renaissance of right-wing narratives of the past in unified Germany—even haunted the national media.[84] After some negotiation with the Bad Frankenhausen council, however, the hotelier has compromised.[85] Hindenburg is to remain underground, but

made visible through a glass plate with a panel explaining the statue's event-
ful history. Lying on one side, Hindenburg's face looks up at the observer
from underground—a rather curious example of Germany's archaeology
of memory: a monument to the once mythical Hindenburg, firmly buried,
yet visible and not entirely forgotten.

# Conclusion

The Hindenburg myth was an exceptionally potent—and all too often overlooked—force in German politics between 1914 and 1934. Hindenburg acquired mythical stature soon after the Battle of Tannenberg and became Germany's undisputed national hero embodying the—typically masculine—virtues of wartime: not just military skill, but determination, strong nerves, sang-froid, the readiness for sacrifice, and a mighty sense of duty. From the outset, Hindenburg appealed to broad sections of German society, not least because his myth corresponded to the traditional structures of popular imagination; it united and personalized older semantic and semiotic traditions, such as the cults of Bismarck, Hermann the Cherusker, and Barbarossa. Hindenburg's veneration was not narrowly restricted to a single class, confessional group, or to a particular region. Because his seminal mythical moment had been the defence and salvation of the homeland—crucially from Tsarist Russia—his allure even penetrated the circles of patriotic and Russophobic Social Democrats. Although German war propaganda consciously promoted his myth from the top down to bolster the war effort and the monarchical idea, within less than two years Hindenburg had eclipsed even his monarch, Wilhelm II. The Hindenburg myth had a life of its own and would outlive the reign of the Hohenzollern dynasty and survive German military defeat—a defeat his leadership had meant to rule out.

The Hindenburg myth remained a lens through which Germans saw events despite their growing insecurity and sense of crisis towards the end of the war. The effectiveness of such propaganda began to encounter its limits, as conveyed by the secret reports on the popular mood, but given Hindenburg's centrality in public discourse on the war it is striking that he was hardly ever held accountable for Germany's military failure. Instead, the democratic left vilified Ludendorff and authoritarian Wilhelmine politics, whilst the right found its scapegoat in the 'stab-in-the-back' theory. Most importantly, however, the Hindenburg myth survived in 1918/19, because it still expressed the social expectations of large sections of German society: to retrieve something positive from war, to continue believing in the national cause, and to recreate order and recapture tranquillity after the disruption of wartime. Re-creating order and preventing chaos were especially important to the democratic left which engaged Hindenburg's mythical authority as a source of legitimacy for the new republican order. This frame of reference in 1918/19 explains why Weimar democrats would be able to believe in Hindenburg as a 'resting pole', a 'lifesaver', and 'beacon of stability' for long into his presidency.

Republican reluctance to criticize the Hindenburg myth, resting on belief as well as calculation, soon turned into a burden for the young Republic. Myths can stabilize a political order as much as they can undermine it. Especially the interconnectedness of the Hindenburg myth and the 'stab-in-the-back' narration—anti-republican to its core—meant that after 1919 his myth was increasingly caught up in the extreme of politics. Anti-republicans discovered Hindenburg-worship as a vital resource of agitation and mobilization, most visibly during his travels around East Prussia and the Tannenberg commemorations in 1924. The Republic increasingly came under siege as a result. The pro-republican parties found themselves faced with the impossible task of defying attacks on democracy camouflaged as veneration of Hindenburg. The Hindenburg myth was thus a decisive factor in shifting the political climate considerably to the right during Weimar's early crisis-ridden years by disarming republican defences. Republicans repeatedly alerted Hindenburg to his polarizing influence but he did nothing to avert this course. On the contrary, he consciously aided in spreading anti-republican ideas and was integral to popularizing the stab-in-the-back legend, not least during the court hearings in 1919.

Because he had not faded from public imagination since his second retirement in 1919, his myth did not have to be resurrected during the presidential contest of 1925. The Reichsblock managed to transform his mythical reputation into political capital in 1925: it helped the right capture, of all things, the highest republican office. Hindenburg's unremittingly broad appeal not only galvanized anti-republicans, but also drew many previous non-voters to the polls and held considerable sway in the realm of political Catholicism. Furthermore, left-wing reluctance to attack Germany's most venerated figure—the result of over a decade of cross-party Hindenburg reverence—substantially weakened and confused the republican campaign and therefore contributed in no small measure to his victory.

Hindenburg's first term as President witnessed profound changes among the attitudes of both his followers and former opponents. As a result of his initial reluctance to implement a thoroughly anti-democratic agenda, the radical right began to turn its back on the President while republicans increasingly began to sing his praises. A republican layer of the Hindenburg myth emerged that fed off his stance during the revolution and demobilization in 1918: that of the dutiful president who stabilized the republican order and helped to consolidate democracy, overcoming the chaos of Weimar's early years by sheer virtue of his character and rock-like presence. The evocative symbol of the 'rock' invoked Hindenburg's masculine gravitas, but also expressed the extent to which his age was portrayed as a benefit; he was likened to matter that resisted the ravages of time.

The immense popularity Hindenburg brought with him into office transformed the face of the Weimar presidency. After 1925 he became more ubiquitous in German public life than ever before. The Hindenburg myth did not just find expression in the party political press but also found new cultural and commercial outlets. That the myth was increasingly disseminated via the new mass media of film, radio, the illustrated papers, and commercial advertising contributed significantly to its scope, endurance, and intensity, and turned it into much more than a political fashion. Hindenburg's omnipresence across the new mass media, whose audiences were more amorphous than the readership of the traditional party press, meant that his myth increasingly transcended the dividing lines of Weimar politics. Republicans, too, were exposed to—and sometimes shaped—Hindenburg's iconic status, blurring the boundaries between cultural entertainment and propagandistic politics.

This considerable overlap of open, if qualitatively different, republican and right-wing veneration of Hindenburg mirrored in the mass cultural sphere during Hindenburg's first term was also evident on his eightieth birthday. Although the orchestrated unity of 2 October 1927 rang hollow, that the Hindenburg myth proved polyvalent enough in this era of sharpening political polarization to attract a diverse band of followers ranging from moderate Social Democrats, such as Gustav Noske, to the DNVP, and the Nazi party was highly significant. No other figure in this fragmented

period was venerated by such a broad social and political coalition. Social
Democratic and bourgeois-republican worship of Hindenburg, of course,
differed qualitatively from that of right-wing bourgeois Germans. One
would probably have searched in vain for Hindenburg portraits in Social
Democratic workers' living rooms and their public praise of Hindenburg
differed in terms of style and substance from that of their bourgeois counterparts. Moderate left leaders and commentators nevertheless subscribed to
significant layers of the mythical narrative, especially when hailing Hindenburg as a beacon of tranquillity and rock of stability. They, too, frequently
emphasized his sense of duty, and based their belief in the constitutionality
of his actions on their trust in this national father figure. Different versions
of the Hindenburg myth thus existed among his body of faithful, but often
did so simultaneously.

The mythical chronology of the nationalist right was unlike that of
republicans: the focus was on the interconnectedness of Hindenburg's early
career with the Kaiserreich's 'glorious past', on victory at Tannenberg and
his wartime leadership, on his first election success, and, from 1933, on
his role in the 'Third Reich'. The pre-Nazi democratic left, meanwhile,
had emphasized a different set of dates: Hindenburg's stabilizing impact
during the revolution and its aftermath, his constitutional stance after 1925,
and his victory over Hitler in 1932. The Hindenburg myth was thus in
a constant process of being re-negotiated and re-interpreted; it was an
ever-evolving phenomenon which had to incorporate the many twists
and turns of Hindenburg's career. This very polyvalence, in fact, made
the Hindenburg myth a more plastic and potent phenomenon than one
trapped in the tight corset of Weimar's right-wing political sphere could
ever have been. Crucially, the belief in Hindenburg as an indispensable
source of stability—a 'rock' of the Republic—would make republicans
less perceptive when it came to recognizing, and holding the President
accountable for, the quiet constitutional takeover from 1930. It also led in
no small measure to Hindenburg's re-election in 1932. Supporting him as
a bulwark or an 'imperturbable dam' against the Nazi 'tide' rested on older
patterns of thought relating to the war and to 1918/19.

So multi-layered, in fact, was his myth that Hindenburg could be
perceived both as a saviour *from* Weimar and saviour *of* Weimar within
the space of a few years; and indeed in the same election campaign, as
the conflicting campaign rhetoric of people such as Otto Braun and Julius
Elbau on the one hand, and Edgar Julius Jung and Count Kuno Westarp

on the other illustrates. Only when grasping the mythical narrative as a multi-layered phenomenon with different layers simultaneously appealing to different groups can we understand its inimitably broad and enduring appeal. This multi-layered nature meant that a bricoleur of the radical right like Joseph Goebbels could peel off Hindenburg's republican stratum once he sided more openly with their political aim of the 'national revolution'. It was precisely because Hindenburg managed to cut across party political lines like no other figure in this period of political polarization, that his myth—and, by extension, his actions—could wield such influence over the course of Weimar's history.

The myth's anti-democratic function was not always evident. Different political groups employed it to further more current agendas. When Hindenburg defied many of his former right-wing voters and signed the Young Plan in March 1930, it looked as though he would, in fact, continue to boost republican stability. Ultimately, however, the myth's function depended in no small measure on what causes he was willing to lend his name to—a key difference between Hindenburg, the living myth and mythical narratives involving abstract concepts or figures from a long gone past. Their capacity as vacant vessels is ultimately greater and more straightforward. Subscribing to the Hindenburg myth, by contrast, entailed potential disappointment. That the trust invested in him by so many of his followers—both on the left and right—survived in spite of military failure and political disappointments is cause to question the notion that the Hindenburg myth was simply moulded in the image of the expectations and desires of German society. If myths nevertheless give us clues to the collective unconscious of the society in which they are worshipped, then German society harboured strong wishes for a national father figure and political saviour, and cherished the sense of order and continuity Hindenburg's mythical presence offered more than the various political—and military—goals associated with his name. As we have seen, for many the trust in Hindenburg was non-negotiable, but his devotees also showed astonishing adaptive abilities; rather than debunking the Hindenburg myth in 1918, 1925, 1930, 1932, or in 1933 they largely settled with what they were offered. While the mythical narrative itself was constantly evolving, with layer after layer being added around the nucleus of his Tannenberg credentials, the belief in Hindenburg's mythical qualities was less ephemeral and more enduring than a narrow application of Weber's model of 'charismatic authority'—which defines projection as key—would suggest.

Crucially, Hindenburg's re-election in April 1932 made him the ultimate arbiter of Hitler. If, as has been argued with reference to the 1932 presidential elections, Hindenburg had had no genuine followers in the last years of Weimar, but had been perceived entirely as the lesser of two evils by the democrats on the one hand and deserted completely by right-wing Germans on the other, there would have been no need to rely on his mythical status during the campaign. Democratic commentators could have focused exclusively on their opposition to Hitler, and Hindenburg's right-wing opponents could simply have brushed their veneration of the Field Marshal and President under the carpet. If the Hindenburg myth had indeed sounded hollow in 1932, the Nazis would not have been able to rely on his mythical authority to the extent that they did when they took power less than a year later. In fact, they stressed Hindenburg's mythical endorsement of their rule from the outset. Given their brutality towards other opponents and competitors, the lengths to which they went to reap the benefits of Hindenburg's authority are striking—and only understandable if the party leadership genuinely believed that they would not fare as well on a more aggressive course. Hindenburg may have lost some of his allure to the political class, but not to the populace. The Nazis continued to accept—and honour—Hindenburg as a parallel authority in the symbolic realm and his myth was a vital tool in the process of consolidating their rule at a time when Hitler's stature as a 'statesman' still had to be fashioned; the 'seizure of power' was ultimately not completed until Hindenburg died. The President did nothing to stop his veneration playing into the hands of the Nazi regime. Quite the contrary: he willingly participated in the stage-managed shows of unity with Hitler. Moreover, his political will provided the regime with invaluable symbolic ammunition after his death.

Without a permanent official myth-maker, or bricoleur, the Hindenburg myth required a variety of thurifers. The Imperial War Press Office encouraged his wartime popularity by means of censorship and carefully orchestrated information management. During the Weimar years, many different personalities, ranging from German Nationalist politicians such as Wilhelm von Gayl, and the members of the Reichsblock to State Secretary Meissner, were involved in promoting Hindenburg. The heterogeneous members of the United Hindenburg Committees of 1932, the Centre Party Chancellor Heinrich Brüning, Goebbels, who orchestrated Hindenburg's appearances and carefully Nazified the mythical narrative in the 'Third

Reich', and crucially, Hindenburg himself were important players in this process of image management and control.

Whilst much of the Hindenburg worship remained spontaneous—or was appropriated strategically by businesses for commercial purposes—and not controlled by a single political agent, Hindenburg's efforts to censor his image in the cultural realm prior to 1933 show how closely he was involved in the mythmaking process—and how aware he was of its power. That he willingly participated in the Nazis' stage-managed propaganda displays thus takes on new meaning—as does the fact that he was of sound mind until his death. Hindenburg was no senile old man oblivious to the powers of image and propaganda, conned by the Nazis' powers of seduction.

Strikingly, Hindenburg remained a rallying point for opponents of the regime in spite of his complicity in the Nazi takeover and his propagandistic support for the party. Many continued to believe in his integrity and considered him a fellow victim of the regime—or at least a senile old man above blame—who was being exploited. A hopeful sense of trust in his rock-like presence and his power to alter people's fortunes remained. As a result, Jewish veterans and Social Democrats were equally overwhelmed by fear and depression when Hindenburg died in August 1934. The intangible belief in Hindenburg as a beacon of stability and order, the belief that he would 'sort things out' and 'save' Germany, had meant different things to different groups of society during the previous twenty years. Ultimately, those who had hoped, as late as 1932, that 'simply by being there' he would save them *from* Nazism were let down bitterly.

Whilst Hindenburg's media presence naturally diminished somewhat after his death, the Nazis continued to invoke his myth. This continuing reliance on his authority was most evident during his second funeral in 1935, and in the fact that the Nazis moved Hindenburg's coffin from the Tannenberg Memorial in early 1945, when Germany's military situation was already extremely desperate. After 1945, their emphasis on Hindenburg's role in the 'Third Reich' remained, albeit now re-interpreted in a largely negative light. In West Germany, Weimar's second President increasingly began to be regarded as Hitler's 'stirrup holder'. Focusing on Hindenburg's role in the Nazi 'seizure of power' was not free from apologetic tendencies, however. Arguing that a politically weak and senile old man had 'delivered' the country to Nazi rule enabled Germans to pinpoint the blame for the Nazis' rise to power on a small group of men. Blaming Hindenburg thus offered an opportunity to skirt the issue of popular consent so vital to Nazi rule, just like blaming Hitler would for the 12 years that followed.

At the same time, however, the renunciation of Hindenburg was not total in the pluralist Federal Republic. Countless streets carry his name to this day and there was a strong undercurrent of Hindenburg worship among select, yet influential, groups, especially among the expellees. Whilst such pluralist memories doubtless also existed in the GDR, the East German state left no space for these to be voiced openly; in official East German accounts Hindenburg featured as the chief representative of the corrupt 'bourgeois-imperialist' system. His name was erased from all street signs and his memorials discarded. In reunified Germany the debates about Hindenburg have gradually lost their urgency. While traces of his erstwhile veneration remain, Hindenburg is by and large no longer subject to self-exculpatory vilification nor still adulated to monumental heights. A Hindenburg myth on the scale of the phenomenon that caught the imagination of an inimitably broad social and political coalition of Germans between 1914 and 1934 and beyond, turning it into one of the most potent forces in German politics in a period otherwise characterized by rupture and fragmentation, has ceased to exist.

# Notes

## INTRODUCTION

1. *WaM*, 27 April 1925.
2. *FZ*, 27 April 1925, ev. edn.
3. *Weltbühne*, no. 12, 22 March 1932.
4. In the Federal Republic of Germany, the President is elected by a special assembly (the so-called *Bundesversammlung*).
5. See his interview in *FAZ*, no. 28, 3 Feb. 2003, 39.
6. Deutsche Bücherei (ed.), *Hindenburg-Bibliographie: Verzeichnis der Bücher und Zeitschriftenaufsätze von und über den Reichspräsidenten Generalfeldmarschall von Hindenburg* (Leipzig, 1938).
7. R. B. Asprey, *The German High Command at War: Hindenburg and Ludendorff and the First World War*, 4th edn. (London, 1994); M. Kitchen, *The Silent Dictatorship: The Politics of the German High Command under Hindenburg and Ludendorff, 1916–1918* (London, 1976); W. J. Astore and D. E. Showalter, *Hindenburg: Icon of German Militarism* (Washington DC, 2005).
8. W. Rauscher, *Hindenburg: Feldmarschall und Reichspräsident* (Vienna, 1997).
9. A. Dorpalen, *Hindenburg and the Weimar Republic* (Princeton, NJ, 1964).
10. W. Görlitz, *Hindenburg: Ein Lebensbild* (Bonn, 1953); W. Hubatsch, *Hindenburg und der Staat: Aus den Papieren des Generalfeldmarschalls und Reichspräsidenten von 1878 bis 1934* (Göttingen, Berlin, Frankfurt/M., and Zurich, 1966); see also W. Scharlau, 'Mit ihm trug sich Preußen selber zu Grabe: Der Mythos Hindenburg und ein wissenschaftlicher Skandal', *Der Monat*, vol. 23 (1971), 56–64.
11. K. D. Bracher, *Die Auflösung der Weimarer Republik: Eine Studie zum Problem des Machtverfalls in der Demokratie* (Stuttgart and Düsseldorf, 1955); A. J. Nicholls, *Weimar and the Rise of Hitler*, 4th edn. (London, 2000); H. Mommsen, *The Rise and Fall of Weimar Democracy* (Chapel Hill, NC, and London, 1996).
12. V. R. Berghahn, 'Die Harzburger Front und die Kandidatur Hindenburgs für die Präsidentschaftswahlen 1932', *VfZ*, 13, no. 1 (1965), 64–82; N. D. Cary, 'The Making of the Reich President, 1925: German Conservatism and the Nomination of Paul von Hindenburg', *CEH*, 23 (1990), 179–204; G. Jasper, 'Die verfassungs- und machtpolitische Problematik

des Reichspräsidentenamtes in der Weimarer Republik: Die Praxis der Reichspräsidenten Ebert und Hindenburg im Vergleich', in R. König, H. Soell, and H. Weber (eds.), *Friedrich Ebert: Bilanz und Perspektiven der Forschung* (Munich, 1990), 147–59; L. E. Jones, 'Hindenburg and the Conservative Dilemma in the 1932 Presidential Elections', *German Studies Review*, vol. 20 (1997), 235–59; E. Matthias, 'Hindenburg zwischen den Fronten: Zur Vorgeschichte der Reichspräsidentenwahlen von 1932 (Dokumentation)', *VfZ*, vol. 8 (1960), 75–84; W. Pyta, 'Die Präsidialgewalt in der Weimar Republik', in M.-L. Recker (ed.), *Parlamentarismus in Europa: Deutschland, England und Frankreich im Vergleich* (Munich, 2004), 65–96.

13. J. Wheeler-Bennett, *The Wooden Titan* (London, 1936).

14. e. g. ibid., 272; Dorpalen, *Hindenburg*; H. A. Turner, *German Big Business and the Rise of Hitler* (New York and Oxford, 1985); H. Schulze, *Weimar: Deutschland 1917–1933* (Berlin, 1982), 100 and 298–300.

15. W. Maser, *Hindenburg: Eine politische Biographie* (Rastatt, 1990); H. Zaun, *Hindenburg und die deutsche Außenpolitik 1925–1934* (Cologne, 1999); W. Pyta, 'Paul von Hindenburg als charismatischer Führer der deutschen Nation', in F. Möller (ed.), *Charismatische Führer der deutschen Nation* (Munich, 2004), 109–48; W. Pyta, *Hindenburg: Herrschaft zwischen Hohenzollern und Hitler* (Munich, 2007) offers the most far-reaching, detailed, and in many ways most convincing re-assessment of Hindenburg's political role. None of these authors gained access to Hindenburg's personal papers, which the family refuse to make available. This author's attempt to gain access was not crowned with success either, see Hindenburg's grandson Hubertus von Hindenburg to the author, 12 October 2004.

16. A few studies are exceptions: A. Menge, 'The Iron Hindenburg—a Popular Icon of Weimar Germany', *German History*, vol. 26, no. 3 (2008), 357–382; A.v.d. Goltz, 'Die Macht des Hindenburg-Mythos: Politik, Propaganda und Popularität in Kaiserreich und Republik' in V. Borsó, C. Liermann, and P. Merziger (eds.) *Die Macht des Populären: Politik und populäre Kultur im 20. Jahrhundert* (Bielefeld, 2010), 31–56. K.-D. Weber, *Das Büro des Reichspräsidenten* (Frankfurt/M., 2001), 250–79; H. Fischer, 'Tannenberg-Denkmal und Hindenburgkult', in M. Hütt et al. (eds.), *Unglücklich das Land, das Helden nötig hat: Leiden und Sterben in den Kriegsdenkmälern des Ersten und Zweiten Weltkriegs* (Marburg, 1990), 28–49; D. Lehnert, 'Die geschichtlichen Bilder von "Tannenberg". Vom Hindenburg-Mythos im Ersten Weltkrieg zum ersatzmonarchischen Identifikationssymbol in der Weimarer Republik', in K. Imhof and P. Schulz (eds.), *Medien und Krieg—Krieg in den Medien* (Zurich, 1995), 37–72; J. v. Hoegen, *Der Held von Tannenberg: Genese und Funktion des Hindenburg-Mythos* (Cologne, Weimar, Vienna, 2007). Hoegen's impressive work, which was published after this study was submitted as a doctoral thesis at Oxford University, focuses mainly on Hindenburg's image in the mainstream press. It pays less attention to the popular press and other

mass media, such as film, radio, and commercial advertising, and leaves out the period between 1919 and 1925, as well as the fate of the myth after Hindenburg's death in 1934.

17. Dorpalen, *Hindenburg*; Hoegen, *Held von Tannenberg*.

18. J. Assmann, *Das kulturelle Gedächtnis* (Munich, 1999); S. Wodianka, 'Mythos und Erinnerung: Mythentheoretische Modelle und ihre gedächtnistheoretischen Implikationen', in G. Oesterle (ed.), *Erinnerung, Gedächtnis, Wissen: Studien zur kulturwissenschaftlichen Gedächtnisforschung* (Göttingen, 2005), 211–30.

19. M. Halbwachs, *On Collective Memory* (Chicago, IL, and London, 1992); L. Niethammer, 'Maurice Halbwachs: Memory and the Feelings of Identity', in B. Strath (ed.), *Myth and Memory in the Construction of Community: Historical Patterns in Europe and Beyond* (Brussels, 2000), 75–94.

20. P. H. Hutton, *History as an Art of Memory* (Hanover and London, 1993), 79.

21. B. Strath, 'Introduction. Myth, Memory and History in the Construction of Community', in idem (ed.), *Myth and Memory*, 33.

22. E. Wolfrum, *Geschichte als Waffe: Vom Kaiserreich bis zur Wiedervereinigung* (Göttingen, 2001), 5–7.

23. P. Nora et al. (eds.), *Realms of Memory: Rethinking the French Past*, 3 vols. (New York, 1996–1998); E. François and H. Schulze (eds.), *Deutsche Erinnerungsorte*, 3 vols. (Munich, 2001).

24. D. Lehnert and K. Megerle (eds.), *Politische Identität und nationale Gedenktage: Zur politischen Kultur in der Weimarer Republik* (Opladen, 1989); idem (eds.), *Politische Teilkulturen zwischen Integration und Polarisierung: Zur politischen Kultur in der Weimarer Republik* (Opladen, 1990); U. Heinemann, *Die verdrängte Niederlage: Politische Öffentlichkeit und Kriegsschuldfrage in der Weimarer Republik* (Göttingen, 1983); A. Thimme, *Flucht in den Mythos: Die Deutschnationale Volkspartei und die Niederlage von 1918* (Göttingen, 1969); B. Barth, *Dolchstoßlegenden und politische Desintegration: Das Trauma der deutschen Niederlage im Ersten Weltkrieg 1914–1933* (Düsseldorf, 2003); J. Verhey, *The 'Spirit of 1914': Militarism, Myth and Mobilization in Germany* (Cambridge, 2000).

25. H.-D. Schmid, 'Der Mythos-Begriff in der neueren Geschichtswissenschaft, Philosophie und Theologie', in A. von Saldern (ed.), *Mythen in Geschichte und Geschichtsschreibung aus polnischer und deutscher Sicht* (Münster, 1996), 40–2, here: 40.

26. I. Kershaw, *The 'Hitler Myth': Image and Reality in the Third Reich* (Oxford and New York, 1987); A. Grunenberg, *Antifaschismus: Ein deutscher Mythos* (Reinbek, 1993); H. Blumenberg, *Arbeit am Mythos* (Frankfurt/M., 1996); A. Dörner, *Politischer Mythos und symbolische Politik: Der Hermannmythos: Zur Enstehung des Nationalbewußtseins der Deutschen* (Reinbek, 1996); R. Gerwarth, *The Bismarck Myth: Weimar Germany and the Legacy of the Iron Chancellor* (Oxford, 2005).

27. S. Behrenbeck, *Der Kult um die toten Helden: Nationalsozialistische Mythen, Riten und Symbole* (Vierow near Greifswald, 1996), 36 and 40; D. Orlow,

'The Conversion of Myths into Political Power: The Case of the Nazi Party, 1925—1926', *AHR*, vol. 72, no. 3 (1967), 906—24; C. Jamme, *Einführung in die Philosophie des Mythos, vol. 2: Neuzeit und Gegenwart* (Darmstadt, 1991), 110.

28. A. Horstmann, 'Der Mythosbegriff vom frühen Christentum bis zur Gegenwart', *Archiv für Begriffsgeschichte*, 23 (1979), 7—54 and 197—245.

29. A. v. Saldern, 'Mythen, Legenden und Stereotypen', in idem (ed.), *Mythen in Geschichte und Geschichtsschreibung* (Münster, 1996), 13—26, here: 14.

30. E. Cassirer, *The Myth of the State* (London, 1946); idem, *Philosophie der symbolischen Formen, vol. 2: Das mythische Denken* (Berlin,1925).

31. See e.g.: W. Scholz, 'Mythos Hindenburg', *Die Woche*, no. 40, 1 Oct. 1927; W. v. Schramm's 'Gegenwärtiger Mythus' in *MNN*, no. 68, 10 March 1932.

32. R. Voigt (ed.), *Symbole der Politik, Politik der Symbole* (Opladen, 1989), 11.

33. T. Ziolkowski, 'Der Hunger nach dem Mythos: Zur seelischen Gastronomie der Deutschen in den Zwanziger Jahren', in R. Grimm and J. Hermand (eds.), *Die Sogenannten Zwanziger Jahre* (Bad Homburg, 1970), 169—201; G. L. Mosse, *The Nationalization of the Masses: Political Symbolism and Mass Movements in Germany from the Napoleonic Wars through the Third Reich* (Ithaca, NY, 1991), 6.

34. Behrenbeck, *Kult*, 36—40; Saldern, 'Mythen, Legenden und Stereotypen'.

35. J. Topolski, 'Historiographische Mythen: Eine methodologische Einführung', Saldern, *Mythen*, 27—35, here: 2.

36. H.-H. Nolte, 'Mythos-Plädoyer für einen engen Begriff', Saldern, *Mythen*, 36—9, here: 36.

37. C. G. Flood, *Political Myth: A Theoretical Introduction* (New York and London, 2004), 44.

38. Saldern, 'Mythen, Legenden und Stereotypen', 15.

39. Orlow, 'The Conversion of Myths', 906; Assmann, *Das kulturelle Gedächtnis*, 76.

40. Behrenbeck, *Kult*, 45; H. Münkler and W. Storch, *Siegfrieden: Politik mit einem deutschen Mythos* (Berlin, 1988), 66—7.

41. J. Topolski, 'Helden in der Geschichte und Geschichtsschreibung (theoretische Überlegungen)', in J. Strzelzyk (ed.), *Die Helden in der Geschichte und Historiographie* (Poznan, 1997), 11—19.

42. H.-J. Wirth, 'Vorwort', in idem (ed.), *Helden: Psychosozial* 10 (Weinheim, 1987), 6.

43. C. Lévi-Strauss, 'La structure des mythes', in idem, *Anthropologie structurale* (Paris, 1958), 235—65, here: 242; Wodianka, 'Mythos und Erinnerung', 215—18.

44. Dörner, *Politischer Mythos*, 28 and 92; Gerwarth, *Bismarck Myth*, 6—7.

45. Cassirer, *Myth of the State*, 280.

46. Orlow, 'The Conversion of Myths', 906; Cassirer, *Myth of the State*, 278; on the Weimar republic as crisis-ridden: D. Peukert, *The Weimar Republic: The Crisis of Classical Modernity* (London, 1991); for a recent alternative reading:

M. Föllmer and R. Graf (eds.), *Die 'Krise' der Weimarer Republik: Zur Kritik eines Deutungsmusters* (Frankfurt/M., 2005).

47. Behrenbeck, *Kult*, 45; Ziolkowski, 'Hunger nach dem Mythos', 170−1.

48. T. Nipperdey, *Deutsche Geschichte 1866−1988: Arbeitswelt und Bürgergeist*, 2nd edn. (Munich, 1991), 814.

49. T. Carlyle, *On Heroes, Hero-Worship, and the Heroic in History* (London, 1841); U. Frevert, 'Herren und Helden: Vom Aufstieg und Niedergang des Heroismus im 19. und 20. Jahrhundert', in R. van Dülmen (ed.), *Erfindung des Menschen: Schöpfungsträume und Körperbilder 1500−2000* (Vienna, 1998), 323−44.

50. Mosse, *Nationalization*, 53; Frevert, 'Herren und Helden', 332 and 335; on Bismarck especially K. Breitenborn, *Bismarck: Kult und Kitsch um den Reichsgründer* (Frankfurt/M. and Leipzig, 1990).

51. Dörner, *Politischer Mythos*, 96.

52. Gerwarth, *Bismarck Myth*, 86−92; H.-U. Wehler, *Deutsche Gesellschaftsgeschichte*, vol. 4: 1914−1949 (Munich, 2003), 547.

53. On these narratives: L. Kettenacker, 'Der Mythos vom Reich', in K.-H. Bohrer (ed.), *Mythos und Moderne: Begriff und Bild einer Rekonstruktion* (Frankfurt,1983), 134−56; K. Schreiner, ' "Wann kommt der Retter Deutschlands?" Formen und Funktionen von politischem Messianismus in der Weimarer Republik', *Saeculum*, 49 (1998), 105−47; Barth, *Dolchstoßlegenden*; Verhey, 'Spirit of 1914'; on the 'mythical web' of Weimar, Dörner, *Politischer Mythos*, 314.

54. Ibid. H. Callies, 'Arminius—Hermann der Cherusker: der deutsche Held', in Strzelzyk, *Helden in der Geschichte und Historiographie*, 49−58; Münkler and Storch, *Siegfrieden*; R. Krohn, 'Friedrich I. Barbarossa. Barbarossa und der Alte vom Berge: Zur neuzeitlichen Rezeption der Kyffhäuser-Sage', in U. Müller and W. Wunderlich (eds.), *Mittelalter-Mythen*, vol. 1 (St. Gallen, 1996), 101−18.

55. Dörner, *Politischer Mythos*, 15.

56. Frevert, 'Herren und Helden', 324; R. Schilling, *Deutungsmuster heroischer Männlichkeit in Deutschland 1813−1945* (Paderborn, 2003), 23−6.

57. P. Demandt, *Luisenkult: Die Unsterblichkeit der Königin von Preussen* (Cologne, 2003).

58. H.-J. Wirth, 'Die Sehnsucht nach Vollkommenheit: Zur Psychoanalyse der Heldenverehrung', in idem *Helden*, 96−113; here: 97; M. Naumann, *Strukturwandel des Heroismus: Vom sakralen zum revolutionären Heldentum* (Königstein and Taunus, 1984).

59. Schilling, *Deutungsmuster*, 257−8; Wirth, 'Sehnsucht nach Vollkommenheit', 97.

60. Kershaw, *Hitler Myth*; H.-U. Wehler, *Deutsche Gesellschaftsgeschichte*, vols. 3 and 4 (Munich, 1995 and 2003); Möller, *Charismatische Führer*.

61. M. Weber, 'Die drei reinen Typen der legitimen Herrschaft', idem, *Gesammelte Aufsätze zur Wissenschaftslehre*, ed. J. Winckelmann (Tübingen, 1985, 6th edition), 475–88.

62. W. J. Mommsen, *Max Weber and German Politics 1890–1920* (Chicago, IL, and London, 1984), 332–89; for an application of Weber's theory to Hindenburg's rule: Pyta, 'Hindenburg'; and his *Hindenburg*, especially 285–93; also Hoegen, *Held von Tannenberg*, 21–5.

63. This is especially true for Hans-Ulrich Wehler's concept of *Fremdcharisma* ('external charisma') that he derived from Weber's theory. The notion of *Fremdcharisma* focuses exclusively on the projection of beliefs and wishes onto a leader. See his *Gesellschaftsgeschichte*, vol. 3, 370.

64. Weber, 'Typen der legitimen Herrschaft', 484. Accordingly, Ian Kershaw asserts that Hitler's image suffered substantially once he was no longer able to prove his worth by delivering foreign policy and military successes: Kershaw, *Hitler Myth*; on this 'Bewährungszwang' also Wehler, *Gesellschaftsgeschichte*, vol. 4, 553.

65. I disagree with Pyta here, who works with the idea of the 'Bewährungszwang' and argues that the projected wishes of his followers corseted Hindenburg, see his, *Hindenburg*, 291.

66. Kurt Hübner has described this obstinate clinging to an idea even in the face of intense pressure with reference to myths. Since the perceived charisma of a leader is also situated in the realm of myth, Hübner's findings can—and should be—applied to Weber's concept. See K. Hübner, 'Wie irrational sind Mythen und Götter?', in H. P. Duerr (ed.), *Der Wissenschaftler und das Irrationale, vol. 3: Beiträge aus der Philosophie* (Frankfurt/M., 1985), 7–32, here: 20.

67. D. Blackbourn and G. Eley, *The Peculiarities of German History* (Oxford, 1984).

68. On Hindenburg's adulation abroad, see Zaun, *Hindenburg*, 195–226; R. W. Faulkner, 'American Reaction to Hindenburg of the Weimar Republic, 1925–1934', *The Historian* 51/3 (1989), 402–22.

69. P. Warner, *Kitchener: The Man behind the Legend* (London, 1985).

70. J. Ramsden, *Man of the Century: Winston Churchill and His Legend Since 1945* (London, 2002).

71. P. Servent, *Le mythe Pétain: Verdun ou les tranchées de la mémoire* (Paris, 1992); The comparability of the Hindenburg myth to other European phenomena of hero-worship has often been denied. See Hoegen, *Held von Tannenberg*, 61, 62 and 427; and Pyta, *Hindenburg*, 69 and 228. For a different reading of its French parallels, see A. v. d. Goltz and R. Gildea, 'Flawed saviours: the myths of Hindenburg and Pétain', *European History Quarterly*, vol. 39, no. 3 (2009), 439–64.

72. S. Hazareesingh, *The Legend of Napoleon* (London, 2004), 261 and 72–89.

73. L. Riall, *Garibaldi: Invention of a Hero* (New Haven, CT, 2007), 392.

74. B. Apor et al. (eds.), *The Leader Cult in Communist Dictatorships: Stalin and the Eastern Bloc* (Basingstoke, 2004).
75. Lehnert and Megerle, *Politische Teilkulturen.*
76. Dörner, *Politischer Mythos*, 295–314; Wehler, *Gesellschaftsgeschichte*, vol. 4, 359.
77. C. Lévi-Strauss, *La pensée sauvage* (Paris, 1962), cited in Wodianka, 'Mythos und Erinnerung', 217.
78. See Wolff's 'Wunsch an Hindenburg', *BT*, 2 Oct. 1932; also O. Meissner, *Staatssekretär unter Ebert-Hindenburg-Hitler: Der Schicksalsweg des deutschen Volkes von 1918–1945, wie ich ihn erlebte* (Hamburg, 1950), 382; and D. v. d. Schulenburg, *Welt um Hindenburg. 100 Gespräche mit Berufenen* (Berlin, 1935), 57; Even the former Prussian Interior Minister Carl Severing (SPD) continued to stress Hindenburg's humility and lack of vanity after 1945. See his article on Hindenburg in *AdsD Bonn*, NL Severing, 1/CSA B000027; Hindenburg's lack of vanity and personal ambition is also a paradigm of some of the more useful scholarly treatments, see e. g. Wheeler-Bennett, *Wooden Titan*, 226.
79. Klaus-Dieter Weber, who charts the mythmaking of Meissner et al. in some detail, bemoans the longevity of notions of an 'apolitical' Hindenburg, but clings to the idea that Hindenburg himself was not at all interested in the way he was portrayed and did not consider public opinion important. Weber, *Büro*, 172–3, 480–1, footnote, 1491.
80. For a more radical interpretation of Hindenburg as an obsessive 'image politician', Pyta, 'Hindenburg'.
81. Wolfram Pyta's monumental biography takes a different line and portrays Hindenburg's obsession with his own public standing as key to understanding much of his political career.
82. *Die Weltbühne*, no. 12, 22 March 1932.


CHAPTER I

1. Pyta, *Hindenburg*, 15.
2. On Hindenburg's early career see especially the first biography by his younger brother, B. v. Hindenburg, *Paul von Hindenburg: Ein Lebensbild* (Berlin, 1915); also Pyta, *Hindenburg*, 13–39.
3. Groener to Laegler, 22 March 1935, cited in D. Groener-Geyer, *General Groener: Staatsmann und Feldherr* (Frankfurt/M., 1955), 339.
4. A. Mombauer, *The Origins of the First World War: Controversies and Consensus* (London, 2002).
5. D. Showalter, *Tannenberg: Clash of Empires* (Hamden, CT, 1991), 329.
6. W. Kruse, *Krieg und nationale Integration: Eine Neuinterpretation des sozialdemokratischen Burgfriedensschlusses 1914/15* (Essen, 1993); N. Stargardt, *The German Idea of Militarism: Radical and Socialist Critics, 1866–1914* (Cambridge, 1994), 143.

7. *Vorwärts*, 28 August 1914, *GStA PK*, 1. HA, Rep. 77, CBS, no. 970a I, 47; Kruse, *Krieg,* 240–42, fn. 206.

8. P. Jahn, ' "Zarendreck, Barbarendreck—Peitscht sie weg!" Die russische Besatzung Ostpreußens 1914 in der deutschen Öffentlichkeit', in Berliner Geschichtswerkstatt (ed.), *August 1914: Ein Volk zieht in den Krieg* (Berlin, 1989), 147–55; P. Hoeres, 'Die Slawen: Perzeptionen des Kriegsgegners bei den Mittelmächten: Selbst- und Feindbild', in G. P. Groß, (ed.), *Die vergessene Front: Der Osten 1914/15: Ereignis, Wirkung, Nachwirkung* (Paderborn, 2006), 179–200.

9. Stargardt, *Militarism,* 155 and 147–8; Kruse, *Krieg,* 65–74.

10. *BT,* 31 August 1914.

11. *BT,* 14 September 1914.

12. See the reports of the local administrations in Osterode, Alleinstein, and Königsberg, *GStA PK*, 1. HA, Rep. 77, no. 1, vol. 1, 113 and 207.

13. V. G. Liulevicius, 'Von "Ober Ost" nach "Ostland"?', in Groß, *Vergessene Front,* 295–310, especially 297; J. Horne and A. Kramer, *German Atrocities 1914: A History of Denial* (New Haven, CT, 2001).

14. Verhey, *Spirit of 1914*; H. Strachan, *The First World War, vol. 1: To Arms* (Oxford, 2001), 103–62.

15. Cassirer, *Myth of the State,* 47–8.

16. c.f. Hoegen, *Held von Tannenberg,* 75.

17. *BT,* 14 September 1914.

18. Showalter, *Tannenberg,* 323.

19. R. Chickering, *Imperial Germany and the Great War: 1914–1918* (Cambridge, 1998), 26.

20. A. Niemann, *Hindenburgs Siege bei Tannenberg und Angerburg August-September 1914: Das Cannae und Leuthen der Gegenwart* (Berlin, 1915).

21. K. Lange, *Marneschlacht und deutsche Öffentlichkeit: Eine verdrängte Niederlage und ihre Folgen 1914–1939* (Düsseldorf, 1974).

22. Wolff, diary entry for 30 August 1914, printed in B. Sösemann (ed.), *Theodor Wolff: Tagebücher 1914–1919,* vol. 1 (Boppard am Rhein, 1984), 95–6; on reactions in Berlin, Jagow's report of 2 September 1914, I. Materna and H.-J. Schreckenbach (eds.), *Dokumente aus Geheimen Archiven, vol. 4: Berichte des Berliner Polizeipräsidenten zur Stimmung und Lage der Bevölkerung in Berlin 1914–1918* (Weimar, 1987), 6; for press reports e.g. *DTAZ,* 11 September 1914, morn. ed.; *Vorwärts,* 11 September 1914.

23. *KZ,* 29 August 1914, ev. ed.; *Vorwärts,* 30 August 1914; c.f. Hoegen, *Held von Tannenberg,* 40.

24. *BAB,* R43, no. 2398, 130.

25. S. Eckdahl, *Die Schlacht bei Tannenberg 1410: Quellenkritische Untersuchungen,* vol. 1 (Berlin, 1982), 17.

26. Cited in Hubatsch, *Hindenburg,* 152; see also Chief of the Naval Cabinet Admiral von Müller's diary entry for 30 August 1914, W. Görlitz (ed.)

*Regierte der Kaiser? Kriegstagebücher, Aufzeichnungen und Briefe des Chefs des Marine-Kabinetts Admiral Georg Alexander von Müller 1914–1918* (Göttingen, Berlin, and Frankfurt a. M., 1959), 52–3; and the diary of the Chief of Wilhelm II's Military Cabinet, Moritz Freiherr von Lyncker for 30 August 1914, printed in H. Afflerbach (ed.), *Kaiser Wilhelm II. als Oberster Kriegsherr im Ersten Weltkrieg: Quellen aus der militärischen Umgebung des Kaisers 1914–1918* (Munich, 2005), 148–9; on others claiming credit, M. Hoffmann, *Tannenberg wie es wirklich war* (Berlin, 1926), 75; E. Ludendorff, *Meine Kriegserinnerungen 1914–1918* (Berlin, 1919), 44–5.

27. Further Pyta, *Hindenburg*, 54–5.

28. *DTAZ*, no. 442, 1 September 1914, c.f. Hoegen, *Held von Tannenberg*, 47.

29. B. Ziemann, ' "Macht der Maschine"—Mythen des industriellen Krieges', in R. Spilker and B. Ulrich (eds.), *Der Tod als Maschinist: Der industrialisierte Krieg 1914–1918* (Bramsche, 1998), 177–89; F. B. Schenk, 'Tannenberg/Grunwald', in Francois and Schulze, *Erinnerungsorte*, vol. 2, 446–57.

30. Hoffmann to his wife, 4 June 1916, letter printed in *FAZ*, no. 7, 10 January 1955; H. H. Herwig, 'Of Men and Myths: The Use and Abuse of History in the Great War', in J. Winter et al. (eds.), *The Great War and the Twentieth Century* (New Haven, CT, and London, 2000), 299–330.

31. e.g. *KZ*, 12 September 1914, morn. ed.; *DTAZ*, 12 September 1914, morn. ed.

32. *KZ*, no. 408, 1 September 1914.

33. *BT*, no. 438, 29 August 1914.

34. Showalter, *Tannenberg*, 329.

35. *DTAZ*, no. 438, 30 August 1914; *KZ*, no. 413, 1 September 1914.

36. *BT*, no. 466, 14 September 1914.

37. *KZ*, no. 434, 12 September 1914.

38. W. v. Scholz, 'Mythos Hindenburg', *Der Heimatdienst*, October 1927; H. Winter, 'Hindenburg', *Volkschriften zum Großen Krieg*, vol. 92/93 (Berlin, 1916), 7.

39. *BT*, no. 443, 30 August 1916.

40. Eduard David's diary entry for 15–20 February 1915, E. Matthias and S. Miller (eds.), *Das Kriegstagebuch des Reichstagsabgeordneten Eduard David 1914 bis 1918* (Düsseldorf, 1966), 105–6.

41. Behrenbeck, *Kult*, 71.

42. P. v. Hindenburg, *Aus meinem Leben* (Leipzig, 1920), 67–8.

43. U. Frevert, 'Pflicht', in Schulze and François, *Erinnerungsorte*, II, 269–85.

44. A. Solzhenitsyn, *August 1914* (London, 1974), 387; on Ludendorff's nerves, Max Hoffmann, cited in D. J. Goodspeed, *Ludendorff: Soldier, Dictator, Revolutionary* (London, 1966), 73; Pyta, *Hindenburg*, 50–2; on equanimity as a wartime virtue: A. Reimann, *Der große Krieg der Sprachen: Untersuchungen zur historischen Semantik in Deutschland und England zur Zeit des Ersten Weltkriegs* (Essen, 2000), 28–31.

45. *BT,* no. 438, 29 August 1914. On the enemy as a 'flood' or 'tide': Reimann, *Krieg der Sprachen,* 40−41; on Hindenburg's 'strong nerves' c.f. Hoegen, *Held von Tannenberg,* 108−12; Pyta, *Hindenburg,* 77−8 and 106−7.

46. R. Krohn, 'Friedrich I. Barbarossa'; *Die Woche,* no. 40, 1 October 1927.

47. Dörner, *Politischer Mythos,* 317−18. The satirical magazine *Kladderadatsch* portrayed Hindenburg as Hermann as early as October 1914, P. Warncke et al. (eds.), *Hindenburg-Album des Kladderadatsch* (Berlin, 1925), 6.

48. Theodor Wolff is a good example as was the well-known national liberal historian Karl Hampe: F. Reichert and E. Wolgast (eds.), *Karl Hampe: Kriegstagebuch 1914−1919* (Munich, 2004), 56−7; for Bavarian Catholic views, W. Albrecht, *Landtag und Regierung in Bayern am Vorabend der Revolution von 1918* (Berlin, 1968), 178−81; on Hindenburg's cross-party and cross-regional appeal during WWI c.f. Hoegen, *Held von Tannenberg,* 130.

49. Kessler, diary entry for 8 April 1932, C. Kessler (ed.), *Diaries of a Cosmopolitan* (London, 1971), 413; c.f. Chapter 7, 163.

50. David, diary entry for 15−20 February 1915, Matthias, *Eduard David,* 105−6; Liebknecht's comments of February 1915 in E. Matthias and E. Pikart (eds.), *Die Reichstagsfraktion der deutschen Sozialdemokratie 1914 bis 1918* (Düsseldorf, 1966), 29−30.

51. *Schaubühne,* no. 38, 23 September 1915.

52. C. M. Clark, *Wilhelm II - Profiles in Power* (London, 2000), 161; on the impact of the mass media on Wilhelm's image M. Kohlrausch, *Der Monarch im Skandal* (Berlin, 2005).

53. M. Kohlrausch (ed.), *Samt und Stahl: Kaiser Wilhelm II. im Urteil seiner Zeitgenossen* (Berlin, 2006), 10−11 and 26; Clark, *Wilhelm II,* 239−40; see further J. C. G. Röhl, *Wilhelm II.: Der Weg in den Abgrund 1900−1941* (Munich, 2008), 689−739.

54. T. A. Kohut, *Wilhelm II and the Germans: A Study in Leadership* (Oxford, 1991), 163 and 233.

55. W. Nicolai, *Nachrichtendienst, Presse und Volksstimmung im Weltkrieg* (Berlin, 1920), 225−6.

56. The War Press Office was established in October 1915, W. Deist (ed.), *Militär und Innenpolitik im Weltkrieg 1914−1918,* 2 vols. (Düsseldorf, 1970), 289−92. On German information management in WWI, K. Koszyk, *Deutsche Pressepolitik im Ersten Weltkrieg* (Düsseldorf, 1968); M. Creutz, *Die Pressepolitik der kaiserlichen Regierung während des Ersten Weltkrieges* (Frankfurt/M., 1996); A. Schmidt, *Belehrung—Propaganda—Vertrauensarbeit: Zum Wandel amtlicher Kommunikationspolitik in Deutschland 1914−1918* (Essen, 2006).

57. *BAK,* N1097, no. 32a, n. p.

58. Plessen, diary entry for 29 June 1915, Afflerbach, *Wilhelm II.,* 794−5.

59. Plessen, diary entry for 2 July 1915, ibid., 795−6. Emphasis as in the original; the picture was printed in the press a few weeks later, Hoegen, *Held von Tannenberg,* 180, fn. 45; and *Times,* 22 July 1915, 5.

60. The German original is '*Hindenburg wird die Sache schon machen*'. Berlin Police Chief Jagow reported that people voiced such sentiments frequently within two months of Tannenberg: Jagow, 16 November 1914, Materna and Schreckenbach, *Berichte*, 24.

61. These were collected and published as edited volumes, e.g. '*Hindenburg-Gedichte*' *gesammelt von Dr. Paul Arras* (Bautzen, 1915); for songs e.g. W. Mannes (ed.), *Hindenburg-Lieder: Den Heldensöhnen Deutschlands gewidmet* (Berlin, 1915); see also the collection of leaflets and brochures in *BAK, ZSG* 2, no. 43.

62. *Schaubühne*, no. 42, 21 October 1915.

63. H. Hoffmann, ' "Schwarzer Peter im Weltkrieg": Die deutsche Spielwarenindustrie 1914–1918', in G. Hirschfeld, G. Krumeich et al. (eds.), *Kriegserfahrungen: Studien zur Sozial- und Mentalitätengeschichte des Ersten Weltkrieges* (Essen, 1997), 323–40; *Times*, 2 June 1915, 5.

64. H. Berghoff, 'Patriotismus und Geschäftssinn im Krieg: Eine Fallstudie aus der Musikinstrumentenindustrie', in Hirschfeld, *Kriegserfahrungen*, 262–82, here: 266; Anonymous, *Hindenburg der Retter der Ostmarken: Sein Leben und Wirken* (Leipzig, 1915).

65. *Liller Kriegszeitung*, no. 21, 1 October 1915; Hoegen cites an earlier version, Hoegen, *Held von Tannenberg*, 83, fn. 188.

66. *Deutsche Spielwarenzeitung*, vol. 18, 10 September 1914.

67. *GStA PK*, 1. HA, Rep. 77, Tit. 332r, no. 68, vol. 1, 346.

68. 'Our Wilhelm' was a term people in the *Kaiserreich*—including members of the working classes—used when talking about the Kaiser affectionately. R. J. Evans (ed.), *Kneipengespräche im Kaiserreich: Stimmungsberichte der Hamburger Politischen Polizei, 1892–1914* (Reinbek, 1989), 328, 329, and 330; on 'Our Hindenburg', P. Lindenberg, 'Unser Hindenburg', in idem (ed.), *Hindenburg-Denkmal für das deutsche Volk* (Berlin, 1923), 1–14. Joseph Goebbels would later emulate this label when he concluded his yearly speech on Hitler's birthday by invoking 'Our Hitler', M. Atze, *"Unser Hitler": Der Hitler-Mythos im Spiegel der deutschsprachigen Literatur nach 1945* (Göttingen, 2003), 15.

69. Bruno Paul of the Werkbund, for example, designed a Hindenburg poster for the seventh war loan campaign in 1917 and was also in charge of visuals during the celebrations at the Berlin stadium for Hindenburg's 80th birthday in 1927. See *BAB*, R601, no. 56, n. p.

70. *Süddeutsche Monadshefte*, July 1915, 561–2.

71. *BAB*, R601, no. 47, n.p.; c.f. Zaun, *Hindenburg*, 62.

72. Warncke, *Hindenburg-Album*, 44; caricature in 'Lustige Blätter', printed in Lindenberg, *Hindenburg-Denkmal*, 141.

73. H. Sachs, 'Vom Hurrakitsch, von Nagelungsstandbildern, Nagelungsplakaten und andren Schönheiten', *Das Plakat*, vol. 1/8, January 1917, 6; G. Schneider, 'Zur Mobilisierung der "Heimatfront": Das Nageln sogenannter Kriegswahrzeichen im Ersten Weltkrieg', *Zeitschrift für Volkskunde*, 95 (1999), 32–62;

S. Goebel, 'Forging the Industrial Home Front: Iron-Nail Memorials in the Ruhr', in J. Macleod and P. Purseigle (eds.), *Uncovered Fields: Perspectives in First World War Studies* (Leiden and Boston, MA, 2004), 159—78; S. Brandt, 'Nagelfiguren: Nailing Patriotism in Germany 1914—18', in N. Saunders (ed.), *Matters of Conflict: Material Culture, Memory and the First World War* (London and New York, 2004), 62—71.

74. J. Winter, *Sites of Memory, Sites of Mourning: The Great War in European Cultural History* (Cambridge, 1995), 82.

75. *GStA PK*, I. HA, Rep. 89, no. 32445.

76. Schneider, 'Mobilisierung', 45.

77. Valentini to Selberg, 6 August 1915, *GStA PK*, I. HA, Rep. 89, no. 32445.

78. *Liller Kriegszeitung*, no. 21, 1 October 1915.

79. Sachs, 'Hurrakitsch', 7.

80. Reimann, *Krieg der Sprachen*, 49.

81. Lederer et al. to Wermuth, October 1915, *GStA PK*, I. HA, Rep. 89, no. 32445.

82. Tuaillon to Wermuth, 16 September 1915, ibid; see further Goltz, 'Die Macht des Hindenburg-Mythos'.

83. *Schaubühne*, no. 42, 21 October 1915. Similar criticism was voiced by the Royal Academy of Arts and Architecture towards the Prussian Parliament in February 1916: *GStA PK*, I. HA, Rep. 169 C52, 74.

84. Wermuth to Tuaillon, 21 September 1915, *GStA PK*, I. HA, Rep. 89, no. 32445.

85. *Liller Kriegszeitung: Vom Pfingsfest zur Weihnacht: Der Auslese erste Folge*, ed. P. O. Hoecker (Lille, 1916), 85.

86. Ibid., 86.

87. Ibid.

88. Selberg to Loebell, n.d. (October 1915), *GStA PK*, I. HA, Rep. 89, no. 14954, 257.

89. Printed in *Schulthess Europäischer Geschichtskalender*, vol. 31: *1915* (Munich, 1919), 455.

90. *BT,* 5 September 1915.

91. 'The waning of faith' was the caption of a caricature of the Iron Hindenburg in *Punch*, 25 April 1917.

92. *DTAZ*, 21 May 1925; P. Weiglin, *Berlin im Glanz: Bilderbuch der Reichshauptstadt von 1888—1918* (Cologne, 1954).

93. *BAB*, R43, no. 2415, 5; *LAB*, A. Pr. Br. Rep. 030, no. 11360, 312.

94. *DTAZ*, no. 500, 4 October 1915; M. Stibbe, 'Germany's "Last Card": Wilhelm II and Germany's Decision for Unrestricted Submarine Warfare in January 1917', in A. Mombauer and W. Deist (eds.), *The Kaiser: New Research on Wilhelm II's Role in Imperial Germany* (Cambridge, 2003), 217—34.

95. Ibid., *GStA PK*, I. HA, Rep. 89, no. 15083, 258, with the Kaiser's marginal comments. The Kaiser had underlined the last sentence; also M. Stibbe, *German Anglophobia and the Great War, 1914—1918* (Cambridge, 2001), 90.

96. Ibid., 252−9. Reventlow had made a career out of criticizing the Kaiser publicly before the war, Kohut, *Wilhelm II*, 137.
97. *GStA PK*, 1. HA, Rep. 89, no. 15083, 252. Matthew Stibbe alludes to the episode, but does not cite the documents in detail. See his 'Germany's "Last Card" ', 228.
98. See further Goltz, 'Die Macht des Hindenburg-Mythos'.
99. Tirpitz to Hindenburg, 16 July 1916, *BA-MA*, N253, no. 453, 11.
100. Lyncker, diary entry for 17 March, 1916, Afflerbach, *Wilhelm II.*, 364−5; on Falkenhayn, H. Afflerbach, *Falkenhayn: Politisches Denken und Handeln im Kaiserreich* (Munich, 1994). Although this study argues that Hindenburg overshadowed the Kaiser publicly, it does not follow the argument that Wilhelm II had been reduced to being a shadow monarch, who had lost all influence in German politics. His continuing influence was especially manifest with regard to political and military appointments, Afflerbach, *Wilhelm II.*, 6 and 30−1; also Clark, *Wilhelm II*, 229. Hindenburg managed to limit the Kaiser's room for manoeuvre even in this realm, however, by continuously threatening his resignation if a particular policy was not pursued, Pyta, *Hindenburg*, 155−66.
101. *Times*, 2 June 1915, 5.
102. M. Kohlrausch, 'Die Deutung der "Flucht" Wilhelms II. als Fallbeispiel der Rezeption des wilhelminischen Kaisertums', in W. Neugebauer and R. Pröve (eds.), *Agrarische Verfassung und politische Struktur: Studien zur Gesellschaftsgeschichte Preußens 1700−1918* (Berlin, 1998) 325−47, here 328.
103. *BAK*, KLE 331, no. 2, 3.
104. *GStA PK*, I. HA, Rep. 77, Tit. 332r, no. 126; also Jagow's remarks of 7 August 1915, Materna and Schreckenbach, *Berichte*, 73.
105. Kohlrausch, *Samt,* 24−5; on Wilhelm II during WWI generally, Röhl, *Der Weg in den Abgrund*, 1167−1245.
106. A. Offer, *The First World War: An Agrarian Interpretation* (Oxford, 1989).
107. H. Reichold and G. Granier (eds.), *Adolf Wild von Hohenborn: Briefe und Tagebuchaufzeichnungen des preußischen Generals als Kriegsminister und Truppenführer im Ersten Weltkrieg* (Boppard am Rhein, 1986), 167.
108. Plessen, diary entry for 22 August 1915, Afflerbach, *Wilhelm II.*, 815.
109. Reichold, *Wild*, 135; also Chief of the Military Cabinet Admiral von Müller's diary entry for 4 July 1916, Görlitz, *Regierte der Kaiser?*, 200; also Afflerbach, *Wilhelm II.*, 41.
110. Reichold, *Wild,* 135 and 175; also Erzberger memorandum in *BAK*, N1097, no. 23, n.p.; Plessen, diary entry for 5 July 1916, Afflerbach, *Wilhelm II.*, 861; generally E. P. Guth, 'Der Gegensatz zwischen dem Oberbefehlshaber Ost und dem Chef des Generalstabes des Feldheeres 1914/1915. Die Rolle des Majors v. Haeften im Spannungsfeld zwischen Hindenburg, Ludendorff und Falkenhayn', *MGM*, 35 (1984), 75−112.
111. Reichold, *Wild*, 180; G. Ritter, *The Sword and the Scepter: The Problem of Militarism in Germany,* vol. 3 (Coral Gables, FL, 1972), 188−200.

112. R. T. Foley, *German Strategy and the Path to Verdun: Erich von Falkenhayn and the Development of Attrition 1879–1916* (Cambridge, 2005).

113. Reichold, *Wild*, 211.

114. Bethmann to Lyncker, 23 June 1916, cited in Ritter, *Sword and Scepter*, 188.

115. See Plessen's letter to Max Freiherr von Holzing-Berstett, 10 November 1914, printed in Afflerbach, *Wilhelm II.*, 691–2; M. Balfour, *The Kaiser and his Times* (London, 1964), 400.

116. *BAB*, R43, no. 2398/7, 128.

117. See the letter Erzberger sent to Bethmann on 30 August 1916, ibid., 133.

118. See the press survey compiled by the Chancellery in ibid., 157; also Müller, diary entry for 30 August 1916, Görlitz, *Regierte der Kaiser?*, 217; Wolff, diary entry for 30 August 1916, printed in Sösemann, *Wolff Diaries*, I, 419; for a summary of reactions in Bavaria, Albrecht, *Regierung in Bayern,* 178–181; c.f. Hoegen, *Held von Tannenberg*, 174–5.

119. *BT*, 30 August 1916, morn. edn.

120. Cited in *Vorwärts*, 31 August 1916.

121. Cited in ibid.

122. *BAB*, R1501, no. 112478, 4. The Deputy General Commands (*Stellvertretende Generalkommandos)* superseded the local civilian administration of the areas where they were stationed during wartime. They were in charge of securing supplies and manpower for their respective armies in the field and compiled secret reports on the mood of the population at the home front. Deist, *Militär*, vol. 1, XL-LI.

123. Ibid., 8; also Ernst von Wrisberg's observations of 30 October 1916, Schiffers, *Hauptausschuss*, vol. 2, 983.

124. Cited in D. Welch, *Germany: Propaganda and Total War 1914–1918* (London, 2000) 85.

125. Lyncker to his wife, 30 August 1916, and 24 September 1916, Afflerbach, *Wilhelm II.*, 419 and 434; Albrecht, *Regierung in Bayern*, 179 and 181.

126. Reichold, *Wild*, 122.

127. Ibid., 216.

128. Karl von Einem to his wife, 16 October 1917, cited in Deist, *Militär,* 425.

129. Plessen, diary entry for 20 January 1917, Afflerbach, *Wilhelm II.*, 887.

130. Plessen to Countess Brockdorff, 29 August 1916, ibid., 873.

131. Meeting of 2–4 October 1916, Schiffers, *Hauptausschuss,* vol. 2, (Düsseldorf, 1983), 771; on the 'Hindenburg Programme': G. Feldman, *Army, Industry and Labour in Germany 1914–1918* (Princeton, NJ, 1966), 149–96; and on a 'Hindenburg Peace' versus a 'Scheidemann Peace': *Kölner Volkszeitung*, no. 318, 24 April 1917; c.f. Hoegen, *Held von Tannenberg*, 193–203, especially 197, fn. 104.

132. *Generalfeldmarschall von Hindenburg* and *Hindenburgs österreichisches Regiment, BA-MA*, RM3, no. 9901, 114; further *Unser Hindenburg* (1917) and *Hindenburg—70. Geburtstag im Grossen Hauptquartier* (1917), which are analysed in

U. Jung and M. Loiperdinger (eds.), *Geschichte des dokumentarischen Films in Deutschland, vol. 1: Kaiserreich 1895−1918* (Stuttgart, 2005), 449−50; on film propaganda in WWI, H. Barkhausen, *Filmpropaganda für Deutschland im Ersten und Zweiten Weltkrieg* (Hildesheim, Zurich, New York, 1982); on the museum: A. Kronthal, 'Das Hindenburgmuseum in Posen', *Museumskunde*, 15 (1920), 152−8.

133. W. Mommsen, 'Die Regierung Bethmann Hollweg und die öffentliche Meinung', *VfZ*, 17 (1969), 117−59.

134. Jagow, 25 November 1916, Materna, *Berichte*, 165, fn. 7.

135. *BAB*, R1501, no. 112478, 154.

136. B. Sösemann, 'Der Verfall des Kaisergedankens im Ersten Weltkrieg', in J. C. G. Röhl (ed.), *Der Ort Kaiser Wilhelms II. in der deutschen Geschichte* (Munich, 1991), 145−70; H. Afflerbach, 'Wilhelm II as Supreme Warlord', Mombauer and Deist, *The Kaiser*, 195−216; also Hoegen, *Held von Tannenberg*, 177−92.

137. Rauscher, *Hindenburg*, 133−63.

138. K. Lehmann, 'Kriegsleistung und Kriegsruhm', *Preussische Jahrbücher*, 27 January 1917.

139. *BAB*, R1501, no. 112478, 33ff; also Gustav Stresemann's comments on the regrettable 'withering away of the monarchical idea', in a meeting of 9 July 1917, Schiffers, *Hauptausschuss*, vol. 3, 1579.

140. *GStA PK*, 1. HA, Rep. 89, no. 668, vol. 2, 33.

141. *BAB*, R1501, no. 112475, vol. 1, 109ff.

142. See Plessen, diary entries for 29 June 1915 and 21 August 1915, Afflerbach, *Wilhelm II.*, 794−5 and 815.

143. Minutes of a meeting between Nicolai, Deutelmoser, Haeften et al. on 25 May 1917, *GStA PK*, 1.HA, no. 668, vol. 2, 130ff.

144. Batocki to Valentini, 18 May 1917, ibid., 88ff.

145. The cinematographer had failed to turn up so that this public display of Wilhelm's veneration had to suffice. Plessen, diary entry for 14 and 15 July 1917, Afflerbach, *Wilhelm II.*, 908.

146. See e.g. Karl von Einem's impression of Wilhelm's behaviour during Hindenburg's birthday celebrations. Einem to his wife, 16 October 1917, cited in Deist, *Militär*, 1137.

147. Gemeinderatsprotokoll of 9 October 1917 cited in Buschmann, N., 'Der verschwiegene Krieg: Kommunikation zwischen Front und Heimat', Hirschfeld, *Kriegserfahrungen*, 214.

148. See the picture printed in *Bayerischer Kurier*, 18 October 1917; P. Koschate, *Hindenburg, hurra! Schul- und Volksfeier zum 70. Geburtstage unseres Feldmarschalls am 2. Oktober 1917* (Breslau, 1917).

149. Bösch has shown that the celebrations of the Kaiser's birthdays were toned down deliberately in 1915 and 1916. Hindenburg's birthday in 1917 became a surrogate event fostering national integration. F. Bösch, 'Das zeremoniell der Kaisergeburtstage (1871−1918)', in A. Biefang, H. Epkenhans, and

K. Tenfelde (eds.), *Das politische Zeremoniell im deutschen Kaiserreich* (Düsseldorf, 2008), 53−76.

150. *Aus dem Ostlande,* vol. 10, October 1917.

151. Barkausen, *Filmpropaganda,* 277; Jung, *Geschichte,* 449−450. For an analysis and summary of *Unser Hindenburg,* U. Oppelt, *Film und Propaganda im Ersten Weltkrieg: Propaganda als Medienrealität im Aktualitäten und Dokumentarfilm* (Stuttgart, 2002), 308−9.

152. *BBC,* 30 September 1917; B. Kiesewetter, 'Plakate und Drucksachen zur 7. Kriegsanleihe', *Das Plakat,* 9 (1918), 33−5, here 34.

153. *BAB,* R2501, no. 396, n.p.

154. H. Gebhardt, 'Organisierte Kommunikation als Herrschaftstechnik: Zur Entwicklungsgeschichte staatlicher Öffentlichkeitsarbeit', *Publizistik,* 39 (1994), 175−89.

155. *BAB,* R 2501, no. 396, n.p.

156. For a detailed list of the funds raised by each war loan see *BAB,* R 2501, no. 6628, 293.

## CHAPTER 2

1. Chickering, *Imperial Germany,* 32−5.

2. Deutscher Nationalausschuss to Ludendorff, 19 September 1916, *BAB,* R43, no. 2398/8, 20−1.

3. Report of 2 September 1916, Materna, *Berichte,* 159; generally B. J. Davis, *Home Fires Burning: Food, Politics and Everyday Life in WWI Berlin* (Chapel Hill, NC, 2000).

4. B. Ziemann, *Front und Heimat: Ländliche Kriegserfahrungen im südlichen Bayern 1914−1923* (Essen, 1997).

5. *BAB,* R1501, no. 112478, 69.

6. Report of 21 July 1917, *GStA PK,* 1. HA, Rep. 77, Tit. 332r, no. 126, 163; also: reports of 3 December 1916, 3 May 1917, and 3 May 1918, *BAB,* R1501, no. 112478, 12ff, 113ff, and 543ff.

7. 3 March 1917, ibid., 75.

8. Ibid., 257ff; also ibid., 292ff.

9. *BAB,* R1501, no. 112478, 273.

10. Ibid., 292ff.

11. Ibid., 356.

12. *GStA PK,* 1. HA, Rep. 77, Tit. 332r, no. 126, 166.

13. About 700,000 German civilians died directly from malnutrition during the war. Davis, *Home Fires,* 180 and 184−5.

14. Ibid., 130 and 175−7.

15. Hindenburg to Bethmann, 27 September 1916, cited in Deist, *Militär,* 327; and his second appeal of 19 November 1916, printed in *Schultheß,* 1 (1916), 543−44; also Pyta, *Hindenburg,* 251−3.

16. See the comments of the War Food Office's Dr Werner, cited in Deist, *Militär*, 346; *BAB*, R1501, no. 112478, 12ff; see further Groener's reports on the collection's success in early 1917, ibid., 33ff and 49ff.
17. *BAB*, R601, no. 218, n. p; *BAK*, ZSG 2, no. 43, 54.
18. *BAB*, R1501, no. 112478, 455.
19. Ibid., 400ff.
20. Jagow, 25 Mar. 1918, *GStA PK*, 1. HA, Rep. 77, Tit. 332r, no. 126, 172; also *BAB*, R1501, no. 112478, 543ff.
21. *BAB*, R1501, no. 112478, 543ff.
22. Ibid., and *BAB*, R1501, no. 112479, 39; see further B. Ziemann, 'Enttäuschte Erwartungen und kollektive Erschöpfung: Die deutschen Soldaten an der Westfront 1918 auf dem Weg zur Revolution', in J. Duppler and G. P. Groß (eds.), *Kriegsende 1918: Ereignis, Wirkung, Nachwirkung* (Munich, 1999), 165−82.
23. *BAB*, R1501, no. 112479, 39ff.
24. See the report of the 17th Deputy General Command of 3 June 1918, cited in ibid., 38ff; also 2ff.
25. According to Nikolaus Buschmann these were the key interpretative frameworks of German soldiers. See his 'Der verschwiegene Krieg: Kommunikation zwischen Front und Heimat', in Hirschfeld, *Kriegserfahrungen*, 208−24.
26. Printed in B. Ulrich and B. Ziemann (eds.), *Frontalltag im Ersten Weltkrieg: Wahn und Wirklichkeit* (Frankfurt/M., 1994), 125−6.
27. Josef Krolldorfer to his parents, 31 January 1918, *BA-MA*, MSG 2/5458. I am grateful to Alexander Watson for making this letter available to me.
28. *BAB*, R1501, no. 112479, 39; the minutes of the press briefing of 30 January 1918, printed in Deist, *Militär*, 1142, and the confidential report from Stuttgart, 16 September 1918, ibid., 961−6.
29. c.f. G. Ritter, *The Sword and the Scepter: The Problem of Militarism in Germany*, vol. 4 (Coral Gables, FL, 1973), 235.
30. *BAB*, R1501, no. 112479, 46ff.
31. Ibid., 45ff.
32. Ibid., 46ff.
33. 4th Deputy General Command, ibid.
34. Cited in K. Mühsam, *Wie wir belogen wurden: Die amtliche Irreführung des deutschen Volkes* (Munich, 1918), 117.
35. See the reports of 3 October 1918, *BAB*, R1501, no. 112479, 46ff.
36. Ibid., 45ff.
37. See their comments made at a press briefing on curbing damaging rumours of 3 September 1918, Deist, *Militär*, 1259−66.
38. c.f. Ziemann, *Front und Heimat*, 266 and 140−63.
39. Report of 21 July 1917, *GStA PK*, 1. HA, Rep. 77, Tit. 332r, no. 126, 163; also reports of December 1916, May 1917, November 1917, and May 1918, *BAB*, R1501, no. 112478, 12ff, 113ff, 356, and 543ff.

40. *BAB*, R1501, no. 112479, 45ff.
41. K.-L. Ay, *Die Entstehung einer Revolution: Die Volksstimmung in Bayern während des Ersten Weltkrieges* (Berlin, 1968), 178−83; F. Höffler, 'Kriegser-fahrungen in der Heimat: Kriegsverlauf, Kriegsschuld und Kriegsende in württembergischen Stimmungsbildern des Ersten Weltkrieges', in Hirschfeld, *Kriegserfahrungen, 68−82.*
42. *GStA PK*, 1. HA, Rep. 89, no. 32404, 30ff.
43. *GStA PK*, 1. HA, Rep. 89, no. 668, vol. 2, 103−105 and 243; and *GStA PK*, 1. HA, Rep. 89, no. 32404, 54−67.
44. Ibid., 30ff.
45. *Daily Mail*, 13 July 1918; *Daily Express*, 23 July 1918; *Nouvelles Haag*, 12 July 1918; *Petit Parisien*, 30 July 1918; *Oeuvre*, 23 August 1918, *Gas. de Laus.*, 21 August 1918, cited in ibid., no. 668, vol. 2, 30−6 and 243ff. In a letter sent to Section IIIb of the OHL, an officer who had spent a few days on leave in Germany in August 1918 also noted with concern that rumours about Hindenburg's death were circulating: *GStA PK*, 1. HA, Rep. 89, no. 32404, 84.
46. Davis, *Home Fires*, 221.
47. On this rumour in September 1918 and other rumours of Hindenburg's murder in July see Deist, *Militär*, 961−6 and 1259−66.
48. *Daily Express*, 21 April 1918, cited in *GStA PK*, 1. HA, Rep. 89, no. 668, vol. 2, 54.
49. *BA-MA*, N253, no. 138, 24.
50. Hindenburg to Seel, 8 August 1918, *BA-MA*, N429, no. 4, 4.
51. In September 1918 the confidential report of a Catholic informant from Southern Germany for the first time suggested that Hindenburg was in-creasingly perceived as 'Prussian' in the South and that this repelled many Bavarians, see Dr Nieder, Volksverein für das katholische Deutschland, report on the mood of the population, September 1918, *BAB*, R43, no. 2440, 239. On the contrary, see the report of the Bavarian 6th DGC of 3 October 1918, according to which the trust in Hindenburg was 'unlimited' in the region. *BAB*, R1501, no. 112479, 46ff; on anti-Prussian sentiments in the South generally C. M. Clark, *Iron Kingdom: The Rise and Downfall of Prussia 1600−1946* (London, 2006), 609.
52. A. Watson, *Enduring the Great War: Combat, Morale and Collapse in the German and British Armies, 1914−1918* (Cambridge, 2008), Chapter 6.
53. Felix Höffler, who has mentioned some of the Hindenburg-related ru-mours in his work, has interpreted them differently. Although this is no focus of his research, he argues that the rumours provide evidence that Hindenburg's reputation had been undermined severely by the summer of 1918. Benjamin Ziemann makes a similar point. This study agrees that his image had *changed* and the blind trust in him *diminished*, but argues that

there was greater complexity to the rumours regarding Hindenburg. Höffler, 'Kriegserfahrungen'; Ziemann, *Front und Heimat*, 267.

54. *Matin*, 3 April 1918, cited in *GStA PK*, 1. HA, Rep. 89, no. 668, vol. 2, 243ff.

55. *Nouvelles Haag*, 12 July 1918, cited in ibid.

56. The War Press Office had already singled out the *Freie Zeitung* in November 1917 for its exceptionally severe attacks on Hindenburg. *GStA PK*, 1. HA, Rep. 89, no. 32404, 30ff.

57. M. Korol, 'Dada, Präexil und "Die Freie Zeitung"' (Bremen. Univ. Diss., 1997).

58. *Freie Zeitung*, 19 September 1917, cited in *GStA PK*, 1. HA, Rep. 89, no. 32404, 30ff.

59. Goodspeed, *Ludendorff*; also the recent right-wing attempt to rehabilitate Ludendorff: F. Uhle-Wettler, *Erich Ludendorff: Soldat-Stratege-Revolutionär. Eine Neubewertung* (Berg, 1996); and M. Pöhlmann, 'Der moderne Alexander im Maschinenkrieg', in S. Förster and M. Pöhlmann (eds.), *Kriegsherren der Weltgeschichte: 22 historische Porträts* (Munich, 2006), 268–86.

60. *VZ*, 8 April 1918, copy in *BAK*, NLBauer, no. 15, 25–33; Hoegen makes similar observations in his *Held von Tannenberg*, 224.

61. E. Kolb, *The Weimar Republic* (London, 2005), 4–5.

62. Goodspeed, *Ludendorff*, 215.

63. See notes on the meeting of 18 October 1918, Matthias, *Baden*, 263–9.

64. Kolb, *Weimar*, 4.

65. Minutes of war cabinet meeting, 17 October 1918, printed in Matthias, *Baden*, 217–20.

66. Ibid.

67. Ibid., 284–8.

68. See Hans von Haeften's report, Matthias, *Baden*, 360–5.

69. Stresemann to Friedberg, 26 October 1918, ibid., 382; also cited in H. Bernhard (ed.), *Gustav Stresemann: Vermächtnis: Der Nachlass in drei Bänden*, 3 vols. (Berlin, 1932), here: vol. 1, 12–13.

70. See Berg's detailed account in *BAK*, KLE 331, no. 2, 71.

71. Matthias, *Baden*, 360–5.

72. Haußmann, notes of 9 November 1919, printed in ibid., 632.

73. *BA-MA*, N46, no. 156, 5.

74. See *KZ, Schlesische Zeitung, Tag,* and others cited in *BA-MA*, N46, no. 156, 10.

75. *VZ*, no. 550, 27 October 1918.

76. Hoegen equally stresses Hindenburg's sense of 'duty' as the German press's interpretative framework in 1918/19, but has less to say about the language of 'sacrifice' as an important part of the Hindenburg myth in 1918/19. Hoegen, *Held von Tannenberg*, 229–41.

77. Hindenburg to Seel, letter of 28 December 1918, *BA-MA*, N429, no. 4, 14; also Hindenburg to his wife, 14 November 1918, cited in Hubatsch,

*Hindenburg*, 48, fn. 1; and Hindenburg to Groener, 26 October 1919 and 25 May 1920, *BA-MA*, N46, no. 37, 14 and 39.

78. *KZ, Schlesische Zeitung, Tag,* and others cited in *BA-MA*, N46, no. 156, 10.

79. *Vorwärts*, no. 296, 27 October 1918; c.f. Hoegen, *Held von Tannenberg*, 227.

80. See Scheidemann's comments in the war cabinet meeting of 17 October 1918, printed in Matthias, *Baden*, 217−20.

81. See the memoirs of the Pan-German leader Heinrich Claß in *BAK*, KLE 499F, 528−30. Claß was especially disappointed with Hindenburg's moderate views on the 'Jewish question'.

82. On 'Ludendorff bashing' after the revolution see e.g. *DZ*, 17 November 1919, ev. ed.; Bauer to Hindenburg, 1919, *BA-MA*, NLBauer, no. 18, 33; and *DRPS,* no. 174, 4 August 1919.

83. See the SPD's response in *Vorwärts*, no. 151, 23 March 1919.

84. Barth, *Dolchstoßlegenden*; F. Frhr. Hiller v. Gaertringen, ' "Dolchstoß"-Diskussion und "Dolchstoßlegende" im Wandel von vier Jahrzehnten', in idem and W. Besson (eds.), *Geschichte und Geschichtsbewußtsein* (Göttingen, 1963), 122−60; W. Deist, 'Der militärische Zusammenbruch des Kaisserreichs: Zur Realität der Dolchstoßlegende', in U. Büttner (ed.), *Das Unrechstregime: Internationale Forschung über den Nationalsozialismus* (Hamburg, 1986), 101−31; J. Petzold, *Die Dolchstosslegende: Eine Geschichtsfälschung im Dienst des deutschen Imperialismus und Militarimus* (Berlin, 1963).

85. See Haußmann's and Erzberger's private notes on the cabinet meeting of 31 October 1918, cited in Matthias, *Baden*, 447, fn. 49; and further the details of the officers' poll: Wilhelm II to Lyncker, letter of 2 February 1922, cited in Afflerbach, *Wilhelm II.*, 580, fn. 2.

86. See Paul Hintze's letter to Solf, 29 October 1918, J. Hürter (ed.), *Paul Hintze: Marineoffizier, Diplamt, Staatssekretär: Dokumente einer Karriere zwischen Militär und Politik 1903−1918* (Munich, 1998), 656.

87. See Loose's report about his visit to the Western front to the OHL, 5 November 1918, cited in *Deist, Militär*, 1356.

88. M. Kohlrausch, 'Die Deutung der "Flucht" Wilhelms II. als Fallbeispiel der Rezeption des wilhelminischen Kaisertums', in W. Neugebauer and R. Pröve (eds*.), Agrarische Verfassung und politische Struktur: Studien zur Gesell-schaftsgeschichte Preußens 1700−1918* (Berlin, 1998), 325−47; on Hindenburg's recommendation to leave Berlin, Pyta, *Hindenburg*, 371.

89. c.f. Kohlrausch, 'Flucht', 339; after intense negotiation with Westarp, Plessen, and others, Hindenburg eventually agreed to a joint statement accepting *some* responsibility for the Kaiser's departure. See the co-authored declaration in *KZ*, no. 348, 27 July 1919; also W. Conze (ed.), *Kuno Graf Westarp: Das Ende der Monarchie am 9. November 1918* (Berlin, 1952), 98−115; Pyta, *Hindenburg*, 414−25.

90. A. J. Ryder, *The German Revolution of 1918: A Study of German Socialism in War and Revolt* (Cambridge, 1967), 160; W. Elben, *Das Problem der Kontinuität*

*in der deutschen Revolution: Die Politik der Staatssekretäre und der militärischen Führung vom November 1918 bis Februar 1919* (Düsseldorf, 1965), 127−8.

91. Decree of 12 November 1918, cited in W. Wette, 'Demobilization in Germany 1918−1919: The Gradual Erosion of the Powers of the Soldiers' Councils', in C. Wrigley (ed.), *Challenges of Labour: Central and Western Europe 1917−1920* (London and New York, 1993), 176−95, here: 179.

92. Ryder, *Revolution*, 161.

93. Printed in Hubatsch, *Hindenburg*, 49.

94. On Groener's and Hindenburg's reasons for backing Ebert, see Groener to his wife, 17 November 1918, *BA-MA*, N46, no. 32, 235; for the historiography on the Ebert-Groener pact e.g. Ryder, *Revolution,* 160, who considers the pact 'inevitable'; see the contrasting assessments, F. L. Carsten, *Revolution in Central Europe 1918−1919* (Aldershot, 1988), chapters 2, 5, 6, and 7; H. A. Winkler, *Der Weg in die Katastrophe: Arbeiter und Arbeiterbewegung in der Weimarer Republik 1930−1933* (Berlin and Bonn, 1987), 13−14; and R. Rürup, 'Die Revolution von 1918/19 in der deutschen Geschichte', *Reihe Gesprächskreis Geschichte der Friedrich-Ebert-Stiftung in Bonn*, vol. 5 (1993), 5−28. For a summary of the historiographical debate see H. A. Winkler, 'Der umstrittene Wendepunkt: Die Revolution von 1918/19 im Urteil der westdeutschen Geschichtswissenschaft', in idem (ed.), *Weimar im Widerstreit: Deutungen der ersten deutschen Republik im geteilten Deutschland* (Munich, 2002), 33−42; Kolb, *Weimar,* 149−59.

95. See Westarp's assessment in F. Frhr. v. Gaertringen (ed.), *Kuno Graf von Westarp: Konservative Politik im Übergang vom Kaiserreich zur Weimarer Republik* (Düsseldorf, 2001), 191−2.

96. Davis, *Home Fires*, 238; W. Mühlhausen, *Friedrich Ebert 1871−1925: Reichspräsident der Weimarer Republik* (Bonn, 2006), 119.

97. Arthur Marwick, cited in S. A. Robson, '1918 and All That: Reassessing the Periodization of Recent German History', in L. E. Jones and J. Retallack (eds.), *Elections, Mass Politics, and Social Change in Modern Germany* (Cambridge, 1992), 331−45, here: 340.

98. R. Krumpholz, *Wahrnehmung und Politik: Die Bedeutung des Ordnungsdenkens für das politische Handeln am Beispiel der deutschen Revolution von 1918−1920* (Münster, 1998), on Ebert, 171−208; on Scheidemann, 212−13; and on Noske especially 243−55; on Ebert's preoccupation with 'tranquillity and order' also Mühlhausen, *Ebert,* 150−64 and 120.

99. *BT*, no. 443, 30 August 1916; Noske would later invoke this image when referring to Hindenburg as an 'imperturbable dam' keeping back the 'floods': *Der Heimatdienst: Mitteilungen der Reichszentrale für Heimatdienst,* 1 October 1927, vol. VII, no. 19.

100. R. Bessel, 'Mobilization and Demobilization in Germany, 1916−1919', in J. Horne (ed.), *State, Society and Mobilization in Europe during the First World War* (Cambridge, 1997), 220.

101. *Preußische Jahrbücher*, vol. 174/3, 27 November 1918.

102. General Hans Henning von Holtzendorff to Walther Hubatsch, 18 January 1955, cited in Hubatsch, *Hindenburg*, 51.

103. Mühlhausen, *Ebert*, 112 and 129, who stresses Ebert's conviction that the existence of the new government depended largely on the support of the old military.

104. e.g. Ebert's response to Ernst Däumig of the USPD, Minutes of Cabinet Meeting of 20 November 1918, printed in S. Miller and H. Potthoff (eds.), *Die Regierung der Volksbeauftragten* (Düsseldorf, 1969), 108−12; also his response to the Bavarian Independent Social Democrat Kurt Eisner in Minutes of *Reichskonferenz* of 25 November 1918, printed in ibid., 182.

105. Minutes of cabinet meeting of 15 March 1919, *Akten der Reichskanzlei: Kabinett Scheidemann*, nos. 14a and 14b, 48−55.

106. Ibid.; on Reinhardt's 'pragmatic republican' politics, W. Mulligan, *The Creation of the Modern German Army: General Walther Reinhardt and the Weimar Republic 1914−1930* (Oxford, 2004), especially 34−5 and 117.

107. Hoth to *FAZ*, letter of 16 January 1955, cited in Hubatsch, *Hindenburg*, 48.

108. S. Haffner, *Die verratene Revolution. Deutschland 1918/19* (Bern, Munich, and Vienna, 1969).

109. I follow Winkler here who argues that the democratic leaders failed to make a moral break with the *Kaiserreich*, see his *Arbeiter*, 13−14; also R. Bessel, '1918−1919 in der deutschen Geschichte', in D. Papenfuss and W. Schieder (eds.), *Deutsche Umbrüche im 20. Jahrhundert* (Cologne and Weimar, 2000), 173−82, here: 174.

110. See the photograph printed in Kunstamt Kreuzberg Berlin und Institut für Theaterwissenschaft der Universität Köln (eds.), *Weimarer Republik* (Berlin and Hamburg, 1977), 241.

111. See e.g. Albert Südekum's notes on a meeting of the *Interfraktioneller Ausschuss* of 18 October 1918, Matthias, *Baden*, 263−9.

112. For details Kolb, *Weimar*, 224.

113. *HA*, 5 July 1919.

114. See Groener to Reinhold Laegler, 11 February 1935, cited in D. Groener-Geyer, *General Groener: Staatsmann und Feldherr* (Frankfurt/M., 1955), 339.

115. *BA-MA*, N46, no. 132, 17−18; also printed in F. Frhr. Hiller v. Gaertringen (ed.), *Wilhelm Groener: Lebenserinnerungen—Jugend, Generalstab, Weltkrieg* (Göttingen, 1957), 511−12. The government further issued a statement expressing its gratitude to Hindenburg for his service, see *Schultheß*, vol. 1, 1919, 281.

116. *FZ*, 27 April 1925, ev. edn.

117. M. Görtemaker, 'Bürger, Ersatzkaiser, Volkstribun: Reichspräsidenten in der Weimarer Republik', in Stiftung Haus der Geschichte der Bundesrepublik Deutschland (ed.), *Bilder und Macht im 20. Jahrhundert* (Bielefeld, 2004), 28−41, here: 34.

118. Wehler, *Gesellschaftsgeschichte*, vol. 4, 554.

CHAPTER 3

1. Kolb, *Weimar*, 35−51.
2. *OZ*, no. 272, 1 October 1919, copy in *BAK*, NL31, no. 5.
3. See also Colonel Max Bauer's 1919 birthday speech: *BAK*, NLBauer, no. 18, 19−31.
4. Dörner, *Politischer Mythos*, 314; Verhey, *Spirit of 1914*, 219−23.
5. Gerwarth, *Bismarck Myth*; U. Heinemann, 'Die Last der Vergangenheit: Zur politischen Bedeutung der Kriegsschuld- und Dolchstoßdiskusssion', in K. D. Bracher et al. (eds.), *Die Weimarer Republik 1918−1933: Politik, Wirtschaft, Gesellschaft* (Bonn, 1987), 371−86; Verhey, *Spirit of 1914*.
6. Kolb, *Weimar*, 36−7.
7. Gaetringen, 'Dolchstoßlegende'.
8. *BT*, no. 309, 20 November 1919.
9. W. Schücking and E. Fischer (eds.), *Das Werk des Untersuchungsausschusses der Verfassungsgebenden Deutschen Nationalversammlung und des Deutschen Reichstages 1919−1928*, vol. 7: *Die Ursachen des Deutschen Zusammenbruches im Jahre 1918* (Berlin, 1928).
10. DDP politician Georg Gothein, chairman of the Investigation Committee in a letter of 22 November 1919, *BAK*, N41, 2.
11. J. G. Williamson, *Karl Helfferich 1872−1924: Economist, Financier, Politician* (Princeton, NJ, 1971), 308−10.
12. The full text is printed in *Schultheß*, vol. 1, 1919, 481−6; English translation cited from Wheeler-Bennett, *Wooden Titan*, 235−7.
13. On Maurice see Gaertringen, 'Dolchstoßlegende', 127; *DTAZ*, 19 November 1919, morn. edn.
14. *BT*, 20 November 1919, morn. edn.
15. *FZ*, 20 November 1919, ev. edn.
16. *Vorwärts*, 19 November, morn. edn.
17. See 'Hindenburg', *Weltbühne*, 18 December 1919; and Tucholsky's 'Zwei Mann in Zivil', *Weltbühne*, 27 November 1919.
18. H. Pogge von Strandmann, 'Rathenau, Wilhelm II, and the Perception of *Wilhelminismus*', in Mombauer and Deist, *The Kaiser*, 259−80, here: 275.
19. SPD functionaries Heller and Caspari to Reich Chancellor Bauer, 10 December 1919, *Akten der Reichskanzlei: Das Kabinett Bauer*, no. 127, 468−70.
20. *Vorwärts*, 13 November 1919, morn. edn.
21. Ibid.
22. *KZ*, no. 549, 12 November 1919; *BT,* 12 November 1919, ev. ed.; *DTAZ*, 12 November 1919, ev. edn.
23. G. Noske, *Erlebtes aus Aufstieg und Niedergang einer Demokratie* (Offenbach/M., 1947), 148−9.
24. *KZ*, 14 November 1919, ev. ed.; *BT*, 14 November 1919, ev. edn.
25. *Vorwärts*, no. 586, 15 November 1919.

26. *Vorwärts*, no. 584, 14 November 1919.

27. On the recruiting of children *Vorwärts*, nos. 583 and 585, 13 and 15 November 1919; *BT*, 14 November 1919, morn. edn.

28. *KZ*, no. 551, 13 November 1919.

29. *KZ*, no. 555, 15 November 1919.

30. *BT*, 14 November 1919, ev. edn.; also *FZ*, 14 November 1919, ev. edn.

31. *BT*, 15 November 1919, morn. edn.; *Vorwärts*, no. 585, 15 November 1919.

32. *DTAZ* and *BT*, 19 November 1919, morn. edn.

33. D. Lehnert, 'Propaganda des Bürgerkriegs? Politische Feindbilder als mentale Destabilisierung der Weimarer Demokratie', in idem, *Politische Teilkulturen*, 61−101.

34. *Vorwärts*, no. 586, 15 November 1919; see also Kurt Tucholsky's short poem (published under his pseudonym Kaspar Hauser) of November 1919: 'Morgenpost', *Weltbühne*, 27 November 1919. After Chancellor Wirth repeated the verdict in a speech about Rathenau's murder in a parliamentary debate on 25 June 1922, it became one of the most frequently cited political slogans of the Weimar era, see *Verhandlungen des Reichstags: Stenographische Berichte. I. Wahlperiode 1920,* vol. 356, session 236 (Berlin, 1922), 8054−8.

35. *BT*, no. 547, 17 November 1919; c.f. also *Weltbühne*, 27 November 1919.

36. Mosse, *Nationalization*.

37. The DVP leadership considered Hindenburg the only viable candidate, because he had 'the people behind him'. See their discussions of 24 August 1919, E. Kolb and L. Richter (eds.), *Nationalliberalismus in der Weimarer Republik: Die Führungsgremien der Deutschen Volkspartei 1918−1933*, 2 vols., here vol. 1 (Düsseldorf, 1999), 187.

38. See the minutes of meetings in Berlin and Leipzig on 13 September and 16 October 1919, Kolb, *Nationalliberalismus*, 192 and 193; also Hindenburg to Berg, 5 January 1920, printed in Hubatsch, *Hindenburg*, 58−59; generally also J. R. C. Wright, *Gustav Stresemann: Weimar's Greatest Statesman* (Oxford, 2002), 148−9.

39. See the correspondence between Wilhelm II and Hindenburg in December 1919 and January 1920, printed in Hubatsch, *Hindenburg*, 58−9.

40. Kolb, *Weimar*, 226.

41. *BL*, no. 122, 6 March 1920; see also Mühlhausen, *Ebert*, 528−30.

42. *BL,* no. 123, 7 March 1920; *KZ*, no. 122, 6 March 1920; on this further B. Asmuss, *Republik ohne Chance? Akzeptanz und Legitimation der Weimarer Republik in der deutschen Tagespresse zwischen 1918 und 1923* (Berlin and New York, 1994), 213. Under the catchier name '*Reichsblock*' the Loebell Committee would also be the driving force behind Hindenburg's nomination in 1925.

43. *BL*, no. 123, 7 March 1920.

44. *BL*, nos. 131 and 132, 11 and 12 March 1920.

45. *BL*, no. 123, 7 March 1920.

NOTES TO PAGES 65–83

46. *BZ am Mittag*, 8 March 1920.
47. *Wochenblatt der FZ*, 10 March 1920.
48. *RF*, 10 and 12 March 1920.
49. H. Hürten (ed.), *Zwischen Revolution und Kapp-Putsch: Militär und Innenpolitik 1918–1920* (Düsseldorf, 1977); idem, *Der Kapp-Putsch als Wende: Über Rahmenbedingungen der Weimarer Republik seit dem Frühjahr 1920* (Opladen, 1989).
50. c.f. Mühlhausen, *Ebert*, 323.
51. The elections were initially postponed to a later date, but after yet another right-wing attack on the Republic, the murder of Foreign Minister Rathenau in June 1922, the Reichstag altered the constitution and extended Ebert's term until 30 June 1925. See Kolb, 'Friedrich Ebert: Vom "vorläufigen" zum definitiven Reichspräsidenten: Die Auseinandersetzungen um die Volkswahl des Reichspräsidenten 1919–1922', in idem (ed.), *Friedrich Ebert als Reichspräsident* (Munich, 1997), 109–56.
52. Hindenburg to Berg, 5 January 1920, printed in Hubatsch, *Hindenburg*, 58–9.
53. Minutes of meeting with leaders of 18 February 1921, *Akten der Reichskanzlei: Kabinett Fehrenbach*, no. 177, 471–5.
54. *Vorwärts*, 30 August 1924, ev. edn.
55. Walter Nicolai's private notes of 11 November 1917, cited in M. Pöhlmann, *Kriegsgeschichte und Geschichtspolitik: Der Erste Weltkrieg: Die amtliche deutsche Militärgeschichtsschreibung 1914–1956* (Paderborn, 2002), 258.
56. Hindenburg to Plessen, letter of 26 July 1919, Afflerbach, *Wilhelm II.*, 948; Schulenburg, *Welt um Hindenburg*, 214.
57. *DTAZ*, 2 October 1922.
58. *DRPS*, no. 210, 15 September 1919 and no. 5, 7 January 1921; *DRPS*, no. 140, 28 June 1920.
59. Hindenburg, *Aus meinem Leben*; also Pyta, *Hindenburg*, 435–9; on Mertz's career: Pöhlmann, *Kriegsgeschichte*, 82–4.
60. See the contract of 10 May 1919, cited in ibid., 60, footnote 39. An early draft with Hindenburg's comments can be found in *BA-MA*, N429, no. 5–8; O. v. Bismarck, *Gedanken und Erinnerungen*, 2 vols. (Stuttgart, 1898 and 1919).
61. Hindenburg, *Aus meinem Leben*, n.p.
62. Ibid., 208 and 314.
63. Hindenburg to Cramon, 6 March 1920, *BA-MA*, N 266, no. 22, 1.
64. See the detailed programme of the visit in *AdSD Bonn*, NL Severing, 1/CSA B000088.
65. Minutes of meeting of 7 June 1922, *Akten der Reichskanzlei: Die Kabinette Wirth I und II*, no. 289, 850; *BAK*, NL31, no. 19; 'Die "Staatsbürgerliche Arbeitsgemeinschaft" zu Königsberg Pr.' (1921), *BAK*, NL31, no. 19.
66. Gayl to Hindenburg, 26 March 1922, *BAK*, N1031, no. 20, vol. 1.
67. Friedensburg to Hindenburg, 26 April 1922, *BAK*, NL 31, no. 20, vol. 1; Friedensburg to Gayl, 27 April 1922, ibid.

68. Friedensburg to Gayl, 27 April 1922, ibid.

69. Gayl to Friedensburg, 13 May 1922, ibid.; Friedensburg memorandum, 14 May 1922, *BAK*, N 1114, no. 11; Friedensburg to Oberpräsident of Königsberg, 16 May 1922, ibid.

70. Friedensburg to Oberpräsident of Königsberg, 16 May 1922, ibid.

71. See the letter of the East Prussian SPD committee to Hindenburg, 19 May 1922, *BAK*, NL31, no. 20, vol. 1; Friedensburg memorandum, 14 May 1922, *BAK*, N 1114, no. 11.

72. Minutes of meeting of 24 May and 7 June 1922, *Kabinette Wirth*, nos. 281 and 289, 822–824 and 850.

73. Gayl complained to Reichswehr Minister Otto Gessler that this would infuriate soldiers. Gayl to Gessler, 8 June 1922, *BAK*, NL31, no. 20, vol. 1; also *KAZ*, 12 June 1922; generally F. L. Carsten, *The Reichswehr and Politics 1918–1933* (London, 1966).

74. *RF*, 11 June 1922.

75. *Schultheß*, vol. 63 (1922), 68; *KV*, 12 June 1922.

76. *KAZ*, 12 June 1922; *OZ*, no. 136, 13 June 1922; Gayl in *KAZ*, 17 June 1922; *KV*, 29 May 1922.

77. R. G. L. Waite, *Vanguard of Nazism: The Free Corps Movement in Post-War Germany 1918–1923* (Cambridge, MA, 1952); M. Sabrow, *Die verdrängte Verschwörung: Der Rathenau-Mord und die deutsche Gegenrevolution* (Frankfurt/M., 1999).

78. *KV*, 27 June 1922.

79. It is therefore surprising that the most important work on political violence in interwar Germany neither mentions Hindenburg's trip to East Prussia nor his stay in Berlin in November 1919: D. Schumann, *Politische Gewalt in der Weimarer Republik 1918–1933: Kampf um die Straße und Furcht vor dem Bürgerkrieg* (Essen, 2001).

80. See Carl Severing's recollection of 1947, *AdsD Bonn*, NL Severing, 1/CSA B000027, 5–6.

81. Siegfried Jacobsohn to Kurt Tucholsky, 6 May 1926, printed in R. v. Soldenhoff (ed.), *Briefe an Kurt Tucholsky 1915–1926: "Der beste Brotherr dem schlechtesten Mitarbeiter"* (Munich, 1989), 409; c.f. also F. Friedensburg, *Die Weimarer Republik* (Berlin, 1946), 365–7.

82. Wheeler-Bennett's argument is that Hindenburg kept his 'dignified silence throughout the early struggles of the Republic', see his *Wooden Titan*, 257.

83. In 1924, Hindenburg once again asked Gayl to organize a month-long trip around East Prussia for him. See Gayl to Hindenburg, 3 July 1924, *BAK*, NL31, no. 21, vol. 2.

84. Kolb, *Weimar*, 39.

85. See Interior Minister Köster's letter to Wirth, 9 September 1922, printed in H. Hürten, *Die Anfänge der Ära Seeckt: Militär und Innenpolitik 1920–1922* (Düsseldorf, 1979), 285–7.

86. Government envoy to Bavaria, 23 August 1922, *Kabinette Wirth,* no. 344, 1030, fn. 12. On the events in Munich also Hellmut von Gerlach's report of August 1922, K. Holl and A. Wild (eds.), *Ein Demokrat kommentiert Weimar: Die Berichte Hellmut von Gerlachs an die Carnegie-Friedensstiftung in New York 1922–1930* (Bremen, 1973), 57–9. It is therefore not true that Hindenburg was 'so appalled' by the East Prussian events that he 'refused to appear in public again' 'for over a year', as Wheeler-Bennett maintains in his *Wooden Titan,* 257.

87. See 'Von der Tannenberg-Feier' (1921), *BAK,* NL31, no. 19, n.p.; and K. Koszyk, *Geschichte der deutschen Presse, vol. 3: Deutsche Presse 1914–1945* (Berlin, 1972), 69.

88. See also the attempt to highlight the working-class contribution to Tannenberg by the Social Democratic *KV,* 10 August 1921.

89. Tietz, *Tannenberg-Nationaldenkmal,* 29; *DRPS,* no. 199, 2 September 1919; and no. 193, 28 August 1920.

90. Koszyk, *Deutsche Presse,* vol. 3, 71.

91. See Pöhlmann, *Kriegsgeschichte,* 131–2.

92. *DRPS,* no. 202, 30 August 1921, no. 218, 17 September 1921; *Vorwärts,* no. 406, 29 August 1921; also the minutes of ministerial council of 29 August 1921, *Kabinette Wirth,* no. 76, 216.

93. *WaM,* 19 June 1922; *KV,* 10 August 1921; also: 'Von der Tannenberg-Feier' (1921), *BAK,* NL31, no. 19, n.p.

94. Tietz, *Tannenberg-Nationaldenkmal,* 29.

95. B. Ziemann, 'Die Deutsche Nation und ihr zentraler Erinnerungsort: Das "Nationaldenkmal für die Gefallenen im Weltkriege" und die Idee des "Unbekannten Soldaten" 1914–1935', in H. Berding et al. (eds.), *Krieg und Erinnerung* (Göttingen, 2000), 67–92.

96. Tietz, *Tannenberg-Nationaldenkmal;* Mosse, *Nationalization,* 69–70.

97. On the fundraising campaign after 1924, *LAB,* A Rep. 001–02, no. 882.

98. Social Democrats and Communists staged an anti-war demonstration in Königsberg on the same day, albeit on a much smaller scale, *Ostpreußische Blätter,* 1 September 1924, copy in *BAK,* NL31, no. 19.

99. Gayl to Hindenburg, 3 July 1924, *BAK,* NL31, no. 21, vol. 2; on Hindenburg's visit to Danzig on 22 August: Schulenburg, *Welt um Hindenburg,* 84–6.

100. *KAZ,* 26 August 1924. The commemorations were not limited to East Prussia, see the supplements of *DTAZ,* 31 August 1924 and 1 September 1924, ev. edn.

101. *Königsberger Hartungsche Zeitung,* no. 373, 24 August 1924.

102. *KAZ,* 26 August 1924.

103. See the second supplement to *DTAZ,* 31 August 1924.

104. See the reports in *BT,* 1 September 1924, ev. ed.; *DTAZ,* 1 September 1924, ev. ed.

CHAPTER 4

1. Mühlhausen, *Ebert,* 967–80.

2. Pyta, 'Präsidialgewalt'; H. Boldt, 'Die Weimarer Reichsverfassung', in K. D. Bracher et al. (eds.), *Die Weimarer Republik 1918–1933: Politik, Wirtschaft, Gesellschaft* (Bonn, 1987), 44–62, especially 52.

3. J. W. Falter et al (eds.), *Wahlen und Abstimmungen in der Weimarer Republik: Materialien zum Wahlverhalten 1919–1933* (Munich, 1986), 70; Dorpalen, *Hindenburg,* 66.

4. On the genesis of Hindenburg's candidacy: Cary, 'Reich President'; also the very detailed account: H.-J. Hauss, *Die erste Volkswahl des deutschen Reichspräsidenten* (Kallmünz, 1965); Pyta, *Hindenburg,* 463–9.

5. Meeting of 12 March 1925, K.-H. Minuth (ed.), *Akten der Reichskanzlei. Die Kabinette Luther I und II,* vol. 1 (Boppard am Rhein, 1977), 170–1.

6. Schulenburg, *Welt um Hindenburg,* 58–9; Hindenburg's appeal published in the DVP's Berlin publication: *Berliner Stimmen,* no. 13, 27 March 1925.

7. Cary, 'Reich President', 187.

8. On the distribution of votes on the first ballot: Falter, *Wahlen,* 46; and table no. 1 in this chapter.

9. Hindenburg to Cramon, 27 March 1925, *BA-MA,* N266, no. 24, 14. Emphasis as in the original; a shorter extract from this letter is cited in Pyta, *Hindenburg,* 466.

10. Confidential circular of Stahlhelm leadership, 10 April 1925, *BAK,* N1031, no. 23.

11. Hindenburg to Cramon, 3 April 1925, *BA-MA,* N266, no. 24, 25; a shorter extract from this letter is cited in Pyta, *Hindenburg,* 471; c.f. Hindenburg to Berg, 5 January 1920, printed in Hubatsch, *Hindenburg,* 58–9.

12. See Keudell's account: 'Mit Tirpitz in Hannover bei Hindenburg 8. April 1925', *BAK,* N1243, no. 102; all other sources state that the visit took place on 7 April 1925, Hauss, *Volkswahl,* 98–103; Dorpalen, *Hindenburg,* 71–3; Hubatsch, *Hindenburg,* 70–1.

13. 'Mit Tirpitz in Hannover bei Hindenburg 8. April 1925' in *BAK,* N1243, no. 102.

14. For a detailed account of the discussions within the Reichsblock and the leading role of Hanover DNVP politician Winkler: Schulenburg, *Welt um Hindenburg,* 58–67.

15. Reich Chancellor Luther's memoirs: 'Hindenburg und Ebert', *BAK,* N1009, no. 669; also Kessler, *Diaries,* 263; also Eduard Dingeldey, memoranda on DVP objections from Bavaria, Hamburg, Frankfurt/Oder, and Halle, cited in Dorpalen, *Hindenburg,* 69, fn. 69; Pyta, 'Präsidialgewalt', 80, fn. 49; and Wright, *Stresemann,* 154–8.

16. *BAK,* N1031, no. 23, n.p.

17. Confidential circular of Stahlhelm leadership, 10 April 1925, ibid.; Cary, 'Reich President', 196; generally also V. R. Berghahn, *Der Stahlhelm: Bund der Frontsoldaten 1918–1935* (Düsseldorf, 1966), 72–5.

18. Confidential circular of Stahlhelm leadership, 10 April 1925, *BAK*, N1031, no. 23.

19. *Die Zeit*, no. 160, 19 April 1925.

20. Cary, 'Reich President', 198.

21. On Feldmann's work for Hindenburg: Pyta, 'Präsidialgewalt', 80, fn. 49; on the organization of the campaign G. Schultze-Pfaelzer, *Wie Hindenburg Reichspräsident wurde: Persönliche Eindrücke aus seiner Umgebung vor und nach der Wahl* (Berlin, 1925). Schultze-Pfaelzer worked as a press secretary to the campaign.

22. *BA-MA*, N266, no. 24, 25; Minutes of meeting of 9 April 1925, *BAK*, N1031, no. 23.

23. A memorandum urging these practices was circulated to all Reichsblock parties, cited in Fritzsche, 'Hindenburg's Election', 213.

24. See the various reports on pro-Hindenburg rallies hosted by different bourgeois societies: *DTAZ*, 15–18 April 1925.

25. *Korrespondenz der DNVP*, 9 April 1925.

26. Appeal of the Reichsblock to the German people, 8 April 1925, printed in J. Hohlfeld (ed.), *Deutsche Reichsgeschichte in Dokumenten 1849–1934*, vol. 2 (Berlin, 1934), 835–6.

27. *Düsseldorfer Nachrichten*, no. 187, 9 April 1925.

28. Hindenburg to Jarres, 9 April 1925, *BAK*, NLJarres, no. 29; Hindenburg to Cramon, 25 April 1925, *BA-MA*, N266, no. 24, 16.

29. *DTAZ*, 22 April 1925, ev. edn.; and 21 April 1925, morn. edn.

30. *DTAZ*, 25 April 1925, ev. edn.

31. *Korrespondenz der DNVP*, 9 April 1925; also Hindenburg's appeal to the German people, 11 April 1925, printed in Hohlfeld, *Reichsgeschichte*, 836–7.

32. *BAK*, ZSG2, no. 187.

33. *Korrespondenz der DNVP*, 16 April 1925.

34. *Frauenkorrespondenz der DNVP*, 15 and 18 April 1925.

35. P. Fritzsche, *Rehearsals for Fascism: Populism and Political Mobilization in Weimar Germany* (Oxford, 1990), 154.

36. *Germania*, no. 195, 27 April 1925; *LAB*, A Pr. Br. Rep. 030, Tit. 90, no. 7592, 45.

37. Ibid., 118–33; *Kölnische Volkszeitung*, nos. 309 and 310, 27 April 1925.

38. Hindenburg to Gayl, 11 April 1925, *BAK*, N1031, no. 23.

39. The Volksblock (People's Bloc) was the republican parties' alliance in the presidential elections.

40. See the hagiographic account of Hindenburg's public appearances by his press secretary: Schultze-Pfaelzer, *Persönliche Eindrücke,* 24–30.

41. Pyta merely covers Hindenburg's radio speech of 31 December 1931.

42. A permanent national broadcasting station would not be established until 1930, K. C. Führer, 'Auf dem Weg zur "Massenkultur"? Kino und Rundfunk in der Weimarer Republik', *HZ*, no. 262 (1996), 739–81, here: 779. Wilhelm Marx was also given airtime immediately after Hindenburg, whereas Ernst Thälmann was not allowed to speak, see Schultze-Pfaelzer, *Persönliche Eindrücke*, 34–6.

43. Statistisches Bundesamt Wiesbaden (ed.), *Bevölkerung und Wirtschaft 1872–1972* (Stuttgart, 1972), 209.

44. *Germania*, no. 195, 27 April 1925; D. Lau, *Wahlkämpfe der Weimarer Republik* (Marburg, 1995), 110.

45. On the myth of the *Reich*: K. Sontheimer, *Antidemokratisches Denken in der Weimarer Republik*, 4th edn. (Munich, 1994), 222–30.

46. *LAB*, A Pr. Br. Rep. 030, Tit. 90, no. 7592, 214.

47. *DTAZ*, 22 April 1925, ev. edn.; *MNN*, nos. 108 and 110, 20 and 22 April 1925. Also H. Regel, 'Die Fridericus-Filme der Weimarer Republik', in A. Marquardt and H. Rathsack (eds.), *Preussen im Film* (Hamburg, 1981), 124–34; K. Kreimeier, *The Ufa Story: A History of Germany's Greatest Film Company 1918–1945* (New York, 1996).

48. Schultze-Pfaelzer, *Persönliche Eindrücke*, 39.

49. Lau, *Wahlkämpfe*, 243.

50. *DTAZ*, 18 April 1925, ev. edn.; c.f. also *Korrespondenz der DNVP*, 17 April 1925; on the 'saviour' theme as an article of faith of the nationalist right in Weimar: Sontheimer, *Antidemokratisches Denken*, 214–22.

51. *Weltbühne*, no. 20, 19 May 1925.

52. *BT*, 21 April 1925, morn. edn.; *Germania*, 9 April 1925.

53. *BT*, 12 April 1925.

54. *Germania*, 11 April 1925, ev. edn.

55. *Vorwärts*, no. 168, 9 April 1925.

56. Cartoon from *Vorwärts*, 18 April 1925, printed in Hauss, *Volkswahl*, 173.

57. In 1932 the Nazis would pick up on this theme, this time accusing Capitalists, Socialists, and Jews of hiding behind Hindenburg's mask. See Chapter 7; 154–5.

58. H. Stehkämper (ed.), *Der Nachlass des Reichskanzlers Wilhelm Marx*, vol. 1 (Cologne, 1968 and 1997), 372–6.

59. *LAB*, A Pr. Br. Rep. 030, Tit. 90, no. 7592, 246.

60. Ibid., 245; also in *BAK*, ZSG2, no. 187.

61. c.f. the article in a large West German Catholic daily: 'Warum nicht Hindenburg?', *Tremonia*, no. 107, 19 April 1925.

62. *RF*, 18 April 1925.

63. *RF*, 25 April 1925.

64. *RF*, 26 April 1925.

65. *Weltbühne*, 21 April 1925.

66. Ibid.; *Vorwärts*, 18 April 1925, ev. edn.; c.f. Hoegen, *Held von Tannenberg*, 308; also Paul Guttmann's article in *Vorwärts*, 22 April 1925, morn. edn.

67. 'Feldherrnkult und Militärische Kritik', *Sozialistische Monatshefte*, 30 January 1922; *Vorwärts*, no. 173, 12 April 1925.
68. *LAB*, A Pr. Br. Rep. 030, Tit. 90, no. 7592, 188.
69. The official election result is in *BAB*, R601, no. 371; Falter et al. also have a breakdown of the results in different constituencies in *Wahlen*, 47.
70. Ibid., 234; Hauss, *Volkswahl*, 137; further K. Schönhoven, *Die Bayerische Volkspartei 1924–1932* (Düsseldorf, 1972), 123–30.
71. J. K. Zeender, 'The German Catholics and the Presidential Election of 1925', *JMH*, 35 (1963), 366–81, here: 348; J. Horstmann, 'Katholiken, Reichspräsidentenwahlen und Volksentscheide', *Jahrbuch für christliche Sozialwissenschaften*, no. 27 (1986), 61–93.
72. M. Buchner, 'Was eint uns mit Hindenburg?', *Gelbe Hefte*, 1 June 1925; on the relationship between Catholics and Social Democracy: S. Ummenhofer, *Wie Feuer und Wasser? Katholizismus und Sozialdemokratie in der Weimarer Republik* (Berlin, 2003), 120–3.
73. Praschma to Marx, 2 April and 11 April 1925, Stehkämper, *Marx*, vol. 1, 394–5 and 398.
74. Hauss, *Volkswahl*, 134.
75. *Germania*, 27 April 1925, ev. edn.
76. *The Evening World*, April 1915, copy in *BAB*, R601, no. 371.
77. Frau Gramm to Freia Jarres, n.d. (May 1925), *BAK*, NLJarres, no. 23, n.p.
78. Falter, *Wahlen*, 81. For literature on women's voting patterns and politics in Weimar see: R. Scheck, *Mothers of the Nation. Right wing Women in Weimar Germany* (Oxford and New York, 2004); J. Sneeringer, *Winning Women's Votes: Propaganda and Politics in Weimar Germany* (Chapel Hill, NC, and London, 2002). Sneeringer's analysis of the political mobilization of women during the parliamentary elections of the Weimar years is immensely valuable, but leaves out the two presidential elections. Scheck includes the presidential campaigns but focuses exclusively on DVP and DNVP women and does not go much beyond what has been established by Falter: J. W. Falter, 'The Two Hindenburg Elections of 1925 and 1932: A Total Reversal of Voter Coalitions', *CEH*, 23 (1990), 225–41.
79. Falter, *Wahlen*, 83.
80. See the tables in *VZ*, 28 April 1925; *BT*, 28 April 1925.
81. e.g. v. Gerlach's report of April 1925, Holl and Wild, *Berichte von Gerlachs*, 138.
82. *Germania*, 28 April 1925, morn. ed.; c.f. also *Tremonia*, nos. 116 and 117, 28 and 29 April 1925.
83. *Weltbühne*, no. 20, 19 May 1925.
84. e.g. Zaun, *Hindenburg*, 65. For an eloquent rebuttal of this argument: Fritzsche, 'Hindenburg's Election', 207.
85. *Weltbühne*, no. 19, 12 May 1925.
86. Kessler, diary entry for 15 May 1925, Kessler, *Diaries*, 267.
87. Fritzsche, 'Hindenburg's Election', 207.

88. *FZ*, 27 April 1925, morn. ed.; on Hindenburg as 'Ersatzkaiser': Wehler, *Gesellschaftsgeschichte*, vol. 4, 513; W. H. Kaufmann, *Monarchism in the Weimar Republic* (New York, 1953), 149 and 151; for a detailed discussion of the impact of Hindenburg's election on the monarchical idea, Hoegen, *Held von Tannenberg*, 320–31.

89. *BT*, 28 April 1925, morn. edn.; c.f. A. Brecht, *Aus nächster Nähe: Lebenserinnerungen 1884–1927* (Stuttgart, 1966), 454.

90. *FZ*, 27 April 1925, ev. edn.; a longer extract of this article is cited in Chapter 2, 63–4.

91. *DT*, 27 April 1925, ev. edn.

92. Confidential circular of Stahlhelm leadership, 10 April 1925, *BAK*, N1031, no. 23, n.p.

93. A detailed programme of the festivities can be found in *BAB*, R601, no. 390, 23–8.

94. *WTB*, 9 May 1925, *BAB*, R 601, no. 390, 94; a list of all the clubs present can be found in *LAB*, A. Pr. Br. Rep. 030, no. 7593, 29–33.

95. *BT*, no. 222, 12 May 1925.

96. Fritzsche, *Rehearsals*, 157.

97. *Vorwärts*, no. 221, 12 May 1925.

98. 'Hindenburg und Ebert', *BAK*, N1009, no. 669.

99. *BT*, no. 222, 12 May 1925. Count Harry Kessler also observed that some of his female acquaintances were so fond of Hindenburg, because they had 'retained the girlish heart that cannot resist the sight of the soldier's tunic'. Diary entry for 15 May 1925, Kessler, *Diaries*, 267.

100. *RF*, 12 May 1925.

101. *Vorwärts*, no. 221, 12 May 1925.

102. *MNN*, no. 131, 13 May 1925; Fritzsche, *Rehearsals*, 157.

103. Ibid.

104. *BAK*, NL5, no. 95, 23.

105. *RF*, 10 May 1925; *LAB*, A Pr. Br. Rep. 030 C Tit. 90, no. 7593, 23 and 163.

106. Ibid., 91.

107. *Die Zeit*, no. 199, 12 May 1925; *LAB*, A Pr. Br. Rep. 030 C Tit. 90, no. 7593, 59.

108. *BAB*, R601, no. 390, 84; also Pünder to Reich Chancellor, 5 May 1925, *BAK*, NL5, no. 95; *Düsseldorfer Nachrichten*, no. 225, 12 May 1925; Funk-Stunde to Meissner, 12 May 1925, *BAB*, R601, no. 390, 157.

109. *BT*, 13 May 1925, morn. ed. Hindenburg's speech had been drafted by State Secretary Meissner and members of the Chancellery.

110. *Vorwärts*, 13 May 1925, morn. edn.; Ernst Feder made similar observations in *BT*; 13 May 1925, morn. edn.

111. Three days later, however, he already sounded much less optimistic: diary entries for 12 and 15 May 1925, printed in Kessler, *Diaries*, 266–7.

CHAPTER 5

* A slightly altered version of this chapter was published under the author's maiden name: Menge, 'The Iron Hindenburg'.

1. *Der Eiserne Hindenburg in Krieg und Frieden* (Allgemeine Film-Union Häussler & Co., 1929), copy in *BA-FA*. All citations are taken from the film's subtitles.

2. Weber, *Büro*, 480–1.

3. K. Maase, *Grenzenloses Vergnügen: Der Aufstieg der Massenkultur 1850–1970* (Frankfurt/M., 1997); C. Ross, 'Mass Politics and the Techniques of Leadership: The Promise and Perils of Propaganda in Weimar Germany', *German History*, 24 (2006), 184–211.

4. G. Rollenbeck, 'Freigesetzte Moderne und diktatorische Optionen. Zur argumentativen Konfliktlage in der Weimarer Republik', in K. Kreimeier et al. (eds.), *Geschichte des dokumentarischen Films in Deutschland*, vol. 2 (Stuttgart, 2005), 229–48, here: 230; A. Kaes, 'Filmgeschichte als Kulturgeschichte: Reflexionen zum Kino der Weimarer Republik', in U. Jung and W. Schatzberg (eds.), *Filmkultur zur Zeit der Weimarer Republik* (Munich, 1992), 54–64, here: 61.

5. J. Goergen, 'Der dokumentarische Kontinent: Ein Forschungsbericht', in Kreimeier, *Geschichte*, 15–43, here: 16. The term 'documentary' to describe non-fictional films was not yet in use in Germany at this time, c.f. ibid., 17–21.

6. B. Kester, *Film Front Weimar: Representations of the First World War in German Films of the Weimar Period (1919–1933)* (Amsterdam, 2003), 11; R. Rother, 'The Experience of the First World War and the German Film', in M. Paris (ed.), *The First World War and Popular Cinema: 1914 to the Present* (Edinburgh, 1999), 217–46; Mühlhausen, *Ebert*, 788.

7. *Stuttgarter Neues Tageblatt*, 22 April 1929, copy in *BAB*, R601, no. 46, n.p.

8. For details of the premiere: ibid.; on 'cinema palaces': Führer, ' "Massenkultur" ', 742–3 and 756.

9. Ibid., 742, 747.

10. The view that cinema and radio completely overcame class divisions has been attacked most forcefully in ibid., especially 766; Lynn Abrams on the other hand maintains that cinema served a socially integrative function. See her 'From Control to Commercialization: The Triumph of Mass Entertainment in Germany 1900–1925?', *German History*, 8 (1990), 278–93.

11. Häussler to Ministerial Council Doehle, 10 April 1929, *BAB*, R601, no. 46, n.p.; on Häussler's career in Nazi Germany: P. Zimmermann and K. Hoffmann, *Geschichte des dokumentarischen Films in Deutschland*, vol. 3 (Stuttgart, 2005), 546–8.

12. *Einer für Alle!* (1932), copy in *BA-FA*; on its use in the 1932 campaign: *BAB*, R601, no. 389, 294. Heinrich Roellenbleg was the head of Ufa's *Wochenschau*.

13. See *BA-FA,* no. 16691: 'Tannenbergfilm'; a copy of the film has also survived on videotape; 'Film der Zeit', *BT,* no. 456, 25 September 1932.

14. Regel, 'Fridericus-Filme'.

15. Kester, *Film Front,* especially 106, and 137−8; on the controversy: M. Eksteins, 'War, Memory and Politics: The Fate of the Film *All Quiet on the Western Front*', *CEH* (1980), 167−85.

16. Paul to Meissner, 1 September 1932, *BAB,* R601, no. 48, n.p.

17. *Illustrierter Filmkurier,* no. 1806, 1932, copy in *BA-FA,* no. 16691.

18. A plot summary is given in U. W. Wolff, *Preussens Glanz und Gloria im Film: Die berühmten deutschen Tonfilme über Preussens glorreiche Vergangenheit* (Munich, 1981), 61−2; see also Walter Redmann's article in *Berliner Morgenpost,* no. 234, 29 September 1932.

19. Seeger to Präsidialkanzlei, 23 September 1932, *BAB,* R601, no. 48, n.p.

20. See H. Liepe (ed.), *Das Lichtspielgesetz vom 12. Mai 1920 mit Ausführungs-verordnung und Gebührenordnung* (Berlin, 1920).

21. See J.-P. Barbian, 'Politik und Film in der Weimarer Republik: Ein Beitrag zur Kulturpolitik der Jahre 1918−1933', *Archiv für Kulturgeschichte,* vol. 80, no. 1 (1998), 213−45; idem, 'Filme mit Lücken: Die Lichtspielzensur in der Weimarer Republik: Von der sozialethischen Schutzmaßnahme zum politischen Instrument', in U. Jung (ed.), *Der deutsche Film: Aspekte seiner Geschichte von den Anfängen bis zur Gegenwart* (Trier, 1993), 51−78.

22. Barbian, 'Politik und Film', 233; on the specific Nazi deployment of film: G. Paul, *Aufstand der Bilder: Die NS-Propaganda vor 1933* (Bonn, 1990).

23. Seeger had already worked for the OHL's *Bild- und Filmamt* during the First World War and would serve as the head of Goebbels's Propaganda Ministry's film department. H.-M. Bock, 'Ernst Seeger—Jurist, Zensor', *CineGraph: Lexikon zum deutschsprachigen Film,* 20th edn. (Hamburg, 1992), 456−9.

24. Barbian, 'Politik und Film', 237.

25. Seeger to Hindenburg's office, 23 September 1932, *BAB,* R601, no. 48, n.p.

26. Ibid. In what way exactly Koerner's performance was 'degrading' was not made clear in the censor's report, but the wording implied that Koerner simply appeared too ordinary and not heroic and 'historically great' enough. See the still from the film printed in Menge, 'Iron Hindenburg', 366.

27. On this Chapter 6; further Pyta, 'Präsidialgewalt'.

28. C. Schmitt, *Der Hüter der Verfassung* (Tübingen, 1931), 89; on the influence of Schmitt's thinking Mommsen, *Max Weber,* 384; Boldt, 'Article 48', 94; on Schmitt's understanding of Hindenburg presidency, Pyta, *Hindenburg,* 731−3.

29. Statistisches Bundesamt Wiesbaden, *Bevölkerung und Wirtschaft,* 209.

30. Führer, ' "Massenkultur" ', 767.

31. U. Heitger, *Vom Zeitzeichen zum politischen Führungsmittel: Entwicklungstenden-zen und Strukturen der Nachrichtenprogramme des Rundfunks in der Weimarer Republik 1923—1932* (Münster, 2003); J.-F. Leonhard (ed.), *Programmgeschichte des Hörfunks in der Weimarer Republik,* vol.1 (Munich, 1997), 482−3.

253

253

32. Lau, *Wahlkämpfe*, 233; T. Mergel, *Parlamentarische Kultur in der Weimarer Republik: Politische Kommunikation, symbolische Politik und Öffentlichkeit im Reichstag* (Düsseldorf, 2002), 348.
33. Paul, *Aufstand*, 195.
34. For details of the speech and listeners' reactions to it see Chapter 7, 151 and 158–9.
35. *NYT*, 23 November 1930, cited in H. Hardt, *In the Company of Media: Cultural Constructions of Communications, 1920s–1930s* (Oxford, 2000), 96.
36. The speech can be listened to at http://www.dhm.de/lemo/objekte/sound/hindenburg/index.ram.
37. *BT*, 3 January 1932; *12-Uhr-Blatt*, 31 December 1931, copies of both articles in *LAB*, A. Pr. Br. Rep. 030, Tit. 90, no. 7522, 168 and 151.
38. Ibid.; *RF*, 3 January 1932; *BT*, 2 January 1932.
39. *LAB*, A. Pr. Br. Rep. 030 Tit. 90, no. 7522.
40. Lau, *Wahlkämpfe*, 232; B. Currid, *A National Acoustics: Music and Mass Publicity in Weimar and Nazi Germany* (Minneapolis, MN, 2006), 31–2.
41. See 'Politisches Weltecho', *VZ*, 2 January 1932.
42. On the Nazis' emulation of the Communist stunt in March 1932: Winkler, *Weimar*, 453; on the coverage of Hindenburg's eightieth birthday (2 October 1927) on the radio see Chapter 6, 132.
43. Führer, '"Massenkultur"', 780–1.
44. See e.g. E. M. Remarque, *Im Westen nichts Neues* (Berlin, 1929); L. Renn, *Krieg* (Frankfurt/M.,1928); E. Jünger, *In Stahlgewittern* (Berlin, 1920); H. Grimm, *Volk ohne Raum*, 2 vols. (Munich, 1926); H. Zöberlein, *Der Glaube an Deutschland* (Munich, 1931); J. M. Wehner, *Sieben vor Verdun* (Munich, 1930); on this genre generally M. Gollbach, *Die Wiederkehr des Weltkrieges in der Literatur: Zu den Frontromanen der späten Zwanziger Jahre* (Kronberg/Ts., 1978); A. Gümbel, 'Instrumentalisierte Erinnerung an den Ersten Weltkrieg: Hans Grimms "Volk ohne Raum"', in Berding et al., *Krieg und Erinnerung*, 93–112; J. W. Baird, 'Literarische Reaktionen auf den Ersten Weltkrieg: Josef Magnus Wehner und der Traum von einem neuen Reich', in Papenfuss and Schieder, *Deutsche Umbrüche*, 15–38.
45. Ibid.; T. F. Schneider and H. Wagener (eds.), *Von Richthofen bis Remarque: Deutschsprachige Prosa zum I. Weltkrieg* (Amsterdam and New York, 2003); J. Hermand and F. Trommler, *Die Kultur der Weimarer Republik* (Munich, 1978), 47.
46. J.-P. Barbian, *Literaturpolitik im 'Dritten Reich': Institutionen, Kompetenzen, Betätigungsfelder* (Munich, 1995), 75–8; Gollbach, *Wiederkehr*, 167–209.
47. Meissner to Gerhard Stalling, 7 August 1929, *BAB*, R601, no. 46, n.p.
48. *Schlachten des Weltkrieges*, 40 vols. (Oldenburg, 1922–1930); *Erinnerungsblätter deutscher Regimenter*, 372 vols. (Oldenburg, 1920–1942); also Pöhlmann, *Kriegsgeschichte*, 55 and 194–202.

49. Stalling to Meissner, 3 August 1929, *BAB*, R601, no. 46, 34a; also Weber, *Büro*, 253–7.
50. By 1930, the book had sold 120,000 copies and by 1940, 328,000 copies had been sold. Gollbach, *Wiederkehr*, 167.
51. Meissner strongly insisted that he himself had been the architect of the changes he put forward and that he had not informed Hindenburg. In spite of Meissner's growing influence this account is questionable—Hindenburg could well have been consulted, but may have preferred not to be involved personally to guard his reputation. See Meissner to Stalling, 7 August 1929, *BAB*, R601, no. 46, n.p.
52. Ibid.
53. Stalling to Meissner, 11 September 1929, *BAB*, R601, no. 46, n.p.; also Pyta, who cites a different passage from the sources in his *Hindenburg*, 536.
54. The last edition of 141,000–145,000 was published in 1935: P. Lindenberg, *Hindenburg-Denkmal für das deutsche Volk* (Berlin, 1935); Lindenberg had published popular illustrated books on Hindenburg since 1917; see his *Generalfeldmarschall von Hindenburg* (Stuttgart, 1917). For a list of all hagiographic Hindenburg books published before 1938, see Deutsche Bücherei, *Hindenburg-Bibliographie*, which lists 3,000 works.
55. Weber, *Büro*, 258.
56. W. Marckwardt, *Die Illustrierten der Weimarer Zeit: Publizistische Funktion, ökonomische Entwicklung und inhaltliche Tendenzen* (Munich, 1982), 100; B. Fulda, *Press and Politics in the Weimar Republic* (Oxford, 2009); idem, 'Die Politik der "Unpolitischen": Die Boulevard- und Massenpresse in den zwanziger und dreißiger Jahren', (MS, 2004). I am grateful to Bernhard Fulda for making this manuscript available to me.
57. H. Stahr, *Fotojournalismus zwischen Exotismus und Rassismus: Darstellungen von Schwarzen und Indianern in Foto-Text-Artikeln deutscher Wochenillustrierter 1919–1939* (Hamburg, 2004).
58. Mühlhausen, *Ebert,* 13 and 991; see the photograph printed in Menge, 'Iron Hindenburg', 372.
59. See e.g. the images in *BIZ*, nos. 24 and 26, 14 and 28 June 1931; and the cover and inside pages of *Hackebeils Illustrierte*, no. 19, 7 May 1925.
60. *Die Woche: Erinnerungsheft* (Berlin, October 1927).
61. For other pictures of Hindenburg in civilian clothes published in Scherl's weekly see *Die Woche*, no. 48, 28 November 1925; no. 13, 26 March 1927; no. 6, 11 February 1928; no. 7, 18 February 1928.
62. *Die Woche*, no. 40, 1 October 1927; *BIZ*, no. 40, October 1927; also *BIZ*, 11 November 1928. Such 'human interest' formats were typical for Weimar's illustrated weeklies: Marckwardt, *Die Illustrierten,* 128; see further Chapter 7, 159–61.
63. e.g. *VB*, special ed., 2 August 1934, copy in *BAB*, R72, no. 1325.
64. Marckwardt, *Die Illustrierten,* 109.

65. Gebhardt, 'Organisierte Kommunikation'.

66. The Nazis, for instance, did not use Hitler's face until 1932, S. Behrenbeck, ' "Der Führer": Die Einführung eines politischen Markenartikels', in R. Gries and G. Diesener (eds.), *Propaganda in Deutschland: Zur Geschichte der politischen Massenbeeinflussung im 20. Jahrhundert* (Darmstadt, 1996), 51–78, here: 55–6.

67. S. Haas, 'Die neue Welt der Bilder: Werbung und visuelle Kultur der Moderne', in P. Borscheid and C. Wischermann (eds.), *Bilderwelt des Alltags: Werbung in der Konsumgesellschaft des 19. und 20. Jahrhunderts* (Stuttgart, 1995), 64–89, here: 69–70; F. Jaspert, 'Werbepsychologie: Grundlinien ihrer geschichtlichen Entwicklung', in F. Stoll (ed.), *Die Psychologie des 20. Jahrhunderts, vol. 13: Anwendungen im Berufsleben. Arbeits-, Wirtschafts- und Verkehrspsychologie* (Zurich, 1981), 170–89, here: 174.

68. T. König, *Die Psychologie der Reklame* (Würzburg, 1922); further A. Schug, 'Wegbereiter der modernen Absatzwerbung in Deutschland: Advertising Agencies und die Amerikanisierung der deutschen Werbebranche in der Zwischenkriegszeit', *WerkstattGeschichte*, 12 (2003), 29–52, especially 34; S. Haas, 'Psychologen, Künstler, Ökonomen: Das Selbstverständnis der Werbetreibenden zwischen Fin de Siècle und Nachkriegszeit', in Borscheid, *Bilderwelt*, 78–89, especially 85.

69. Schug, 'Wegbereiter', 35.

70. Meissner to Stocker, 10 September 1932, *BAB*, R601, 49, n.p.; c.f. Weber, *Büro*, 250.

71. Haus der Geschichte der Bundesrepublik Deutschland (ed.), *Prominente in der Werbung: Da weiss man, was man hat* (Mainz, 2001), especially the articles by Jürgen Reiche, 'Von Bismarck zu Zlatko oder wer ist prominent', 15–38; and Clemens Wischermann, 'Wirtschaftswerbung in der Konsumgesellschaft: Historische Entwicklung', 78–95.

72. G. Bechstein, *Automobilwerbung von 1890 bis 1935: Versuch einer semiotischen Analyse früher Automobilannoncen* (Bochum, 1987), 413–14. On promoting an object of every day use—an ashtray—see Meissner to Reinmann, 8 April 1930, *BAB*, R601, no. 10, n. p.

73. On 2 October 1927 Hindenburg did not stand upright in his car as the advert suggests. It was probably modelled on a photograph taken during Hindenburg's inaugural celebrations on 11 May 1925. The actual car used at the time, however, was a Mercedes. See the picture printed in *Die Woche: Erinnerungsheft* (October 1927), n.p.

74. H. Edelmann, *Vom Luxusgut zum Gebrauchsgegenstand: Die Geschichte der Verbreitung von Personenkraftwagen in Deutschland* (Frankfurt/M., 1989).

75. *BAB*, R601, no. 9, n.p.

76. *Verband deutscher Sektkellereien* to Meissner, 25 July 1925, *BAB*, R601, no. 9, n.p..

77. C. Wischermann, 'Grenzenlose Werbung? Die gesellschaftliche Akzeptanz der Werbewelt im 20. Jahrhundert', in Borscheid, *Bilderwelt*, 372–440.

78. The correspondence between Meissner and Linstow shows that the whole affair was dragged out over four years, with Linstow still selling bottles of his *Hindenburg-Sekt* in 1929, see *BAB*, R601, no. 9, n. p..

79. Metzler to Meissner, 20 July 1928, *BAB*, R601, no. 9, n. p..

80. *BAB*, R601, no. 9, n. p.

81. Meissner to Metzler, 27 July 1928, *BAB*, R601, no. 9, n. p.

82. Harald Zaun's assessment of Hindenburg's stance towards advertising is therefore one-sided. See his *Hindenburg*, 64, fn. 21.

83. I would therefore contend that there is some reason to doubt Pyta's assessment that Hindenburg insisted on controlling his image at all costs. See his *Hindenburg*, 144.

84. Weber, *Büro*, 292.

85. P. Melograni, 'The Cult of the Duce', *JCH*, 2 (1976) 178–95; Hitler, for instance, avoided any hint of human frailty and was never pictured wearing spectacles, Kershaw, *Hitler Myth*, 3.

86. Accordingly, advertising was coordinated (*gleichgeschaltet*) in 1933, U. Westphal, *Werbung im Dritten Reich* (Berlin, 1989); B. Lammers, *Werbung im Nationalsozialismus* (Weimar, 1999). In the mid-1930s, the term '*Führer*' was registered as a trademark, Behrenbeck, 'Der Führer', 67.

87. e.g. Messerschmidt to Hindenburg, 6 May 1933, *BAB*, R601, no. 11, n.p.

88. NSDAP Gauleitung of Greater Berlin to Ministry of Propaganda, 28 April 1933, *BAB*, R601, no. 11, n. p..

89. Behrenbeck, 'Der Führer'.

90. Wischermann, 'Grenzenlose Werbung?', 388–91.

91. Recent scholarship has thoroughly revised the idea of 'Weimar Culture' being defined by the avant-garde, e.g. G. Bollenbeck, *Tradition, Avantgarde, Reaktion: Deutsche Kontroversen um die kulturelle Moderne 1880–1945* (Frankfurt/M., 1999); R. Schneider and W. Wang (eds.), *Moderne Architektur in Deutschland 1900 bis 2000,* vol. 3 (Ostfildern, 1998); K. Leyendecker (ed.), *German Novelists of the Weimar Republic: Intersections of Literature and Politics* (Columbia, SC, 2006); for a summary of the historiographical debate: Kolb, *Weimar,* 106; the most important synthetic surveys remain P. Gay, *Weimar Culture: The Outsider as Insider* (London, 1969); W. Laqueur, *Weimar: A Cultural History 1918–1933* (London, 1974).

## CHAPTER 6

1. *Weltbühne*, no. 17, 27 April 1926; also the similar criticism by Kurt Tucholsky (under his pseudonym Ignaz Wrobel), *Weltbühne*, no. 32, 9 August 1927; generally I. Deák, *Weimar Germany's Left-Wing Intellectuals: A Political History of the Weltbühne and its Circle* (Berkeley and Los Angeles, CA, 1968).

2. On Ossietzky's politics, H.-U. Wehler, 'Leopold Schwarzschild contra Carl v. Ossietzky: Politische Vernunft für die Verteidigung der Republik gegen

ultralinke "Systemkritik" und Volksfront-Illusionen', in idem, *Preußen ist wieder chic... Politik und Polemik in zwanzig Essays* (Frankfurt/M., 1983), 77–83.

3. On this standard periodization of Weimar German history: Schulze, *Weimar*, 287–303; H. A. Winkler, *Weimar 1918–1933: Die Geschichte der ersten deutschen Demokratie* (Munich, 1993), 244–84 and 306–33.

4. Wright, *Stresemann*, 330–9.

5. Holl and Wild, *Ein Demokrat kommentiert Weimar*, 150; on Hindenburg's stance towards Locarno, and right-wing agitation against the treaty: Hubatsch, *Hindenburg*, 216–17; Zaun, *Hindenburg*, 387–437.

6. See Keudell's memorandum on Germany's entry into the League of Nations and other foreign policy questions, 18 March 1926, BA-MA, N253, no. 250, 129–30; on Hindenburg's reservations: P. Haungs, *Reichspräsident und parlamentarische Kabinettsregierung: Eine Studie zum Regierungssystem der Weimarer Republik in den Jahren 1924 bis 1929* (Cologne and Opladen, 1968), 194–201; Zaun, *Hindenburg*, 387–456; on Germany's entry generally: Z. Steiner, *The Lights that Failed: European International History 1919–1933* (Oxford, 2005), 418–20.

7. Pyta, 'Präsidialgewalt', 85; see also the liberal publicist Ernst Feder's diary entry for 25 February 1926, C. Lowenthal-Hensel and A. Paucker (eds.), *Ernst Feder: Heute sprach ich mit... Tagebücher eines Berliner Publizisten 1926–1932* (Stuttgart, 1971), 42.

8. On the rumours concerning Gayl as a candidate: BAK, N131, no. 2, 195–6; on Walter von Keudell: Tirpitz to Rupprecht of Bavaria, letter of 3 August 1925, BA-MA, N253, no. 190, 6; regarding Otto v. Feldmann: Weber, *Büro*, 152; Pyta, *Hindenburg*, 482–3.

9. Meissner, *Staatssekretär*; Weber, *Büro*, 151–76; Pyta, *Hindenburg*, 559–61; on Meissner's role during Ebert's presidency: Mühlhausen, *Ebert*, 226–8.

10. See e.g. *DAZ*, 26 April 1926; and *BT*, 2 October 1926.

11. Friedensburg, *Weimarer Republik*, 195–6.

12. On Hindenburg appearing as a 'resting pole': Winkler, *Weimar*, 331–2.

13. See e.g. the Reichsbanner poster of 1927 highlighting Hindenburg's republican credentials, in: BAB, R1507, no. 1104e, 224; on the Reichsbanner: B. Ziemann, 'Republikanische Erinnerung in einer polarisierten Öffentlichkeit: Das Reichsbanner Schwarz-Rot-Gold als Veteranenverband der sozialistischen Arbeiterschaft', *HZ*, 267 (1998), 357–98.

14. On right-wing disappointment: Tirpitz to Rupprecht of Bavaria, 3 August 1925, BA-MA, N253, no. 190, 6; Tirpitz to Elard von Oldenburg-Januschau, 8 December 1926, ibid., no. 250, 56–7; O. Schmidt-Hannover, *Umdenken oder Anarchie: Männer-Schicksale-Lehren* (Göttingen, 1959), 201; Haungs, *Reichspräsident*, 182.

15. Berghahn, *Stahlhelm*, 138–42, 148–53, and 161–3.

16. U. Schüren, *Der Volksentscheid zur Fürstenenteignung 1926* (Düsseldorf, 1978); H. Pleyer, *Politische Werbung in der Weimarer Republik* (Münster, 1960).

17. See Hindenburg to Loebell, 19 May 1926, Hubatsch, *Hindenburg*, 236−9; also *Akten der Reichskanzlei: Weimarer Republik: Die Kabinette Marx III und IV*, 2 vols., ed. G. Abramowski (Boppard am Rhein, 1988), 40−1; Weber, *Büro*, 274−7; also Feder, diary entry for 21 January 1927, *Heute sprach ich mit . . .*, 98−9.

18. See e.g. the cartoon 'Beware of the Dogs' (*Achtung Hunde*) depicting Hindenburg as a bull dog chewing on the constitution: *RF*, no. 160, 13 July 1926. Hindenburg consequently sued the *RF*'s editor Arnim Hauswirth for libel. On Hauswirth's trials: *BAB*, R1501, no. 125648, especially 11−30.

19. 'Der Hindenburgbrief', *Sozialistische Politik und Wirtschaft*, no. 23, 10 June 1926; c.f. also Ernst Funke's 'Unser Hindenburg', *Weltbühne*, no. 14, 2 April 1929, which makes a similar case.

20. Holl and Wild, *Ein Demokrat kommentiert Weimar*, 164−5; c.f. Hoegen, *Held von Tannenberg*, 340.

21. 'Der Hindenburgbrief', *Sozialistische Politik und Wirtschaft*, no. 23, 10 June 1926.

22. On the memorial's design, construction, and the unveiling ceremony: Tietz, *Tannenberg-Nationaldenkmal*, 45−74.

23. The full text is printed in *Schultheß Europäischer Geschichtskalender* (Munich, 1927), 153.

24. On the international reactions to Hindenburg's speech: Stresemann to Marx, 21 September 1927, Stehkämper, *Marx*, vol. 2, 71−2; also Zaun, *Hindenburg*, 216.

25. Heinemann, 'Kriegsschuld- und Dolchstoßdiskusssion'; idem, *Verdrängte Niederlage*.

26. Hoegen offers a slightly different assessment of republican attitudes from 1925 onwards. He downplays the republicans' increasingly congenial relationship with Hindenburg and emphasizes their lasting suspicion of the Field Marshal. In a later chapter, however, he highlights the 'integrative function' of the Hindenburg myth during the early years of his presidency.

27. Friedensburg, *Weimarer Republik*, 366; c.f. M. Bosch, *Liberale Presse in der Krise: Die Innenpolitik der Jahre 1930 bis 1933 im Spiegel des "Berliner Tageblatts", der "Frankfurter Zeitung" und der "Vossischen Zeitung"* (Frankfurt/M. and Munich, 1976), 208.

28. *BBZ*, no. 461, 2 October 1927.

29. 'Der Einiger des Volkes', *Die Woche*, no. 40, 1 October 1927.

30. K. W. Wipperman, *Politische Propaganda und staatsbürgerliche Bildung: Die Reichszentrale für Heimatdienst in der Weimarer Republik* (Cologne, 1976), especially 11−20; J. K. Richter, *Die Reichszentrale für Heimatdienst: Geschichte der ersten politischen Bildungsstelle in Deutschland und Untersuchung ihrer Rolle in der Weimarer Republik* (Berlin, 1963).

31. *Der Heimatdienst: Mitteilungen der Reichszentrale für Heimatdienst*, 1 October 1927, vol. VII, no. 19.

32. Krumpholz, *Wahrnehmung und Politik*, 255.
33. Hoegen does not discuss Noske's crucial birthday eulogy and instead argues that the SPD did not take an active interest in Hindenburg's birthday. He therefore regards Hindenburg as an icon of the German right in this period.
34. On planning the event: Weber, *Büro*, 318–35; further Pünder to Meissner, 4 March 1927, *BAB*, R601, no. 55, 4–5; also the minutes of the cabinet meeting of 20 May 1927, *Kabinette Marx III und IV*, vol. 1, 759–60.
35. Berlin's Chief of Police to State Secretary of the Interior, 21 September 1927, *LAB*, A Pr. Br. Rep. 030, Tit. 89–90, no. 7537, 49–50 and 39.
36. *BAB*, R601, no. 56, n. p.
37. Fritzsche, *Rehearsals*, 157, 159, and 222; Mosse, *Nationalization*, 92; Biefang et al., *Zeremoniell;* on Ebert: Mühlhausen, *Ebert*, 991.
38. Stehkämper, *Marx*, vol. 4, 213.
39. *WTB*, no. 1704, 2 October 1927; *BAB*, R601, no. 56, n. p.
40. *LAB*, A Pr. Br. Rep. 030, Tit. 89–90, no. 7537, 49–50; also the letter from the *Schulkollegium* of 24 June 1927, ibid., 2–3.
41. *BAB*, R601, no. 55, 3.
42. H. Schallenberger, *Untersuchungen zum Geschichtsbild der Wilhelminischen Ära und der Weimarer Zeit* (Ratingen near Düsseldorf, 1964), 168–9, 177, and 242.
43. Ibid., 177, also fn. 63.
44. Hindenburg featured especially prominently in illustrations: ibid., 180 and 183.
45. A. Henche (ed.), *Geschichtliches Unterrichtswerk: Ein Arbeits- und Tatsachenbuch für höhere Lehranstalten*, vol. 2 (Breslau, 1926), 15.
46. A. Reimann (ed.), *Geschichtswerk für höhere Schulen,* vol. 1 (Munich and Berlin, 1926).
47. Ibid., chapter 15, 134ff.
48. F. Schnabel (ed.), *Grundriss der Geschichte für die Oberstufe höherer Lehranstalten*, vol. 4 (Leipzig and Berlin, 1924), 152; on Schnabel's politics: Schallenberger, *Geschichtsbild*, 204.
49. *KAZ*, no. 462, 3 October 1927.
50. Fritzsche, *Rehearsals*, 158.
51. On celebrations in East Prussia: *KAZ*, no. 462, 3 October 1927; on the Rhineland: *Düsseldorfer Nachrichten*, no. 499, 2 October 1927; on East Prussia, Upper Silesia, Danzig, the Saarland, and Vienna: ibid., no. 501, 3 October 1927; on Dortmund and Cologne: *Tremonia*, no. 271, 3 October 1927; *Kölnische Volkszeitung*, no. 729, 3 October 1927.
52. *Düsseldorfer Nachrichten*, no. 500, 3 October 1927.
53. *MNN*, no. 269, 3 October 1927.
54. Fritzsche, *Rehearsals*, 158.
55. *BAB*, R601, no. 56, n.p.
56. The hand-written appeal in *Tägliche Rundschau*, n.d., copy in *BAB*, R601, no. 1100, 68.

57. *BBZ*, 31 July 1927, copy in *BAB*, R601, no. 1100, 70.

58. *BAB*, R601, no. 55, 26; for Meissner's reasoning: *LAB*, A Pr. Br. Rep. 030, Tit. 89–90, no. 7537, 17–20; also *BAB*, R601, no. 1100, 18; and the official appeal in ibid., 24.

59. See Karstedt's report to the State Secretary of Labour, 8 December 1927, *BAB*, R601, no. 1102, 3–20.

60. Ibid.; *BAB*, R601, no. 57, 5. The *Hindenburg Dank* was organized, amongst others by Hindenburg's close associates Oldenburg-Januschau and Gayl as well as the Reichsverband der Industrie. The endowment of Neudeck was by no means uncontroversial. To avoid high taxation, the property was officially signed over to Hindenburg's son Oskar, an incident that caused great misgivings when it became public. See *BAK*, NL31, Erinnerungen, 109–110; *BAB*, R601, no. 57, 1a-2; Weber, *Büro*, 326–35. Oskar von Hindenburg and the Neudeck property were also caught up in the so-called 'Eastern Aid Scandal', involving the abuse of German emergency state subsidies for East Prussian farmers, W. Weßling, 'Hindenburg, Neudeck und die deutsche Wirtschaft. Tatsachen und Zusammenhänge einer "Affäre" ', *Vierteljahrshefte für Sozial-Wirtschaftsgeschichte,* 64 (1977), 41–73.

61. *RF*, no. 220, 18 September 1927; *BAB*, R601, no. 1102, 3–20.

62. Ibid.; *BAB*, R601, no. 57, 5.

63. *BAB*, R601, no. 1102, 3–20; *BAB*, no. 1100, 253.

64. *BBZ,* no. 462, 3 October 1927.

65. *VZ,* 4 October 1927, copy in *BAB*, R72, no. 1320, 52; Holl and Wild, *Ein Demokrat kommentiert Weimar,* 195–6; and Feder, diary entries for 2 and 3 October 1927, *Heute sprach ich mit . . . ,* 138; v. Hoegen cites articles from the broadsheet press that convey similar observations. See his *Held von Tannenberg,* 345–7.

66. 'Nachklänge zu den Hindenburg-Tagen', *BA-MA*, N714, no. 10.

67. See 'Die Hindenburgfeier', *Sozialistische Politik und Wirtschaft,* 30 September 1927, copy in *AdsD Bonn*, NLLevi, 1/PLAA000308; c.f. Ignaz Wrobel (Kurt Tucholsky) in *Weltbühne*, no. 32, 9 August 1927.

68. Hindenburg really seems to have made this statement to an American journalist during the First World War, W. Ruge, *Hindenburg: Porträt eines Militaristen* (Berlin, 1975), 123 and 520, fn. 63; on invoking the quotation see the KPD guidelines on agitprop slogans in *LAB*, A Pr. Br. Rep., Tit 89–90, no. 7537. The anarcho-pacifist Ernst Friedrich had also juxtaposed images of unspeakably disfigured veterans with the headline 'The health spa' in his famous illustrated book *Krieg dem Kriege* (Berlin, 1924).

69. *LAB*, A Pr. Br. Rep., Tit 89–90, no. 7537.

70. Ibid.

71. The leaflet was distributed in the streets of Berlin and also printed in *RF*, 30 September 1927, see *BAB*, R1501, no. 125648, 36–40.

72. On the 'bogus victory', C. v. Ossietzky, 'Hindenburg's Ruhm', *Weltbühne*, no. 39, 27 September 1927.

73. Theodor Fritsch, one of Weimar's most prolific anti-Semites, for instance, had drafted an article headlined 'What Hindenburg still owes us' in 1927, but did not dare to print it until January 1929. *Hammer: Blätter für deutschen Sinn*, no. 637, 1 January 1929; also the explanatory letter from Fritsch to Hindenburg, *BAB*, R601, 46, n.p.

74. See his own account in *BAK*, KLE499F, 891–5.

75. Claß' speech cited on the front pages of *DZ*, 8 September 1928; and *Der Abend, Spätausgabe des Vorwärts*, no. 426, 8 September 1928.

76. *BT*, 8 September 1928, ev. edn.; *FZ*, no. 676, 9 September 1928.

77. *DTAZ* and *KZ* (both affiliated to the anti-Hugenberg wing of the DNVP), 9 September 1928. Claß also received many letters of complaint from outraged citizens over the following days and weeks, see *DZ*, 3 December 1928, ev. cdn.

78. c.f. Winkler, *Weimar*, 348–9.

79. K. A. Holz, *Die Diskussion um den Dawes- und Young-Plan in der deutschen Presse* (Frankfurt/M., 1977), 375.

80. *BAB*, R 8005, nos. 72 and 73, especially the draft of the law in no. 73; also Holz, *Young-Plan*, 377.

81. Holz, *Young-Plan*; V. R. Berghahn, 'Das Volksbegehren gegen den Young-Plan und die Ursprünge des Präsidialregimes 1928–30', in D. Stegmann (ed.), *Industrielle Gesellschaft und politisches System: Beiträge zur politischen Sozialgeschichte* (Bonn, 1978), 431–46; also Wippermann, *Heimatdienst*, 323–39.

82. Hindenburg to Müller, 13 March 1932, printed in *Akten der Reichskanzlei, Müller II*, doc. 474, 1568; on Hindenburg's attitude towards the Young Plan, Zaun, *Hindenburg*, 462–85.

83. *Vorwärts*, no. 104, 3 March 1930.

84. *KV* and *FZ*, both cited in Holz, *Young-Plan*, 475 and 486.

85. Cited in ibid., 479.

86. *FZ*, 14 March 1930, second morn. edn.

87. Hindenburg signed the Polish treaty on 18 March 1930, see *BT*, no. 133, 19 March 1930; H. v. Riekhoff, *German-Polish Relations 1918–1933* (Baltimore, MD, 1971), 131–60; Zaun, *Hindenburg*, 486–95.

88. The full text is printed in *DAZ*, no. 122, 13 March 1930.

89. *KZ*, no. 74, 14 March 1930; on the DNVP's shift to the right: T. Mergel, 'Das Scheitern des deutschen Tory-Konservatismus: Die Umformung der DNVP zu einer rechtsradikalen Partei 1928–1932', *HZ*, 276 (2003), 323–68.

90. *DTAZ*, no. 132, 19 March 1930; also *DTAZ*, 14 March 1930, morn. edn.

91. *KZ*, no. 77, 16 March 1930; also *KZ*, no. 80, 20 March 1930; Gottfried Treviranus, who had left the DNVP in opposition to Hugenberg and would later found the Conservative People's Party together with Westarp, equally

declared his loyalty to Hindenburg after the ratification of the treaty: *FZ*, 14 March 1930, ev. edn.; on the Stahlhelm's stance: Berghahn, *Stahlhelm*, 143−5.

92. *BAK*, KLE499F, 906−13; v. Hoegen also cites this article in his *Held von Tannenberg*, 313.

93. *DZ*, no. 61b, 13 March 1930; the issue was re-printed as a special edition: *DZ*, Sonderdruck, n.d., *BAB*, R72, no. 1321.

94. On republican reactions: Theodor Wolff's editorial in *BT*, no. 128, 16 March 1930; further *Germania*, 16 March 1930. More moderate conservatives rejected Claß' article outright, see *KZ*, no. 77, 16 March 1930; *DTAZ*, 14 March 1930, morn. edn.; on the Nazis' attitude: 'Hindenburg finally ad acta', Goebbels, diary entries for 12 and 14 March 1930, printed in R. G. Reuth (ed.), *Joseph Goebbels Tagebücher 1924−1945*, 5 vols. (Munich, 1992), here: vol. 2, 468−9.

95. O. Jung, 'Plebiszitärer Durchbruch 1929? Zur Bedeutung von Volksbegehren und Volksentscheid gegen den Young-Plan für die NSDAP', *GG*, 15 (1989), 489−510.

96. See the memoirs of Goebbels's lawyer, v.d. Goltz: *BAK*, KLE653, no. 2, 148−51; also Goebbels, diary entry for 19 September 1929, Reuth, *Goebbels Tagebücher*, 406−8.

97. *Angriff*, no. 65, 29 Dec., 1929; also Doehle to the Reich Justice Minister, 29 December 1929, *BAB*, R601, no. 53, n.p..

98. Goebbels, diary entries for 4 January, 12 and 14 March and 22, 28, and 29 May 1930, Reuth, *Goebbels Tagebücher*, vol. 2, 449 and 468−9, 481 and 485.

99. *DZ*, no. 126b, 31 May 1930; *BAK*, KLE 653, no. 2, 155; State Attorney Sethe to the Prussian Justice Minister, 2 June 1930, *BAB*, R601, no. 53, n.p.; on Hauswirth: *BAB*, R1501, no. 125648, especially 11−30.

100. See G. Zarnow, 'Politische Prozesse', *DS*, vol. 23, 6 June 1930, copy in *BAB*, R601, no. 53, n.p.; *DZ*, no. 126b, 31 May 1930; on Goebbels's preparations for the trial: Goebbels, diary entries for 29, 30, and 31 May 1930, Reuth, *Goebbels Tagebücher*, vol. 2, 485−6.

101. *BAK*, KLE 653, no. 2, 155.

102. Diary entry for 1 June 1930, Reuth, *Goebbels Tagebücher*, vol. 2, 486−7.

103. See Goltz to Meissner, 5 July 1930; and Goltz to Hindenburg, 7 August 1930, *BAB*, R601, no. 53, n.p.; see also Goebbels, diary entries for 5 and 6 July 1930, Reuth, *Goebbels Tagebücher*, vol. 2, 496−8.

104. See Hindenburg's statement of 9 August 1930, *BAB*, R601, no. 53, n.p.

105. Copy of the verdict, ibid.

106. c.f. Goebbels, diary entries for 14 and 15 August 1930, Reuth, *Goebbels Tagebücher*, vol. 2, 507; also *BAK*, KLE 653, no. 2, 156−7.

107. Hindenburg sued for libel more often than Ebert although the latter was subject to much fiercer public criticism, see the memorandum of 27 May 1930, *BAB*, R601, no. 53, n.p.; further Weber, *Büro*, 481, fn. 1492.

108. E. Kolb, 'Rettung der Republik: Die Politik der SPD in den Jahren 1930 bis 1933', in Winkler, *Weimar im Widerstreit*, 85–104, here: 88.

109. Pyta, 'Präsidialgewalt'; Kolb, *Weimar*, 119–20.

110. Pyta, *Hindenburg*, 578–9.

111. Kolb, 'Rettung der Republik', 92–3.


## CHAPTER 7

1. *DZ*, 17 June 1931.
2. Jones, 'Conservative Dilemma', 247.
3. A detailed list of all the supporting organizations can be found in *BAB*, R601, no. 375, 193–201.
4. G. Opitz, *Der Christlich Soziale Volksdienst: Versuch einer protestantischen Partei in der Weimarer Republik* (Düsseldorf, 1969), 231–3.
5. Hugenberg had consequently recommended that DNVP voters should abstain on 10 April and focus on the local elections of 24 April instead. *Mitteilungen der Deutschnationalen Volkspartei*, 21 March 32; Claß to Hugenberg, 19 March 1932, *BAK*, N1231, no. 36, 88; Hugenberg to Hitler, 20 March 1932, *BAK*, N1231, no. 37, 38–47.
6. c.f. Falter, 'Hindenburg Elections', 239–41.
7. c.f. Pünder memorandum, n.d., *BAK*, NL5, no. 97, 39–40, Falter, 'Hindenburg Elections', 239–41; Winkler, *Arbeiter*, 531.
8. Bracher, *Auflösung*, 421, fn. 150.
9. Falter, *Wahlen*, 83; Bracher, *Auflösung*, 419, fn.132.
10. Ummenhofer, *Wie Feuer und Wasser?*, 194.
11. Falter, *Wahlen*, 41.
12. Falter, 'Hindenburg Elections', 236.
13. Jones, 'Conservative Dilemma', 244.
14. Dorpalen, *Hindenburg*, 294.
15. Jones, 'Conservative Dilemma', 245; Bracher, *Auflösung*, 419.
16. Falter, 'Hindenburg Elections'; Cary, 'Reich President', 203–4.
17. See e.g. the accounts in I. Kershaw, *Hitler 1889–1936: Hubris* (London, 1998), 360–3; R. J. Evans, *The Coming of the Third Reich* (London, 2003), 279–82; D. Peukert, *The Weimar Republic* (London, 1991), 263–4, who barely mentions the presidential elections at all.
18. Berghahn, 'Harzburger Front'; and Bracher, *Auflösung* 391–423, who offers a useful synthesis.
19. Kershaw, *Hubris*, 363; T. Childers, *The Nazi Voter: The Social Foundations of Fascism in Germany, 1919–1933* (Chapel Hill, NC, and London, 1983), 197; Paul, *Aufstand*, 202–10.

20. Dorpalen, *Hindenburg*, 254–77; H. Hömig, *Brüning: Kanzler in der Krise der Republik: Eine Weimarer Biographie* (Paderborn, 2000), 486–524.
21. Jones, 'Conservative Dilemma'.
22. Monographs on Weimar election campaigns typically leave out the presidential contests: Lau, *Wahlkämpfe;* Sneeringer, *Women's Votes*; T. Engelmann, *'Wer nicht wählt, hilft Hitler': Wahlkampfberichterstattung in der Weimarer Republik* (Cologne, 2004); on the state of research Jones, 'Conservative Dilemma', 236; a brief sketch of the campaign in Bracher, *Auflösung*, 414–18. Hoegen limits his discussion to the coverage in the party press, see his *Held von Tannenberg*, 296–300 and 316–18 and 357–62; Pyta does not deal with the campaign in great detail, see his *Hindenburg*, 679–83.
23. Dorpalen argues that the myth 'sounded hollow' in his *Hindenburg*, 265; Nicholls suggests that Brüning had to 'create a "Hindenburg myth" ' during the campaign: A. J. Nicholls, *Weimar and the Rise of Hitler*, 4th edn. (London, 2000), 157.
24. H. A. Winkler, 'Choosing the Lesser Evil: The German Social Democrats and the Fall of the Weimar Republic', *JCH*, vol. 25 (1990), 205–27.
25. Bracher pointed out the striking centrality of the Hindenburg myth in 1932, but offered no detailed explanation: *Auflösung*, 423.
26. *Der Jungdeutsche*, 20 January, 25 February, and 2 October 1931; 'Hindenburg-Begehren', *Der Meister. Jungdeutsche Monatsschrift*, vol. 6, March 1931; A. Mahraun, *Die neue Front. Hindenburgs Sendung* (Berlin, 1928); on Westarp: W. Pyta, 'Das Zerplatzen der Hoffnungen auf eine konservative Wende: Kuno Graf von Westarp und Hindenburg', in L. E. Jones and W. Pyta (eds.), *"Ich bin der letzte Preuße": Der politische Lebensweg des konservativen Politikers Kuno Graf von Westarp (1864–1945)* (Cologne, Weimar, and Vienna, 2006), 163–87; E. Jonas, *Die Volkskonservativen 1928–1933: Entwicklung, Struktur, Standort und politische Zielsetzung* (Düsseldorf, 1965), 33–79 and 110–13.
27. Mommsen, *Weimar Democracy*, 367; D. Blasius, *Bürgerkrieg und Politik 1930–1933* (Göttingen, 2005), 32–47.
28. The events leading up to Hindenburg's second nomination are well-known and do not merit explanation in greater detail here, Jones, 'Conservative Dilemma', 236; Bracher, *Auflösung*, 397–404; Pyta, *Hindenburg*, 645–69; on Brüning's role: Hömig, *Brüning*, 486–524; Dorpalen, *Hindenburg*, 254–77; and Brüning's own account in his *Memoiren 1918–1934* (Stuttgart, 1970), 504–8.
29. Pünder, diary entry for 7 January 1932, T. Vogelsang (ed.), *Hermann Pünder: Politik in der Reichskanzlei. Aufzeichnungen aus den Jahren 1929–1932* (Stuttgart, 1961), 110; Pünder, memos of 5, 8, 10, 13 January 1932, T. Koops, (ed.), *Die Kabinette Brüning I und II*, vol. 1, no. 617, 2139–40, and 2159–67.
30. Bracher, *Auflösung*, 360–90; J. A. Leopold, *Alfred Hugenberg: The Radical Nationalist Campaign against the Weimar Republic* (New Haven, CT, and London, 1977), 68–83.

31. Hugenberg to Brüning, 11 January 1932, *BAK*, N1231, no. 36, n.p.; also printed in Koops, *Brüning*, vol. 1, no. 622, 2153–4; Hitler to Brüning, 12 January 1932, printed in ibid., no. 623, 2155; and *BAK*, NL5, no. 97, 205. On the negotiations in January and the caveats presented by the Nazis and DNVP: Meissner, confidential memorandum, 12 December 1931, *BAK*, NL5, no. 97, 275–7; c.f. Dorpalen, *Hindenburg*, 151–2; Bracher, *Auflösung*, 393–6.

32. Pünder, memorandum, 27 January 1932, printed in Koops, *Brüning*, no. 646, 2227–32; see also Jones, 'Conservative Dilemma', 237. On Sahm, H. Sprenger, *Heinrich Sahm: Kommunalpolitiker und Staatsmann* (Cologne, 1969).

33. Sahm, letter of 30 January 1932, *BAB*, R601, no. 373, 91–2; an exemplar of the lists in *BAB*, R601, no. 373, 101.

34. Westarp's appeal and letter to Hindenburg, 22 February 1932, *BAB*, R601, no. 375, 55–7; Dorpalen, *Hindenburg*, 257.

35. Kempner to Meissner, 16 February 1932, *BAB*, R601, no. 373, 126–7; also *WTB*, no. 361, 18 February 1932; 'Protokoll der konstituierenden Sitzung der "Hindenburgausschüsse"', 22 February 1932, printed in Wengst, *Quellen zur Ära Brüning*, vol. 2, 1291–94; further Jones, 'Conservative Dilemma', 237.

36. Pünder, memorandum, 15 February 1932 and Hindenburg's public announcement, printed in Koops, *Brüning*, vol. 1, no. 673, 2293–4.

37. 'Persönliche Darlegung des Herrn Reichspräsidenten über die Vorgänge und Vorgeschichte seiner Wiederkandidatur', *BAB*, R601, 375, 12–20; *BAK*, NL15, no. 422, n.p.; also printed in Wengst, *Quellen zur Ära Brüning*, vol. 2, 1306–10; on drafting the statement see Pünder's notes in *BAK*, NL5, no. 97, 103; also E. Matthias, 'Hindenburg zwischen den Fronten. Zur Vorgeschichte der Reichspräsidentenwahlen von 1932', *VfZ*, vol. 8 (1960), 75–84; and Mackensen to Hindenburg, 5 February 1932 and 13 February 1932, *BAB*, R601, no. 375, 5 and 2; further Einem to Hindenburg, 22 February 1932, ibid., 97–8; further T. Schwarzmüller, *Zwischen Kaiser und 'Führer': Generalfeldmarschall August von Mackensen. Eine politische Biographie* (Paderborn, 1996), 243–53; and Pyta, *Hindenburg*, 665–6.

38. Matthias, 'Hindenburg zwischen den Fronten', 82.

39. See Einem's long reply to Hindenburg, 3 March 1932, *BAB*, R601, no. 375, 108–117, Mackensen's similar comments in his letter to Hindenburg, 13 February 1932, ibid., 2; Mackensen to Hindenburg, 4 March 1932, ibid., 21–2. see also a similar letter by Cramon to Bernhard Schwertfeger, 7 April 1932, *BAK*, NL15, no. 423, n.p.

40. *Deutsches Adelsblatt*, no. 6, 6 February 1932, copy in *BAB*, R601, no. 372, 47–9; also *Deutsches Adelsblatt*, no. 9, 27 February 1932; further Dorpalen, *Hindenburg*, 257.

41. Hindenburg Committees to Meissner, 9 March 1932, *BAB*, R601, no. 373, 43.

42. Minutes of Reich committee meeting of 28 Feb 1932, Kolb, *Nationalliberalismus*, vol. 2, 1206–9; also the letter of an ordinary DVP member (name illegible) to Jarres, 3 February 1932, *BAK*, NL Jarres, no. 29, 18–19.

43. On the negotiations with Stahlhelm and Kyffhäuser in January and February see the notes of the deputy chairman of the Kyffhäuser League, Enckevort, *NSDAP Hauptarchiv*, Reel 44, fol. 930, n.p.; also 'Aufzeichnung des Kyffhäuserbundes über Verhandlungen zur Wiederwahl des Reichspräsidenten', printed in G. Schulz et al. (eds.), *Politik und Wirtschaft in der Krise 1930–1932: Quellen zur Ära Brüning*, vol. 2 (Düsseldorf, 1980), 1278–86; further Berghahn, *Stahlhelm*, 195–219.

44. *Kyffhäuser: Zeitschrift für das deutsche Haus*, no. 8, 21 February 1932, copy in *BAB*, R601, no. 375, 59; *NSDAP Hauptarchiv*, Reel 44, fol. 930, n.p.

45. Ibid.

46. Open letter of Enckevort et al. to the members of the Kyffhäuser League, n.d., and Enckevort's confidential report, 2 May 1932, ibid.

47. See the letter of a local Silesian leader to his superiors, ibid.; generally also K. Führer, 'Der Deutsche Reichskriegerbund Kyffhäuser 1930–1934: Politik, Ideologie und Funktion eines "unpolitischen" Verbandes', *MGM*, 36 (1984), 57–76.

48. Most of these letters are located in *BAB*, R601, no. 37; *NSDAP Hauptarchiv*, Reels 44–5, fol. 930.

49. Gruhl to Horn, 18 February 1932, *NSDAP Hauptarchiv*, Reel 44, fol. 930, n.p.; c.f. Curt Ankermann to Horn, 13 February 1932, ibid; and illegible name, 21 February 1932, ibid.

50. Zoepke to Horn, 23 February 1932, ibid.; and the letter of writer Alwin Rath to Horn accusing the General of violating the Kyffhäuser League's 'legendary name', 22 February 1932, ibid.

51. The letters complaining against Horn's decision outnumbered the statements of support. Those opposed to Horn were, however, probably more likely to feel the need to voice their anger than his supporters were to state their approval. The high number of disapproving letters is thus not necessarily representative of members' opinions.

52. Illegible name, Heidelberg, 14 February 1932, ibid.; Schulz to Horn, 17 February 1932, ibid.

53. Illegible name, Berlin-Karow, 16 February 1932, ibid.

54. Vollmers to Kyffhäuser leadership, 15 April 1932, *NSDAP Hauptarchiv*, Reel 45, fol. 931, n.p.

55. Puls to Horn, 24 February 1932, *NSDAP Hauptarchiv*, Reel 44, fol. 930, n.p.; see also Ernst Strauss to Horn, 22 February 1932, ibid.

56. Illegible name to Horn, 15 March 1932, *NSDAP Hauptarchiv*, Reel 45, fol. 930, n.p.; his impressions were vindicated by Hindenburg's election results in the south. See Falter, *Wahlen*, 47.

57. See e.g. the letter of Dr Regenganz to Kriegerverein Dahlem, 1 March 1932, *NSDAP Hauptarchiv*, Reel 45, fol. 930, n.p.

58. Tiburtius to Paul Neukranz, 19 March 1932, *NSDAP Hauptarchiv*, Reel 45, fol. 931, n.p.; copy in *BAB*, R601, no. 376, 275.

59. Hilbert to Hindenburg, 10 March 1932, ibid., 53.

60. *BAB*, R601, no. 376, 52.

61. *BAK*, NL1377, no. 47, chapter 19.

62. 'Ritterlicher Kampf', *Der Stahlhelm*, 21 February 1932.

63. *BAB*, R601, no. 389, 32–33.

64. e.g. *Nachtausgabe*, 15 March 1932; on the election coverage in the DNVP-affiliated press: *BAB*, R8034 II, no. 9146.

65. *OZ*, 21 February 1932.

66. *Oberschlesischer Landmann*, 15 March 1932. On the Reichslandbund's role in the campaign: *BAB*, R8034 II, no. 9152 and 9153.

67. Goebbels, diary entry for 2 February 1932, E. Fröhlich (ed.), *Die Tagebücher von Joseph Goebbels: Sämtliche Fragmente*, Part 1, vol. 2 (Munich, 1987), 120.

68. c.f. Childers, *Nazi Voter,* 197; Z. A. B. Zeman, *Nazi Propaganda* (Oxford, 1964), 30; R. Bessel, 'The Rise of the NSDAP and the Myth of Nazi Propaganda', *Wiener Library Bulletin*, no. 33 (1980), 20–9.

69. *Reichsparteileitung*, memorandum of 4 February 1932, *NSDAP Hauptarchiv*, Reel 30, fol. 565, n.p.; see also Goebbels, diary entry for 4 February 1932, Fröhlich, *Goebbels Tagebücher*, 121–2, in which he mentions drafting the memorandum.

70. See Duesterberg's memoirs in *BAK*, NL1377, no. 47, chapter 19, 171–201.

71. Report from Nuremberg, 24 May 1932, *BAB*, R1501, no. 126043, 182; also the leading article in *Der Nationalsozialist*, 17 February 1932; and the brochure by 'Spectator Germaniae', *NSDAP Hauptarchiv*, Reel 13A, fol. 1399, n.p.

72. The Berlin police also noted this: *LAB*, A Pr. Br. Rep. 030, no. 7594, 63.

73. Fröhlich, *Goebbels Tagebücher*, 132–3.

74. 'Was ist Pflicht?', *Angriff*, 18 February 1932. See also a similar article by Count Rüdiger von der Goltz, 'Klare Fronten—klare Begriffe', *DZ*, 22 February 1932.

75. 'Wir wählen Hindenburg nicht', *Angriff*, 23 February 1932.

76. Winkler, *Weimar*, 446; also *Vorwärts*' late-night edn. *Der Abend*, 24 February 1932; on Goebbels's speech also Mergel, *Parlamentarische Kultur*, 459.

77. In his diary he even accused the republican parties of forging the minutes of his speech so that they sounded as though he had challenged the President directly: diary entries for 23 and 24 February 1932, Fröhlich, *Goebbels Tagebücher*, 131–2.

78. See e.g. Hitler's speech in the *Sportpalast, VB*, no. 100, 28 February 1932; also Goebbels, diary entries for 22 and 27 February 1932, Fröhlich, *Goebbels Tagebücher*, 130–1 and 134.

79. 'Die Tragödie des Marschalls', *Westdeutscher Beobachter*, 20 February 1932.

80. 'Wir alten Soldaten', *VB*, 19 February 1932.

81. *Angriff*, 26 February 1932; also the brochure written by Goebbels's deputy Heinz Franke, 'Why Hindenburg', *BAB*, R1501, no. 126042, 308–18.

82. See e.g. Goebbels, diary entry for 24 February 1932, Fröhlich, *Goebbels Tagebücher*, 132.

83. *Reichspropagandaleitung*, circular of 23 March 1932, cited in Childers, *Nazi Voter*, 198.

84. Goebbels, diary entry for 29 February 1932, Fröhlich, *Goebbels Tagebücher*, 134–5.

85. Copy of WTB announcement of 19 March 1932, *BAK*, NL5, no. 97, 62; Paul, *Aufstand*, 97–8.

86. Ibid., 206; Kershaw, *Hubris*, 362.

87. Paul, *Aufstand*, 193.

88. Hardt, *In the Company of Media*, 76; R. Grunberger, *A Social History of the Third Reich* (London, 1971), 391.

89. Paul, *Aufstand*, 187–94; Lau, *Wahlkämpfe*, 241.

90. Report of party member Körner from Berlin, *NSDAP Hauptarchiv*, Reel 30, fol. 564, n.p.; *Reichsrundfunkanstalt* to Erich Lachmann, letter in ibid.; Paul, *Aufstand*, 195.

91. Ibid., 198 and 257.

92. Jones, 'Conservative Dilemma', 239. Gereke was the president of the Association of the Prussian Rural Communities. See his self-critical account of the committee's work, published in the GDR in 1970: G. Gereke, *Ich war königlich-preußischer Landrat* (Berlin, 1970), 176–87.

93. Jones, 'Conservative Dilemma', 240.

94. Duisberg alone donated one million Reichsmark to the Hindenburg campaign. According to Gereke, Kurt von Schleicher contributed a further one million illegally from a secret Reichswehr fund, Gereke, *Landrat*, 177 and 184–5. By contrast, Hitler's campaign cost 6.5 million Reichsmark. See Jones, 'Conservative Dilemma', 241; Hömig, *Brüning*, 515.

95. Kempner memorandum on election propaganda, printed in Koops, *Brüning*, vol. 1, no. 680, 2310–13.

96. *BAK*, NL15, no. 422, n.p.

97. *BAB*, R601, no. 389, 293–6; 'Berlin im Zeichen der Hindenburg-Propaganda', *Vorwärts*, no. 119, 11 March 1932.

98. *BAK*, N1005, no. 98, 121–26; Fox Tönende Wochenschau A. G. to Zechlin, 16 February 1932, *BAB*, R601, no. 372, 118.

99. *BAB*, R601, no. 389, 289 and 293–6. For a discussion of the film's content see Chapter 6, 107.

100. Pünder, diary entry for 12 February 1932, Vogelsang, *Pünder*, 113–4; Dorpalen, *Hindenburg*, 269.

101. *WTB*, no. 535, 10 March 1932, copy in *BAB*, R601, no. 372, 185.

102. Weber, *Büro*, 450.

103. *BAK*, N1005, no. 98, 121–6; also Hindenburg Committees to Schwertfeger, 29 February 1932, *BAK*, NL15, no. 422, n.p.; Gereke, *Landrat*, 181.

104. See the report by Erich Tulenda, which was filed as an 'average' impression, *BAB*, R601, no. 389, 125–7; on impressions from the small town of Northeim: W. S. Allen, *The Nazi Seizure of Power: The Experience of a Single German Town 1922–1945*, 3rd edn. (London, 1989), 92–106.

105. *BAK*, N1005, no. 98, 197–220.

106. M. Lau, *Pressepolitik als Chance: Staatliche Öffentlichkeitsarbeit in den Ländern der Weimarer Republik* (Stuttgart, 2003), 174.

107. *BAK*, N1005, no. 98, 158 and 197–220.

108. 'Der Reporter in Wort und Bild', copy in *BAB*, R601, no. 389, 66.

109. Walter Riemer, for instance, designed posters for both campaigns, see *BAK*, posters no. 002-014-018 and 002-016-012.

110. *Tremonia*, no. 65, 5 March 1932; also Behrenbeck, 'Der Führer'.

111. Copies in *BAB*, R601, no. 389, n.p.

112. *BAK*, poster no. 002–016–008.

113. See e.g. Arthur Mahraun's 'Hindenburg, the Citizen', *BAK*, NL15, no. 422, n.p.

114. *BAK*, NL15, no. 423, n.p.; further Jones, 'Conservative Dilemma', 242.

115. *BAK*, N1005, no. 98, 223–230; Catholic publications or those distributed predominantly in Catholic areas generally featured more images of Hindenburg as a family man, e.g. *Tremonia*, no. 73, 13 March 1932; and *Die Welt: Illustrierte Beilage zur Kölnischen Volkszeitung*, no. 11, 13 March 1932.

116. *NSDAP Hauptarchiv*, Reel 30, fol. 566, 1–18; also in *BAK*, NL15, no. 424, 1–9; *BAK*, NL15, no. 422, n. p.; Gereke, *Landrat*, 181.

117. *NSDAP Hauptarchiv*, Reel 29, fol. 563, n.p.

118. 'Hindenburg unsere Rettung. Material für einen Vortrag', *NSDAP Hauptarchiv*, Reel 29, fol. 2563, n.p.; also in *BAK*, NL15, no. 422, n.p.

119. Jung, cited in H. Jahnke, *Edgar Julius Jung: Ein konservativer Revolutionär zwischen Tradition und Moderne* (Pfaffenweiler, 1998), 165; on the pro-Hindenburg stance of the so-called 'Conservative Revolution', also K. Fritzsche, *Politische Romantik und Gegenrevolution: Fluchtwege in der Krise der bürgerlichen Gesellschaft: Das Beispiel des Tat-Kreises* (Frankfurt, 1976), 270.

120. Opitz, *Volksdienst*, 233.

121. Bracher, *Auflösung*, 416–17.

122. Dorpalen, *Hindenburg*, 271; Winkler, *Weimar*, 448; Bömig, *Brüning*, 516–7; Bracher, *Auflösung*, 413; on the coverage of the elections in the Centre-affiliated press, *BAB*, R8034 II, no. 9165.

123. *Nationalliberale Correspondenz*, 1 and 3 March 1932; DVP appeal printed in *WTB*, no. 448, 29 February 1932; on the coverage of the elections in the DVP-affiliated press: *BAB*, R8034 II, no. 9149.

124. D. Harsch, *German Social Democracy and the Rise of Nazism* (Chapel Hill, NC, 1993); Bracher, *Auflösung*, 410–11.

125. Kolb, 'Rettung der Republik', 103.

126. Bracher, *Auflösung*, 401, fn. 39.

127. See e.g. *Vorwärts*, no. 97, 27 February 1923, 5 and 13 March 1932; further Winkler, *Arbeiter*, 511–32.

128. 'Gedanken zu Eberts Todestag', *Vorwärts*, 28 February 1932; on the coverage of the elections in the SPD-affiliated press see: *BAB*, R 8034 II, no. 9154.

129. Winkler, *Arbeiter*, 514–15; also R. Albrecht, 'Symbolkampf in Deutschland 1932: Sergej Tschachotin und der "Symbolkrieg" der Drei Pfeile gegen den Nationalsozialismus als Episode im Abwehrkampf der Arbeiterbewegung gegen den Faschismus in Deutschland', *IWK*, vol. 22, no. 4 (1986), 498–533; Harsch, *Social Democracy*, 169–87; also the pro-Hindenburg appeal of the ADGB, copy in *BAB*, R601, no. 373, 69.

130. *Der Abend*, no. 112, 7 March 1932; Allen, *Seizure of Power*, 94.

131. Kessler, diary entry for 8 April 1932, Kessler, *Diaries*, 413; c.f. Chapter 1, 23.

132. In a crucial meeting of 5 February, Mathilde Wurm, a moderate leftist, was the only one who upheld her opposition to supporting Hindenburg, Harsch, *Social Democracy*, 179.

133. Cited in ibid., 180.

134. Bömig, *Brüning*, 517; Gereke, *Landrat*, 177.

135. Cited in Winkler, *Arbeiter*, 516.

136. See his diary entry for 5 August 1914, cited in Kruse, *Krieg*, 72; also Harsch, *Social Democracy*, 179; Gereke, *Landrat*, 185; O. Braun, *Von Weimar zu Hitler* (New York, 1940), 204; M. Jeretin-Kopf, *Der Niedergang der Weimarer Republik im Spiegel der Memoirenliteratur* (Frankfurt/M., 1992), 146.

137. *Vorwärts*, no. 111, 10 March 1932; Bracher, *Auflösung*, 417.

138. Hömig, *Brüning*, 507.

139. B. Sösemann, *Das Ende der Weimarer Republik in der Kritik demokratischer Publizisten: Theodor Wolff, Ernst Feder, Julius Elbau, Leopold Schwarzschild* (Berlin, 1976), 145.

140. On his previous Hindenburg praise see *BT*, no. 466, 14 September 1914; *BT*, 20 November 1919, morn. edn.; and *BT*, 12 April 1925.

141. 'Die Fahne', *BT*, 6 March 1932, morn. edn.

142. *VZ*, no. 125, 14 March 1932.

143. Sösemann, *Ende*, 140–7. Bosch, who also surveyed liberal commentary on this period, comes to the more convincing conclusion that liberals thought of Hindenburg as the venerable epitome of constitutionality; see his *Liberale Presse*, 210, 219, 229.

144. Dorpalen, *Hindenburg*, 269.

145. Gereke, *Landrat*, 187. In his memoirs, Gereke, who defected to the GDR in the 1950s, nevertheless styled himself as a long-term KPD sympathizer and admitted to misjudging Hindenburg in 1932.

146. *FZ*, 15 March 1932; *VZ*, 15 March 1932, morn. edn.; *BT*, no. 125, 14 March 1932.

147. *Nationalliberale Korrespondenz*, 15 March 1932.
148. *Demokratischer Zeitungsdienst*, 12 April 1932.
149. On the KPD campaign for Ernst Thälmann: *BAB*, R8034 II, no. 9148, 56; on Ossietzky's support for Thälmann: *Die Weltbühne*, no. 9, 1 March 1932; for a Socialist historiographical perspective: E. Kücklich, *Ernst Thälmann und die Reichspräsidentenwahl 1932* (Berlin, 1986).
150. *Weltbühne*, no. 12, 22 March 1932. A shorter extract from Ossietzky's article is cited in the Introduction, 12.
151. *Angriff*, no. 53, 14 March 1932; also Goebbels, diary entries for 13 and 14 March 1932, Fröhlich, *Goebbels Tagebücher*, 140–2.
152. *Angriff*, 11 April 1932.
153. Kershaw, *Hubris*, 363.

## CHAPTER 8

1. Kolb, *Weimar*, 117; Pyta, 'Präsidialgewalt'.
2. Generally Bracher, *Auflösung*, 287–732; on Brüning, G. Schulz, *Zwischen Demokratie und Diktatur: Verfassungspolitik und Reichsreform in der Weimarer Republik*, vol. 3: (Berlin, 1992), 768–70; Pyta, *Hindenburg*, 685–98.
3. On Papen's idea of a 'new state' and the centrality of Hindenburg's mythical authority to this concept: Bracher, *Auflösung*, 544–5.
4. G. Schulz, ' "Preussenschlag" oder Staatsstreich?', *Der Staat*, vol. 17 (1978), 553–81; Clark, *Iron Kingdom*, 645–8.
5. c.f. Bosch, *Liberale Presse*, 212–13 and 228.
6. Hindenburg mistook Hitler's birthplace Braunau am Inn in Austria for Braunau in Bohemia, Meissner, *Staatssekretär*, 322.
7. On the meeting of 13 August 1932 and the communiqué, see the minutes in Minuth, *Kabinett Papen*, 391–7; Bracher, *Auflösung*, 615–8.
8. *BT*, 15 August 33, ev. edn.; 'Wunsch an Hindenburg', *BT*, 2 October 1932; H. Hömig, *Brüning: Politiker ohne Auftrag: Zwischen Bonner und Weimarer Demokratie* (Paderborn, Munich, Vienna, and Zurich, 2006), 31; also Bosch, *Liberale Presse*, 232–3.
9. On the birthday festivities, which roughly 50,000 people attended, *BT* and *DTAZ*, 3 October 1932.
10. *Vorwärts*, no. 465, 2 October 1932; c.f. Hoegen, *Held von Tannenberg*, 354.
11. *DZ*, no. 232a, 2 October 1932.
12. *FZ*, 2 October 1932, ev. edn.
13. W. G., 'Hindenburg', *Germania*, 2 October 1932.
14. G. Schreiber, *Brüning, Hitler, Schleicher: Das Zentrum in der Opposition* (Cologne, 1932), 16–17.
15. Evans, *Coming*, 298–9.
16. Further Pyta, *Hindenburg*, 754–6.
17. Kolb, *Weimar*, 116.

18. On the option of and preparations for declaring a state of emergency in 1932/33: E. Kolb and W. Pyta, 'Die Staatsnotstandsplanung unter den Regierungen Papen und Schleicher' in H. A. Winkler (ed.), *Die deutsche Staatskrise 1930–1933: Handlungsspielräume und Alternativen* (Munich, 1992), 155–81; W. Pyta, 'Vorbereitungen für den militärischen Ausnahmezustand unter Papen/Schleicher', *MGM*, 51 (1992), 385–428.

19. Further Pyta, 'Hindenburg'.

20. The background of Hitler's appointment in the winter of 1932/33 is well known and does not merit being outlined in greater detail here. For a summary in English, Kolb, *Weimar*, 128–35; generally also Bracher, *Auflösung*.

21. Kolb, *Weimar*, 222.

22. Hitler's public appeal of 30 January 1933, printed in M. Domarus (ed.), *Hitler: Reden und Proklamationen 1932–45*, vol. 1 (Wiesbaden, 1973), 188.

23. *DAZ*, 31 January 1933, morn. ed.; *BBC*, 31 January 1933, morn. edn.

24. See e.g. *BA-FA*, DTW, no. 57/1933 and Ufa-Tonwoche, no. 428/1938.

25. *Angriff*, 31 January 1933. The numbers given here are vastly exaggerated and photographs of the scene clearly show that the paper's account was embellished.

26. 'War das Berlin?', *Vorwärts*, no. 53, 1 February 1933.

27. Kershaw, *Hitler Myth*, 55–6; Behrenbeck, 'Der Führer', 61.

28. e.g. *BAK*, posters nos. 002–042–156 and 003–003–003; on street violence after 30 January 1933, Schumann, *Gewalt*, 331–4.

29. See e.g. the film *Unser Führer* (1934), *BA-FA*.

30. On early Nazi festivals, B. Sösemann, ' "Auf Bajonetten läßt sich schlecht sitzen": Propaganda und Gesellschaft in der Anfangsphase der Nationalsozialistischen Diktatur', in T. Stamm-Kuhlmann et al. (eds.), *Geschichtsbilder* (Stuttgart, 2003), 381–409.

31. For images of the *Volkstrauertag*, see *BA-FA*, DTW, no. 63/1933; and *Dr. Frick* (Sonderfilm, 1931/38).

32. Diary entry for 20 March 1933, V. Klemperer, *I Shall Bear Witness: The Diaries of Victor Klemperer 1933–1941* (London, 1999), 9.

33. c.f. on this pattern of thought: Bosch, *Liberale Presse*, 217.

34. See e.g. the memoirs of Hindenburg's doctor Ferdinand Sauerbruch, *A Surgeon's Life* (London, 1957), 212; also Meissner, *Staatssekretär*, 214; F. v. Papen, *Der Wahrheit eine Gasse* (Munich, 1952), 368; and the memoirs of Papen's private secretary: F. G. v. Tschirschky, *Erinnerungen eines Hochverräters* (Stuttgart, 1972), 146; on Hindenburg's mental agility further Zaun, *Hindenburg*, 80–4; Pyta, *Hindenburg*, 605, 835–6, and 855.

35. Wheeler-Bennet includes the story about Hindenburg mistaking the SA men for Russian POWs in his book. Given the reports about the President's mental agility until mid-1934, however, it is likely that this anecdote mirrors people's perceptions rather than a true story. Wheeler-Bennet, *Wooden Titan*,

434–5 and 442; on the other jokes: H.-J. Gamm, *Der Flüsterwitz im Dritten Reich* (Munich, 1963), 16–19.

36. *BT*, 4 March 33, morn. edn., 5 March 1933; *VZ*, 31 January 1933, morn. edn.; *Vorwärts*, no. 95, 25 February 1933; c.f. Bosch, *Liberale Presse*, 212–13; K.-D Bracher et al., *Die nationalsozialistische Machtergreifung: Studien zur Errichtung des totalitären Herrschaftssystems in Deutschland 1933/34* (Cologne and Opladen, 1962), 967; Wheeler-Bennet, *Wooden Titan*, 437; Dorpalen, *Hindenburg*, 459 and 482.

37. e.g. *FZ*, 19 March, 1 April, 9 April; *VZ*, 5 February, morn. edn., 24 February, morn. edn., *BT*, 13 March 1933, ev. edn.; Opitz describes similar beliefs among Protestant nationalists in his *Volksdienst*, 293.

38. Löwenstein to Hindenburg, 23 March 1934, K.-H. Minuth (ed.), *Die Regierung Hitler*, vol. 1 (Boppard am Rhein, 1983), 1222–3; on the RjF: U. Dunker, *Der Reichsbund jüdischer Frontsoldaten 1919–1938: Geschichte eines jüdischen Abwehrvereins* (Düsseldorf, 1977); Leipart to Hindenburg, 10 March 1933, ibid., Minuth, *Hitler*, 188–9; further the minutes of the meeting with a delegation from Bavaria, 17 February 1933, ibid., 89; Wilhelm H. Thomas, a member of a union in the formerly occupied western territories to Hindenburg, 28 February 1933, and the DDP's former State Minister Moeller to Hindenburg, ibid., 133–5.

39. P. Longerich, *Politik der Vernichtung* (Munich, 1998), 42; Meissner, *Staatssekretär*, 322–4. Hindenburg did, for instance, explicitly support the move to make 'racial purity' a precondition for DAG membership, Wehler, *Gesellschaftsgeschichte*, vol. 4, 748.

40. Goebbels, diary entries for 14 and 12 March 1933, Reuth, *Goebbels Tagebücher*, vol. 2: 1930–1934, 780 and 778; on the *Volkstrauertag* also Minuth, *Hitler*, 157–9.

41. W. Freitag, 'Nationale Mythen und kirchliches Heil: Der "Tag von Potsdam"', *Westfälische Forschungen*, 41 (1991), 379–430, here: 382.

42. Minutes of meeting of 7 March 1933, Minuth, *Hitler,* 159; Goebbels, diary entries for 17 and 19 March 1933, Reuth, *Goebbels Tagebücher*, vol. 2: 1930–1934, 781 and 782; Meissner, *Staatssekretär*, 294; generally K.-J. Müller, 'Der Tag von Potsdam und das Verhältnis der preussisch-deutschen Militär-Elite zum Nationalsozialismus', in B. Kröner (ed.), *Postdam: Stadt, Armee, Residenz in der preussisch-deutschen Militärgeschichte* (Frankfurt/M., 1993), 435–49; Freitag, 'Potsdam'; c.f. Hoegen, *Held von Tannenberg*, 383–400.

43. Meissner's memorandum on the meeting between Hitler, Hindenburg et al. on 7 March 1933, printed in Minuth, *Hitler,* 157–9; also *Angriff*, no. 69, 22 March 1933, first supplement.

44. See the special supplement of *BT*, no. 134, 22 March 1933; 'Die Wallfahrt der Hunderttausend', *DZ*, no. 68b, 21 March 1933; further Freitag, 'Potsdam', 389.
45. *DZ*, no. 68b, 21 March 1933.
46. c.f. G. Kaufmann, 'Der Händedruck von Potsdam: Die Karriere eines Bildes', *GWU*, 48 (1997), 295–315, here: 312–3; Evans, *Coming*, 350–1; Kershaw, *Hitler Myth*, 54.
47. The full texts were printed on the front page of the major papers, e.g. *DZ*, no. 69a, 22 March 1933; *BT*, no. 133, 21 March 1933; *Angriff*, no. 68, 21 March 1933; also Domarus, *Reden,* vol. 1, 224–9.
48. Domarus, *Reden,* vol. 1, 224–9.
49. *DZ*, no. 69a, 22 March 1933; *DAZ*, no. 136, 21 March 1933.
50. Freitag, 'Potsdam', 399–400. The photograph of a handshake which has since become the most widely distributed image of that day does not show the ceremonial handshake inside the church, but was taken outside just before Hindenburg departed, see Kaufmann, 'Händedruck'; further Chapter 9, 199.
51. See the special illustrated supplement of *BT*, no. 134, 22 March 1933.
52. See the supplements of *DZ*, no. 69a, 22 March 1933; *BT*, no. 134, 22 March 1933; *Angriff*, no. 69, 22 March 1933.
53. Freitag, 'Potsdam', 407; Allen, *Seizure of Power*, 207.
54. *BT*, no. 134, 22 March 1933; also Goebbels, diary entries for 17 and 19 March 1933, Reuth, *Goebbels Tagebücher*, vol. 2: 1930–1934, 781–2.
55. *BT*, no. 134, 22 March 1933; Freitag, 'Potsdam', 425; also *Hindenburg und Hitler sprechen am Tag von Potsdam* (1933), *BA-FA*.
56. Diary entry for 31 March 1933, Klemperer, *Witness*, 12.
57. Kershaw, *Hitler Myth*, 55.
58. Freitag, 'Potsdam', 404; Bracher et al., *Machtergreifung*, 151.
59. Freitag, 'Potsdam', 380 and 394, rightly stresses the importance of religion in broadening the Nazis' base of support, but neglects the centrality of the Hindenburg myth in making the ceremony work; also *BAK*, NL 1377, no. 47, 202–6.
60. Goebbels, diary entry for 12 March 1933, Reuth, *Goebbels Tagebücher*, vol. 2, 778.
61. Kershaw, *Hitler Myth*, 54.
62. Bracher et al., *Machtergreifung*, 150–2.
63. R. Morsey (ed.), *Das 'Ermächtigungsgesetz' vom 24. März 1933: Quellen zur Geschichte und Interpretation des 'Gesetzes zur Behebung der Not von Volk und Reich'* (Düsseldorf, 1992).
64. Meissner, *Staatssekretär*, 297; Goebbels, diary entry for 24 March 1933, Reuth, *Goebbels Tagebücher*, vol. 2, 784–5.
65. Sösemann, 'Bajonetten'; S. Behrenbeck, 'Durch Opfer zur Erlösung: Feierpraxis im nationalsozialistischen Deutschland', in idem and A. Nützenadel (eds.), *Inszenierung des Nationalstaats. Politische Feiern in Italien und Deutschland*

*seit 1860/71* (Cologne, 2000), 149–70; The speeches of 1 May are printed in Domarus, *Reden*, vol. 1, 258–64.

66. *VB*, ed. A, no. 239/40, 27/28 August 1933; *Angriff*, no. 201, 28 August 1933.

67. Ibid.

68. Domarus, *Reden*, vol. 1, 293–4.

69. Ibid.; *DAZ*, 29 August 1933; *BBZ*, 29 August 1933; on the controversy surrounding the tax for the property and allegations of corruption: Minutes of 14 July 1933 and 26 September 1933, Minuth, *Hitler*, 665 and 828; *Reichsgesetzblatt*, 1933, vol. 1, no. 95, copy in *BAB*, R601, no. 58, 2; as well as Hindenburg's letter of thanks to Hitler, 30 August 1933, *BAB*, R601, no. 58, 3; further Meissner, *Staatssekretär*, 325–6; *BAK*, NL31, no. 2, 112.

70. Breitenborn, *Bismarck*, 119–20; also *DZ*, no. 200b, 28 August 1933; *Angriff*, no. 201, 28 August 1933.

71. *FZ*, 27 August 1933, morn. edn.

72. *VB*, ed. A, no. 241, 29 August 1933; both events were covered in the *Wochenschauen, BA-FA*, DTW, no. 87/1933.

73. Kershaw, *Hitler Myth*.

74. *BBC*, 12 November 1933.

75. See the press order of 10 November 1933, printed in G. Toepser-Ziegert (ed.), *NS-Presseanweisungen der Vorkriegszeit*, 7 vols. here: vol. 1. (Munich, 1984–2001), here: vol. 1, 215–6.

76. Press order of 16 March 1934, printed in ibid., vol. 2, 140.

77. *VB*, ed. A, 3 October 1933; *DZ*, no. 231a, 3 October 1933; Domarus, *Reden*, vol. 1, 305.

78. *VB*, ed. A, 1/2 October 1933.

79. Toepser-Ziegert, *NS-Presseanweisungen*, vol. 1, 21–44; K.-F. Abel, *Presselenkung im NS-Staat* (Berlin, 1968).

80. P. Longerich, *Die braunen Bataillone: Geschichte der SA* (Munich, 1989), 206–19; on public reactions Kershaw, *Hitler Myth*, 84–95.

81. Domarus, *Reden*, vol. 1, 405.

82. Gamm, *Flüsterwitz*, 18.

83. e.g. 'Hindenburg as a prisoner' by Otto Strasser's *Schwarze Front*, Gestapo report from Osnabrück, August 1934, G. Steinwascher (ed.), *Gestapo Osnabrück meldet... Polizei- und Regierungsberichte aus dem Regierunsbezirk Osnabrück aus den Jahren 1933–1936* (Osnabrück, 1995), 121; and from Oldenburg, 16 November 1934, A. Eckhardt and K. Hoffmann (eds.), *Gestapo Oldenburg meldet... Berichte der Geheimen Staatspolizei und des Innenministers aus dem Freistaat und Land Oldenburg 1933–1936* (Hanover, 2002), 168.

84. Gamm, *Flüsterwitz*, 18; on the actress: J. Ahlemann, *Ich bleibe die große Adele: Die Sandrock: Eine Biografie* (Düsseldorf, 1988).

85. He seems to have believed Hitler's version, however, and signed the congratulatory telegrams personally: Tschirschky, *Erinnerungen*, 237–40; also Sauerbruch, *Surgeon's Life*, 215, who says Hindenburg's knowledge was hazy;

Meissner, *Staatssekretär*, 375, who argues that Hindenburg objected to the events, but did not blame Hitler personally; further Pyta, *Hindenburg*, 843–53.

86. Sauerbruch, *Surgeon's Life*, 212–15; Meissner, *Staatssekretär*, 376.

87. Goebbels, diary entries for 19 July and 25 August 1933, Reuth, *Goebbels Tagebücher*, vol. 2: 1930–1934, 822 and 829.

88. *Reichsgesetzblatt*, no. 89, 2 August 1934; also the minutes of the cabinet meeting of 1 August 1934, Minuth, *Hitler*, 1384–86; Domarus, *Reden*, vol. 1, 429–31.

89. *Reichsgesetzblatt*, no. 92, 2 August 1934, copy in *BAB*, R72, no. 1332.

90. Evans, *Third Reich*, 43–4.

91. Diary entry for 4 August 1934, Klemperer, *Witness*, 97–8.

92. *Reichsgesetzblatt*, no. 93, 3 August 1934; also printed in *BBZ*, 3 August 1934.

93. Schultze-Pfaelzer, 'Die Wahrheit über das Hindenburg-Testament', *SZ*, no. 46, 2 August 1946; see also his correspondence with Bernhard Schwertfeger in the 1940s, *BAK*, NL15, no. 566; and his personal papers: *BAK*, KLE 608, especially 43–6 and 58–62.

94. See press orders of 31 July and 1 August 1934, printed in Toepser-Ziegert, *NS-Presseanweisungen*, vol. 2, 296–9.

95. V. Ackermann, *Nationale Totenfeiern in Deutschland* (Stuttgart, 1990), 47–52 and 79.

96. *LAB*, A Pr. Br. Rep. 042, vol. 1, no. 236.

97. *Berliner Illustrierte Nachtausgabe*, no. 179, 3 August 1934; *BL*, 2 August 1934, ev. ed.; *VB*, special ed., 2 August 1934, copy in *BAB*, R72, no. 1325.

98. *Nationalsozialistische Partei-Korrespondenz*, 2 August 1934; also printed in *Der Deutsche*, no. 128, 3 August 1934, copies in *BAB*, R72, no. 1325.

99. *Angriff*, 6 August 1934; Hitler himself had referred to Hindenburg as his 'fatherly friend' in a cabinet meeting a few days earlier, Minuth, *Hitler*, 1386–9.

100. See the press clippings in *BA-MA*, N429, nos. 12 and 15; *BAB*, R8034 III, no. 198; *BAB*, R72, nos. 1325, 1326 and 1328.

101. Diary entry for 7 August 1934, Klemperer, *Witness*, 98.

102. *BT*, no. 367, 6 August 1934; Domarus, *Reden*, vol. 1, 434–7; Ackermann, *Totenfeiern*, 69.

103. As a concession the body of Hindenburg's wife Gertrud, who had been buried at Neudeck, was moved and buried alongside that of her husband's inside the Tannenberg Memorial in 1936. Some soil from the family estate was also taken to Tannenberg so that Hindenburg's wish—to be buried in the ground of Neudeck—was honoured formally. See Minutes of cabinet of 2 August 1934, Minuth, *Hitler*, 1386–9; Meissner, *Staatssekretär*, 376–8; *BAK*, NL1377, no. 47, 202–6; and the press order of 24 June 1936, Toepser-Ziegert, *NS-Presseanweisungen*, vol. 4, 667.

104. Minutes of cabinet meeting, 2 August 1934, Minuth, *Hitler*, 1386–9; *VB*, ed. A, 8 August 1934.

105. Ackermann, *Totenfeiern*, 14 and 66–8.

106. Albert Speer was involved in 'designing' the funeral: Tietz, *Tannenberg-Nationaldenkmal*, 86–9; see the photographs in *BIZ*, special edn., 9 August 1934, copy in *BA-MA*, N429, 15; *DAZ*, special Hindenburg memorial edn., August 1934.

107. Copy in *BA-MA*, N429, no. 20.

108. Domarus, *Reden*, vol. 1, 437–8; Tietz, *Tannenberg-Nationaldenkmal*, 85–8; On Valhalla as a German national myth: Mosse, *Nationalization*, 53–5.

109. See the Gestapo report from Kassel, 5 September 1934, printed in T. Klein (ed.), *Die Lageberichte der Geheimen Staatspolizei über die Provinz Hessen Nassau 1933–1936*, 2 vols. (Cologne and Vienna, 1986), 152; Meissner, *Staatssekretär*, 378.

110. *Berliner Illustrierte Nachtausgabe*, no. 182, 7 August 1934; Ackermann, *Totenfeiern*, 237.

111. *VB*, Berlin edn. A, 8 August 1934.

112. See the report on public opinion from the *Oberpräsident* of Hessen-Nassau, 8 September 1934, printed in Klein, *Lageberichte Hessen Nassau*, 912; the reports from Magdeburg, for July and August 1934, and for Saxony, 8 September 1934, printed in H.-J. Rupieper and A. Sperk (eds.), *Die Lageberichte der Geheimen Staatspolizei zur Provinz Sachsen 1933–1936*, vol. 1 (Halle, 2003), 87, 99, and 104; and the report from Osnabrück for August 1934, printed in Steinwascher, *Gestapo Osnabrück*, 85. According to Ackermann's comparative study on funeral rites the scale and spontaneity of people's reactions to Hindenburg's death were only matched by those to that of Wilhelm I in 1888: *Totenfeiern*, 80.

113. See the report from Nuremberg in *Sopade*, vol. 1, 296.

114. Diary entry for 7 August 1934, P. de Mendelssohn (ed.), *Thomas Mann: Tagebücher 1933–1934* (Frankfurt/M., 1977), 500–1.

115. Diary entry for 2 August 1934, ibid., 97; Wheeler-Bennett, *Wooden Titan*, 437.

116. Diary entry for 4 August 1934, Klemperer, *Witness*, 97–8.

117. *Sopade*, vol. 1, 299–300.

118. Diary entry for 5 February 1938, J. Klepper, *Unter dem Schatten Deiner Flügel: Aus den Tagebüchern der Jahre 1932 bis 1942* (Berlin, 1967), 333.

119. See the Gestapo report from Kassel, 5 September 1934 in Klein, *Lageberichte Hessen Nassau*, 153; and the report from Erfurt in Rupieper and Sperk, *Lageberichte Sachsen*, vol. 1, 110.

120. Diary entry for 5 August 1934, Mann, *Tagebücher*, 496–7.

121. According to the standard periodization of the 'Third Reich' August 1934 was a pivotal moment when the 'seizure of power' was completed and a period of 'consolidation and consensus' began: Bracher, *Machtergreifung*, 967–8; G. Plum, 'Übernahme und Sicherung der Macht 1933/34', in M. Broszat and N. Frei (eds.), *Ploetz: Das Dritte Reich. Ursprünge, Ereignisse, Wirkungen*

(Freiburg and Würzburg, 1983), 28–44; and W. Benz, 'Konsolidierung und Konsens 1934–1939', ibid., 45–62.

122. Printed in *Deutsches Nachrichtenbüro*, no. 1738, 15 August 1934, copy in *BAB*, R 8034 III, no. 198; also *BL*, no. 384, 16 August 1934; Domarus, *Reden*, vol. 1, 439–45.

123. Tschirschky, *Erinnerungen*, 224–5.

124. Ibid., 151–4; Papen, *Wahrheit*, 368–9; Meissner, *Staatssekretär*, 379; also the extracts of the verdict against Papen of 26 January 1949, copy in *AdsD Bonn*, NL Meissner, box. 11, n.p.; further the memoirs of Papen's deputy v. Kageneck, 'Hans Graf von Kageneck: Wo blieb Hindenburgs Testament', *FAZ*, no. 146, 26 June 2004, 39; further Pyta, *Hindenburg*, 855–71; the most detailed account is by H. Mühleisen, 'Das Testament Hindenburgs vom 11. Mai 1934', *VfZ*, 44 (1996), 355–71;

125. On the campaign: *Sopade,* vol. 1, 275–80; Klemperer, diary entry for 21 August 1934, Klemperer, *Witness*, 100–1; and Goebbels, diary entry for 10 August 1934, Reuth, *Goebbels Tagebücher*, vol. 2, 846.

126. *Germania*, 17 August 1934, c.f. Hoegen, *Held von Tannenberg*, 418–19; also the similar articles in *Berliner Morgenpost*, 16 August 1934; *DZ*, 18 August 1934; and 'Herr Hitler's Campaign' in *The Times*, 17 August 1934, copy in *BAK*, Zsg. 117, no. 14, 44.

127. Printed in H. Michaelis and E. Schraepler (eds.), *Ursachen und Folgen,* vol. 10 (Berlin, 1966), 277; in his de-Nazification trial in 1949, Hindenburg testified that the Propaganda Ministry had presented him with a draft even more explicit in its support for Hitler. He then wrote his own, allegedly less strongly worded speech: *Die Welt*, n.d. (March, 1949), copy in *AdsD Bonn*, NLMeissner, box 27, n.p.; Mühleisen, 'Testament', 370. Otto Dietrich ordered the press to print Oskar's speech prominently. See press order of 17 August 1934, Toepser-Ziegert, *NS-Presseanweisungen*, vol. 2, 318–19.

128. Diary entry for 22 August 1934, Reuth, *Goebbels Tagebücher*, vol. 2: 1930–1934, 847; on rigging the vote, *Sopade,* vol. 1, 282–7 and 290–5.

129. Diary entry for 17 August 1934, *Tagebücher,* 508–9.

130. Even after 1945 the notion of the will being a forgery was still virulent. Hindenburg devotees Schultze-Pfaelzer and Schwertfeger, for instance, poured considerable energy into proving that Papen, Meissner, Oskar v. Hindenburg or others forged the will, *BAK*, NL15, no. 566; *BAK*, KLE608. None of the studies on Hindenburg's political will consult their papers.

131. *BAK*, picture no. 183–2006–0429–501.

132. *VB*, 3 October 1934; *BL*, no. 465, 2 October 1934; press order of 27 July 1935, Toepser-Ziegert, *NS-Presseanweisungen,* vol. 3, 472; *Times*, 3 August 1935, 10.

133. *DAZ*, 4 August 1936; *VB*, 3 August 1940, *VB*, 2 August 1941; *DAZ*, 3 August 1942; *VB*, 2 August 1944; *VB*, 2 October 1937.

134. *VB*, 11 August 1937.

135. Order of 27 March 1936, Toepser-Ziegert, *NS-Presseanweisungen*, vol. 4, 356.

136. *DAZ*, 26 April and 2 October 1935.

137. *Times*, 29 February 1936, 11; 5 March 1936, 13; H. G. Dick and D. H. Robinson, *The Golden Age of the Great Passenger Airships: Graf Zeppelin and Hindenburg* (Washington, DC, 1985), 83–137.

138. *Times*, 28 and 30 March 1936, 12.

139. *Times*, 1, 7, and 8 May 1937; on the real reason of the crash which the Nazis initially covered up: 'Funke am Lack', *Der Spiegel*, 15 (1991), 246–7.

140. *BA-FA, Hindenburg* (1936).

141. *DAZ*, 24 May 1935, 2 October 1935, and 24 August 1935.

142. F. Lauritzen, 'Propaganda Art in the Postage Stamps of the Third Reich', *The Journal of Decorative and Propaganda Arts*, 10 (1988), 62–79, here: 62 and 65; on the original stamp: *BAB*, R601, no. 1100, 4.

143. J. M. Wehner, *Hindenburg* (Leipzig, 1935), 9.

144. Schenk, 'Tannenberg/Grunwald'.

145. *Kyffhäuser*, no. 40, 6 October 1935; *BBZ*, 2 October 1935; *VB*, no. 276, 3 October 1935, copies in *BAB*, R72, no. 1331.

146. Speer had initially wanted to have a say in the reconstruction, but was ousted by the Krüger brothers, Tietz, *Tannenberg-Nationaldenkmal*, 90–91; generally ibid., 85–154.

147. Ibid., 119.

148. *VB*, 5 March 1935; *BBZ*, 18 December 1934; *Hamburger Nachrichten*, 12 December 1934, copies in *BAB*, R72, no. 1331.

149. 'Tannenberg als Hindenburg-Denkmal', *BBZ*, 11 December 1934, copy in *BAB*, R72, no. 1331; Ackermann, *Totenfeiern*, 237.

150. Ian Kershaw, for instance, pays relatively scant attention to the Hindenburg myth in his *Hitler Myth* and *Hubris*. Similarly, Wehler who analyses the *Führer* cult in some detail does not mention Hitler's reliance on Hindenburg's mythical glorification at all—with the exception of a brief reference to the 'Day of Potsdam': Wehler, *Gesellschaftsgeschichte*, vol. 4, 606–7.

CHAPTER 9

1. 'MG Reburies 3 German Rulers in Secret Operation', in *Stars and Stripes*, 23 August 1946, cited in I. Krüger-Bulcke, 'Der Hohenzollern-Hindenburg-Zwischenfall in Marburg 1947: Wiederaufleben nationalistischer Strömungen oder Sturm im Wasserglas?', *Hessisches Jahrbuch für Landesgeschichte*, 39 (1989), 311–52, here: 329–30.

2. M. Zeidler, *Kriegsende im Osten: Die Rote Armee und die Besetzung Deutschlands östlich von Oder und Neiße 1944–45* (Munich, 1996), 86–7; Weber, *Büro*, 458.

3. Zeidler, *Kriegsende*, 129.

4. Although the whole memorial was not actually blown up, as the Nazis claimed, almost no trace of it has survived. Most of its material was used for local reconstruction efforts after 1945, Tietz, *Tannenberg-Nationaldenkmal*, 201.

5. Zeidler, *Kriegsende*, 87; also Hermann Bauer's account, 12 January 1963, StM, NLBauer, no. 725; Görlitz, *Hindenburg*, 431–2.

6. 'Prussian relics found', *Times*, 18 June 1945, 4; 'Hidden shrine yields two Kaisers' bodies', *NYT*, 18 June 1945.

7. Robert Murphy, the State Department's Political Adviser for Germany, and James Byrnes, the US Secretary of State, amongst others, were involved in the decision-making process, Krüger-Bulcke, 'Hohenzollern-Hindenburg-Zwischenfall', 317–18.

8. Ibid., 319.

9. Ibid., 324–5.

10. Bauer to Hans-Ulrich v. Sperling, 2 August 1960, StM, NLBauer, no. 728. While the mortal remains of the two Prussian Kings were re-located to the Hohenzollern ancestral home in Hechingen in 1952 and re-buried in Potsdam in 1991, the remains of Hindenburg and his wife remain in Marburg to this day.

11. 'An den Gräbern in der Elisabethkirche', *Marburger Presse*, no. 68, 27 August 1946, copy in StM, NLBauer, no. 727.

12. Anthony F. Kleitz to Bauer, 8 October 1946, StM, NLBauer, no. 728; also Bauer's account in StM, NLBauer, no. 725; on the ICD: U. M. Bausch, *Die Kulturpolitik der US-amerikanischen Information Control Division in Württemberg-Baden von 1945 bis 1949: Zwischen militärischem Funktionalismus und schwäbischem Obrigkeitsdenken* (Stuttgart, 1992), 66–80; C. Kleßman, *Die doppelte Staatsgründung: Deutsche Geschichte 1945–1955* (Göttingen, 1982), 393–4.

13. C. F. Latour and T. Vogelsang, *Okkupation und Wiederaufbau: Die Tätigkeit der Militärregierung in der amerikanischen Besatzungszone Deutschlands 1944–1947* (Stuttgart, 1973), 132; B. Braun, *Umerziehung in der amerikanischen Besatzungszone: Die Schul- und Bildungspolitik in Württemberg-Baden von 1945 bis 1949* (Münster, 2004), 94.

14. The IMT acquitted Papen in October 1945, but he was tried by German courts for his role in the Nazi 'seizure of power' in 1947: 'Papen before his own countrymen', *Times*, 25 January 1947, 3; 'Hand in will forgery denied by von Papen', *NYT*, 30 January 1947; also Oskar von Hindenburg to Meissner, 11 August 1949, AdsD Bonn, NL Meissner, box 10, n.p.; press cutting from *Die Welt*, n.d. (March 1949), ibid., box 27, n.p.

15. 'Hindenburgs Testament gefälscht', *Neue Zeitung*, no. 12, 26 November 1945; further the pretty much accurate account (albeit with a misleading headline): 'Hitler fraud Hindenburg will', *NYT*, 11 February 1945, 5.

16. 'Das Testament Hindenburgs—keine Fälschung? Zwei historische Dokumente zerstören eine Legende', *SZ*, no. 67, 20 August 1946.

17. 'Nationalheilige' der Republik?', *FR*, 17 September 1946, *StM*, NLBauer, no. 727.
18. 'Hindenburg der Wegbereiter Hitlers. Der "Feldmarschall-Präsident" als Totengräber der deutschen Demokratie', *Neue Presse*, 4 September 1946, 3.
19. Cited in Krüger-Bulcke, 'Hohenzollern-Hindenburg-Zwischenfall', 327; on Brill generally: M. Overesch, *Hermann Brill in Thüringen 1895–1946: Ein Kämpfer gegen Hitler und Ulbricht* (Bonn, 1992).
20. See e.g. 'Hindenburg der Wegbereiter Hitlers'; M. Freund, 'Totengräber eines Kaiserreichs und einer Republik. Paul von Hindenburg', *FAZ*, 24 December 1962; on the '*Steigbügelhalter*': W. Dirks, 'Rechts und links', *Frankfurter Hefte* I, no. 6 (1946), 24–37, here: 25; the majority of memoirs painted Hindenburg as a tragic figure with political shortcomings, who was nevertheless not to blame personally, c.f. Jeretin-Kopf, *Memoirenliteratur*, 147.
21. E. Marcks, *Hindenburg: Feldmarschall und Reichspräsident* (Göttingen, Berlin, and Frankfurt/M., 1963), 67–8. Marcks's popular biography that likened Hindenburg to Bismarck had originally been written in 1932 and was re-printed including explanatory remarks by Hubatsch in 1963.
22. M. Salewski, *Der Erste Weltkrieg* (Paderborn, 2003), 339.
23. F. Meinecke, *Die deutsche Katastrophe* (Wiesbaden, 3rd edn., 1947), 97.
24. Bracher, *Auflösung*, 631, fn. 176 and 637.
25. N. Frei, *1945 und wir: Das Dritte Reich im Bewusstsein der Deutschen* (Munich, 2005), 87; R. G. Moeller, *War Stories: The Search for a Usable Past in the Federal Republic of Germany* (Berkeley, CA, 2001).
26. Kaufmann, 'Händedruck', 307.
27. The idea of the 'conned' Hindenburg who fell victim to the Nazis is, for instance, still evident in Werner Maser's biography published in 1990, see his *Hindenburg: Eine politische Biographie* (Rastatt, 1990), 369.
28. S. Ullrich, 'Im Schatten einer gescheiterten Demokratie: Die Weimarer Republik und der demokratische Neubeginn in den Westzonen 1945–1949', Winkler, *Deutungsmacht*, 185–208, especially 200–7; F. K. Fromme, *Von der Weimarer Verfassung zum Bonner Grundgesetz: Die verfassungspolitischen Folgerungen des Parlamentarischen Rates aus Weimarer Republik und nationalsozialistischer Diktatur* (3rd edn., Berlin, 1999).
29. Mühlhausen, *Ebert*, 989–90.
30. M. Jochum, *Worte als Taten: Der Bundespräsident im demokratischen Prozess der Bundesrepublik Deutschland* (Gütersloh, 2000).
31. E. Noelle and P. Neumann (eds.), *Jahrbuch der öffentlichen Meinung 1947–1955* (Allensbach, 1956), 132. Because Hitler continued to be venerated by a considerable number, however, Hindenburg's association with the Nazis cannot suffice to explain his relatively low standing after 1945. His memory must have begun to fade into obscurity in the 'Third Reich' already.

32. G. Knopp and P. Arens, *Unsere Besten: Die 100 größten Deutschen* (Berlin, 2003); E. Wolfrum, 'Konrad Adenauer: Politik und Vertrauen', Möller, *Charismatische Führer*, 171–91.

33. Schwertfeger to Schultze-Pfaelzer, letter of 17 September 1946, *BAK*, NL15, no. 566.

34. Schultze-Pfaelzer to Schwertfeger, 13 October 1946, ibid.

35. Margarete v. Hindenburg to Keudell, 25 October 1967, *BAK*, N1243, no. 122.

36. Görlitz, *Hindenburg*; Hubatsch, *Hindenburg*.

37. See Margarete v. Hindenburg to Keudell, 4 February 1963, *BAK*, N1243, no. 55 and 26 March 1966, *BAK*, N1243, 122; also Oskar v. Hindenburg to Meissner, 11 August 1949, *AdsD Bonn*, NL Meissner, box 10, n.p.

38. c.f. Herbert Hupka's review of Hubatsch, *Das Parlament*, January 1966, copy in *BAK*, N1243, no. 55.

39. 'Die Tragödie Paul von Hindenburgs. Die Nation hat ihn überfordert', *FAZ*, no. 294, 18 December 1954; 'Ein armer alter Mann ... General Hoffman über den Feldmarschall von Hindenburg', *FAZ*, no. 7, 10 January 1955; also the clippings from the *FAZ*, no. 163, 18 July 1959, 11, *BAK*, N1243, no. 55.

40. 'Blick in die Westzone', *Leipziger Zeitung*, 26 November 1946, *StM*, NLBauer, no. 727. Because Hindenburg's grave is located in a part of the church accessible free of charge the exact number visiting the grave itself cannot be established. In the 1960s, over 50,000 people a year paid to gain entrance to see the shrine of the Holy Elizabeth. All of these would have passed Hindenburg's grave: Werner Mascos of the Hessian league of journalists to Bauer, 6 April 1966, *StM*, NLBauer, no. 728.

41. See Agency Press, 'Tausende pilgern zu Hindenburgs Grab', 4 April 1966, *StM*, NLBauer, no. 727.

42. Such services were held e.g. in August 1954 and 1959 to mark the twentieth and twenty-fifth anniversary of Hindenburg's death and also in 1962, when a veterans' organization laid a wreath in the Imperial colours—thereby defying church policy, see *StM*, NLBauer, no. 725.

43. Moeller, *War Stories*, 3.

44. Ibid.

45. M. Lüders, *Der Soldat und das Reich: Paul von Hindenburg: Generalfeldmarschall und Reichspräsident* (Freising, 1961), 252.

46. See e.g. the report on the commemoration of Tannenberg's fiftieth anniversary in 1964, *Oberhessische Presse*, 31 August 1964, copy in *StM*, NLBauer, no. 727. A similar service had been held in 1951, see *StM*, NLBauer, no. 725; also the critical account of these celebrations in the *Geschichtswerkstatt Marburg's* open letter to all visitors and members of the parish of the Elizabeth Church of 1 Sept. 1985, ibid., no. 810.

47. See, for instance, the article by Hindenburg's grandson Hubertus published by the *Landsmannschaft Ostpreußen*: 'Weimars letzter Präsident', *Preußische Allgemeine Zeitung*, 31 July 2004.

48. Bauer's remarks cited in Agency Press, 'Tausende pilgern zu Hindenburgs Grab'; also W. Lasek, '"Revisionistische" Autoren und ihre Publikationen', in B. Bailer-Galanda, W. Benz, and W. Neugebauer (eds.), *Die Auschwitzleugner: Geschichtslüge und Historische Wahrheit* (Berlin, 1996), 320–80, particularly 360–1.

49. G. Jasper, *Der Schutz der Republik: Studien zur staatlichen Sicherung der Demokratie in der Weimarer Republik 1922–1930* (Tübingen, 1963).

50. Krüger-Bulcke, 'Hohenzollern-Hindenburg Zwischenfall'; and the account by Geschichtswerkstatt Marburg, *StM*, NLBauer, no. 810.

51. Protestant Lutheran Congregation of Marburg to the editorial office of the *Oberhessische Presse*, 1 September 1951, *StM*, NLBauer, no. 810; also ibid., no. 725; further Krüger-Bulcke, 'Hohenzollern-Hindenburg Zwischenfall', 349.

52. H.-A. Jacobsen, 'Wehrmacht und Bundeswehr—Anmerkungen zu einem umstrittenen Thema soldatischer Traditionspflege', in R.-D. Müller and H.-E. Volkmann (eds.), *Die Wehrmacht: Mythos und Realität* (Munich, 1999), 1184–91, here: 1187.

53. *NYT*, 1 December 1957, 269.

54. 'Hindenburg hat wenig Freunde', *SZ*, no. 38, 16 February 1999.

55. c.f. Moeller, *War Stories*, 19.

56. D. Niemetz, *Das feldgraue Erbe: Die Wehrmachteinflüsse im Militär der SBZ/DDR* (Berlin, 2006).

57. J. Danyel, 'Die Erinnerung an die Wehrmacht in beiden deutschen Staaten: Vergangenheitspolitik und Gedenkrituale', in Müller and Volkmann, *Wehrmacht*, 1139–49, here: 1144–5; J. Danyel, 'Die Vergangenheitspolitik in der SBZ-DDR 1945–1989', in W. Borodziej and K. Ziemer (eds.), *Deutschpolnische Beziehungen: 1939–1945–1949* (Osnabrück, 2000), 265–96, here: 274.

58. M. Sabrow, 'Kampfplatz Weimar: DDR-Geschichtsschreibung im Konflikt von Erfahrung, Politik und Wissenschaft', Winkler, *Weimar im Widerstreit*, 163–84, here: 176.

59. Ibid., 166.

60. c.f. The law on the democratization of schools in Saxony, 22 May 1946, cited in Kleßman, *Doppelte Staatsgründung*, 392–3, also 525; generally: N. M. Naimark, *The Russians in Germany: A History of the Soviet Zone of Occupation 1945–1949* (Cambridge, MA, 1995).

61. Danyel, 'Vergangenheitspolitik', 279; A. Dorpalen, *German History in Marxist Perspective: The East German Approach* (London, 1985); M. Sabrow (ed.), *Geschichte als Herrschaftsdiskurs: Der Umgang mit der Vergangenheit in der DDR* (Cologne, Weimar, and Vienna, 2000).

62. Ruge, *Hindenburg*.

63. Ibid., 25.

64. Ibid., 23.

65. Ibid., 513. In spite of its polemical overtones, Ruge's account is based on extensive original research. When one cuts through the obligatory Marxist-Leninist jargon, it is extremely useful.

66. B. Brecht, *The Resistable Rise of Arturo Ui* (New York, 1972).

67. J. Danyel, 'Die geteilte Vergangenheit. Gesellschaftliche Ausgangslagen und politische Dispositionen für den Umgang mit Nationalsozialismus und Widerstand in beiden deutschen Staaten nach 1949', in J. Kocka (ed.), *Historische DDR-Forschung: Aufsätze und Studien* (Berlin, 1993), 129−48, especially: 134 and 140.

68. I. Mittenzwei, *Friedrich der II. von Preußen: Eine Biographie* (Berlin, 1980); E. Engelberg, *Bismarck: Urpreuße und Reichsgründer* (Berlin, 1985); Gerwarth, *Bismarck Myth*, 168; further T. C. W. Blanning, 'The Death and Transfiguration of Prussia', *The Historical Journal*, 29 (1986), 433−59, particularly 445.

69. An article by Klaus Drobisch of 1967 exemplified the tendency to suggest links between the role of the 'financial oligarchy' in the Weimar Republic, the Nazi state and the FRG, see his 'Hindenburg-, Hitler-, Adenauerspende', *ZfG*, (1967), 447−58.

70. On street signs as media of collective memory: J. Sänger, *Heldenkult und Heimatliebe: Straßen- und Ehrennamen im offiziellen Gedächtnis der DDR* (Berlin, 2006), 42−4.

71. In 2000, the square was given its current name, Platz des 18. März, commemorating both the revolution of 1848 and the first free elections in the GDR in 1990, S. Lais and H.-J. Mende (eds.), *Lexikon Berliner Straßennamen* (Berlin, 2004), 199; on its name-change in 1934: *Berliner Illustrierte Nachtausgabe*, no. 182, 7 August 1934.

72. Sänger, *Heldenkult,* 75−6.

73. M. Azaryahu, 'Street Names and Political Identity: The Case of East Berlin', *JCH*, vol. 21 (1986), 581−604, here 587.

74. Sänger, *Heldenkult*, 76.

75. Individual street names are listed in Deutsche Post AG (ed.), *Die Postleitzahlen* (Bonn, 2005); see also R. Euler, 'Ist Hindenburg noch eine Straße wert?', *FAZ*, no. 34, 25 August 2002.

76. Ibid.; 'Umstrittener Hindenburg', *FAZ*, no. 75, 1 April 2005, 58; 'Dem "Militaristen" Hindenburg eine geklebt', *TAZ* (Hamburg edition), 27 July 1988, 18.

77. See e.g. the debate in Marburg's Chamber of Deputies in 1983, *StM*, no. 127, tape recording; further N. Haase and C. Hühne: 'Höchste Auszeichnung', *TAZ*, 21 April 1989, 11.

78. The debate raged between January and March 2003. Heinrich August Winkler even gave an expert evaluation of Hindenburg at a hearing of the Chamber of Deputies' cultural committee: J. Bisky, 'Helden wie ihr: Hindenburg und Bersarin: Die neue Berliner Geschichtspolitik', *SZ*, no. 37, 14 February

2003, 13; 22; P. Bahners, 'Paul von Hindenburg: Ehrenmann', *FAZ*, no. 26, 31 January 2003, 44.

79. Cited in 'Hindenburg gar nicht honorig', *TAZ* (Berlin edn.), 22 January 2003, 22.

80. *FAZ*, no. 28, 3 February 2003, 39, c.f. Introduction, 2.

81. The Berlin Chamber of Deputies decided on 10 March 2003 that Hindenburg's honorary citizenship would not be revoked. The same decision had been made in Potsdam the previous January: 'Berliner Liste. Hindenburg bleibt Ehrenbürger', *FAZ*, no. 59, 11 March 2003, 39.

82. See e.g. Winkler, *Weimar*; Mommsen, *Weimar Democracy*, who both have relatively little to say about Hindenburg's political role and his personality. Traces of an older interpretative framework remain in Schulze's account. He portrays Hindenburg as an entirely constitutional President with the 'best of intentions', who became a victim of circumstance and his 'out of control' and 'irresponsible' advisers: Schulze, *Weimar*, 100 and 298−300.

83. 'Der heroische Schein', *FAZ*, no. 200, 28 August 2004.

84. T. Gerlach, 'Hindenburg, die Kyffhäuser-Mumie', *FAS*, no. 8, 27 February 2005, 8; 'Statuenfund', *Sächsische Zeitung*, 9 June 2004.

85. 'Hindenburg bleibt', *FAZ*, no. 6, 8 January 2005, 33.

# Bibliography

ARCHIVAL SOURCES

**Bundesarchiv Berlin**
R 32 Reichskunstwart
R 43 Alte Reichskanzlei
R 45 II Deutsche Volkspartei
R 72 Stahlhelm—Bund der Frontsoldaten
R 601 Büro des Reichspräsidenten
R 703 Stellvertreter des Reichskanzlers, Friedrich von Payer
R 1501 Reichsministerium des Innern
R 1507 Reichskommissar für Überwachung der öffentlichen Ordnung
R 2501 Reichsbank
R 8005 Deutschnationale Volkspartei
R 8034 I-III Reichslandbund
N 2329 Count Kuno von Westarp Papers

**Bundesarchiv Koblenz**
NL Max Bauer
KLE 331 Friedrich von Berg Papers
KLE 499F Heinrich Claß Papers
NL Eduard Dingeldey
N 1377 Theodor Duesterberg Papers
N 1097 Matthias Erzberger Papers
N 1114 Ferdinand Friedensburg Papers
NL 31 Wilhelm Freiherr von Gayl Papers
NL 1032 Otto Gessler Papers
KLE 653 Count Rüdiger von der Goltz Papers
NL Georg Gothein
N 1123 Karl Helfferich Papers
KLE 332 Paul von Hindenburg Papers
N 1231 Alfred Hugenberg Papers
NL Karl Jarres
N 1243 Walter von Keudell Papers
NL 45 Friedrich Wilhelm Freiherr von Loebell Papers
N 1009 Hans Luther Papers
N 1046 Gustav Noske Papers

NL 5 Hermann Pünder Papers
KLE 608 Gerhard Schultze-Pfaelzer Papers
NL 15 Bernhard Schwertfeger
N 1324 Martin Spahn Papers
ZSG 2/208 Flugschriftensammlung zur Reichspräsidentenwahl 1932
ZSG 2 Kriegsflugblattsammlung
ZSG 117 Presseausschnittssammlung NSDAP
Picture collection
Poster collection

### Bundesarchiv-Militärarchiv Freiburg
N 386 Erich Freiherr von dem Bussche-Ippenburg Papers
N 266 August von Cramon Papers
N 46 Wilhelm Groener Papers
N 714 Count Rüdiger von der Goltz Papers
N 429 Paul von Hindenburg Papers
N 78 Helmuth von Moltke Papers
N 101 Adalbert Scholtz v. Krechowce Papers
N 253 Alfred Tirpitz Papers

### Bundesarchiv-Filmarchiv Berlin
Deulig-Tonwoche no. 57/1933; no. 63/1933; no. 69/1933; no. 87/1933
File 16691 Tannenbergfilm
*Der Eiserne Hindenburg in Krieg und Frieden* (1929)
*Dr. Frick* (Sonderfilm, 1931/38)
*Einer für Alle!* (1932)
*Hindenburg* (1936)
*Hindenburg und Hitler sprechen am Tag von Potsdam* (1933)
*Unser Führer* (1934)
Ufa-Tonwoche no. 428/1938

### Geheimes Staatsarchiv Preußischer Kulturbesitz, Berlin Dahlem
1. HA, Rep. 77 Preußisches Ministerium des Innern
1. HA, Rep. 89 Geheimes Zivilkabinett—Jüngere Periode

### Landesarchiv Berlin
Magistrat der Stadt Berlin, Generalbüro, A Rep. 001-02
Polizeipräsidium Berlin, A Pr. Br. Rep. 030
Preußische Bau- und Finanzdirektion, A Pr. Br. Rep. 042

### Deutsches Historisches Museum Berlin
Picture collection: file 'Hindenburg'

### Archiv der sozialen Demokratie der Friedrich-Ebert-Stiftung, Bonn
NL Adolph Köster (1/AKAF0000)
NL Paul Levi (1/PLAA000)

NL Otto Meissner (Not catalogued)
NL Hermann Müller
NL Heinrich Ritzel (1/HRAB000)
NL Carl Severing (1/CSAB000)

**Stadtarchiv Marburg**
NL Hermann Bauer
D1118

**St Antony's College, Oxford**
NSDAP Hauptarchiv

## Newspapers and periodicals

*Der Angriff, Aus dem Ostlande, Berliner Tageblatt, Berliner Börsen-Courier, Berliner Börsen-Zeitung, Berliner Illustrirte Zeitung, Berliner Lokalanzeiger, Deutsche Allgemeine Zeitung, Deutsche Tageszeitung, Deutschen-Spiegel, Deutsche Zeitung, Düsseldorfer Nachrichten, Frankfurter Allgemeine Zeitung, Frankfurter Allgemeine Sonntagszeitung, Frankfurter Zeitung, Hackebeils Illustrierte, Gelbe Hefte, Germania, Hannoverscher Anzeiger, Kölnische Volkszeitung, Königsberger Allgemeine Zeitung, Königsberger Volkszeitung, Korrespondenz der Deutschnationalen Volkspartei, Liller Kriegszeitung, Münchener Neueste Nachrichten, Neue Preussische Kreuz-Zeitung, The New York Times, Ostpreussische Zeitung, Das Plakat, Preussische Jahrbücher, Rote Fahne, Die Schaubühne, Sozialistische Monatshefte, Süddeutsche Zeitung, Taz, The Times, Tremonia, Völkischer Beobachter, Vossische Zeitung, Welt am Montag, Die Weltbühne, Die Woche, Die Zeit*

## PRINTED PRIMARY SOURCES

### The Files of the Federal Chancellory

*Akten der Reichskanzlei: Weimarer Republik: Das Kabinett Scheidemann*, ed. Hagen Schulze (Boppard am Rhein, 1971)

*Akten der Reichskanzlei: Weimarer Republik: Das Kabinett Bauer*, ed. Anton Golecki (Boppard am Rhein, 1980)

*Akten der Reichskanzlei: Weimarer Republik: Das Kabinett Müller I*, ed. Martin Vogt (Boppard am Rhein, 1971)

*Akten der Reichskanzlei: Weimarer Republik: Das Kabinett Fehrenbach*, ed. Peter Wulf (Boppard am Rhein, 1972)

*Akten der Reichskanzlei: Weimarer Republik: Die Kabinette Wirth I und II*, 2 vols., ed. Ingrid Schulze-Bidlingmaier (Boppard am Rhein, 1973)

*Akten der Reichskanzlei: Weimarer Republik: Das Kabinett Cuno*, ed. Karl-Heinz Harbeck (Boppard am Rhein, 1968)

*Akten der Reichskanzlei: Weimarer Republik: Die Kabinette Stresemann I und II*, 2 vols., ed. Karl-Dietrich Erdmann and Martin Vogt (Boppard am Rhein, 1978)

*Akten der Reichskanzlei: Weimarer Republik: Die Kabinett Marx I und II*, 2 vols., ed. Günther Abramowski (Boppard am Rhein, 1973)

*Akten der Reichskanzlei: Weimarer Republik: Die Kabinette Luther I und II*, 2 vols., ed. Karl-Heinz Minuth (Boppard am Rhein, 1977)

*Akten der Reichskanzlei: Weimarer Republik: Die Kabinette Marx III und IV*, 2 vols., ed. Günter Abramowski (Boppard am Rhein, 1988)

*Akten der Reichskanzlei: Weimarer Republik: Das Kabinett Müller II*, 2 vols., ed. Martin Vogt (Boppard am Rhein, 1970)

*Akten der Reichskanzlei: Weimarer Republik: Die Kabinette Brüning I und II*, 3 vols., ed. Tilman Koops (Boppard am Rhein, 1982)

*Akten der Reichskanzlei: Weimarer Republik: Das Kabinett von Papen*, 2 vols., ed. Karl-Heinz Minuth (Boppard am Rhein, 1989)

*Akten der Reichskanzlei: Weimarer Republik: Das Kabinett von Schleicher*, ed. Anton Golecki (Boppard am Rhein, 1986)

*Akten der Reichskanzlei: Die Regierung Hitler 1933–1938*, 2 vols., ed. Karl-Heinz Minuth (Boppard am Rhein, 1983)

## Other printed collections of primary documents

Afflerbach, Holger (ed.), *Kaiser Wilhelm II. als Oberster Kriegsherr im Ersten Weltkrieg: Quellen aus der militärischen Umgebung des Kaisers 1914–1918* (Munich, 2005)

Behnken, Klaus (ed.), *Deutschland-Berichte der Sozialdemokratischen Partei Deutschlands (Sopade) 1934–1940*, 4th edn (Munich, 1980)

Conze, Werner (ed.), *Kuno Graf Westarp: Das Ende der Monarchie am 9. November 1918* (Berlin, 1952)

Deist, Wilhelm (ed.), *Militär und Innenpolitik im Weltkrieg 1914–1918*, 2 vols. (Düsseldorf, 1970)

Domarus, Max (ed.), *Hitler: Reden und Proklamationen 1932–45*, 4 vols. (Wiesbaden, 1973)

Eckhardt, Albrecht and Hoffmann, Katharina (eds.), *Gestapo Oldenburg meldet... Berichte der Geheimen Staatspolizei und des Innenministers aus dem Freistaat und Land Oldenburg 1933–1936* (Hanover, 2002)

Evans, Richard J. (ed.), *Kneipengespräche im Kaiserreich: Stimmungsberichte der Hamburger Politischen Polizei, 1892–1914* (Reinbek, 1989)

Hohlfeld, Johannes, *Deutsche Reichsgeschichte in Dokumenten 1849–1934*, vol. 2 (Berlin, 1934)

Holl, Karl and Wild, Adolf (eds.), *Ein Demokrat kommentiert Weimar: Die Berichte Hellmut von Gerlachs an die Carnegie-Friedensstiftung in New York 1922–1930* (Bremen, 1973)

Hürter, Johannes (ed.), *Paul von Hintze, Marineoffizier, Diplomat, Staatssekretär: Dokumente einer Karriere zwischen Militär und Politik, 1903–1918* (Munich, 1998)

Kaes, Anton, Martin, Jay and Dimendberg, Edward (eds.), *The Weimar Republic Sourcebook* (Berkeley, Los Angeles and London, 1994)

Klein, Thomas (ed.), *Die Lageberichte der Geheimen Staatspolizei über die Provinz Hessen Nassau 1933–1936*, 2 vols. (Cologne and Vienna, 1986)

Kolb, Eberhard (ed.), *Nationalliberalismus in der Weimarer Republik: Die Führungsgremien der Deutschen Volkspartei 1918–1933*, 2 vols. (Düsseldorf, 1999)

Materna, Ingo and Schreckenbach, Hans-Joachim (eds.), *Berichte des Berliner Polizeipräsidenten zur Stimmung und Lage der Bevölkerung in Berlin 1914–1918* (Weimar, 1987)

Matthias, Erich and Morsey, Rudolf (eds.), *Die Regierung des Prinzen Max von Baden* (Düsseldorf, 1962)

Matthias, Erich and Pikart, Eberhard (eds.), *Die Reichstagsfraktion der deutschen Sozialdemokratie 1914 bis 1918* (Düsseldorf, 1966)

Maurer, Ilse and Wengst, Udo (eds.), *Politik und Wirtschaft in der Krise 1930–1932: Quellen zur Ära Brüning* (Düsseldorf, 1980)

Michaelis, Herbert and Schraepler, Ernst (eds.), *Ursachen und Folgen, vol. 10: Das Dritte Reich: Die Errichtung des Führerstaates: Abwendung von dem System der kollektiven Sicherheit* (Berlin, 1966)

Miller, Susanne and Potthoff, Heinrich (eds.), *Die Regierung der Volksbeauftragten 1918/19*, 2 vols. (Düsseldorf, 1969)

Morsey, Rudolf (ed.), *Das 'Ermächtigungsgesetz' vom 24. März 1933: Quellen zur Geschichte und Interpretation des 'Gesetzes zur Behebung der Not von Volk und Reich'* (Düsseldorf, 1992)

Noelle, Elisabeth and Neumann, Erich Peter (eds.), *Jahrbuch der öffentlichen Meinung 1947–1955* (Allensbach, 1956)

Rupieper, Hermann-J. and Sperk, Alexander (eds.), *Die Lageberichte der Geheimen Staatspolizei zur Provinz Sachsen 1933–1936*, 3 vols. (Halle, 2003)

Schiffers, Reinhard and Koch, Manfred (eds.), *Der Hauptausschuss des Deutschen Reichstages 1915–1918*, 4 vols. (Düsseldorf, 1983)

Schücking, Walther and Fischer, Eugen (eds.), *Das Werk des Untersuchungsausschusses der Verfassungsgebenden Deutschen Nationalversammlung und des Deutschen Reichstages 1919–1928, vol. 7: Die Ursachen des Deutschen Zusammenbruches im Jahre 1918* (Berlin, 1928)

Statistisches Bundesamt Wiesbaden (ed.), *Bevölkerung und Wirtschaft 1872–1972* (Stuttgart, 1972)

Steinwascher, Gerd (ed.), *Gestapo Osnabrück meldet . . . Polizei- und Regierungsberichte aus dem Regierunsbezirk Osnabrück aus den Jahren 1933–1936* (Osnabrück, 1995)

Toepser-Ziegert, Gabriele (ed.), *NS-Presseanweisungen der Vorkriegszeit*, 7 vols. (Munich, New York, London, Paris, 1984–2001)

Ziemann, Benjamin and Ulrich, Bernd (eds.), *Krieg im Frieden: Die umkämpfte Erinnerung an den Ersten Weltkrieg: Quellen und Dokumente* (Frankfurt/M., 1997)

### Printed diaries, notes, memoirs, and contemporary texts

Arras, Paul (ed.), *Hindenburg-Gedichte* (Bautzen, 1915)

Bernhard, Henry (ed.), *Gustav Stresemann: Vermächtnis: Der Nachlass in drei Bänden*, 3 vols. (Berlin, 1932)

Bloch, Eduard (ed.) *Hindenburgs 70. Geburtstag* (Berlin, 1917)

Bismarck, Otto von, *Gedanken und Erinnerungen*, 2 vols. (Stuttgart, 1898 and 1919)

Braun, Otto, *Von Weimar zu Hitler* (New York, 1940)

Brecht, Bertolt, *The Resistable Rise of Arturo Ui* (New York, 1972)

Brüning, Heinrich, *Memoiren 1918–1934* (Stuttgart, 1970)

Carlyle, Thomas, *On Heroes, Hero-Worship, and the Heroic in History* (London, 1841)

Deutsche Bücherei (ed.), *Hindenburg-Bibliographie: Verzeichnis der Bücher und Zeitschriftenaufsätze von und über den Reichspräsidenten Generalfeldmarschall von Hindenburg* (Leipzig, 1938)

Dreßler, Max, *Auf Arminius-Siegfrieds Spuren: Ein Buch vom ersten Befreier Deutschlands* (Leipzig, 1921)

*Erinnerungsblätter deutscher Regimenter*, 372 vols. (Oldenburg, 1920–1942)

Friedensburg, Ferdinand, *Die Weimarer Republik* (Berlin, 1946)

Friedrich, Ernst, *Krieg dem Kriege* (Berlin, 1924)

Gaertringen, Friedrich Freiherr Hiller von (ed.), *Wilhelm Groener: Lebenserinnerungen—Jugend, Generalstab, Weltkrieg* (Göttingen, 1957)

—— (ed.), *Kuno Graf von Westarp: Konservative Politik im Übergang vom Kaiserreich zur Weimarer Republik* (Düsseldorf, 2001)

Gereke, Günther, *Ich war königlich-preußischer Landrat* (Berlin, 1970)

Görlitz, Walter (ed.), *Regierte der Kaiser? Kriegstagebücher, Aufzeichnungen und Briefe des Chefs des Marine-Kabinetts Admiral Georg Alexander von Müller 1914–1918* (Göttingen, Berlin, Frankfurt a. M., 1959)

Grimm, Hans, *Volk ohne Raum*, 2 vols. (Munich, 1926)

Henche, Albert (ed.), *Geschichtliches Unterrichtswerk: Ein Arbeits- und Tatsachenbuch für höhere Lehranstalten*, vol. 2 (Breslau, 1926)

Hindenburg, Bernhard von, *Paul von Hindenburg: Ein Lebensbild* (Berlin, 1915)

Hindenburg, Paul von, *Aus meinem Leben, Illustrierte Volksausgabe* (Leipzig, 1934)

*Hindenburg der Retter der Ostmarken—sein Leben und Wirken*, ed. Anonymous (Leipzig, 1915)

Hindenburgspende (ed.), *Reichspräsident Hindenburg* (Berlin, 1927)

Hoecker, Paul Oskar and Ompteda, Rittmeister Freiherr von (eds.), *Liller Kriegszeitung: Eine Auslese aus Nummer 1–40* (Berlin, Leipzig, Vienna, 1915)

Hoecker, Paul Oskar (ed.), *Liller Kriegszeitung: Vom Pfingsfest zur Weihnacht: Der Auslese erste Folge* (Lille, 1916)

—— *Drei Jahre Liller Kriegszeitung: Eine Denkschrift zum 2. Dezember 1917* (Lille, 1917)

Hoffmann, Max, *Tannenberg wie es wirklich war* (Berlin, 1926)

Hubatsch, Walther, *Hindenburg und der Staat: Aus den Papieren des Generalfeldmarschalls und Reichspräsidenten von 1878 bis 1934* (Göttingen, Berlin, Frankfurt/M. and Zurich, 1966)

Jünger, Ernst, *In Stahlgewittern* (Berlin, 1920)

Kessler, Charles (ed.), *Diaries of a Cosmopolitan: Count Harry Kessler 1918–1937* (London, 1971)

Kiesewetter, B., 'Plakate und Drucksachen zur 7. Kriegsanleihe', *Das Plakat*, 9 (1918), 33–5

Klemperer, Victor, *I Shall Bear Witness: The Diaries of Victor Klemperer 1933–1941* (London, 1999)

Klepper, Jochen, *Unter dem Schatten Deiner Flügel: Aus den Tagebüchern der Jahre 1932 bis 1942* (Berlin, 1967)

König, Theodor, *Die Psychologie der Reklame* (Würzburg, 1922)

Koschate, Paul, *Hindenburg, hurra! Schul- und Volksfeier zum 70. Geburtstage unseres Feldmarschalls am 2. Oktober 1917* (Breslau, 1917)

Kronthal, Arthur, 'Das Hindenburgmuseum in Posen', *Museumskunde: Zeitschrift für Verwaltung und Technik öffentlicher und privater Sammlungen*, 15 (1920), 152–8

Lindenberg, Paul, *Generalfeldmarschall von Hindenburg* (Stuttgart, 1917)

—— *Das Buch vom Feldmarschall Hindenburg* (Oldenburg, 1920)

—— (ed.), *Hindenburg-Denkmal für das deutsche Volk* (Berlin, 1922–1935)

Loebell, Friedrich Wilhelm von (ed.), *Hindenburg: Was er uns Deutschen ist* (Berlin, 1927)

Lowenthal-Hensel, Cécile and Paucker, Arnold (eds.), *Ernst Feder: Heute sprach ich mit . . . Tagebücher eines Berliner Publizisten 1926–1932* (Stuttgart, 1971)

Ludendorff, Erich, *Meine Kriegserinnerungen 1914–1918* (Berlin, 1919)

Ludwig, Emil, *Hindenburg* (Chicago, Philadelphia and Toronto, 1935)

Mahraun, Artur, *Die neue Front: Hindenburgs Sendung* (Berlin, 1928)

Mannes, Wilhelm, *Hindenburg-Lieder: Den Heldensöhnen Deutschlands gewidmet* (Berlin, 1915)

Matthias, Erich and Miller, Susanne (eds.), *Das Kriegstagebuch des Reichstagsabgeordneten Eduard David 1914 bis 1918* (Düsseldorf, 1966)

Meissner, Otto, *Staatssekretär unter Ebert-Hindenburg-Hitler: Der Schicksalsweg des deutschen Volkes von 1918–1945, wie ich ihn erlebte* (Hamburg, 1950)

Mendelssohn, Peter de (ed.), *Thomas Mann: Tagebücher 1933–1934* (Frankfurt/M., 1977)

Mühsam, Kurt, *Wie wir belogen wurden: Die amtliche Irreführung des deutschen Volkes* (Munich, 1918)

Nicolai, Walter, *Nachrichtendienst, Presse und Volksstimmung im Weltkrieg* (Berlin, 1920)

Niemann, Alfred, *Hindenburgs Siege bei Tannenberg und Angerburg August-September 1914: Das Cannae und Leuthen der Gegenwart* (Berlin, 1915)

Noske, Gustav, *Erlebtes aus Aufstieg und Niedergang einer Demokratie* (Offenbach/M., 1947)

Papen, Franz von, *Der Wahrheit eine Gasse* (Munich, 1952)

Pünder, Heinrich, *Politik in der Reichskanzlei* (Stuttgart, 1961)

Reichert, Folker and Wolgast, Eike (eds.), *Karl Hampe: Kriegstagebuch 1914–1918* (Munich, 2004)

Reichold, Helmut and Granier, Gerhard (eds.), *Adolf Wild von Hohenborn: Briefe und Tagebuchaufzeichnungen des preußischen Generals als Kriegsminister und Truppenführer im Ersten Weltkrieg* (Boppard am Rhein, 1986)

Reimann, Arnold (ed.), *Geschichtswerk für höhere Schulen, vol. 1: Das Heldenbuch* (Munich and Berlin, 1926)

Remarque, Erich Maria, *Im Westen nichts Neues* (Berlin, 1929)

Renn, Ludwig, *Krieg* (Frankfurt/M., 1928)

Reuth, Ralf Georg (ed.), *Joseph Goebbels Tagebücher 1924–1945*, 5 vols. (Munich, 1992)

Sachs, Hans, 'Vom Hurrakitsch, von Nagelungsstandbildern, Nagelungsplakaten und andren Schönheiten', *Das Plakat,* 8, vol. 1 (January 1917), 3—21

Sauerbruch, Ferdinand, *A Surgeon's Life* (London, 1957)

*Schlachten des Weltkrieges,* 40 vols. (Oldenburg, 1922—1930)

Schnabel, Franz (ed.), *Grundriß der Geschichte für die Oberstufe höherer Lehranstalten, vol. 4: Neueste Zeit* (Leipzig, Berlin, 1924)

Schulenburg, Dieter von der, *Welt um Hindenburg: 100 Gespräche mit Berufenen* (Berlin, 1935)

Schultze-Pfaelzer, Gerhard, *Wie Hindenburg Reichspräsident wurde: Persönliche Eindrücke aus seiner Umgebung vor und nach der Wahl* (Berlin, 1925)

—— *Hindenburg* (Leipzig und Zurich, 1930)

—— *Hindenburg: Peace, War, Aftermath* (Glasgow, 1931)

Soldenhoff, Richard von (ed.), *Briefe an Kurt Tucholsky 1915—1926: 'Der beste Brotherr dem schlechtesten Mitarbeiter'* (Munich, 1989)

Solzhenitsyn, Alexander, *August 1914* (London, 1974)

Sösemann, Bernd (ed.) *Theodor Wolff, Tagebücher 1914—1919: Der Erste Weltkrieg und die Enstehung der Weimarer Republik in Tagebüchern, Leitartikeln und Briefen des Chefredakteurs am 'Berliner Tageblatt' und Mitbegründers der 'DDP',* 2 vols., (Boppard am Rhein, 1984)

Stehkämper, Hugo (ed.), *Der Nachlaß des Reichskanzlers Wilhelm Marx,* 5 vols. (Cologne, 1968 and 1997)

Tschirschky, Fritz Günther von, *Erinnerungen eines Hochverräters* (Stuttgart, 1972)

Vogel, Hugo, *Als ich Hindenburg malte* (Berlin, 1927)

—— *Erlebnisse und Gespräche mit Hindenburg* (Berlin, 1935)

Vogelsang, Thilo (ed.), *Hermann Pünder: Politik in der Reichskanzlei: Aufzeichnungen aus den Jahren 1929—1932* (Stuttgart, 1961)

Warncke, Paul, Brandt, Gustav and Hoffmann, Wolfgang (eds.), *Hindenburg-Album des Kladderadatsch* (Berlin, 1927)

Wehner, Joseph Magnus, *Sieben vor Verdun* (Munich, 1930)

—— *Hindenburg* (Leipzig, 1935)

Zöberlein, Hans, *Der Glaube an Deutschland* (Munich, 1931)

## PRINTED SECONDARY WORKS

Abel, Karl-Friedrich, *Presselenkung im NS-Staat* (Berlin, 1968)

Abrams, Lynn, 'From Control to Commercialization: The Triumph of Mass Entertainment in Germany 1900—1925?', *German History,* 8 (1990), 278—93

Ackermann, Volker, *Nationale Totenfeiern in Deutschland: Von Wilhelm I. bis Franz Josef Strauß: Eine Studie zur politischen Semiotik* (Stuttgart, 1990)

Afflerbach, Holger, *Falkenhayn: Politisches Denken und Handeln im Kaiserreich* (Munich, 1994)

—— 'Wilhelm II as Supreme Warlord in the First World War', in Mombauer, Annika and Deist, Wilhelm (eds.), *The Kaiser: New Research on Wilhelm II's Role in Imperial Germany* (Cambridge, 2003), 195—216

Ahlemann, Jutta, *Ich bleibe die große Adele: die Sandrock: Eine Biografie* (Düsseldorf, 1988)

Albrecht, Richard, 'Symbolkampf in Deutschland 1932: Sergej Tschachotin und der "Symbolkrieg" der Drei Pfeile gegen den Nationalsozialismus als Episode im Abwehrkampf der Arbeiterbewegung gegen den Faschismus in Deutschland', *IWK*, vol. 22, no. 4 (1986), 498–533

Albrecht, Willy, *Landtag und Regierung in Bayern am Vorabend der Revolution von 1918: Studien zur gesellschaftlichen und staatlichen Entwicklung Deutschlands von 1912–1918* (Berlin, 1968)

Allen, William Sheridan, *The Nazi Seizure of Power: The Experience of a Single German Town 1922–1945*, 3rd edn (London, 1989)

Apor, Balasz et al. (eds.), *The Leader Cult in Communist Dictatorships: Stalin and the Eastern Bloc* (Basingstoke, 2004)

Asmuss, Burkhard, *Republik ohne Chance? Akzeptanz und Legitimation der Weimarer Republik in der deutschen Tagespresse zwischen 1918 und 1923* (Berlin and New York, 1994)

Asprey, Robert B., *The German High Command at War: Hindenburg and Ludendorff and the First World War*, 4th edn (London, 1994)

Assmann, Aleida, *Erinnerungsräume: Formen und Wandlungen des kulturellen Gedächtnisses* (Munich, 1999)

Astore, William J. and Showalter, Dennis E., *Hindenburg: Icon of German Militarism* (Washington, DC, 2005)

Atze, Marcel, *'Unser Hitler': Der Hitler-Mythos im Spiegel der deutschsprachigen Literatur nach 1945* (Göttingen, 2003)

Ay, Karl-Ludwig, *Die Entstehung einer Revolution: Die Volksstimmung in Bayern während des Ersten Weltkrieges* (Berlin, 1968)

Azaryahu, Maoz, 'Street Names and Political Identity: The Case of East Berlin', *JCH*, vol. 21 (1986), 581–604

Bailer-Galanda, Brigitte, Benz, Wolfgang and Neugebauer, Wolfgang (eds.), *Die Auschwitzleugner: Geschichtslüge und Historische Wahrheit* (Berlin, 1996)

Baird, Jay W., 'Literarische Reaktionen auf den Ersten Weltkrieg: Josef Magnus Wehner und der Traum von einem neuen Reich', in Papenfuss, Dietrich and Schieder, Wolfgang (eds.), *Deutsche Umbrüche im 20. Jahrhundert* (Cologne and Weimar, 2000), 63–76

Balfour, Michael, *The Kaiser and his Times* (London, 1964)

Barbian, Jan-Pieter, 'Filme mit Lücken: Die Lichtspielzensur in der Weimarer Republik: von der sozialethischen Schutzmaßnahme zum politischen Instrument', in Jung, Uli (ed.), *Der deutsche Film: Aspekte seiner Geschichte von den Anfängen bis zur Gegenwart* (Trier, 1993), 51–78

——— *Literaturpolitik im 'Dritten Reich': Institutionen, Kompetenzen, Betätigungsfelder* (Munich, 1995)

——— 'Politik und Film in der Weimarer Republik: Ein Beitrag zur Kulturpolitik der Jahre 1918–1933', *Archiv für Kulturgeschichte*, vol. 80, no. 1 (1998), 213–45

Barkhausen, Hans, *Filmpropaganda für Deutschland im Ersten und Zweiten Weltkrieg* (Hildesheim, 1982)

Barth, Boris, *Dolchstoßlegenden und politische Desintegration: Das Trauma der deutschen Niederlage im Ersten Weltkrieg 1914–1933* (Düsseldorf, 2003)

Bausch, Ulrich M., *Die Kulturpolitik der US-amerikanischen Information Control Division in Württemberg-Baden von 1945 bis 1949: Zwischen militärischem Funktionalismus und schwäbischem Obrigkeitsdenken* (Stuttgart, 1992)

Bavaj, Riccardo and Fritzen, Florentine (eds.), *Deutschland—ein Land ohne revolutionäre Traditionen? Revolutionen im Deutschland des 19. und 20. Jahrhunderts im Lichte neuerer geistes- und kulturwissenschaftlicher Erkenntnisse* (Frankfurt/M., 2005)

Bechstein, Gabriele, *Automobilwerbung von 1890 bis 1935: Versuch einer semiotischen Analyse früher Automobilannoncen* (Bochum, 1987)

Behrenbeck, Sabine, '"Der Führer": Die Einführung eines politischen Markenartikels', in Diesener, Gerald and Gries, Rainer (eds.), *Zur politischen Massenbeeinflussung im 20. Jahrhundert* (Darmstadt, 1996), 51–78

—— *Der Kult um die toten Helden: Nationalsozialistische Mythen, Riten und Symbole* (Vierow near Greifswald, 1996)

—— 'Durch Opfer zur Erlösung: Feierpraxis im nationalsozialistischen Deutschland', in Behrenbeck, Sabine and Nützenadel, Alexander (eds.), *Inszenierung des Nationalstaats: Politische Feiern in Italien und Deutschland seit 1860/71* (Cologne, 2000), 149–70

—— and Nützenadel, Alexander (eds.), *Inszenierung des Nationalstaats: Politische Feiern in Italien und Deutschland seit 1860/71* (Cologne, 2000)

Benz, Wolfgang, 'Konsolidierung und Konsens 1934–1939', in Broszat, Martin and Frei, Norbert (eds.), *Ploetz: Das Dritte Reich: Ursprünge, Ereignisse, Wirkungen* (Freiburg and Würzburg, 1983), 45–62

Berding, Helmut, Heller, Klaus and Speitkamp, Winfried (eds.), *Krieg und Erinnerung* (Göttingen, 2000)

Berghahn, Volker R., *Der Stahlhelm: Bund der Frontsoldaten 1918–1935* (Düsseldorf, 1966)

—— 'Die Harzburger Front und die Kandidatur Hindenburgs für die Präsidentschaftswahlen 1932', *VfZ*, 13, no. 1 (1965), 64–82

—— 'Das Volksbegehren gegen den Young-Plan und die Ursprünge des Präsidialregimes 1928–1930', in Stegmann, Dirk (ed.), *Industrielle Gesellschaft und politisches System: Beiträge zur politischen Sozialgeschichte* (Bonn, 1978), 431–48

Berghoff, Hartmut, 'Patriotismus und Geschäftssinn im Krieg: Eine Fallstudie aus der Musikinstrumentenidustrie', in Hirschfeld, Gerhard, Krumeich, Gerd, Langewiesche, Dieter and Ullmann, Hans-Peter (eds.), *Kriegserfahrungen: Studien zur Sozial- und Mentalitätengeschichte des Ersten Weltkrieges* (Essen, 1997), 262–82

Berliner Geschichtswerkstatt (ed.), *August 1914: Ein Volk zieht in den Krieg* (Berlin, 1989)

Bessel, Richard, 'The Rise of the NSDAP and the Myth of Nazi Propaganda', *Wiener Library Bulletin*, no. 33 (1980), 20–9

Bessel, Richard, *Germany after the First World War* (Oxford, 1993)

—— 'Mobilization and Demobilization in Germany, 1916–1919', in Horne, John (ed.), *State, Society and Mobilization in Europe during the First World War* (Cambridge, 1997), 212–22

—— '1918–1919 in der deutschen Geschichte', in Papenfuss, Dietrich and Schieder, Wolfgang (eds.), *Deutsche Umbrüche im 20. Jahrhundert* (Cologne and Weimar, 2000), 173–82

Bialas, Wolfgang and Stenzel, Burkhard (eds.), *Die Weimarer Republik zwischen Metropole und Provinz* (Weimar, Cologne and Vienna, 1996)

Biefang, Andreas, Epkenhans, Hans, and Tenfelde, Klaus (eds.), *Das politische Zeremoniell im deutschen Kaiserreich* (Düsseldorf, 2008)

Blackbourn, David and Eley, Geoff, *The Peculiarities of German History* (Oxford, 1984)

Blanning, Timothy C. W., 'The Death and Transfiguration of Prussia', *The Historical Journal, 29* (1986), 433–59

Blasius, Dirk, *Bürgerkrieg und Politik 1930–1933* (Göttingen, 2005)

Blauert, Elke (ed.), *Walter Krüger, Johannes Krüger: Architekten* (Berlin, 2004)

Blumenberg, Hans, *Arbeit am Mythos* (Frankfurt/M., 1996)

Bock, Hans-Michael, 'Ernst Seeger-Jurist, Zensor', CineGraph: lexikon zum deutschsprachigen Film, 20th edn (Hamburg, 1992), 465–9

Boldt, Hans, 'Article 48 of the Weimar Constitution: Its Historical and Political Implications', in Anthony J. Nicholls and Erich Matthias (eds.), *German Democracy and the Triumph of Hitler: Essays in Recent German History* (London, 1971), 79–98

—— 'Die Weimarer Reichsverfassung', in Bracher, Karl Dietrich, Funke, Manfred, and Jacobsen, Hans-Adolf (eds.), *Die Weimarer Republik 1918–1933: Politik, Wirtschaft, Gesellschaft* (Bonn, 1987), 44–62

Bollenbeck, Georg, *Tradition, Avantgarde, Reaktion: Deutsche Kontroversen um die kulturelle Moderne 1880–1945* (Frankfurt/M., 1999)

Borodziej, Wlodzimierz and Ziemer, Klaus (eds.), *Deutsch-polnische Beziehungen: 1939–1945–1949* (Osnabrück, 2000)

Borscheid, Peter and Wischermann, Clemens (eds.), *Bilderwelt des Alltags: Werbung in der Konsumgesellschaft des 19. und 20. Jahrhunderts* (Stuttgart, 1995)

—— 'Am Anfang war das Wort: Die Wirtschaftswerbung beginnt mit der Zeitungsannonce', Borscheid, Peter and Wischermann, Clemens (eds.), *Bilderwelt des Alltags: Werbung in der Konsumgesellschaft des 19. und 20. Jahrhunderts* (Stuttgart, 1995), 20–43

Borsó, Vittoria, Liermann, Christiane and Merziger, Patrick (eds.) *Die Macht des Populären: Politik und populäre Kultur im 20. Jahrhundert* (Bielefeld, 2010)

Bosch, Michael, *Liberale Presse in der Krise: Die Innenpolitik der Jahre 1930 bis 1933 im Spiegel des ''Berliner Tageblatts'', der ''Frankfurter Zeitung'' und der ''Vossischen Zeitung''* (Frankfurt/M. and Munich, 1976)

Bösch, Frank, 'Das zeremoniell der Kaisergeburtstage (1871–1918)', in Biefang,
    Andreas, Epkenhans, Hans and Tenfelde, Klaus (eds.), *Das politische Zeremoniell
    im deutschen Kaiserreich* (Düsseldorf, 2008), 53–76
Bracher, Karl Dietrich, Sauer, Wolfgang and Schulz, Gerhard, *Die nationalsozialis-
    tische Machtergreifung: Studien zur Errichtung des totalitären Herrschaftssystems in
    Deutschland 1933/34* (Cologne and Opladen, 1962)
Bracher, Karl Dietrich, Sauer, Wolfgang and Schulz, Gerhard, *Die Auflösung der
    Weimarer Republik: Eine Studie zum Problem des Machtverfalls in der Demokratie*,
    5th edn (Düsseldorf, 1984)
——Funke, Manfred, and Jacobsen, Hans-Adolf (eds.), *Die Weimarer Republik
    1918–1933: Politik, Wirtschaft, Gesellschaft* (Bonn, 1987), 44–62
Brandt, Susanne, 'Nagelfiguren: Nailing Patriotism in Germany 1914–18', in
    Saunders, Nicholas J. (ed.), *Matters of Conflict: Material Culture, Memory and the
    First World War* (London and New York, 2004), 62–71
Braun, Birgit, *Umerziehung in der amerikanischen Besatzungszone: Die Schul- und
    Bildungspolitik in Württemberg-Baden von 1945 bis 1949* (Münster, 2004)
Breitenborn, Konrad, *Bismarck: Kult und Kitsch um den Reichsgründer* (Frankfurt/M.
    and Leipzig, 1990)
Broszat, Martin and Frei, Norbert (eds.), *Ploetz: Das Dritte Reich: Ursprünge,
    Ereignisse, Wirkungen* (Freiburg and Würzburg, 1983)
Buschmann, Nikolaus, 'Der verschwiegene Krieg: Kommunikation zwischen
    Front und Heimat', in Hirschfeld, Gerhard, Krumeich, Gerd, Langewiesche,
    Dieter and Ullmann, Hans-Peter (eds.), *Kriegserfahrungen: Studien zur Sozial- und
    Mentalitätengeschichte des Ersten Weltkrieges* (Essen, 1997), 208–24
Callies, Horst, 'Arminius—Hermann der Cherusker: der deutsche Held', in
    Strzelzyk, Jerzy (ed.), *Die Helden in der Geschichte und Historiographie* (Poznan,
    1997), 49–58
Carsten, Francis L., *Revolution in Central Europe 1918–1919* (Aldershot, 1988)
Cary, Noel D., 'The Making of the Reich President, 1925: German Conservatism
    and the Nomination of Paul von Hindenburg', *CEH*, 23 (1990), 179–204
Cassirer, Ernst, *Philosophie der symbolischen Formen, vol. 2: Das mythische Denken*
    (Berlin, 1925)
—— *The Myth of the State* (London, 1946)
Chickering, Roger, *Imperial Germany and the Great War: 1914–1918* (Cam-
    bridge, 1998)
Childers, Thomas, *The Nazi Voter: The Social Foundations of Fascism in Germany,
    1919–1933* (Chapel Hill, NC, and London, 1983)
Clark, Christopher M., *Wilhelm II - Profiles in Power* (London, 2000)
—— *Iron Kingdom: The Rise and Downfall of Prussia 1600–1946* (London, 2006)
Conze, Werner, 'Hindenburg', *Das Parlament*, 18 March 1953, no. 11 (1953), 3
Creutz, Martin, *Die Pressepolitik der kaiserlichen Regierung während des Ersten
    Weltkrieges: Die Exekutive, die Journalisten und der Teufelskreis der Berichterstattung*
    (Frankfurt/M., 1996)

Danyel, Jürgen, 'Die geteilte Vergangenheit: Gesellschaftliche Ausgangslagen und politische Dispositionen für den Umgang mit Nationalsozialismus und Widerstand in beiden deutschen Staaten nach 1949', in Kocka, Jürgen (ed.), *Historische DDR-Forschung: Aufsätze und Studien* (Berlin, 1993), 129–48

—— 'Die Erinnerung an die Wehrmacht in beiden deutschen Staaten: Vergangenheitspolitik und Gedenkrituale', in Müller, Rolf-Dieter and Volkman, Hans-Erich (eds.), *Die Wehrmacht: Mythos und Realität* (Munich, 1999), 1139–49

—— 'Die Vergangenheitspolitik in der SBZ-DDR 1945–1989', in Borodziej, Wlodzimierz and Ziemer, Klaus (eds.), *Deutsch-polnische Beziehungen: 1939–1945–1949* (Osnabrück, 2000), 265–96

Davis, Belinda J., *Home Fires Burning: Food, Politics and Everyday Life in WWI Berlin* (Chapel Hill, NC, 2000)

Déak, István, *Weimar Germany's Left-Wing Intellectuals: A Political History of the Weltbühne and its Circle* (Berkeley and Los Angeles, CA, 1968)

Deist, Wilhelm, 'Der militärische Zusammenbruch des Kaiserreichs: Zur Realität der "Dolchstoßlegende"', in Büttner, Ute (ed.), *Das Unrechtsregime: Internationale Forschung über den Nationalsozialismus* (Hamburg, 1986), 101–31

—— *Militär: Staat und Gesellschaft: Studien zur preußisch-deutschen Militärgeschichte* (Munich, 1991)

Demandt, Philipp, *Luisenkult: Die Unsterblichkeit der Königin von Preussen* (Cologne, 2003)

Dick, Harold G. and Robinson, Douglas H., *The Golden Age of the Great Passenger Airships: Graf Zeppelin and Hindenburg* (Washington, DC, 1985)

Dörner, Andreas, *Politischer Mythos und symbolische Politik: Der Hermannmythos: Zur Entstehung des Nationalbewußtseins der Deutschen* (Reinbek near Hamburg, 1996)

Dorpalen, Andreas, *Hindenburg and the Weimar Republic* (Princeton, NJ, 1964)

—— *German History in Marxist Perspective: The East German Approach* (London, 1985)

Drobisch, Klaus, 'Hindenburg-, Hitler-, Adenauerspende', *ZfG*, (1967), 447–58

Duerr, Hans Peter (ed.), *Der Wissenschaftler und das Irrationale, vol. 2: Beiträge aus Philosophie und Psychologie* (Frankfurt/M., 1981)

Dülffer, Jost and Krumeich, Gerd (eds.), *Der verlorene Frieden: Politik und Kriegskultur nach 1918* (Essen, 2002)

Dülmen, Richard van (ed.), *Erfindung des Menschen: Schöpfungsträume und Körperbilder 1500–2000* (Vienna, 1998)

Dunker, Ulrich, *Der Reichsbund jüdischer Frontsoldaten 1919–1938: Geschichte eines jüdischen Abwehrvereins* (Düsseldorf, 1977)

Duppler, Jörg and Groß, Gerhard P. (eds.), *Kriegsende 1918: Ereignis, Wirkung, Nachwirkung* (Munich, 1999)

Echterhoff, Gerald and Saar, Martin (eds.), *Kontexte und Kulturen des Erinnerns: Maurice Halbwachs und das Paradigma des kollektiven Gedächtnisses* (Konstanz, 2002)

Eckdahl, Sven, *Die Schlacht bei Tannenberg 1410, vol. 1: Quellenkritische Untersuchungen* (Berlin, 1982)

Ehrke-Rotermund, Heidrun, '"Durch die Erkenntnis des Schrecklichen zu seiner Überwindung"? Werner Beumelburg: Gruppe Bosemüller (1930)', in Schneider, Thomas F. and Wagener, Hans (eds.), *Von Richthofen bis Remarque: Deutschsprachige Prosa zum I. Weltkrieg* (Amsterdam and New York, 2003), 299–318

Eksteins, Modris, 'War, Memory and Politics: The Fate of the Film *All Quiet on the Western Front*', *CEH*, 13 (1980), 60–82

Engelberg, Ernst, *Bismarck: Urpreuße und Reichsgründer* (Berlin, 1985)

Engelmann, Tanja, '*'Wer nicht wählt, hilft Hitler''*: *Wahlkampfberichterstattung in der Weimarer Republik* (Cologne, 2004)

Evans, Richard J., *The Coming of the Third Reich* (London, 2003)

—— *The Third Reich in Power* (London, 2005)

Falter, Jürgen W. 'The Two Hindenburg Elections of 1925 and 1932: A Total Reversal of Voter Coalitions', *CEH*, 23 (1990), 225–41

——, Lindenberger, Thomas and Schumann, Siegfried (eds.), *Wahlen und Abstimmungen in der Weimarer Republik: Materialien zum Wahlverhalten 1919–1933* (Munich, 1986)

Faulkner, Ronnie W. 'American Reaction to Hindenburg of the Weimar Republic, 1925–1934', *The Historian*, 51/3 (1989), 402–22

Fischer, Heike, 'Tannenberg-Denkmal und Hindenburgkult', in Hütt, Michael, Kunst, Hans-Joachim, Matzner, Florian and Pabst, Ingeborg (eds.), *Unglücklich das Land das Helden nötig hat: Leiden und Sterben in den Kriegsdenkmälern des Ersten und Zweiten Weltkriegs* (Marburg, 1990), 28–49

Fischer, Heinz-Dietrich (ed.), *Deutsche Zeitschriften des 17. bis 20. Jahrhunderts* (Pullach near Munich, 1973)

Flood, Christopher G., *Political Myth: A Theoretical Introduction* (New York and London, 2004)

Foley, Robert T., *German Strategy and the Path to Verdun: Erich von Falkenhayn and the Development of Attrition 1879–1916* (Cambridge, 2005)

Föllmer, Moritz and Graf, Rüdiger (eds.), *Die "Krise" der Weimarer Republik: Zur Kritik eines Deutungsmusters* (Frankfurt/M., 2005)

François, Etienne and Schulze, Hagen (eds.), *Deutsche Erinnerungsorte*, 3 vols. (Munich, 2001)

Frei, Norbert, *1945 und wir: Das Dritte Reich im Bewusstsein der Deutschen* (Munich, 2005)

Freitag, Werner, 'Nationale Mythen und kirchliches Heil: Der "Tag von Potsdam"', *Westfälische Forschungen*, 41 (1991), 379–430

Frevert, Ute, 'Herren und Heroen: Vom Aufstieg und Niedergang des Heroismus im 19. und 20. Jahrhundert', in Dülmen, Richard van (ed.), *Erfindung des Menschen: Schöpfungsträume und Körperbilder 1500–2000* (Vienna, 1998), 323–44

—— 'Vertrauen: Historische Annäherungen an eine Gefühlshaltung', in Benthien, Claudia, Fleig, Anne and Kasten, Ingrid (eds.), *Emotionalität: Zur Geschichte der Gefühle* (Cologne, Weimar, and Vienna, 2000), 178–97

—— 'Pflicht', in François, Etienne and Schulze, Hagen (eds.), *Erinnerungsorte*, vol. 2 (Munich, 2001) 269–85

—— 'Männer in Uniform: Habitus und Signalzeichen im 19. und 20. Jahrhundert',
in Benthien, Claudia and Stephan, Inge (eds.), *Männlichkeit als Maskerade:
Kulturelle Inszenierungen vom Mittelalter bis zur Gegenwart* (Cologne, Weimar,
Vienna, 2003), 277–95

Fricke, Dieter (ed.), *Lexikon zur Parteiengeschichte 1789–1945*, 4 vols. (Leipzig,
1983–1986)

Fries, Helmut, *Die große Katharsis: Der Erste Weltkrieg in der Sicht deutscher Dichter
und Gelehrter*, 2 vols. (Konstanz, 1994)

Fritzsche, Klaus, *Politische Romantik und Gegenrevolution: Fluchtwege in der Krise der
bürgerlichen Gesellschaft: Das Beispiel des Tat-Kreises* (Frankfurt, 1976)

Fritzsche, Peter, 'Presidential Victory and Popular Festivity in Weimar Germany:
Hindenburg's 1925 Election', *CEH*, 23 (1990), 205–24

—— *Rehearsals for Fascism: Populism and Political Mobilization in Weimar Germany*
(Oxford, 1990)

Fromme, Friedrich Karl, *Von der Weimarer Verfassung zum Bonner Grundgesetz: Die
verfassungspolitischen Folgerungen des Parlamentarischen Rates aus Weimarer Republik
und nationalsozialistischer Diktatur*, 3rd edn (Berlin, 1999)

Führer, Karl, 'Der Deutsche Reichskriegerbund Kyffhäuser 1930–1934: Politik,
Ideologie und Funktion eines "unpolitischen" Verbandes', *MGM*, 36 (1984),
57–76

Führer, Karl Christian, 'Auf dem Weg zur "Massenkultur"? Kino und Rundfunk
in der Weimarer Republik', *HZ*, no. 262 (1996), 739–81

Fulda, Berhard, *Press and Politics in the Weimar Republic* (Oxford, 2009)

—— 'Die Politik der "Unpolitischen": Die Boulevard- und Massenpresse in den
zwanziger und dreissiger Jahren' (MS, 2004)

Gaetringen, Friedrich Freiherr Hiller von (ed.), 'Die Deutschnationale Volkspartei',
in Matthias, Erich and Morsey, Rudolf (eds.), *Das Ende der Parteien 1933:
Darstellungen und Dokumente* (Bonn, 1960), 391–400

—— '"Dolchstoß"-Diskussion und "Dolchstoßlegende" im Wandel von vier
Jahrzehnten', in Gaertringen, Friedrich Freiherr Hiller von and Besson, Waldemar (eds.), *Geschichte und Geschichtsbewußtsein* (Göttingen, 1963), 122–60

—— and Besson, Waldemar (eds.), *Geschichte und Geschichtsbewußtsein* (Göttingen,
1963)

Gamm, Hans-Joachim, *Der Flüsterwitz im Dritten Reich* (Munich, 1963)

Gay, Peter, *Weimar Culture: The Outsider as Insider* (New York and Evanston,
IL, 1968)

Gerwarth, Robert, *The Bismarck Myth: Weimar Germany and the Legacy of the Iron
Chancellor* (Oxford, 2005)

Glatzer, Dieter and Glatzer, Ruth, *Berliner Leben 1914–1918: Eine historische Reportage
aus Erinnerungen und Berichten* (Berlin, 1983)

Goebel, Stefan, 'Forging the Industrial Home Front: Iron-Nail Memorials in
the Ruhr', in Macleod, Jenny and Purseigle, Pierre (eds.), *Uncovered Fields:
Perspectives in First World War Studies* (Leiden and Boston, MA, 2004), 159–78

Goergen, Jeanpaul, 'Der dokumentarische Kontinent: Ein Forschungsbericht', in Kreimeier, Klaus, Ehmann, Antje and Goergen, Jeanpaul (eds.), *Geschichte des dokumentarischen Films in Deutschland: vol. 2: Weimarer Republik 1918–1933* (Stuttgart, 2005), 15–43

Gollbach, Michael, *Die Wiederkehr des Weltkrieges in der Literatur: Zu den Frontromanen der späten Zwanziger Jahre* (Kronberg/Ts., 1978)

Goltz, Anna von der, 'Die Macht des Hindenburg-Mythos: Politik, Propaganda und Popularität in Kaiserreich und Republik' in Borsó, Vittoria, Liermann, Christiane and Merziger, Patrick (eds.) *Die Macht des Populären: Politik und populäre Kultur im 20. Jahrhundert* (Bielefeld, 2010)

——and Gildea, Robert, '"Flawed Saviours": The Myths of Hindenburg and Pétain', *EHQ* vol. 39, no. 3 (2009), 439–64

Goodspeed, Donald J., *Ludendorff: Soldier, Dictator, Revolutionary* (London, 1966)

Görlitz, Walter, *Hindenburg: Ein Lebensbild* (Bonn, 1953)

Görtemaker, Manfred, 'Bürger, Ersatzkaiser, Volkstribun: Reichspräsidenten in der Weimarer Republik', in Stiftung Haus der Geschichte der Bundesrepublik Deutschland (ed.), *Bilder und Macht im 20. Jahrhundert* (Bielefeld, 2004), 28–41

Gries, Rainer, Ilgen, Volker and Schindelbeck, Dirk (eds.), *'Ins Gehirn der Masse kriechen!' Werbung und Mentalitätsgeschichte* (Darmstadt, 1995)

Grimm, Reinhold and Hermand, Jost (eds.), *Die Sogenannten Zwanziger Jahre* (Bad Homburg, 1970)

Groener-Geyer, Dorothea, *General Groener: Staatsmann und Feldherr* (Frankfurt/M., 1955)

Groß, Gerhard P. (ed.), *Die vergessene Front: Der Osten 1914/15: Ereignis, Wirkung, Nachwirkung* (Paderborn, 2006)

Grunberger, Richard, *A Social History of the Third Reich* (London, 1971)

Grunenberg, Antonia, *Antifaschismus—ein deutscher Mythos* (Reinbek, 1993)

Gümbel, Annette, 'Instrumentalisierte Erinnerung an den Ersten Weltkrieg: Hans Grimms "Volk ohne Raum" ', in Berding, Helmut, Heller, Klaus and Speitkamp, Winfried (eds.), *Krieg und Erinnerung* (Göttingen, 2000), 93–112

Guth, Eckehard P., 'Der Gegensatz zwischen dem Oberbefehlshaber Ost und dem Chef des Generalstabes des Feldheeres 1914/1915: Die Rolle des Majors v. Haeften im Spannungsfeld zwischen Hindenburg, Ludendorff und Falkenhayn', *MGM*, 35 (1984), 75–112

Haas, Stefan, 'Die neue Welt der Bilder: Werbung und visuelle Kultur der Moderne', in Borscheid, Peter and Wischermann, Clemens (eds.), *Bilderwelt des Alltags: Werbung in der Konsumgesellschaft des 19. und 20. Jahrhunderts* (Stuttgart, 1995), 64–89

Haffner, Sebastian, *Die verratene Revolution: Deutschland 1918/19* (Bern, Munich, and Vienna, 1969)

Halbwachs, Maurice, *On Collective Memory* (Chicago, IL, and London, 1992)

Hardtwig, Wolfgang (ed.), *Politische Kultur in der Zwischenkriegszeit 1918–1939* (Göttingen 2005)

Harsch, Donna, *German Social Democracy and the Rise of Nazism* (Chapel Hill, NC, 1993)

Hartwig, Gebhardt, 'Organisierte Kommunikation als Herrschaftstechnik: Zur Entwicklungsgeschichte staatlicher Öffentlichkeitsarbeit', *Publizistik: Vierteljahrshefte für Kommunikationsforschung*, 39 (1994), 175–89

Haungs, Peter, *Reichspräsident und parlamentarische Kabinettsregierung: Eine Studie zum Regierungssystem der Weimarer Republik in den Jahren 1924 bis 1929* (Cologne and Opladen, 1968)

Haus der Geschichte der Bundesrepublik Deutschland (ed.), *Prominente in der Werbung: Da weiss man, was man hat* (Mainz, 2001)

Hauss, Hans-Jochen, *Die erste Volkswahl des deutschen Reichspräsidenten: Eine Untersuchung ihrer verfassungspolitischen Grundlagen, ihrer Vorgeschichte und ihres Verlaufs unter besonderer Berücksichtigung des Anteils Bayerns und der Bayerischen Volkspartei* (Kallmünz, 1965)

Hazareesingh, Sudhir, *The Legend of Napoleon* (London, 2004)

Heinemann, Ulrich, *Die verdrängte Niederlage: Politische Öffentlichkeit und Kriegsschuldfrage in der Weimarer Republik* (Göttingen, 1983)

—— 'Die Last der Vergangenheit: Zur politischen Bedeutung der Kriegsschuld- und Dolchstoßdiskussion', in Bracher, Karl Dietrich, Funke, Manfred, and Jacobsen, Hans-Adolf (eds.), *Die Weimarer Republik: Politik—Wirtschaft—Gesellschaft* (Bonn, 1987), 371–86

Heitger, Ulrich, *Vom Zeitzeichen zum politischen Führungsmittel: Entwicklungstendenzen und Strukturen der Nachrichtenprogramme des Rundfunks in der Weimarer Republik 1923—1932* (Münster, 2003)

Henke, Klaus-Dietmar, *Die amerikanische Besetzung Deutschlands* (Munich, 1995)

Hermand, Jost and Trommler, Frank, *Die Kultur der Weimarer Republik* (Munich, 1978)

Hertzmann, Lewis, *DNVP: Right-wing Opposition in the Weimar Republic 1918–1924* (Lincoln, NE, 1963)

Herwig, Holger H., 'Of Men and Myths: The Use and Abuse of History in the Great War', in Winter, Jay M. (ed.) *The Great War and the Twentieth Century* (New Haven, CT, and London, 2000), 299–330

Hettling, Manfred (ed.), *Revolution in Deutschland? 1789–1989 Sieben Beiträge* (Göttingen, 1991)

Hey'l, Bettina, *Geschichtsdenken und literarische Moderne: Zum historischen Roman in der Zeit der Weimarer Republik* (Tübingen, 1994)

Hirschfeld, Gerhard and Krumeich, Gerd (eds.), *Keiner fühlt sich hier mehr als Mensch . . . Erlebnis und Wirkung des Ersten Weltkrieges* (Essen, 1993)

—— —— Langewiesche, Dieter and Ullmann, Hans-Peter (eds.), *Kriegserfahrungen: Studien zur Sozial- und Mentalitätengeschichte des Ersten Weltkrieges* (Essen, 1997)

Hoegen, Jesko von, *Der Held von Tannenberg: Genese und Funktion des Hindenburg-Mythos* (Cologne, Weimar, Vienna, 2007)

Hoeres, Peter, 'Die Slawen: Perzeptionen des Kriegsgegners bei den Mittelmächsten: Selbst- und Feindbild', in Groß, Gerhard P. (ed.), *Die vergessene*

*Front: Der Osten 1914/15: Ereignis, Wirkung, Nachwirkung* (Paderborn, 2006), 179–200

Höffler, Felix, 'Kriegserfahrungen in der Heimat: Kriegsverlauf, Kriegsschuld und Kriegsende in würtemmbergischen Stimmungsbildern des Ersten Weltkrieges', in Hirschfeld, Gerhard, Krumeich, Gerd, Langewiesche, Dieter and Ullmann, Hans-Peter (eds.), *Kriegserfahrungen: Studien zur Sozial- und Mentalitätengeschichte des Ersten Weltkrieges* (Essen, 1997), 68–82

Hoffmann, Heike, '"Schwarzer Peter im Weltkrieg": Die deutsche Spielwaren-industrie 1914–1918', in Hirschfeld, Gerhard, Krumeich, Gerd, Langewiesche, Dieter and Ullmann, Hans-Peter (eds.), *Kriegserfahrungen: Studien zur Sozial- und Mentalitätengeschichte des Ersten Weltkrieges* (Essen, 1997), 323–40

Holz, Kurt A., *Die Diskussion um den Dawes- und Young-Plan in der deutschen Presse* (Frankfurt/M., 1977)

Hömig, Hermann, *Brüning: Kanzler in der Krise der Republik: Eine Weimarer Biographie* (Paderborn, Munich, Vienna, and Zurich, 2000)

—— *Brüning: Politiker ohne Auftrag: Zwischen Bonner und Weimarer Demokratie* (Paderborn, Munich, Vienna, and Zurich, 2006)

Horne, John (ed.), *State, Society and Mobilization in Europe during the First World War* (Cambridge, 1997)

—— and Kramer, Alan, *German Atrocities 1914: A History of Denial* (New Haven, CT, 2001)

Horstmann, Axel, 'Der Mythosbegriff vom frühen Christentum bis zur Gegenwart', *Archiv für Begriffsgeschichte*, 23 (1979), 7–54, 197–245

Horstmann, Johannes, 'Katholiken, Reichspräsidentenwahlen und Volksent-scheide', *Jahrbuch für christliche Sozialwissenschaften*, no. 27 (1986), 61–93

Hübner, Kurt, 'Wie irrational sind Mythen und Götter?', in Duerr, Hans Peter (ed.), *Der Wissenschaftler und das Irrationale, vol. 3: Beiträge aus der Philosophie* (Frankfurt/M., 1985), 7–32

Hürten, Heinz (ed.), *Zwischen Revolution und Kapp-Putsch: Militär und Innenpolitik 1918–1920* (Düsseldorf, 1977)

—— *Die Anfänge der Ära Seeckt: Militär und Innenpolitik 1920–1922* (Düsseldorf, 1979)

—— *Der Kapp-Putsch als Wende: Über Rahmenbedingungen der Weimarer Republik seit dem Frühjahr 1920* (Opladen, 1989)

Hutton, Patrick H., *History as an Art of Memory* (Hanover and London, 1993)

Imhof, Kurt and Schulz, Peter (eds.), *Medien und Krieg—Krieg in den Medien* (Zurich, 1995)

Jacobsen, Hans-Adolf, 'Wehrmacht und Bundeswehr—Anmerkungen zu einem umstrittenen Thema soldatischer Traditionspflege', in Müller, Rolf-Dieter and Volkmann, Hans-Erich (eds.), *Die Wehrmacht: Mythos und Realität* (Munich, 1999), 1184–91

Jahn, Peter '"Zarendreck, Barbarendreck—Peitscht sie weg!" Die russische Besetzung Ostpreußens 1914 in der deutschen Öffentlichkeit', in Berliner Geschichtswerkstatt (ed.), *August 1914: Ein Volk zieht in den Krieg* (Berlin, 1989), 147–55

Jahnke, Helmut, *Edgar Julius Jung: Ein konservativer Revolutionär zwischen Tradition und Moderne* (Pfaffenweiler, 1998)

Jahr, Christoph, 'Revolution im Schatten: Kulturgeschichtliche Aspekte des Umsturzes in Bayern 1918/19', in Bavaj, Riccardo and Fritzen, Florentine (eds.), *Deutschland—ein Land ohne revolutionäre Traditionen? Revolutionen im Deutschland des 19. und 20. Jahrhunderts im Lichte neuerer geistes- und kulturwissenschaftlicher Erkenntnisse* (Frankfurt/M., 2005), 43–59

Jamme, Christoph, *Einführung in die Philosophie des Mythos, vol. 2: Neuzeit und Gegenwart* (Darmstadt, 1991)

Jasper, Gotthard, *Der Schutz der Republik: Studien zur staatlichen Sicherung der Demokratie in der Weimarer Republik 1922–1930* (Tübingen, 1963)

—— 'Die verfassungs- und machtpolitische Problematik des Reichspräsidentenamtes in der Weimarer Republik: Die Praxis der Reichspräsidenten Ebert und Hindenburg im Vergleich', in König, Rudolf, Soell, Hartmut and Hermann Weber (eds.), *Friedrich Ebert: Bilanz und Perspektiven der Forschung* (Munich, 1990), 147–59

Jaspert, Friedhelm, 'Werbepsychologie: Grundlinien ihrer geschichtlichen Entwicklung', in Francois Stoll (ed.), *Die Psychologie des 20. Jahrhunderts, vol. 13: Anwendungen im Berufsleben: Arbeits-, Wirtschafts- und Verkehrspsychologie* (Zurich, 1981), 170–89

Jeretin-Kopf, Maja, *Der Niedergang der Weimarer Republik im Spiegel der Memoirenliteratur* (Frankfurt/M., 1992)

Jesse, Eckhard, 'Die Bundespräsidenten von 1949 bis zur Gegenwart. Über den protokollarisch höchsten Repräsentanten des deutschen Staates', *Das Parlament*, 20 (10 May 2004)

Jochum, Michael, *Worte als Taten: Der Bundespräsident im demokratischen Prozess der Bundesrepublik Deutschland* (Gütersloh, 2000)

Jonas, Erasmus, *Die Volkskonservativen 1928–1933: Entwicklung, Struktur, Standort und politische Zielsetzung* (Düsseldorf, 1965)

Jones, Larry Eugene and Retallack, James (eds.), *Elections, Mass Politics, and Social Change in Modern Germany* (Cambridge, 1992)

—— 'Hindenburg and the Conservative Dilemma in the 1932 Presidential Elections', *German Studies Review*, vol. 20 (1997), 235–59

—— and Pyta, Wolfram (eds.), *'Ich bin der letzte Preuße'': Der politische Lebensweg des konservativen Politikers Kuno Graf von Westarp (1864–1945)* (Cologne, Weimar, and Vienna, 2006), 163–87

Jung, Otmar, 'Plebiszitärer Durchbruch 1929? Zur Bedeutung von Volksbegehren und Volksentscheid gegen den Young-Plan für die NSDAP', *GG*, 15 (1989), 489–510

Jung, Uli and Schatzberg, Walter (eds.), *Filmkultur zur Zeit der Weimarer Republik* (Munich, 1992)

—— (ed.), *Der deutsche Film: Aspekte seiner Geschichte von den Anfängen bis zur Gegenwart* (Trier, 1993)

Jung, Uli and Loiperdinger, Martin (eds.), *Geschichte des dokumentarischen Films in Deutschland: vol. 1: Kaiserreich 1895–1918* (Stuttgart, 2005)

Kaufmann, Günter, 'Der Händedruck von Potsdam: Die Karriere eines Bildes', *GWU,* 48 (1997), 295–315

Kaufmann, Walter H., *Monarchism in the Weimar Republic* (New York, 1953)

Kerbs, Diethart, 'Die illustrierte Presse am Ende der Weimarer Republik', in Kerbs, Diethart and Stahr, Henrick (eds.), *Berlin 1932: Das letzte Jahr der ersten deutschen Republik* (Berlin, 1992), 68–89

—— and Stahr, Henrick (eds.), *Berlin 1932: Das letzte Jahr der ersten deutschen Republik: Politik, Symbole, Medien* (Berlin, 1992)

Kershaw, Ian, *The 'Hitler Myth': Image and Reality in the Third Reich* (Oxford and New York, 1987)

—— *Hitler 1889–1936: Hubris* (London, 1998)

Kester, Bernadette, *Film Front Weimar: Representations of the First World War in German Films of the Weimar Period (1919–1933)* (Amsterdam, 2003)

Kettenacker, Lothar, 'Der Mythos vom Reich', in Bohrer, Karl-Heinz (ed.) *Mythos und Moderne: Begriff und Bild einer Rekonstruktion* (Frankfurt/M., 1983), 134–56

Kitchen, Martin, *The Silent Dictatorship: The Politics of the German High Command under Hindenburg and Ludendorff, 1916–1918* (London, 1976)

Kleßman, Christoph, *Die doppelte Staatsgründung: Deutsche Geschichte 1945–1955* (Göttingen, 1982)

Kluge, Ulrich, *Soldatenräte und Revolution: Studien zur Militärpolitik in Deutschland 1918/19* (Göttingen, 1975)

—— *Die deutsche Revolution 1918/1919* (Frankfurt/M., 1985)

Knopp, Guido and Arens, Peter, *Unsere Besten: Die 100 größten Deutschen* (Berlin, 2003)

Kocka, Jürgen (ed.), *Historische DDR-Forschung: Aufsätze und Studien* (Berlin, 1993)

Koebner, Thomas et al. (eds.), *'Mit uns zieht die neue Zeit.' Der Mythos Jugend* (Frankfurt/M., 1985)

Kohlrausch, Martin, 'Die Deutung der "Flucht" Wilhelms II. als Fallbeispiel der Rezeption des wilhelminischen Kaisertums', in Neugebauer, Wolfgang and Pröve, Ralf (eds.), *Agrarische Verfassung und politische Struktur: Studien zur Gesellschaftsgeschichte Preußens 1700–1918* (Berlin, 1998) 325–47

—— *Der Monarch im Skandal: Die Logik der Massenmedien und die Transformation der wilhelminischen Monarchie* (Berlin, 2005)

—— (ed.), *Samt und Stahl: Kaiser Wilhelm II. im Urteil seiner Zeitgenossen* (Berlin, 2006)

Kohut, Thomas A., *Wilhelm II and the Germans: A Study in Leadership* (Oxford, 1991)

Kolb, Eberhard and Pyta, Wolfram, 'Die Staatsnotstandsplanung unter den Regierungen Papen und Schleicher', in Winkler, Heinrich August (ed.), *Die deutsche Staatskrise 1930–1933: Handlungsspielräume und Alternativen* (Munich, 1992), 155–81

Kolb, 'Friedrich Ebert: Vom "vorläufigen" zum definitiven Reichspräsidenten: Die Auseinandersetzungen um die Volkswahl des Reichspräsidenten 1919–1922', in Kolb, Eberhard (ed.), *Friedrich Ebert als Reichspräsident* (Munich, 1997), 109–56

—— (ed.), *Friedrich Ebert als Reichspräsident* (Munich, 1997)

—— 'Rettung der Republik: Die Politik der SPD in den Jahren 1930 bis 1933', in Winkler, Heinrich August (ed.), *Weimar im Widerstreit: Deutungen der ersten deutschen Republik im geteilten Deutschland* (Munich, 2002), 85–104

—— *The Weimar Republic* (London, 2005)

König, Rudolf, Soell, Hartmut and Weber, Hermann (eds.), *Friedrich Ebert: Bilanz und Perspektiven der Forschung* (Munich, 1990)

Koszyk, Kurt, *Deutsche Pressepolitik im Ersten Weltkrieg* (Düsseldorf, 1968)

—— *Geschichte der deutschen Presse, vol. 3: Deutsche Presse 1914–1945* (Berlin, 1972)

Kreimeier, Klaus, *The Ufa Story: A History of Germany's Greatest Film Company 1918–1945* (New York, 1996)

—— Ehmann, Antje and Goergen, Jeanpaul (eds.), *Geschichte des dokumentarischen Films in Deutschland: vol. 2: Weimarer Republik 1918–1933* (Stuttgart, 2005)

Krohn, Rüdiger, 'Friedrich I. Barbarossa: Barbarossa und der Alte vom Berge: Zur neuzeitlichen Rezeption der Kyffhäuser-Sage', in Müller, Ulrich and Wunderlich, Werner (eds.), *Mittelalter-Mythen*, vol. 1 (St. Gallen, 1996), 101–18

Krollpfeiffer, Gerhard, *Die Lustigen Blätter im Weltkrieg 1914/18: Der publizistische Kampf eines deutschen Witzblattes* (München, 1935)

Kroener, Bernhard R. (ed.), *Potsdam—Stadt, Armee, Residenz in der preußisch-deutschen Militärgeschichte* (Frankfurt/M., 1993)

Krüger-Bulcke, Ingrid, 'Der Hohenzollern-Hindenburg-Zwischenfall in Marburg 1947: Wiederaufleben nationalistischer Strömungen oder Sturm im Wasserglas?', *Hessisches Jahrbuch für Landesgeschichte*, 39 (1989), 311–52

Krumpholz, Ralf, *Wahrnehmung und Politik: Die Bedeutung des Ordnungsdenkens für das politische Handeln am Beispiel der deutschen Revolution von 1918–1920* (Münster, 1998)

Kruse, Wolfgang, *Krieg und nationale Integration: Eine Neuinterpretation des sozialdemokratischen Burgfriedensschlusses 1914/15* (Essen, 1993)

Kücklich, Erika, *Ernst Thälmann und die Reichspräsidentenwahl 1932* (Berlin, 1986)

Kunstamt Kreuzberg Berlin und Institut für Theaterwissenschaft der Universität Köln (eds.), *Weimarer Republik* (Berlin and Hamburg, 1977)

Kurze, Dietrich (ed.), *Aus Theorie und Praxis: Festschrift für Hans Herzfeld zum 80. Geburtstag* (Berlin and New York, 1972)

Lais, Sylvia and Mende, Hans-Jürgen (eds.) *Lexikon Berliner Straßennamen* (Berlin, 2004)

Lammers, Britta, *Werbung im Nationalsozialismus: Die Kataloge der 'Großen Deutschen Kunstausstellung' 1937–1944* (Weimar, 1999)

Lange, Karl, *Marneschlacht und deutsche Öffentlichkeit: Eine verdrängte Niederlage und ihre Folgen 1914–1939* (Düsseldorf, 1974)

Laqueur, Walter, *Weimar: A Cultural history 1918—1933* (London, 1974)

Lasek, Wilhelm, ' "Revisionistische" Autoren und ihre Publikationen', in Bailer-Galanda, Brigitte, Benz, Wolfgang and Neugebauer, Wolfgang (eds.), *Die Auschwitzleugner: Geschichtslüge und Historische Wahrheit* (Berlin, 1996), 320–80

Latour, Conrad F. and Vogelsang, Thilo, *Okkupation und Wiederaufbau. Die Tätigkeit der Militärregierung in der amerikanischen Besatzungszone Deutschlands 1944–1947* (Stuttgart, 1973)

Lau, Dirk, *Wahlkämpfe der Weimarer Republik: Propaganda und Programme der politischen Parteien bei den Wahlen zum Deutschen Reichstag von 1924 bis 1930* (Marburg, 1995)

Lau, Matthias, *Pressepolitik als Chance: Staatliche Öffentlichkeitsarbeit in den Ländern der Weimarer Republik* (Stuttgart, 2003)

Lauritzen, Frederick, 'Propaganda Art in the Postage Stamps of the Third Reich', *The Journal of Decorative and Propaganda Arts*, vol. 10 (1988), 62–79

Lehnert, Detlef, 'Auf dem Weg zur "nationalen Volksgemeinschaft"? Die Durchsetzung der NSDAP als republikfeindliche Sammlungsbewegung im Parteiensystem und in der politischen Öffentlichkeit', in Megerle, Klaus (ed.), *Warum gerade die Nationalsozialisten?* (Berlin, 1983), 12–67

——and Megerle, Klaus (eds.), *Politische Identität und nationale Gedenktage: Zur politischen Kultur in der Weimarer Republik* (Opladen, 1989)

——and Megerle, Klaus (eds.) *Politische Teilkulturen zwischen Integration und Polarisierung: Zur politischen Kultur in der Weimarer Republik* (Opladen, 1990)

——and Megerle, Klaus (eds.), *Pluralismus als Verfassungs- und Gesellschaftsmodell: Zur politischen Kultur in der Weimarer Republik* (Opladen, 1993)

——'Von der politisch-kulturellen Fragmenteriung zur demokratischen Sammlung? Der "Volksblock" des "Reichsbannerlagers" und die katholischen Republikaner', in Lehnert, Detlef and Megerle, Klaus (eds.), *Pluralismus als Verfassungs- und Gesellschaftsmodell: Zur politischen Kultur in der Weimarer Republik* (Opladen, 1993), 77–129

——'Die geschichtlichen Bilder von "Tannenberg": Vom Hindenburg-Mythos im Ersten Weltkrieg zum ersatzmonarchischen Identifikationssymbol in der Weimarer Republik', in Imhof, Kurt and Schulz, Peter (eds.), *Medien und Krieg—Krieg in den Medien* (Zurich, 1995), 37–72

Leonhard, Joachim-Felix (ed.), *Programmgeschichte des Hörfunks in der Weimarer Republik*, 2 vols. (Munich, 1997)

Leopold, John A., *Alfred Hugenberg: The Radical Nationalist Campaign against the Weimar Republic* (New Haven, CT, and London, 1977)

Lepsius, Rainer, *Demokratie in Deutschland: Soziologisch-historische Konstellationsanalysen* (Göttingen, 1993) 95–119

Lévi-Strauss, Claude, *Anthropologie structurale* (Paris, 1958)

——*Mythologiques* (Paris, 1964–1971)

Leyendecker, Karl, (ed.), *German Novelists of the Weimar Republic: Intersections of Literature and Politics* (Columbia, SC, 2006)

Linden, Marcel van der and Mergner, Gottfried (eds.), *Kriegsbegeisterung und mentale Kriegsvorbereitung: Interdisziplinäre Studien* (Berlin, 1991)

Lipp, Anne, 'Heimatwahrnehmung und soldatisches "Kriegserlebnis" ', in Hirschfeld, Gerhard, Krumeich, Gerd, Langewiesche, Dieter and Ullmann, Hans-Peter (eds.), *Kriegserfahrungen: Studien zur Sozial- und Mentalitätengeschichte des Ersten Weltkrieges* (Essen, 1997), 225–42

Liulevicius, Vejas Gabriel, *War Land on the Eastern Front: Culture, National Identity, and German Occupation in World War I* (Cambridge, 2000)

—— 'Von "Ober Ost" nach "Ostland"?', in Gerhard P. Groß (ed.), *Die vergessene Front: Der Osten 1914/15: Ereignis, Wirkung, Nachwirkung* (Paderborn, 2006), 295–310

Longerich, Peter, *Die braunen Bataillone: Geschichte der SA* (Munich, 1989)

—— *Politik der Vernichtung* (Munich, 1998)

Lüders, Martin, *Der Soldat und das Reich: Paul von Hindenburg: Generalfeldmarschall und Reichspräsident* (Freising, 1961)

Maase, Kaspar, *Grenzenloses Vergnügen: Der Aufstieg der Massenkultur 1850–1970* (Frankfurt/M., 1997)

Macleod, Jenny and Purseigle, Pierre (eds.), *Uncovered Fields: Perspectives in First World War Studies* (Leiden and Boston, MA, 2004)

Marcks, Erich, *Hindenburg: Feldmarschall und Reichspräsident* (Göttingen, Berlin, and Frankfurt/M., 1963)

Marquardt, Axel and Rathsack, Heinz (eds.), *Preussen im Film* (Hamburg, 1981)

Marckwardt, Wilhelm, *Die Illustrierten der Weimarer Zeit: Publizistische Funktion, ökonomische Entwicklung und inhaltliche Tendenzen* (Munich, 1982)

Maser, Werner, *Hindenburg: Eine politische Biographie* (Rastatt, 1990)

Matthias, Erich, 'Hindenburg zwischen den Fronten: Zur Vorgeschichte der Reichspräsidentenwahlen von 1932 (Dokumentation)', *VfZ*, vol. 8 (1960), 75–84

—— and Morsey, Rudolf (eds.), *Das Ende der Parteien 1933: Darstellungen und Dokumente* (Bonn, 1960)

Meinecke, Friedrich, *Die deutsche Katastrophe* (Wiesbaden, 1946)

Melograni, Piero, 'The Cult of the Duce in Mussolini's Italy', *JCH*, vol. 2, no. 4, (1976), 221–37

Menge, Anna, 'The Iron Hindenburg—A Popular Icon of Weimar Germany', *German History*, vol. 26, no. 3 (2008), 357–382

Mergel, Thomas, *Parlamentarische Kultur in der Weimarer Republik: Politische Kommunikation, symbolische Politik und Öffentlichkeit im Reichstag* (Düsseldorf, 2002)

Mittenzwei, Ingrid, *Friedrich der II. von Preußen: Eine Biographie* (Berlin, 1980)

Moeller, Robert G., *War Stories: The Search for a Usable Past in the Federal Republic of Germany* (Berkeley, CA, 2001)

Möller, Frank (ed.), *Charismatische Führer der deutschen Nation* (Munich, 2004)

Mombauer, Annika, *The Origins of the First World War: Controversies and Consensus* (London, 2002)

Mombauer, Annika, and Deist, Wilhelm (eds.), *The Kaiser: New Research on Wilhelm II's Role in Imperial Germany* (Cambridge, 2003)

Mommsen, Hans, *The Rise and Fall of Weimar Democracy* (Chapel Hill, NC, and London, 1996)

Mommsen, Wolfgang J., 'Die Regierung Bethmann Hollweg und die öffentliche Meinung 1914–1917', *VfZ*, 17 (1969), 117–59

—— *Max Weber and German Politics 1890–1920* (Chicago and London, 1984)

Mosse, George L., *The Nationalization of the Masses: Political Symbolism and Mass Movements in Germany from the Napoleonic Wars through the Third Reich* (Ithaca, NY, 1991)

Mühleisen, Horst, 'Das Testament Hindenburgs vom 11. Mai 1934', *VfZ*, 44 (1996), 355–71

Mühlhausen, Walter, *Friedrich Ebert 1871–1925: Reichspräsident der Weimarer Republik* (Bonn, 2006)

Müller, Klaus-Jürgen, 'Der Tag von Potsdam und das Verhältnis der preußisch-deutschen Militär-Elite zum Nationalsozialismus', Kroener, Bernhard R. (ed.), *Potsdam—Stadt, Armee, Residenz in der preußisch-deutschen Militärgeschichte* (Frankfurt/M., 1993), 435–49

Müller, Rolf-Dieter and Volkmann, Hans-Erich (eds.), *Die Wehrmacht: Mythos und Realität* (Munich, 1999)

Müller, Ulrich and Wunderlich, Werner (eds.), *Mittelalter-Mythen*, vol. 1 (St. Gallen, 1996)

—— 'Kaiser Friedrich II.: "Jener große Freigeist, das Genie unter den deutschen Kaisern"?', in Müller, Ulrich and Wunderlich, Werner (eds.), *Mittelalter-Mythen*, vol. 1 (St. Gallen, 1996), 197–211

Mulligan, William, *The Creation of the Modern German Army: General Walther Reinhardt and the Weimar Republic 1914–1930* (Oxford, 2004)

Münkler, Herfried and Storch, Wolfgang, *Siegfrieden: Politik mit einem deutschen Mythos* (Berlin, 1988)

Naumann, Michael, *Strukturwandel des Heroismus: Vom sakralen zum revolutionären Heldentum* (Königstein/Taunus, 1984)

Neugebauer, Wolfgang and Pröve, Ralf (eds.), *Agrarische Verfassung und politische Struktur: Studien zur Gesellschaftsgeschichte Preußens 1700–1918* (Berlin, 1998)

Nicholls, Anthony J., *Weimar and the Rise of Hitler*, 4th edn (London, 2000)

Niemetz, Daniel, *Das feldgraue Erbe: Die Wehrmachteinflüsse im Militär der SBZ/DDR* (Berlin, 2006)

Niethammer, Lutz, 'Maurice Halbwachs: Memory and the Feelings of Identity', in Strath, Bo (ed.) *Myth and Memory in the Construction of Community: Historical Patterns in Europe and Beyond* (Brussels, 2000), 75–94

Nolte, Hans-Heinrich, 'Mythos—Plädoyer für einen engen Begriff', in Saldern, Adelheid von (ed.), *Mythen in Geschichte und Geschichtsschreibung aus polnischer und deutscher Sicht* (Münster, 1996), 36–9

Nora, Pierre et al. (eds.), *Realms of Memory: Rethinking the French Past*, 3 vols. (New York, 1996–1998)

Offer, Avner, *The First World War: An Agrarian Interpretation* (Oxford, 1989)

Opitz, Günther, *Der Christlich Soziale Volksdienst: Versuch einer protestantischen Partei in der Weimarer Republik* (Düsseldorf, 1969)

Oppelt, Ulrike, *Film und Propaganda im Ersten Weltkrieg: Propaganda als Medienrealität im Aktualitäten und Dokumentarfilm* (Stuttgart, 2002)

Orlow, Dietrich, 'The Conversion of Myths into Political Power: The Case of the Nazi Party, 1925–1926', *The AHR*, vol. 72, no. 3 (1967), 906–24

Papenfuß, Dietrich and Schieder, Wolfgang (eds.), *Deutsche Umbrüche im 20. Jahrhundert* (Cologne, Weimar, and Vienna, 2000)

Paris, Michael (ed.), *The First World War and Popular Cinema: 1914 to the Present* (Edinburgh, 1999)

Paul, Gerhard, *Aufstand der Bilder: Die NS-Propaganda vor 1933* (Bonn, 1990)

Petzold, Joachim, *Die Dolchstoßlegende: Eine Geschichtsfälschung im Dienst des deutschen Imperialismus und Militarimus* (Berlin, 1963)

Peukert, Detlev, *The Weimar Republic* (London, 1991)

Pleyer, Hildegard, *Politische Werbung in der Weimarer Republik* (Münster, 1960)

Plum, Günther, 'Übernahme und Sicherung der Macht 1933/34', in Broszat, Martin and Frei, Norbert (eds.), *Ploetz: Das Dritte Reich: Ursprünge, Ereignisse, Wirkungen* (Freiburg and Würzburg, 1983), 28–44

Pogge von Strandmann, Hartmut, 'Rathenau, Wilhelm II, and the Perception of Wilhelminismus', in Mombauer, Annika and Deist, Wilhelm (eds.), *The Kaiser: New Research on Wilhelm II's Role in Imperial Germany* (Cambridge, 2003), 259–80

Pöhlmann, Markus, *Kriegsgeschichte und Geschichtspolitik: Der Erste Weltkrieg: Die amtliche deutsche Militärgeschichtsschreibung 1914–1956* (Paderborn, 2002)

—— 'Der moderne Alexander im Maschinenkrieg', Förster, Stig and Pöhlmann, Markus (eds.), *Kriegsherren der Weltgeschichte: 22 historische Porträts* (Munich, 2006), 268–86

Pyta, Wolfram, 'Vorbereitungen für den militärischen Ausnahmezustand unter Papen/Schleicher', *MGM*, 51 (1992), 385–428

—— 'Paul von Hindenburg als charismatischer Führer der deutschen Nation', in Möller, Frank (ed.), *Charismatische Führer der deutschen Nation* (Munich, 2004), 109–48

—— 'Die Präsidialgewalt in der Weimar Republik', in Recker, Marie-Luise (ed.), *Parlamentarismus in Europa: Deutschland, England und Frankreich im Vergleich* (Munich, 2004), 65–96

—— 'Das Zerplatzen der Hoffnungen auf eine konservative Wende: Kuno Graf von Westarp und Hindenburg', in Jones, Larry Eugene and Pyta, Wolfram (eds.), *'Ich bin der letzte Preuße''': Der politische Lebensweg des konservativen Politikers Kuno Graf von Westarp (1864–1945)* (Cologne, Weimar, and Vienna, 2006), 163–87

—— *Hindenburg: Herrschaft zwischen Hohenzollern und Hitler* (Munich, 2007)

Ramsden, John, *Man of the Century: Winston Churchill and His Legend Since 1945* (London, 2002)

Rauscher, Walter, *Hindenburg: Feldmarschall und Reichspräsident* (Vienna, 1997)

Recker, Marie-Luise (ed.), *Parlamentarismus in Europa: Deutschland, England und Frankreich im Vergleich* (Munich, 2004)

Regel, Helmut, 'Die Fridericus-Filme der Weimarer Republik', Marquardt, Axel and Rathsack, Heinz (eds.), *Preussen im Film* (Hamburg, 1981), 124–34

Reiche, Jürgen, 'Von Bismarck zu Zlatko oder wer ist prominent', in Haus der Geschichte der Bundesrepublik Deutschland (ed.), *Prominente in der Werbung: Da weiss man, was man hat* (Mainz, 2001), 18–25

Reimann, Aribert, *Der große Krieg der Sprachen: Untersuchungen zur historischen Semantik in Deutschland und England zur Zeit des Ersten Weltkriegs* (Essen, 2000)

Riall, Lucy, *Garibaldi: Invention of a Hero* (New Haven, CT, 2007)

Richter, Johannes Karl, *Die Reichszentrale für Heimatdienst: Geschichte der ersten politischen Bildungsstelle in Deutschland und Untersuchung ihrer Rolle in der Weimarer Republik* (Berlin, 1963)

Riekhoff, Harald von, *German-Polish Relations 1918–1933* (Baltimore, MD, 1971)

Ritter, Gerhard, *The Sword and the Scepter: The Problem of Militarism in Germany, vol. 3.: The Tragedy of Statesmanship—Bethmann Hollweg as War Chancellor (1914–1917)* (Coral Gables, FL, 1972)

—— *The Sword and the Scepter: The Problem of Militarism in Germany, vol. 4: The Reign of German Militarism and the Disaster of 1918* (Coral Gables, FL, 1973)

Ritter, Gerhard A. (ed.), *Wahlen und Wahlkämpfe in Deutschland: Von den Anfängen im 19. Jahrhundert bis zur Bundesrepublik* (Düsseldorf, 1997)

Robson, Stuart T., '1918 and All That: Reassessing the Periodization of Recent German History', Jones, Larry Eugene and Retallack, James (eds.), *Elections, Mass Politics, and Social Change in Modern Germany* (Cambridge, 1992), 331–45

Röhl, John C. G. (ed.), *Der Ort Kaiser Wilhelms II. in der deutschen Geschichte* (Munich, 1991)

——, *Wilhelm II.: Der Weg in den Abgrund 1900–1941* (Munich, 2008)

Ross, Corey, 'Mass Politics and the Techniques of Leadership: The Promise and Perils of Propaganda in Weimar Germany', *German History*, 24 (2006), 184–211

Rother, Rainer (ed.), *Die letzten Tage der Menschheit—Bilder des Ersten Weltkriegs: Ausstellungskatalog des Deutsche Historischen Museums Berlin* (Berlin, 1994)

—— (ed.), *The First World War and Popular Cinema: 1914 to the Present* (Edinburgh, 1999), 217–46

Ruge, Wolfgang, *Hindenburg—Porträt eines Militaristen* (Berlin, 1975)

Rürup, Reinhard, 'Die Revolution von 1918/19 in der deutschen Geschichte', *Reihe Gesprächskreis Geschichte der Friedrich-Ebert-Stiftung in Bonn*, vol. 5 (1993), 5–28

—— (ed.), *The Problem of Revolution in Germany 1789–1989* (Oxford and New York, 2000)

Ryder, Arthur John, *The German Revolution of 1918: A Study of German Socialism in War and Revolt* (Cambridge, 1967)

Sabrow, Martin, *Die verdrängte Verschwörung: Der Rathenau-Mord und die deutsche Gegenrevolution* (Frankfurt/M., 1999)

—— (ed.), *Geschichte als Herrschaftsdiskurs: Der Umgang mit der Vergangenheit in der DDR* (Cologne, Weimar, and Vienna, 2000)

—— 'Kampfplatz Weimar: DDR-Geschichtsschreibung im Konflikt von Erfahrung, Politik und Wissenschaft', in Winkler, Heinrich August (ed.), *Weimar im Widerstreit: Deutungen der ersten deutschen Republik im geteilten Deutschland* (Munich, 2002), 163–84

Saldern, Adelheid von (ed.), *Mythen in Geschichte und Geschichtsschreibung aus polnischer und deutscher Sicht* (Münster, 1996)

—— 'Mythen, Legenden und Stereotypen', in idem (ed.), *Mythen in Geschichte und Geschichtsschreibung aus polnischer und deutscher Sicht* (Münster, 1996), 13–26

Salewski, Michael, *Der Erste Weltkrieg* (Paderborn, 2003)

Sänger, Johanna, *Heldenkult und Heimatliebe: Straßen- und Ehrennamen im offiziellen Gedächtnis der DDR* (Berlin, 2006)

Schallenberger, Horst, *Untersuchungen zum Geschichtsbild der Wilhelminischen Ära und der Weimarer Zeit: Eine vergleichende Schulbuchanalyse deutscher Schulgeschichtsbücher aus der Zeit von 1888 bis 1933* (Ratingen near Düsseldorf, 1964)

Scharlau, Winfried, 'Mit ihm trug sich Preußen selber zu Grabe: Der Mythos Hindenburg und ein wissenschaftlicher Skandal', *Der Monat*, vol. 23 (1971), 56–64

Scheck, Raffael, *Mothers of the Nation: Right-wing Women in Weimar Germany* (Oxford and New York, 2004)

Schenk, Frithjof Benjamin, 'Tannenberg/Grunwald', in Etienne Francois and Hagen Schulze, (eds.), *Deutsche Erinnerungsorte*, vol. 2, (Munich, 2001), 446–57

Schilling, Rene, *Deutungsmuster heroischer Männlichkeit in Deutschland 1813–1945* (Paderborn, 2003)

Schmid, Hans-Dieter, 'Der Mythos-Begriff in der neueren Geschichtswissenschaft, Philosophie und Theologie', in Saldern, Adelheid von (ed.), *Mythen in Geschichte und Geschichtsschreibung aus polnischer und deutscher Sicht* (Münster, 1996), 40–2

Schmidt, Anne, *Belehrung - Propaganda - Vertrauensarbeit: Zum Wandel amtlicher Kommunikationspolitik in Deutschland 1914–1918* (Essen, 2006)

Schmitt, Carl, *Der Hüter der Verfassung* (Tübingen, 1931)

Schneider, Gerhard, 'Zur Mobilisierung der "Heimatfront": Das Nageln sogenannter Kriegswahrzeichen im Ersten Weltkrieg', *Zeitschrift für Volkskunde* 95 (1999), 32–62

Schneider, Romana and Wang, Wilfried (eds.), *Moderne Architektur in Deutschland 1900 bis 2000, vol. 3: Macht und Monument* (Ostfildern, 1998)

Schneider, Thomas F. and Wagener, Hans (eds.), *Von Richthofen bis Remarque: Deutschsprachige Prosa zum I. Weltkrieg* (Amsterdam and New York, 2003)

Schoch, Rainer (ed.), *Politische Plakate in der Weimarer Republik 1918–1933* (Darmstadt, 1980)

Schönhoven, Klaus, *Die Bayerische Volkspartei 1924–1932* (Düsseldorf, 1972)

Schreiner, Klaus, ' "Wann kommt der Retter Deutschlands?" Formen und Funktionen von politischem Messianismus in der Weimarer Republik', *Saeculum,* 49 (1998), 107–60

Schug, Alexander, 'Wegbereiter der modernen Absatzwerbung in Deutschland: Advertising Agencies und die Amerikanisierung der deutschen Werbebranche in der Zwischenkriegszeit', *WerkstattGeschichte,* 12 (2003), 29–52

Schulz, Gerhard, ' "Preussenschlag" oder Staatsstreich?', *Der Staat,* vol. 17 (1978), 553–81

—— *Zwischen Demokratie und Diktatur: Verfassungspolitik und Reichsreform in der Weimarer Republik, vol. 3: Von Brüning zu Hitler* (Berlin, 1992)

Schulze, Hagen, *Weimar: Deutschland 1917–1933* (Berlin, 1982)

Schumann, Dirk, *Politische Gewalt in der Weimarer Republik 1918–1933: Kampf um die Straße und Furcht vor dem Bürgerkrieg* (Essen, 2001)

Schüren, Ulrich, *Der Volksentscheid zur Fürstenenteignung 1926: Die Vermögensauseinandersetzung mit den depossedierten Landesherren als Problem der deutschen Innenpolitik unter besonderer Berücksichtigung der Verhältnisse in Preussen* (Düsseldorf, 1978)

Schwarzmüller, Theo, *Zwischen Kaiser und 'Führer': Generalfeldmarschall August von Mackensen: Eine politische Biographie* (Paderborn, Munich, Vienna, and Zurich, 1996)

Servent, Pierre, *Le mythe Pétain: Verdun ou les tranchées de la mémoire* (Paris, 1992)

Showalter, Dennis E., *Tannenberg: Clash of Empires* (Hamden, CT, 1991)

Sneeringer, Julia, *Winning Women's Votes: Propaganda and Politics in Weimar Germany* (Chapel Hill, NC, and London, 2002)

Sontheimer, Kurt, *Antidemokratisches Denken in der Weimarer Republik: Die politischen Ideen des deutschen Nationalismus zwischen 1918 und 1933* (Munich, 1968)

Sösemann, Bernd, *Das Ende der Weimarer Republik in der Kritik demokratischer Publizisten: Theodor Wolff, Ernst Feder, Julius Elbau, Leopold Schwarzschild* (Berlin, 1976)

—— 'Der Verfall des Kaisergedankens im Ersten Weltkrieg', in Röhl, John C. G. (ed.), *Der Ort Kaiser Wilhelms II. in der deutschen Geschichte* (Munich, 1991), 145–70

—— ' "Auf Bajonetten läßt sich schlecht sitzen": Propaganda und Gesellschaft in der Anfangsphase der nationalsozialistischen Diktatur', in Stamm-Kuhlmann, Thomas et al. (eds.), *Geschichtsbilder: Festschrift für Michael Salewski zum 65. Geburtstag* (Stuttgart 2003), 381–409

Spilker, Rolf and Ulrich, Bernd (eds.), *Der Tod als Maschinist: Der industrialisierte Krieg 1914–1918* (Bramsche, 1998)

Sprenger, Heinrich, *Heinrich Sahm: Kommunalpolitiker und Staatsmann* (Cologne, 1969)

Stahr, Henrick, *Fotojournalismus zwischen Exotismus und Rassismus: Darstellungen von Schwarzen und Indianern in Foto-Text-Artikeln deutscher Wochenillustrierter 1919–1939* (Hamburg, 2004)

Stamm-Kuhlmann, Thomas (ed.), *Geschichtsbilder: Festschrift für Michael Salewski zum 65. Geburtstag* (Stuttgart, 2003)

Stargardt, Nicholas, *The German Idea of Militarism: Radical and Socialist Critics, 1866–1914* (Cambridge, 1994)

Steiner, Zara, *The Lights that Failed: European International History 1919–1933* (Oxford, 2005)

Stibbe, Matthew, *German Anglophobia and the Great War, 1914–1918* (Cambridge, 2001)

—— 'Germany's "Last Card": Wilhelm II and Germany's Decision for Unrestricted Submarine Warfare in January 1917', in Mombauer, Annika and Deist, Wilhelm (eds.), *The Kaiser: New Research on Wilhelm II's Role in Imperial Germany* (Cambridge, 2003), 217–34

Stoll, Francois (ed.), *Die Psychologie des 20. Jahrhunderts, vol. 13: Anwendungen im Berufsleben: Arbeits-, Wirtschafts- und Verkehrspsychologie* (Zurich, 1981)

Strachan, Hew, *The First World War, vol. 1: To Arms* (Oxford, 2001)

Strath, Bo (ed.), *Myth and Memory in the Construction of Community: Historical Patterns in Europe and Beyond* (Brussels, 2000)

Stiftung Haus der Geschichte der Bundesrepublik Deutschland (ed.), *Bilder und Macht im 20. Jahrhundert* (Bielefeld, 2004)

Strzelzyk, Jerzy (ed.), *Die Helden in der Geschichte und Historiographie* (Poznan, 1997)

Thimme, Anneliese, *Flucht in den Mythos: Die Deutschnationale Volkspartei und die Niederlage von 1918* (Göttingen, 1969)

Thoß, Bruno and Volkmann, Hans Erich (eds.), *Erster Weltkrieg—Zweiter Weltkrieg: Ein Vergleich: Krieg, Kriegserlebnis, Kriegserfahrung in Deutschland* (Paderborn, 2002)

Tietz, Jürgen, *Das Tannenberg Nationaldenkmal: Architektur, Geschichte, Kontext* (Berlin, 1999)

—— 'Ostpreussisches Stonehenge—Das Tannenberg-Nationaldenkmal', in Blauert, Elke (ed.), *Walter Krüger, Johannes Krüger: Architekten* (Berlin, 2004), 47–52

Topolski, Jerzy, 'Historiographische Mythen: Eine methodologische Einführung', in Saldern, Adelheid von (ed.), *Mythen in Geschichte und Geschichtsschreibung aus polnischer und deutscher Sicht* (Münster, 1996), 27–35

—— 'Helden in der Geschichte und Geschichtsschreibung', in Strzelzyk, Jerzy (ed.), *Die Helden in der Geschichte und Historiographie* (Poznan, 1997), 11–19

Turner, Henry Ashby, *German Big Business and the Rise of Hitler* (New York and Oxford, 1985)

Uhle-Wettler, Franz, *Erich Ludendorff in seiner Zeit: Soldat-Stratege-Revolutionär: Eine Neubewertung* (London, 1996)

Ullrich, Sebastian, 'Im Schatten einer gescheiterten Demokratie: Die Weimarer Republik und der demokratische Neubeginn in den Westzonen 1945–1949', in Winkler, Heinrich August (ed.), *Griff nach der Deutungsmacht: Zur Geschichte der Geschichtspolitik in Deutschland* (Göttingen, 2004), 185–208

Ullrich, Volker, *Kriegsalltag: Hamburg im Ersten Weltkrieg* (Cologne, 1982)

Ulrich, Bernd and Ziemann, Benjamin (eds.), *Frontalltag im Ersten Weltkrieg: Wahn und Wirklichkeit* (Frankfurt/M., 1994)

—— 'Die umkämpfte Erinnerung: Überlegungen zur Wahrnehmung des Ersten Weltkrieges in der Weimarer Republik', in Duppler, Jost and Groß, Gerhard P. (eds.), *Kriegsende 1918: Ereignis, Wirkung, Nachwirkung* (Munich, 1999), 367–76

Ummenhofer, Stefan, *Wie Feuer und Wasser? Katholizismus und Sozialdemokratie in der Weimarer Republik* (Berlin, 2003)

Verhey, Jeffrey, *The 'Spirit of 1914': Militarism, Myth and Mobilization in Germany* (Cambridge, 2000)

Vogelsang, Thilo, *Reichswehr, Staat und NSDAP: Beiträge zur deutschen Geschichte 1930–32* (Stuttgart, 1962)

Voigt, Rüdiger (ed.), *Symbole der Politik, Politik der Symbole* (Opladen, 1989)

Waite, Robert George Leeson, *Vanguard of Nazism: The Free Corps Movement in Post-War Germany 1918–1923* (Cambridge, MA, 1952)

Warner, Philip, *Kitchener: The Man behind the Legend* (London, 1985)

Watson, Alexander, *Enduring the Great War: Combat, Morale and Collapse in the German and British Armies, 1914–1918* (Cambridge, 2008)

Weber, Klaus-Dieter, *Das Büro des Reichspräsidenten* (Frankfurt/M., 2001)

Weber, Max, 'Die drei reinen Typen der legitimen Herrschaft', in idem *Gesammelte Aufsätze zur Wissenschaftslehre*, ed. Winckelmann, Johannes (Tübingen, 1985, 6th edn), 475–88

Wehler, Hans-Ulrich, 'Leopold Schwarzschild contra Carl v. Ossietzky: Politische Vernunft für die Verteidigung der Republik gegen ultralinke "Systemkritik" und Volksfront-Illusionen', in idem (ed.), *Preußen ist wieder chic . . . Politik und Polemik in zwanzig Essays* (Frankfurt a.M, 1983), 77–83

—— (ed.), *Preußen ist wieder chic . . . Politik und Polemik in zwanzig Essays* (Frankfurt a.M, 1983)

—— *Deutsche Gesellschaftsgeschichte, vol. 3: Von der "Deutschen Doppelrevolution" bis zum Beginn des Ersten Weltkriegs: 1849–1914* (Munich, 1995)

—— *Deutsche Gesellschaftsgeschichte, vol. 4: Vom Beginn des Ersten Weltkriegs bis zur Gründung der beiden deutschen Staaten 1914–1949*

Weiglin, Paul, *Berlin im Glanz: Bilderbuch der Reichshauptstadt von 1888–1918* (Cologne, 1954)

Welch, David, *Germany: Propaganda and Total War 1914–1918: The Sins of Omission* (London, 2000)

Weßling, Wolfgang, 'Hindenburg, Neudeck und die deutsche Wirtschaft: Tatsachen und Zusammenhänge einer "Affäre" ', *Vierteljahrshefte für Sozial- Wirtschaftsgeschichte*, 64 (1977), 41–73

Westphal, Uwe, *Werbung im Dritten Reich* (Berlin, 1989)

Wette, Wolfram, 'Demobilization in Germany 1918–1919: The Gradual Erosion of the Powers of the Soldiers' Councils', in Wrigley, Chris (ed.), *Challenges of Labour: Central and Western Europe 1917–1920* (London and New York, 1993), 176–95

Wheeler-Bennett, John W., *Wooden Titan: Hindenburg in Twenty Years of German History, 1914–1934,* 2nd edn (London, 1967)

Williamson, John G., *Karl Helfferich 1872–1924: Economist, Financier, Politician* (Princeton, NJ, 1971)

Winkler, Heinrich August, *Der Weg in die Katastrophe: Arbeiter und Arbeiterbewegung in der Weimarer Republik 1930–1933* (Bonn, 1990)

—— 'Choosing the Lesser Evil: The German Social Democrats and the Fall of the Weimar Republic', *JCH*, vol. 25 (1990), 205–27

—— (ed.), *Die deutsche Staatskrise 1930–1933: Handlungsspielräume und Alternativen* (Munich, 1992)

—— *Weimar 1918–1933: Die Geschichte der ersten deutschen Demokratie* (Munich, 1993)

—— (ed.), *Weimar im Widerstreit: Deutungen der ersten deutschen Republik im geteilten Deutschland* (Munich, 2002)

—— (ed.), *Griff nach der Deutungsmacht: Zur Geschichte der Geschichtspolitik in Deutschland* (Göttingen, 2004)

Winter, Jay M., *Sites of Memory, Sites of Mourning: The Great War in European Cultural History* (Cambridge, 1995)

—— (ed.), *The Great War and the Twentieth Century* (New Haven, CT, and London, 2000)

Wipperman, Klaus W., *Politische Propaganda und staatsbürgerliche Bildung. Die Reichszentrale für Heimatdienst in der Weimarer Republik* (Cologne, 1976)

Wirth, Hans-Jürgen (ed.), *Helden. Psychosozial* 10 (Weinheim, 1987)

—— 'Die Sehnsucht nach Vollkommenheit. Zur Psychoanalyse der Heldenverehrung', in Wirth, Hans-Jürgen (ed.), *Helden. Psychosozial* 10 (Weinheim, 1987), 96–113

Wischermann, Clemens, 'Grenzenlose Werbung? Die gesellschaftliche Akzeptanz der Werbewelt im 20. Jahrhundert', in Borscheid, Peter and Wischermann, Clemens (eds.), *Bilderwelt des Alltags. Werbung in der Konsumgesellschaft des 19. und 20. Jahrhunderts* (Stuttgart, 1995), 372–407

—— 'Wirtschaftswerbung in der Konsumgesellschaft—historische Entwicklung', in Haus der Geschichte der Bundesrepublik Deutschland (ed.), *Prominente in der Werbung: Da weiss man, was man hat* (Mainz, 2001), 38–45

Wodianka, Stefanie, 'Mythos und Erinnerung: Mythentheoretische Modelle und ihre gedächtnistheoretischen Implikationen', in Oesterle, Günter (ed.), *Erinnerung, Gedächtnis, Wissen: Studien zur kulturwissenschaftlichen Gedächtnisforschung* (Göttingen, 2005), 211–30

Wolff, Udo W., *Preussens Glanz und Gloria im Film: Die berühmten deutschen Tonfilme über Preussens glorreiche Vergangenheit* (Munich, 1981)

Wolfrum, Edgar, *Geschichte als Waffe: Vom Kaiserreich bis zur Wiedervereinigung* (Göttingen, 2001)

Wright, Jonathan R. C., *Gustav Stresemann: Weimar's Greatest Statesman* (Oxford, 2002)

Wrigley, Chris (ed.), *Challenges of Labour: Central and Western Europe 1917–1920* (London and New York, 1993)

Zaun, Harald, *Paul von Hindenburg und die deutsche Außenpolitik 1925–1934* (Cologne, Weimar and Vienna, 1999)

Zeender, John K., 'The German Catholics and the Presidential Election of 1925', *JMH, 35* (1963), 366–81

Zeidler, Manfred, *Kriegsende im Osten: Die Rote Armee und die Besetzung Deutschlands östlich von Oder und Neiße 1944/45* (Munich, 1996)

Zeman, Zbynek Anthony Bohuslav, *Nazi Propaganda* (Oxford, 1964)

Ziemann, Benjamin, *Front und Heimat: Ländliche Kriegserfahrungen im südlichen Bayern 1914–1923* (Essen, 1997)

——'Republikanische Erinnerung in einer polarisierten Öffentlichkeit: Das Reichsbanner Schwarz-Rot-Gold als Veteranenverband der sozialistischen Arbeiterschaft', *HZ, 267* (1998), 357–98

——'"Macht der Maschine"—Mythen des industriellen Krieges', in Spilker, Rolf and Ulrich, Bernd (eds.), *Der Tod als Maschinist: Der industrialisierte Krieg 1914–1918* (Bramsche, 1998), 177–89

——'Enttäuschte Erwartungen und kollektive Erschöpfung: Die deutschen Soldaten an der Westfront 1918 auf dem Weg zur Revolution', in Duppler, Jörg and Groß, Gerhard P. (eds.), *Kriegsende 1918: Ereignis, Wirkung, Nachwirkung* (Munich, 1999), 165–82.

——'Die Deutsche Nation und ihr zentraler Erinnerungsort: Das "Nationaldenkmal für die Gefallenen im Weltkriege" und die Idee des "Unbekannten Soldaten" 1914–1935', in Berding, Helmut, Heller, Klaus and Speitkamp, Winfried (eds.), *Krieg und Erinnerung* (Göttingen, 2000), 67–92

Zimmermann, Peter and Hoffmann, Kay (eds.), *Geschichte des dokumentarischen Films in Deutschland, vol. 3: 'Drittes Reich' 1933–1945* (Stuttgart, 2005)

Ziolkowski, Theodor, 'Der Hunger nach dem Mythos: Zur seelischen Gastronomie der Deutschen in den Zwanziger Jahren', in Grimm, Reinhold and Hermand, Jost (eds.), *Die Sogenannten Zwanziger Jahre* (Bad Homburg, 1970), 169–201

## UNPUBLISHED THESES

Korol, Martin,, Dada, Präexil und "Die Freie Zeitung"—Ernst Bloch, Homo Ludens und Tänzer; Hugo Ball, Rastlos auf der Suche nach Heimat; und ihre Frauen, Weggefährten und Gegner in der Schweiz 1916–1919' (Bremen, Univ. Diss., 1997)

# Index

Adenauer, Konrad 201
advertising 105, 108, 114–23, 171
*All Quiet on the Western Front* 107, 109
anti-Jewish agitation *see* anti-semitism
anti-semitism 57, 65, 66, 69, 70–2, 80,
    133–5, 153, 154, 174, 186, 238,
    261
Arminius *see* Hermann
armistice of 1918 53, 58–9, 62, 65, 91,
    129

Bad Kreuznach 23, 39, 163
Baden, Prince Max von 52–5, 57–8,
    61, 72
Ball, Hugo 51
Barbarossa (Friedrich I) 7, 22, 28, 211
Basic Law 201
Bauer, Hermann 196–8
Benjamin, Walter 51
Berg, Friedrich von 54, 73, 82, 149
Bernhard, Georg 52, 55, 137
Bernhard, Lucian 115
Bernstein, Eduard 95
Bethmann Hollweg, Theobald von 24,
    31, 35, 37
Beumelburg, Werner 112–13, 122–3
Bismarck, Otto von 7, 8, 12, 22, 28, 66,
    76, 104–5, 118, 132–3, 201,
    206–7, 211, 281
Blasius, Rainer 209
Bloch, Ernst 51
Blomberg, Werner von 181
Böse, Wilhelm 207
Bracher, Karl-Dietrich 199
branding *see* advertising
Braun, Otto 85, 96, 143, 164, 167, 214
Brecht, Bertolt 206

Brest-Litovsk 46, 49
Breuer, Robert 25, 30
Brill, Hermann 198
Brüning, Heinrich 109, 142–3, 146,
    147, 148, 152, 154, 156–7, 162,
    164, 167–8, 173, 216
Bundeswehr 204
Burckhardt, Jakob 7
*Burgfrieden* 31, 66
BVP 85, 87, 96–7, 99, 144–6, 162, 165

Cannae 18
Carlyle, Thomas 7
Cassirer, Ernst 5–6
CDU 208
Centre Party 62, 79, 85, 93, 97, 99, 128,
    142, 144–7, 162, 165, 167–8, 216
'Charismatic leadership' 8, 9, 215, 224
Christian Social People's Service 144
Churchill, Winston 8
cinema *see* Hindenburg films
Claß, Heinrich 136, 139, 140, 143–4,
    150, 168
Communists 11, 74, 78, 85, 90, 94–5,
    99, 101, 110–11, 126, 135, 141,
    145, 147, 163, 171, 176, 188, 198,
    204–5, 207, 209, 261
'Conservative Revolution' 162, 165
council movement 58–61, 63
Council of the People's Delegates 58,
    128
Cramon, August von 76, 85, 86
Crown Princess Auguste Wilhelm 31

Daily Telegraph Affair 23
David, Eduard 23, 163
'Day of German Labour' 178

'Day of Potsdam' 10, 174–78, 183, 199, 208
DDP 55, 60, 62, 67, 77, 84, 85, 93, 94, 125, 144, 166
defensive war (notion of) 15–16, 22
Delbrück, Hans 60
demobilization 58–60, 63
denazification 197, 207
*Der Eiserne Hindenburg in Krieg und Frieden (The Iron Hindenburg in War and Peace)* 104, 106, 120, 123
Deutsche Adelsgenossenschaft 82, 149
Deutsche Staatspartei 144, 146
Deutscher Nationalausschuss 43
Deutscher Ostbund 75
Dietrich, Otto 179, 181–2
DNVP 67, 73, 76–7, 85, 86–8, 99, 100, 133, 137, 138–9, 144, 146, 149, 152–3, 213, 262, 263
Doehle, Heinrich 113
Dorpalen, Andreas 165
Drews, Bill 57
Duesterberg, Theodor 144–5, 148, 152–3, 161
Duisberg, Carl 148, 158, 268
Düwell, Wilhelm 16
DVP 72, 73, 85, 87–8, 128, 144, 149, 162, 165

East Prussia 15–7, 19, 20–1, 26, 76–81, 83, 94, 97, 107–8, 134, 149, 152, 161, 164, 178, 193, 203
Eastern Aid Scandal *see* Osthilfe
Ebert, Friedrich 53, 58–61, 72–3, 75, 84, 105–6, 114, 125, 130, 201, 263
'Ebert-Groener Pact' 57–64
Economic Party (WP) 87, 144
Einem, Karl von 37, 148
*Einer für Alle!* 107, 158
Eisner, Kurt 51
Elbau, Julius 164–5, 214
Enabling Act 177
Empress Auguste Viktoria of Prussia 24, 39
Erzberger, Matthias 24, 41, 75, 67, 79
expellees 202–4, 218
expropriation of the German Princes 126

Falkenhayn, Erich von 33–5
FDP 208
Feder, Ernst 99, 164, 250
Feldmann, Otto von 88, 257
Franco-Prussian War (1870–1) 14, 19
Free corps 70, 74, 79, 107
Friedberg, Robert 54
Friedensburg, Ferdinand 77, 125, 128
Friedrich, Ernst 261
food supplies 43–6, 49
Fortschrittliche Volkspartei 53
Frank, Jakob 73–4
Frederick 'the Great' 175–6, 194–6, 203, 206, 280
*Freie Zeitung* 51–2, 62
Friedrich Wilhelm I 175–6, 280
front novels 112–3

Gareis, Karl 79
Garibaldi, Guiseppe 10
Gayl, Wilhelm von 65, 77, 80–2, 87, 216, 257, 260
Gereke, Günther 157, 165, 268
Gerlach, Hellmut von 125, 126
German Order 18–19
Gerold, Karl 197
Gessler, Otto 84
Gestapo 180, 186
Gilgenburg 18–19
Goebbels, Joseph 11, 120, 123, 140–3, 150, 153–4, 156, 166, 174–77, 181, 198, 207, 215–6, 267
Goltz, Count Rüdiger von der (leader of the Patriotic Leagues) 134–5
Goltz, Count Rüdiger von der (Goebbels's lawyer) 141
Göring, Hermann 178, 180, 207,
Görlitz, Walter 201
Gothein, Georg 67
Green Party 207–8
Grimm, Hans 112
Groener, Wilhelm 15, 55, 59–60, 62, 65, 154
Grzesinski, Albert 59

Haeften, Hans von 54
Halbwachs, Maurice 4
Hanover 21, 22, 62, 75, 85–6, 88–9, 90, 94, 100, 194

Haußmann, Conrad 53, 55
Häussler, Johannes 107
Hauswirth, Arnim 141, 258
Heilmann, Ernst 163
Helfferich, Karl 67, 70
Hellpach, Willy 85, 96
Hermann 7, 12, 22, 211
Hiller, Kurt 99
Hindenburg, Gertrud von 15, 190,
    193–4, 202, 277
Hindenburg, Hubertus von 220, 283
Hindenburg, Margarete von 201
Hindenburg, Oskar von 3, 86, 148, 188,
    197, 201, 260, 278, 279
Hindenburg, Paul von
  age/alleged senility 15, 41, 50, 86, 89,
      91, 120, 161, 173, 180, 192,
      198–9, 205, 213, 217,
  appointment to 'third Supreme
      Command' 33–38
  birthdays 23, 32, 39–42, 46, 65, 104,
      114, 116, 118, 128–36, 143,
      150, 163, 179, 188–9, 190, 202,
      213, 233, 271
  burial in Marburg 193–7, 202–4, 208
  'camarilla' 3, 199
  death 173, 180–88, 190–1, 202–3,
      207, 209, 216–7, 277, 282
  'duty', theme of 21, 25, 55, 59, 63,
      69, 75, 89, 97, 137–38, 148,
      150, 152, 154, 158, 168,
      179–80, 183, 213–14, 237
  film 37, 39, 42, 57, 104–9, 112–14,
      120, 122–3, 134, 157–8, 170,
      173, 177, 189, 213
  iconography 27, 41–2, 74–5, 91–3,
      94, 104–23, 130, 134, 154, 158,
      161, 171–3, 182, 185, 189–90,
      199, 213
  illustrated publications 105, 113–6,
      123, 134, 159, 161, 168, 182,
      199, 213
  'indebtedness', theme of 60, 73, 89,
      94, 97, 152, 168
  'loyalty', theme of 8, 14, 41, 55, 63,
      75, 89, 97, 125, 128, 148–52,
      154, 158, 163, 164, 172, 174–5,
      179, 183, 186

masculinity 20, 22, 27, 89, 116, 164,
    211, 213
memoirs 21, 75–6, 83
memorabilia 25–6, 33, 34, 65, 91,
    116–20, 171
nomination for the office of Reich
    President (1920) 72–5, 83
political will 187–89, 191, 197–8,
    216,
products (Hindenburg) see
    memorabilia
radio, use of/coverage of Hindenburg
    on 90–1, 102, 105, 110–12,
    123, 132, 134, 151, 157–8, 176,
    179, 182, 185, 188–9
religious dimension of myth 21, 26,
    86, 148, 151, 175, 177, 190, 202
rumours/jokes 46–52, 173–4, 180,
    236
'sacrifice', language of 21, 25, 31, 41,
    53, 55, 60, 89, 127, 151, 165,
    211, 237
'saviour' image 7, 9, 33, 51, 66, 78,
    84, 91, 93, 97, 100, 104–7, 125,
    129, 132, 140, 143, 150–1, 157,
    161–2, 164–5, 180, 192, 198,
    203, 209, 214–15, 217
tranquillity/strong nerves/rock-like
    quality 14–15, 20–2, 25, 36,
    50, 56, 60–1, 91, 107, 113, 125,
    129, 143, 162, 164, 166, 174,
    186, 211, 212–4, 217
women's perceptions of 89, 97–99,
    101, 130, 249–50
Hindenburg (film) 189
Hindenburgbund 162
Hindenburg Dank 134, 260
'Hindenburg Donation' 46, 133–5, 189
'Hindenburg Games' 133
'Hindenburg Museum' 37
'Hindenburg Peace' 37, 42
'Hindenburg Programme' 37, 45
Hindenburg Zeppelin 189
Hitler, Adolf 2, 8, 10, 11, 83, 120–3,
    125, 140, 144–7, 152–4, 156–7,
    162–66, 193, 198–9, 201, 207,
    214, 216–8, 268, 282
Hitzberger, Otto 130

Hoetzsch, Otto 76
Hoffmann, Max 19
Hohenstein 19, 80, 81, 183, 185, 190,
    193
Horn, Rudolf von 149–51, 266
Hosaeus, Hermann 209
Hoth, Hermann 61
Hubatsch, Walther 198, 201
Hugenberg, Alfred 139, 144, 146–7,
    152–3, 263

Independent Social Democrats 47, 58,
    60
Information Control Division 197
Iron Front 163, 165
'Iron Hindenburg' (statue) see nailing
    ritual

Jarres, Freia 98
Jarres, Karl 85–7, 96, 98, 128
Jagow, Traugott von 32, 34
Jung, Edgar Julius 162
Jünger, Ernst 112

Kahr, Gustav von 80
Kaiser see Wilhelm II
Kapp, Wolfgang 74
Kapp-Lüttwitz coup 74, 83
Karstedt, Oskar 133
Kempner, Franz 157–8
Kershaw, Ian 177
Kessler, Count Harry von 99, 102–3,
    163
Keudell, Walter von 86, 257
Kitchener, Herbert 8
Klemperer, Victor 173–4, 177, 181–2,
    185–6, 192
Klenze, Leo von 7
Klepper, Jochen 186
Koch, Erich 181
Koerner, Karl 108–9, 252
Kohlrausch, Martin 34
Kohut, Thomas A. 23
Königgrätz 14, 19
KPD see Communists
Kriegk, Otto 88
Krüger, Johannes 128
Kunsturheberrecht 118
Kyffhäuser League 75, 130, 149–51, 202

Lang, Fritz 106
Langemarck 19
League of Nations 125, 179, 189
Lederer, Hugo 28
Lehmann, Konrad 38
Leipart, Theodor 174
Levi, Paul 126, 135
Levi-Strauss, Claude 6, 11
Liebknecht, Karl 23, 58
Liège, Battle of 15
Lindenberg, Paul 113
Lloyd George, David 9
Locarno, Treaty of 85, 124–5
Löbe, Paul 163
Loebell, Friedrich Wilhelm von 32, 73,
    84, 87, 126, 133
Löwenstein, Leo 174
Ludendorff, Erich 3, 15, 19, 20, 22, 35,
    36, 39, 43, 47–9, 52, 53–7, 61,
    63–4, 67–9, 71, 74, 80–1, 85, 96,
    108, 113, 173, 212
Lüders, Martin 203
Luise of Prussia 8
Luther, Hans 101, 128
Lüttwitz, Walther von 74
Lyncker, Moritz Freiherr von 36

Mahraun, Artur 147
Mann, Thomas 185–6, 188
Mao Zedong 10
Marne (Battle of) 18
Marschall, Georg 28
Marx, Wilhelm 85, 90, 94–8, 110,
    128–30, 147
Maser, Werner 3
Masurian Lakes (Battles of) 17, 156
Matschoss, Professor 38
Maurice, Sir Frederick 68
Meinecke, Friedrich 199
Meissner, Otto 3, 108, 113, 116,
    118–19, 125, 133, 141, 148, 158,
    197, 216, 254, 279
Mertz von Quirnheim, Hermann Ritter
    von 76
Mierendorff, Carlo 163
Milestone, Lewis 107
Moltke, Helmuth von 15, 18, 23, 34
Momper, Walter 2, 208
morale 43–6, 46–8, 50, 57, 64

MSPD (Majority Social
    Democrats) 58–62
Müller, Hermann 136, 142

nailing ritual 27–33, 39, 42, 61, 69, 104,
    161
Napoleon Bonaparte 10
National Assembly 60, 62, 73
'National Foundation for the Surviving
    Dependents of Fallen Soldiers' 32
National Liberal Party 54
National People's Army 204
National Rural League
    (Reichslandbund) 144, 152–3
National Socialist Cultural
    Community 2
Nazi party (Nazism) 32, 85, 87, 94,
    119–22, 137, 140–3, 145–6, 148,
    153–58, 161–6, 168–192, 193,
    196–7, 199, 205–8, 213–4, 216–8
'seizure of power' 170–4, 187, 191,
    198–9, 216–7, 278, 280
Neue Sachlichkeit 106
Nibelungen saga 7, 76
Nicolai, Walter 23
Niederwald Memorial 178
'Night of the Long Knives' 180
Nipperdey, Thomas 7
Noske, Gustav 60, 128–9, 143, 164, 213

OHL 2, 23, 44–5, 47–9, 52, 53–6, 59,
    60, 62, 66–7
    Section IIIb 23, 38, 49
    Picture and Film Section 39
Oldenburg-Januschau, Elard von 77,
    260
Opel 116–18
Oppenheim, Louis 40, 41, 115
Organization Consul 79
Ossietzky, Carl von 1, 12, 51, 124–5,
    166
Osthilfe 138, 260
Ostpreußischer Heimatbund 77

Pan-Germans 56, 136–7, 139, 140, 144
Papen, Franz von 109, 140, 167–9, 178,
    187, 197, 279
Paul, Bruno 130, 299
Paul, Heinz 107–9, 113, 122

Payer, Friedrich von 54
people's community
    (Volksgemeinschaft) 10, 12, 89,
    107, 177
Pétain, Philippe 9–10
Plessen, Hans Georg von 24, 35, 37–9
Pol, Heinz 95
'Polish Liquidation Agreement' 138
Praschma, Count Hans von 97
Presidential elections (1925) 1, 74–5,
    84–103, 110–11, 116, 123, 138,
    144–7, 150, 152–4, 161–2, 165,
    183, 205, 212, 214–15
Presidential elections (1932) 1, 74, 103,
    110, 116, 123, 144–66, 167, 171,
    191, 205, 214–7
Prittwitz und Gaffron, Maximilian
    von 15

Rathenau, Walther 67, 79
Reich Press Chief see Dietrich, Otto
Reichlichtspielgesetz 108–9
Reichsarchiv 76
Reichsbank 41, 115, 137
Reichsbanner 90, 126, 163
Reichsblock 84–91, 94–6, 99, 102, 212,
    216, 242
Reichsbund jüdischer
    Frontsoldaten 133, 174, 186
Reichsbürgerrat 73, 84
Reichswehr 69, 70, 78, 137, 167,
    181–2, 186, 268
Reichszentrale für Heimatdienst 128
Reimann, Arnold 132
Reinhard, Wilhelm 70
Reinhardt, Walther 60, 61
Remarque, Erich Maria 109, 112
Remer, Ernst Otto 203
Renn, Ludwig 112
Rennenkampf, Paul von 17
Reventlow, Ernst von 32–4, 69
revolution of 1918 1, 52, 57–64, 65, 68,
    70, 72, 74, 82, 104, 128–9, 163,
    213–4
Riall, Lucy 10
Richter, Ernst von 72
Risorgimento 10
Roedern, Siegfried von 53, 54
Roellenbleg, Heinrich 107

Röhm, Ernst 188
Ruge, Wolfgang 205
Russia
    German perceptions of
        Russia/Russophobia 16–18,
        19, 20–1, 27, 50–1, 106–7,
        127, 132, 163–4, 190, 193, 204,
        211

SA 170–1, 173, 175, 178, 180, 183
Sachs, Hans 28
Sahm, Heinrich 147–8
Saint-Privat 14
Salewski, Michael 198
Samsonov, Alexander 17
Sandrock, Adele 180
Scheidemann, Philipp 58, 60, 72, 79
Schenkendorf, Max von 175
Scherl (publishing house) 114, 116
Scheüch, Heinrich 44
Schiffer, Eugen 60, 61
Schleicher, Kurt von 169, 268
Schlieffen, Alfred von 15
Schmitt, Carl 109, 252
Schnabel, Franz 132
Scholz, Wilhelm von 20
Schöningh, Franz Josef 197
school textbooks 7, 130, 132, 199,
    205
Schreiber, Georg 168
Schriftleitergesetz 179
Schultze-Pfaelzer, Gerhard 181, 201,
    279
Schulze-Wechsungen, Walter 120
Schützinger, Hermann 95
Schwarz van Berk, Hans 182
Schwertfeger, Bernhard 201, 279
Sedan (Battle of) 14, 19
Seeger, Ernst 109
Seel, Franz von 50
Selberg, Emil 32
Seldte, Franz 87
Sethe, Paul 202
Severing, Carl 79, 163, 225
Siegfried myth 7, 76
Siemens, Carl Friedrich von 158
Social Democracy/Social Democrats
    (SPD) 11, 16, 23, 54, 67, 74,
    79–80, 85, 95, 97, 101, 123, 126,
    128–9, 135, 136, 142–6, 148–9,
    154, 158, 162–8, 170–1, 176, 186,
    192, 197–8, 203, 205, 208, 211,
    213, 217
soldiers's councils see council
    movement
Solf, Wilhelm 53, 54
Solzhenitsyn, Alexander 22
Sozialistische Reichspartei 203
Spartacist uprising 61, 69
'special path' 9, 224
Sperrfeuer um Deutschland see
    Beumelburg, Werner
'spirit of 1914' 7, 17, 66, 88
SS 178, 180, 183, 190
Staatsbürgerliche
    Arbeitsgemeinschaft 77, 78, 81
Staatsbürgerliche Vereinigung see
    Staatsbürgerliche
    Arbeitsgemeinschaft
'stab-in-the-back-legend' 7, 56–7, 64,
    66–8, 71–2, 74, 76, 81–3, 104,
    127, 150, 198, 212
Stahlhelm 75, 87, 100, 126, 133, 137
Stalin, Joseph 10
Stalling, Gerhard 112–13
Steinborn, Paul 159
Stinnes, Hugo 75
Stock, Christian 203
Stocker, Rudolf 116
street names 206–8, 218
Stresemann, Gustav 54, 72, 84, 87,

Tannenberg (Battle of) 5, 14, 17–22,
    24–5, 28, 36, 66, 68, 80–3, 86, 89,
    91, 97, 104, 107, 108–9, 113, 124,
    127, 129, 139–40, 148, 150, 152,
    154, 156, 161, 164, 173, 178, 182,
    190, 203–4, 207, 209, 211–2,
    214–5,
Tannenberg (film) 107–9, 122–3
Tannenberg Memorial 81–2, 126–8,
    134, 182–91, 193, 196, 217, 277,
    280
Thälmann, Ernst 85, 96, 99–100, 145,
    166, 205, 207, 271
Tirpitz, Alfred von 33, 86, 94
Treviranus, Gottfried 262
Tuaillon, Louis 28

Tucholsky, Kurt 69
'turnip winter' 45

Ullstein (publishing house) 114
unrestricted submarine warfare 32, 33, 67

Valentini, Rudolf von 32
Verdun (Battle of) 9, 18–19, 112
Vereinigte Vaterländische Verbände (Patriotic Leagues) 85–6, 144
Versailles Treaty 61, 62, 66, 81–2, 105, 125–7, 137, 178
Vichy government 9
Volksblock 90, 93–6, 154
Volkstrauertag 173–5

War Food Office 45
war guilt/'war guilt lie' 66–7, 81–2, 126, 127, 137
war loan 28, 40, 41, 46, 91, 115, 130, 133, 161, 234
War Office 44
War Press Office 38, 48–9, 95
war weariness see morale
Weber, Max 8, 9, 215
Wehner, Josef Magnus 112, 190
Werkbund 41
Wermuth, Adolf 28, 30
Wessel, Kurt 107
Westarp, Count Kuno von 138–40, 147, 157, 161, 165, 214, 262

Wheeler-Bennett, John 3
Wild von Hohenborn, Adolf 35, 37
Wilhelm I 7, 14, 89, 176, 178, 277
Wilhelm II 3, 7, 15, 19, 21, 23–4, 26, 28, 32–9, 41, 48–54, 57–8, 61, 64, 73, 86, 105, 113, 132, 149, 211
image of/relationship with Hindenburg myth 33–5, 38, 49–51, 54, 57–9, 62–4, 211, 231
abdication of 57–8, 113, 238
Wilmowsky, Tilo von 158
Wilson, Woodrow 53, 57
Winnig, August 80
Winterfeld, Detlof von 157
Wirth, Joseph 78
Wolff, Theodor 12, 16, 20, 66, 68, 72, 93, 164, 227
Wolffs Telegraphisches Büro (WTB) 18–19, 24
Wollenberg, Erich 198
workers' councils see council movement

Young, Owen D. 137
Young German Order 144, 147
Young Plan 137–42, 154, 161, 215

Zaun, Harald 3
Zöberlein, Hans 112